Creating Learning-Centered Courses for the World Wide Web

Related Titles of Interest

Successful College Teaching: Problem Solving Strategies of Distinguished Professors
Sharon A. Baiocco and Jamie N. DeWaters
ISBN: 0-205-26654-1

Colleges and Universities as Citizens
Robert G. Bringle, Richard Games, and Reverend Edward A. Malloy, CSC
ISBN: 0-205-28696-8

Faculty Work and Public Trust: Restoring the Value of Teaching and Public Service in American Academic Life
James S. Fairweather
ISBN: 0-205-17948-7

Emblems of Quality in Higher Education: Developing and Sustaining High-Quality Programs
Jennifer Grant Haworth and Clifton F. Conrad
ISBN: 0-205-19546-6

Writing for Professional Publication: Keys to Academic and Business Success
Kenneth T. Henson
ISBN: 0-205-28313-6

Learner-Centered Assessment on College Campuses: Shifting the Focus from Teaching to Learning
Mary E. Huba and Jann E. Freed
ISBN: 0-205-28738-7

Revitalizing General Education in a Time of Scarcity: A Navigational Chart for Administrators and Faculty
Sandra L. Kanter, Zelda F. Gamson, and Howard B. London
ISBN: 0-205-26257-0

The Adjunct Professor's Guide to Success: Surviving and Thriving in the College Classroom
Richard E. Lyons, Marcella L. Kysilka, and George E. Pawlas
ISBN: 0-205-28774-3

Teaching Tips for College and University Instructors: A Practical Guide
David Royse
ISBN: 0-205-29839-7

Designing and Teaching an On-Line Course: Spinning Your Web Classroom
Heidi Schweizer
ISBN: 0-205-30321-8

Leadership in Continuing and Distance Education in Higher Education
Cynthia C. Jones Shoemaker
ISBN: 0-205-26823-4

Shaping the College Curriculum: Academic Plans in Action
Joan S. Stark and Lisa R. Lattuca
ISBN: 0-205-16706-3

For more information or to purchase a book, please call 1-800-278-3525.

Creating Learning-Centered Courses for the World Wide Web

William B. Sanders
University of Hartford

Allyn and Bacon
Boston • London • Toronto • Sydney • Tokyo • Singapore

Executive Editor and Publisher: Stephen D. Dragin
Series Editorial Assistant: Barbara Strickland
Marketing Manager: Stephen Smith

A Pearson Education Company
Needham Heights, MA 02494

Internet: www.abacon.com

Between the time Web site information is gathered and then published, it is not unusual for some sites to have closed. Also, the transcription of URLs can result in unintended typographical errors. The publisher would appreciate notification where these occur so that they may be corrected in subsequent editions. Thank you.

Library of Congress Cataloging-in-Publication Data

Sanders, William B.
Creating learning-centered courses for the World Wide Web / William B. Sanders.
p. cm.
Includes bibliographical references and index.
ISBN 0-205-31513-5
1. Education, Higher—Computer-assisted instruction. 2. World Wide Web—Study and teaching (Higher) 3. Internet in education. I. Title.
LB2395.7 .S27 2001

378.1'7344678—dc21 00-055813

Printed in the United States of America

10 9 8 7 6 5 4 3 2 1 04 03 02 01 00

Dedicated to my wife, Delia

Contents

Preface

This book is a conversation with faculty about technology and pedagogy. Over the past few years the Internet and World Wide Web have grown at an unimaginable rate. Administrators, faculty, and businesses selling Internet hardware, software, and connection technology have espoused a breathless string of promises to educators who are willing to use the new technology. With the recentness of the Web phenomenon, one wonders how those who promote Web technology in education can be so assured that the results will be any better than traditional methods. There has not been time for sufficient research or development of tools to really know, and what research has been conducted appears to be equivocal.

Because the Web is so new, the venture of writing a book on how to go about creating Web pages is a nervy enterprise. Nevertheless, it is a good idea because it is a starting point for dialog, and it represents actual applications with typical university students used in courses. This book shows how to create Web pages with students in mind, but it does not represent itself as a definitive tome. It is a discussion in a faculty lounge, not in a departmental meeting. It is a chat in the hallways of a conference and not a presentation in a session. It brings the conceptual together with actual practices but makes no claims that it represents the final word on the matter.

Of the two elements that make up this book—Web technology and good practices in teaching and learning—the latter is more important. The good practices are borrowed from different places. First, the American Association of Higher Education (AAHE) provides a neat list of seven promising practices that help students learn. To the extent that these practices are relevant, practical, and applicable, they are employed in the examples using different parts of Web technology. Many of the practices are derived from National Science Foundation (NSF) research to find better ways to recruit and educate students in science, math, engineering, and technology. Second, Edward Tufte, a political science statistician and information designer at Yale University, took on the daunting task of explaining how to take complex information and clearly communicate it in pictures and words. His ideas regarding information display, contained in three books, are a second source of illumination on how content should best be presented on Web pages. Finally, Web pages have the capacity to be interactive. Eschewing conventional material on interactive multimedia, the works of Erving Goffman furnish some of the finest insights on social interaction available. So, where possible, Goffman's concepts give Web pages and sites some elements of interaction—a back-and-forth between page and student.

Most of the good ideas I've seen in teaching and learning come from faculty who try out ideas in class. Students invited to participate in their professor's own research are the most fortunate, and I think they learn the most. However, undergraduates usually are left out of the research enterprise and must be content with lab routines (at best) and simply reading about someone else's findings. In the humanities the situation is somewhat mitigated by the nature of the content, yet some very creative forms of learning have been developed by faculty who fully involve students in the content inside and outside of the classroom. The lab and field research models in the natural and behavioral sciences have counterparts in humanities where students explore museums, historical sites, architecture, and libraries. Professional fields have practices, internships, and case studies.

Grand schemes in education come and go, as education is restructured to fix real and perceived problems. Higher education has been somewhat immune from such schemes, but a number of colleges and universities are rethinking how to go about helping students get more out of education. In some part the considerations are guided by financial crises as enrollment changes in composition and number. Retaining and recruiting students are seen as ways to keep the campus financially healthy. Faculty members are handed the scheme in a series of workshops, selected readings, and forums. However, only when important connections are made between students and professors do students actually come away with a better understanding of the content. Whether a scheme actually works is often a point of contention between faculty and administration.

Educational technology has been one scheme to serve diverse populations, enlighten students, and retain students. Of the many technologies available, one is the World Wide Web on the Internet. The advantage of the Web and Internet for distance learning lies in the fact that anyone on the Web and Internet can connect to anyone else. Because students and instructors need not coordinate time and place, there is great flexibility. However, the Web has other elements that faculty may find useful and should think about as possible tools for their own classes.

By and large the world is a pretty fluid and dynamic place. However, paper and lectures tend to be relatively static. Instructors have worked around teaching students about active elements using a rich language and diagrams and flapping arms. Good lectures are *word pictures* of fluid and changing events and states. Demonstrations and films provide more convincing evidence that the word or picture on the page indeed represents something with change and movement. Actual involvement in a process, of course, provides an authentic rendering of what has been described. Students who learn sociological research methods in class are surprised to find that the neatness of a research method in the book does not exactly fit that of the actual research situation and learn a valuable lesson from their involvement in the process. Likewise, the bug under the microscope looks different from the one in the book or chalked on the board.

A final stage in most courses is some kind of problem solving. The process of learning how to take concepts and ideas and apply them is accomplished with exercises in class, in essays, and in field and lab experiments. The application of knowledge and using it to solve a problem clearly show a solid understanding of the content and not simply a rote repeating of what was said in class or written in a book.

Because Web pages and sites can generate processes that actually move, they can more closely approximate an active state and the process described. Arranged correctly, Web pages can serve as a problem-solving tool by which students are led through a series of problems and corrections so that they are engrossed and engaged in the process. A psychology lab requiring mice or pigeons can be simulated so that no caged animals are required and there is no expense for their upkeep and care. But more to the point, professors are given flexible and dynamic alternatives using the Web in helping students learn content. The Internet and Web as a communication system and the Web page and site as a learning tool provide *possibilities yet to be fully explored*. This book is an invitation to such an exploration.

To add flexibility to the book, the HTML and JavaScript listings for some of the more elaborate examples have been placed in appendices at the end of some chapters. For those interested in writing JavaScript or HTML script, these listings can be written in a text file and loaded in a browser. Allyn and Bacon at http://www.abacon.com have a link to the book so that the scripts can be seen at work on the Web. Likewise, each chapter ends with a *Glossary of Terms* used in the chapter. With all of the technical terms introduced by the Internet and Web, the Glossary should help readers get through the new vocabulary. Other terms introduced in the book but not necessarily from technology are included as well.

The best lesson one can take away from this book is not a set of answers to be applied in class, but rather the *idea* to explore what can be done with Web pages. The book provides ample examples and HTML, Dynamic HTML, a little JavaScript, and suggestions for tools and resources on the technology side of the equation. Ideas taken from AAHE, Tufte, Goffman, and others are added as possible frameworks to stimulate and perhaps even aggravate modes of teaching and learning. Ultimately, though, the professor who fully understands his or her course content and explores what can be done using Web pages will gain the most. They will also add the most to understanding the possibilities and limitations of the Web and learning.

Acknowledgments

Most of what I discovered about learning and technology came by way of faculty members with whom I worked in one capacity or another. Also, a number of staff members and nonacademics were most helpful and instructive. At the University of Hartford Steve Misovich, Lou Boudreau, David Demers, Don Sukosky, Art Auden, Dave Kelley, Sebby Sorentino, John Kalkbrenner, Jerry Katrichis, Margaret Finch, Al DiChiara, J. Stewart, Marilyn Schaffer, Fred Sweitzer, Mark Snyder, Catherine Stevenson, Chuck Colarulli, John Roderick, John Gray, and Ed Gray were among the many with whom I worked in an attempt to bring technology and learning together. They all added to my understanding of what the Web can and cannot do for education. Laura Spitz, a talented artist and Web designer, became a good friend and colleague and gave some great tips on design and creative uses of JavaScript and *Flash*. I also want to thank Merle Harris and Ed Klonoski of Charter Oak College and the Connecticut Distance Learning Consortium. Grants from the Sloan Foundation and State of Connecticut in conjunction with CDLC and the University of Hartford enabled me to get the needed equipment, software, and artistic talent from students at the Hartford Art School at the University of Hartford to complete three Web courses.

My appreciation goes to the following reviewers for their helpful comments on the manuscript: Heidi Schweizer, Marquette University and Mary Ellen Nourse, University of Idaho.

Chapter 1

Introduction—Technology Following Learning

Swimming in a Pond of Knowledge

The purpose of this book is to explore ways that Web sites designed by professors can help students learn. Universities have a great deal to accomplish, and one university goal, however worded, is to pass knowledge from the professors to the students. The knowledge may be contained in exercises in how to solve problems, how to think, analyze, collect data, evaluate experiments, or appreciate art, music, literature, and theater. Web pages and Web sites are part of a communicative technology that supplements textbooks, lectures, and the other paraphernalia professors use to stimulate interest, skills, and thought about content. They are not magic tools, but professors can do things with Web pages that cannot be done with textbooks and lectures alone. For the most part Web sites will not replace lectures and texts, but they can *extend* and *supplement* both. This book explores strategies in both learning and technology, and instead of being a definitive work, it is an invitation to explore what might be done.

Without being facetious, students in universities are literally swimming in ponds of knowledge. Considering how little of the sum total of their knowledge that professors impart on students, the students seem to wade in the shallow end of the pond. To get students to absorb more and *desire to know* more during their brief stay in universities is still an important goal. Were it the case that students arrived at universities with an unquenchable thirst for knowledge, professors' jobs as instructors would be considerably eased. (Indeed, if students were voracious in their want of knowledge, the library may suffice with little or no need for professors at all for instruction.)

The goal here is to explore learning practices and their link to Web technology. Further, the basic assumption is that students can learn just about anything if they have the right materials, and they work at it. This assumption is no revelation, but it is in stark contrast to nineteenth-century notions about inherited intelligence, that only a chosen few can achieve university-level knowledge. Some students will have to work harder and longer than others do, but like everything else in life, as one develops skills the tasks are less difficult. However, there are many deadly assumptions in universities about students and learning that we need to be clear about at the outset. The most important one is that only some students have the *capacity* to learn, and this capacity is revealed in some kind of statistical curve.

Teaching Bomb Defusing 101 or Why Grading on the Curve Can Be Dangerous

When I was an undergraduate, I had the opportunity to take a course that was divided between graduate students and undergraduates. We attended the same seminar, were involved in the same general research project, and had the same assignments. When it was time to prepare for an examination, the undergraduates were invited to study with the graduate students. This was not the first time I had been involved in group study, but it was the most memorable. In my mind, the graduate students were brilliant, and we undergraduates were lucky to be allowed to study with them. However, I remember wanting to prepare for the study session so that I wouldn't look too dull to my academic betters. When the study session began I listened, asked questions, and made a few well-chosen contributions. After the exam I found that all of those who participated in the session did pretty well on the test.

Had I spent the better part of my undergraduate years studying with others, I would have learned more than I did, but there were few times that I participated in a group study session. Back then grading on the curve was a norm, and if you helped someone else, it would "bring up the curve" and negatively affect one's own grade. An 80 percent would be a "C" grade instead of a "B" if everyone did well, but that same 80 percent would be an "A" if the rest of the class bombed. Other than studying with the graduate students, group study usually signaled some state of desperation by groups of unprepared students; so there was not a lot of correlation between group study and academic success.

Nevertheless, when I became a professor I encouraged students to study collectively and refused to grade on the curve. Not only did this appeal to a sense of democratic ability, but it allowed me to set standards that could be measured and evaluated. Students would not be artificially arranged in a curve but would have to prepare to a certain level of understanding that had been established.

When I was a new professor, I read a book about the bomb disposal units in London during the Blitz in World War II and how these units were trained to defuse unexploded bombs. Imagine grading on the curve teaching a class on bomb disposal. The graduates would be blown to smithereens on the same curve. If the class were made up of particularly dull students who were allowed to defuse unexploded bombs, even the "A" students would not last long. "Dumbing down" was not an option either because the consequences were too grave. Similarly, pilots are trained to certain standards for the different licenses they receive. There is no curve, and there is no dumbing down. I would not want to get into an airliner where the pilot was judged by anything other than high standards that she had met and by which she stayed current. Because there are lots of pilots who meet these standards, we can assume that it is possible to have high standards and require students to meet these standards with no curve or compromise in quality. Some pilots learn faster than others do, but whether they learn quickly or slowly is less important than they meet the standards and maintain them throughout their careers. (Lest one believes an airline pilot is merely an airborne bus driver, all one needs to do is to look at the conceptual understanding required for meteorology, aerodynamics, avionics, and global navigation.) As will be discussed later in the book, cooperative learning and setting high standards are key good practices for undergraduate education, and a good Web-based syllabus can enhance cooperative learning and help in communicating high standards.

Communicating the Complex

When personal computers and laser printers became widely available in the mid-1980s a remarkable thing occurred—desktop publishing. Prior to that time, anyone who wanted to publish a work that looked professional had to rely on typesetters, experienced printers, high press runs, and a substantial investment. Desktop publishing meant that anybody who taught a course was able to churn out materials to help students learn. Rather than relying solely on textbooks, professors could fine-tune their courses with helpful handouts that combined text and graphics that clearly communicated lesson materials. However, many of the early efforts by self-publishing amateurs looked like ransom notes where the kidnapper cuts out pieces of different publications to make the note and hide his handwriting. There appeared a dizzying array of fonts and styles that cluttered the page with the occasional graphic. Students were more likely to get long streams of text that could have just as well been done with a typewriter, but some instructors actually produced very helpful material for students to use in learning a subject. Copy-machine budgets and the mechanics of collating and binding materials for a class set other limitations. However, there was a tool available if only it could be used wisely.

About the same time *The Visual Display of Quantitative Information* (Tufte, 1983) was published. Written by a Yale professor of political science and statistics, the book set out to examine the design of statistical graphics and how to communicate information through the simultaneous presentations of words, numbers, and pictures. As its author, Edward Tufte, eloquently put the purpose of the book,

> *What is to be sought in designs for the display of information is the clear portrayal of complexity. Not the complication of the simple; rather the task of the designer is to give visual access to the subtle and the difficult—that is, the revelation of the complex (191).*

Those words, *the revelation of the complex*, struck me as precisely what universities and colleges are all about. As a sociologist, I was immediately attracted to the idea of better communicating quantitative data, but more important was the idea that complex concept, whether from English literature or quantum physics, could be presented in ways that better revealed complexity.

In later works Tufte explored how to escape the "flatland" of two-dimensional pages in *Envisioning Information* (1990), and how to effectively show cause and effect in *Visual Explanations* (1997). More simply put, the first work is about pictures of numbers, the second about pictures of nouns, and the third about pictures of verbs. These were exactly the kind of things that colleges and universities needed to know to effectively communicate complex concepts, processes, and structures.

Moreover, Tufte's works are universal in time and culture. In *Envisioning Information*, for example, Tufte draws on Euclid's *The Elements of Geometrie* (London, 1570) for a new idea. Pasted to the page is a folding pyramid that can be pulled into a three-dimensional object so that students can better understand the concept in solid geometry. One would think that a good idea from the sixteenth century would have been passed on and improved on, but instead we find contemporary books presenting solid geometry in two dimensions. Likewise, Tufte gathers examples from such diverse sources as Czechoslovakian airline schedules created in the 1930s and postwar Japanese travel guides. Good and bad examples are not limited to one period or culture. Tufte does an exceptional job in getting the reader to do what used to be called "thinking out of the box" in corporate America. However, Tufte shows that the way out of the "box" can be found in a wide variety of sources in time and place and explains how to look for them. For developing Web pages to help students understand a wide range of complex subject matters, Tufte's works will be used throughout this book.

Enter Hypertext and the World Wide Web

The next major event in recent years that has begun to reshape the thinking in education has been hypertext and the World Wide Web. As a concept, hypertext was designed to promote nonlinear computing in the late 1960s by Ted Nelson, a computer scientist (Gralla, 1998, 164). Rather than going sequentially from A to Z with all of the 24 stops in between, hypertext was designed to go directly from any one place to another. For many, nonlinear thinking is a closer approximation of what goes on in people's heads when they learn than is linear thought. Works in Gestalt psychology and ethnomethodology in sociology all clearly pointed to the importance of context in understanding. Rather than learning sequentially, people seemed to learn by constructing a sense of occasion retrospectively and prospectively (Garfinkel, 1967). Learning occurs more like seeing a picture emerge from a mosaic or jigsaw puzzle than by clearly understanding each step sequentially. As each piece is put into place, the viewer understands what the other parts meant retrospectively, and prospectively looks to the meaning of the rest of the emerging picture. All understanding occurs in some context, and building the context tells both about the context and the exact meaning of the elements that make up the context. Thus, hypertext had appeal beyond mere computing because it better reflected how learning and understanding occur.

The World Wide Web is set on HTML, or HyperText Markup Language. Importantly, we see the extension of the hypertext concept. Applied to a Web page, hypertext means that any Web page can be linked to any other Web page anywhere in the World Wide Web. It need not go sequentially from one to another. What's more, HTML is a "tag" language and not a computer language. That means a series of tags can be written to create a page, such as those used in early word processing programs. It is a relatively simple language, and even the most computer-phobic can learn how to create a Web page. For example, all text between the <B> tag and the </B> tag is made bold. Other simple tags organize text, graphics, and links into pages that can be viewed by anyone connected to the Web. Moreover, the Web was set up to be cross-platform so that Macintosh, Windows, and UNIX computer systems could talk to one another.

The Web as a source of teaching and learning has generated a great deal of excitement and hyperbole. Some view the Web as a way to effectively and inexpensively extend education beyond the classroom to "anywhere, any time" learning. Others view it as a way to dismantle the colleges and universities as teaching institutions. Both extremes are at odds with the facts of history. Books are wonderful tools for "anywhere, any time" learning as is television, and neither has spelled doom for the halls of higher education. The Web is neither a panacea nor a demon, but it can be a valuable tool. It effectively can give the professor the power to produce his own program. In the same way that desktop publishing provided everyone with the ability to be a publisher, the Web extends that ability to a video screen. What's more, the Internet connects every computer with a modem or Internet card to every other computer in the world. Unlike the desktop publisher, the desktop producer is not constrained by the costs of paper copies and distribution. Once a Web page is placed on a server connected to the Internet, the distribution is worldwide.

In addition, the Web has made it easy for students and professors to explore the world. Instead of having to gather all information solely from the library, students are able to explore a broad range of subjects easily from their desktops. (Actually, the library has become more important because it is an online source of material as well as the paper materials.) Powerful search engines can find a dizzying array of Web sites with everything from nanotechnology to Irish poetry. However, because the Web is wide open, the quality of information on the Web varies from Nobel Prize insights to raving bigotry, and anyone who has a point of view or what they consider "facts" is able to put that information on the Web. Such unrestricted, unreviewed, and clearly unedited materials set off academic alarm bells. With so much junk on the Web, many viewed it as an unreliable source of knowledge, and therefore concluded that students or professors doing serious research should not use it. However, others saw quite the opposite. If the Web is a source of universal access, good information should be launched, and the professors should teach students how to separate informational wheat from chaff. Review procedures needed to be put into place and reference systems similar to those used with books and journals could be used to trace a source.

How Do Students Learn?

In their article, "From Teaching to Learning: A New Paradigm for Undergraduate Education" (*Change*, 1995), R. B. Barr and J. Tagg laid the groundwork for learning-based education. Coming as it did when the Internet and World Wide Web were new but growing fast in academic circles, many of the issues raised in the article were seen as pertinent to both the use of the Web and the larger issue of instructional technology. Central to their article Barr and Tagg asked how a learning-centered environment could be created to enhance students' ability to leave college with real knowledge. The question shifted the focus from what is being taught to what is being learned and how does learning take place. In turn, this posed the question of how can technology be used to help students learn.

In a similar vein and around the same time, the National Science Foundation (NSF) had been asking the same questions Barr and Tagg addressed. The NSF's focus had been in the areas of science, math, engineering, and technology—SMET, for short. Concerned with the lack of students in the SMET subject areas, the NSF had launched programs to encourage students to select SMET majors and looked for ways to assist student learning, especially minority and women students where the dearth of SMET students and professors was most pronounced.

From NSF-sponsored research a number of findings and themes emerged (National Research Council, 1999). Among the findings active learning was found to be more effective than passive learning. Students who actively participated in learning activities did better than students who passively attempted to learn by reading and listening to lectures. Students in labs where they solved problems and worked with the tools of science, math, engineering, and technology were better able to comprehend the concepts than those who got their knowledge only from reading or lectures alone were.

Such a finding was important for instructional technology, especially multimedia technology where a student could interact with computer-generated images and data. The interaction makes up a virtual reality where she can take an active role in doing something to learn. Some virtual realities made active learning economical, such as those that simulated electron microscopes. An off-the-shelf electron microscope costs upward from $250,000 whereas the virtual microscope on a video monitor could be made available to students for a few hundred dollars. Both gave the students an active and valuable experience, and the same learning goal was accomplished, but the new technology made it affordable for far more institutions.

Evolution of the Web and Learning

Early versions of HTML gave the user little more than limited text and graphics placement along with links. There were a lot of pages with gray backgrounds, black text, a few awkwardly placed graphics, and underlined links. Evolving versions of HTML added tables, layers, frames, more graphic options, and improved text formatting. In addition, a language called JavaScript added dynamic feedback and multimedia. Importantly, JavaScript could be integrated with HTML, and it was simple enough that someone other than a computer programmer could add it. Many of the multimedia tools soon had Web page options whereby a multimedia presentation with full animation and sound was possible. Most noteworthy was a Web browser plug-in called Shockwave that allowed multimedia developed in certain programs to be streamed into the Web. It was built into the two major browsers produced by Netscape and Microsoft and was one of the emerging technologies that was able to stream small amounts of data over the Internet to produce dramatic multimedia results.

Development Tools: From Word Processors to GoLive

At the same time that new languages and streaming technologies were evolving, so too were development tools to make it easy to create Web pages. Most notable were options in word processors to save a page as HTML. Now faculty could use their word processors to make Web pages, and all handouts and syllabi could be put on the Web. (These efforts did shift the burden of copying and distribution from the departmental paper and copying budget to the student's inkjet cartridge and paper budget or to the college lab's budget.)

Powerful tools dedicated to creating Web pages were emerging as well. Most exceptional was a program called GoLive. It was an early tool that created Dynamic HTML (DHTML) pages for faculty who knew little or no HTML or JavaScript. With DHTML, it was possible to include dynamic feedback and interaction in Web pages. In another Web page development program, called Dreamweaver Attain, faculties were able to generate a variety of online tests and quizzes in addition to DHTML. Other developmental tools included Adobe's ImageStyler and Macromedia's Fireworks, which included built-in JavaScript generators and tools for enhancing Web graphics.

In addition to HTML development tools, special tools were developed for dealing with Web graphics. Initially, Web graphics were limited to the GIF format. Later JPEG was added and then PNG. New versions of popular graphics programs like Adobe *Photoshop* were revised to include special characteristics for dealing with Web graphics. Other graphic tools, such as Adobe's *ImageReady*, were developed specifically for creating Web graphics. Such tools made it possible to more easily create effective images to be integrated with text on Web pages.

All, Some, or a Little: Using the Web for Different Learning Goals

Among the many misunderstandings about the use of Web pages for teaching and learning is a view that such efforts must encompass an entire course. Like any other tool in a course, Web pages and related online materials can be incorporated in the same way. Lectures, discussions, books, labs, films, and field trips all constitute tools used to help students learn. The same is true with Web pages. It is a tool that used properly with other learning tools enhances the learning experience.

The best way to start using the Web and Web pages in a course is with small steps. Developing a single lesson or assignment, a syllabus, or a few well-chosen links makes more sense than trying to develop a whole course alone without sufficient support, training, or experience. Given the wide array of courses being offered and styles of offering them, a faculty member needs to get to know where and how to best incorporate Web pages for her own course. Testing Web materials with a class that regularly meets face to face helps a faculty member gauge how well a lesson using the Web works. Making adjustments within the context of a traditional class helps fine-tune Web lessons that may later be offered in distance education without face-to-face interaction.

In the same way that introducing Web pages into a class is not an all-or-nothing proposition, omitting traditional tools with any instructional technology tool is equally misinformed. Recording and interpreting materials found on the Web are usually best accomplished using paper. In many of the Web-based lessons discussed in this book, there are paper components for the students to use. Likewise books can be used to understand working with Web pages. While the computer is on, a book is a handy tool to use to learn how to do everything from programming to learning how to build a Web page. (Flipping back and forth from a Web page that shows how to build a Web page to actually building a Web page can be tiresome—it's easier to use a book.) So, the moral to the story is to use all the tools on hand, and use them together.

Learning and the Tail of the Dog

A major misconception about instructional technology is that it is somehow inherently instructional. The technology, like blank pages in a book, is the delivery system. How knowledge is best transmitted is the domain of good educational practices and communication design. Thus, it is important to remember that the technology is the tail of the dog. The dog is the rich tradition of practice, content, and design.

The new technology in Web pages allows faculty to do many things not easily done with traditional materials. However, if this new technology is used either as a continuation of earlier technology or in such a way as not to take advantage of what the technology has to offer, it does no good at all. We might as well use chalk and typewriters. Therefore, by beginning with good practices in learning, we ask not how the new technology can help us do a better job of getting students to learn a set of knowledge, but rather we ask how can good pedagogy be better implemented with the new technology. The strong educational practices are first and foremost, followed by excellent content, and concluded in good communication design.

Good Design

Any perusal of the World Wide Web demonstrates the wide variety of design skills. Design professionals create most of the good sites and all of the great sites. They use graphics, text, color, and arrangement of components to create interesting pages that lure the viewer into wanting to find out more. The navigation is clear, and the viewer knows at all times where she is, where she has been, and where she is going.

Unfortunately, if we look at Web pages created by most university and college faculty, we often see poor designs hiding excellent content. For example, one company that makes Web course administrative software shows off its wares with lessons created by faculty using their product. In one sample, the professor uses a turquoise blue text against a swirling turquoise and black background. It is very difficult to read, and a handout would better serve the students with black text on white paper. There are no graphics or links integrated with the long scrolls of text, and so in addition to being difficult to read, it really does not use the Web for anything that cannot be done with paper. The administrative template surrounding the faculty member's page is well designed, having the effect of drawing more attention to the poorly designed faculty page.

Throughout this book there will be design tips, but any faculty member who plans to use Web pages effectively should look at books on page design. Edward Tufte's works cited above provide a wealth of tips, and although very little is explicitly for Web pages, most of his insights apply to Web design. Two other excellent works include *The Non-Designer's Web Book* (1997) by Robin Williams and John Tollett and *Creating Killer Web Sites* (1997) by David Siegel. Both of these books address the common design problems encountered by novice Web page designers and explain how to make pages to effectively communicate a message.

Good Ideas

To effectively work with Web pages, faculty needs good ideas. Ideas for using Web pages as learning tools come from understanding one's own area of expertise and the limitations and opportunities possible in Web pages. One art historian used Web pages to let students explore Italian art through a series of links she designed to let the students browse through the Italian landscape geographically and historically. In addition, she let students view art from different perspectives to better show what the artist was attempting to accomplish. She spent a considerable amount of time in developing her project, but once she came up with the core idea, she was able to weave together a wonderful learning tool for her students.

Faculties who think creatively in research and writing can take the same kind of creative genius and apply it to teaching and learning. Good ideas can come from just about anywhere on the Web, not just university pages. Look for ideas all over the Web. If something is eye-catching and informative for one area, it may be the impetus for an idea for one's own course. Also, try thinking in more dynamic terms. In a recent discussion with a social psychologist, it occurred to me that social and behavioral scientists have taken dynamic behavior and frozen it in text. With new tools available for interactive media, we need to begin thinking of ways that these new tools could be employed to better explain a moving, flowing, and changing process that better reflects the reality of the social world.

Good Practices

In a report sponsored by the American Association for Higher Education, the Education Commission of the States, and the Johnson Foundation (Chickering and Gamson, 1987, p. 4.) six powerful forces were identified in education:

- Activity
- Cooperation
- Diversity
- Expectations
- Interaction
- Responsibility

Each of these forces was identified as key in the teaching and learning process. Taking them together seven good practices were derived for effective undergraduate education and serve as a starting point for effective pedagogy. Experienced faculty will find many of these practices to be nothing new to them, but each is important enough to bear repeating.

1. **Good practice encourages student-faculty contact**. Students who have frequent contact with faculty in and out of class enhance their intellectual commitment, motivation, and understanding of course material. Those faculty who demonstrate a concern and willingness to help students over difficult materials are more likely to be contacted by their students, and students are more willing to believe they can overcome roadblocks in learning.
2. **Good practice encourages cooperation among students**. Above I noted the personal benefit of working with other students. As cultural values, Americans hold individualism and competition very high. However, the society also recognizes the importance of community and teamwork to achieve excellence. Around these latter values it is possible to rally students to a cooperative

effort to excel. Students are social animals, and the sociability can be encouraged and enhanced to include scholarly study.

3. **Good practice encourages active learning**. Active learning immerses students in the learning process. Rather than sitting as spectators and learning, students who are involved physically in an activity are more likely to be involved mentally. Students' daily lives are affected in one way or another by everything they learn, and getting students to think, talk, and actively employ and develop knowledge better instills the facts, figures, and processes. Students who solve problems, participate in internships, or in some other way employ knowledge retain and comprehend better than those who do not.
4. **Good practice gives prompt feedback**. Learning is a process of adjustment. Everything from a rat learning to navigate a maze to a student understanding the importance of the Ottoman Empire requires feedback. Much of the feedback is through traditional assessment whereby a student writes a paper or takes an exam. Sometimes, busy faculties don't get the results back to the students until weeks after the exam. By then the class is off on other topics, and the purpose of the feedback is often lost. Assessment and feedback need to be seen as guides for students and not hurdles or means of stratifying students. The more feedback and the more immediate feedback students get the better they are served.
5. **Good practice emphasizes time on task**. It would surprise me if there were any faculty who is unaware of this practice for students. The more time a student spends with study materials, the better the student is likely to do. The quality of the materials is important, as is the quality of the time a student spends, but accumulating knowledge and understanding requires time. Of all of the practices, to me, this practice best exemplifies the concept of a learning-centered approach to education. Students must understand that they themselves are the best resource for learning, and they need to budget time and effort to do it right. By the same token, good faculty knows it takes time on their part to prepare lessons and help students.
6. **Good practice communicates high expectations**. Course expectations set the context for what students will expect of themselves. Everything from budgeting time to taking a course and faculty member seriously requires a sense that there will be a high-quality outcome. Students who believe that they can get by on a minimal effort will exert a minimal effort. Therefore, it is crucial that students are given both the message of high expectations and the means to meet those expectations.
7. **Good practice respects diverse talents and ways of learning.** Students learn in a variety of methods and have a variety of skills. Some students are great with theory and miserable in the lab. Others perform brilliantly in the lab but cannot understand theories and formula. Students talented in art may falter in computer programming and vice versa. Just as there are types of effective professors, there are different types of effective students. Recognizing the different ways students learn helps faculty create different learning environments.

Bringing all the parts together creates a learning-centered environment. Of the three key elements—good design, good ideas, and good practices—the most important is a good idea. Good ideas virtually always come from faculty trying to think up new ways to communicate or express an idea. Examples used throughout this book will be based on good ideas I've seen other faculty use to stimulate, provoke, inform, or elucidate. However, the reader needs to be the source of genius for really good ideas in one's own subject matter. What may be a good idea for a course in French literature may not work so well for biochemistry. Although this book will not be a source of good ideas, I hope it will serve as a catalyst for good ideas. The Web opens up possibilities not previously available to faculty. Using the Web creatively and effectively depends on faculty understanding its possibilities.

It is possible to teach good design, but it is far more difficult to be a good designer. In my own experience, I've fared better hiring student artists to help me design a decent looking Web page than doing it on my own. However, knowing how to avoid really bad design will go a long way to making anyone a better page designer. Tufte's work will serve as a guide for effectively designing Web pages that clearly convey complex relationships using text, graphics, and links. Other tips for incorporating good design specifically for the Web will be discussed throughout the book.

The ideas and design will be integrated with good practices in teaching and learning. In preparing course materials, the first question that needs to be posed is "What is the student expected to learn?" Next, it is necessary to ask, "Which practices can be incorporated to assist students in meeting this goal?" At this point good ideas need to be reviewed, created, and borrowed. Then, and only then, should we inquire about the role of a Web page in implementing the idea and good practice.

Glossary of Terms

Note Throughout the book glossary terms will be developed and expanded in the text. The glossaries at the end of each chapter are provided to give a working vocabulary to some of the more technical terms used in Web technology.

Browser A Web browser is the operating system that provides a mechanism for calling for Web pages and then reading and translating Web pages to display them on a computer screen. Netscape Navigator and Microsoft Internet Explorer are two major Web browsers.

DHTML (Dynamic HTML). This is an advanced version of HTML that includes more robust handling of text formatting and animated components on a Web page.

HTML Acronym for HyperText Markup Language. This is the main language used to describe a Web page. The browser contains the HTML interpreter.

Hypertext This is a nonlinear concept whereby text can be read and accessed in any order. The World Wide Web is organized so that any link on a Web page can go directly to another Web page using this nonlinear concept.

Internet This is a network of communication that connects computers using modems and other digital data communication devices and Internet protocol software.

Plug-in To add functionality to a browser, several companies provide plug-ins for Web browsers so that their product can be used on the Web.

Shockwave Provided as a plug-in, multimedia programs, including animation and sound, can be viewed and heard on the Web. Developed by Macromedia, files developed with *Flash* and *Director* can be run as Shockwave files.

World Wide Web The World Wide Web refers to all of the Web pages that can be accessed with a browser on the Internet.

References

Barr, R. B., and J. Tagg. "From Teaching to Learning: A New Paradigm for Undergraduate Education." *Change* 4: 13–25 (November/December 1995).

Chickering, Arthur W., and Zelda F. Gamson. "Principles for Good Practice in Undergraduate Education." *The Wingspread Journal* (June 1997). Published as a special insert.

Garfinkel, Harold. *Studies in Ethnomethodology* (Englewood Cliffs, NJ: Prentice-Hall, 1967).

Gralla, Preston. *How the Internet Works* (Indianapolis, IN: Que Books, 1998).

National Research Council (ed.). *Transforming Undergraduate Education in Science, Mathematics, Engineering, and Technology* (Washington, DC: National Academy Press, 1999).

Siegel, David. *Creating Killer Web Sites: The Art of Third Generation Site Design* 2nd ed. (Indianapolis, IN: Hayden Books, 1997).

Tufte, Edward. *The Visual Display of Quantitative Information* (Graphics Press: Cheshire, CT: 1983).

Tufte, Edward, *Envisioning Information* (Graphics Press: Cheshire, CT: 1990).

Tufte, Edward. *Visual Explanations* (Graphics Press: Cheshire, CT: 1997).

Williams, Robin, and John Tollett. *The Non-Designer's Web Book: An Easy Guide to Creating, Designing, and Posting Your Own Web Site* (Berkeley, CA: Peachpit Press, 1997).

Chapter 2

Basic Parts of a Web Page: Text, Graphics, and Links

What Is a Web Page?

Web pages can be anything from robust interactive multimedia to simple screens of text. On the most basic level a Web page shows three elements on a computer screen:

1. Text
2. Graphics (and sound)
3. Links

Understanding the role of text in a Web page is not much different from understanding text in a paper, article, or book. However, making an effective and well-designed Web page using text can be misunderstood even though most of the design conventions for using text on a Web page are taken directly from general principles of page design.

Graphics on a Web page require acquisition or preparation and placement on a page. Included in graphics are photographs, drawings, videos, and animation. A fourth element of a Web page, sound, is included with graphics because of similar computer requirements, and often sound is played simultaneously as part of a video. A major consideration with graphics and sound is the amount of bandwidth they consume, and so in addition to discussing their effective use in teaching and learning, we need to know something about keeping their size within the restrictions of bandwidth.

Links are at the heart of understanding how to effectively use Web pages. Not only are they the essential hypertext structure, they are the gateway to organizing learning. Our discussion of links is essentially a discussion of organizing Web pages. Links are the strands in the World Wide Web, and the way in which pages are linked to one another determines the students' experience of a Web site.

Before going on, there are some very basic understandings of the Internet and the World Wide Web that need clarification. This will provide a context for much of the discussion and considerations that will follow. For readers who are fully knowledgeable about the Internet and World Wide Web, feel free to skip over to the next section.

How the Internet and World Wide Web Work

The World Wide Web lives on the Internet. Without being overly technical, the Internet is an international network of computers that are linked together. There is no "giant brain" that controls it. Rather through a series of computers, routers, power lines, microwave links, cables, and protocols, all of the computers can communicate with one another. The World Wide Web Consortium (W3C) is an international organization that sets standards, but they do not control the Web. Email and the World Wide Web run over the Internet.

The most basic components on the World Wide Web are **servers** and **clients**. *Servers* are computers and software that store Web pages. *Clients* are computers and software that use the Web pages—essentially everyone who uses the Web. Web browsers such as Netscape Communicator or Microsoft Internet Explorer constitute *client software,* and your computer is the *client hardware* when you view a Web page. Browsers are the "brains" or effective operating systems that deal with the Web on a personal computer. Browsers make contact with the servers and get them to send Web pages to the desktop computer and then read the code that tells how to present the Web page on the computer screen. When you prepare course material for the Web, you will need to put the Web pages on a server—a computer with software configured to send your Web pages to clients who request them. In the case of course materials, the clients will be your students.

Every Web page has a Uniform Resource Locator or URL. That's another way of saying that it has an *address*. Every address (URL) on the Web is unique, and so when you put your page on a server, it will be the only page in the whole world with its unique address.

When a link to a Web page is clicked the computer sends a request to the URL for the page indicated in the link (see Figure 2-1). The server then sends the Web page to the client. As soon as the client (your computer) receives the Web page, the connection between the client and server is broken. Now the Web page is in your computer's RAM—dynamic memory. (RAM stands for "random access memory" and it refers to the electronic memory capacity your computer has while it is turned on.) In fact, if two seconds after you received the Web page from the server, the server broke, it would not affect the Web page you received. All of the graphics, text, and code required now reside in your computer's memory. If you save the page to your hard disk, all of the information is now permanently saved and can be viewed again by having your browser retrieve it from your permanent

Client requests Web page.
Client
Server
Server sends page to client.

FIGURE 2-1 The client requests a Web page from the server. The server sends the Web page to the client and disconnects. It reconnects as soon as a new page is requested from the client.

storage—a hard drive, floppy, or high-capacity removable disks such as a Zip, Jaz, or SuperDisks. Browsers allow your computer to keep many Web pages in memory at the same time. In this way, you don't have to wait for the page to be re-sent from the server if you go back to it again. You may notice that sometimes the same page that takes a long time to load initially will load very quickly when you go back to it. The reason for that is it is already in your computer, and your browser just brings it to the current window.

Why Do Some Pages Take a Lot of Time to Load?

The more information that is in a page, the longer it takes to load. The speed at which a Web page is sent over the Internet depends on the available bandwidth. Think of bandwidth as a pipeline. The bigger a pipeline, the more water that is able to flow swiftly through the pipeline. During a particularly bad storm or flood, the pipelines become overwhelmed with water and debris that collect, and things get backed up. The same is true with the Internet. The more information going through the Internet at any one time, the more time it takes to get from one place to another. Rush hour on the freeway is slower because everyone is using it at the same time.

Bigger Web pages take more time. The "size" of a Web page refers to the amount of text, graphics, and other associated files it has with it. *Associated files* are simply those files—such as graphics, sound, or video—that the Web page calls up when the page is loaded. A Web page made entirely of text is relatively "small" even if it is several pages long. Web pages with lots of graphics and other associated files can be very "big." The size of a Web page depends on the amount of information required to get the entire page on your computer. Most Web pages have the bulk of their "weight" or "size" in the graphic images. There are tricks to both reduce graphic sizes and increase speeds, but it is important to remember that whenever a graphic is added to a page, it slows the page. By no means should this dissuade one from using graphics, but they need to be used wisely and well.

In considering the amount of bandwidth that is being used and the amount available to the user, it is important to keep in mind that the user may be dealing with much less bandwidth than you have. At this writing, most colleges and universities are connected to the Internet through T1 lines. These lines run at speeds of up to 1.5 mps (megabits per second). Most private homes have modems that have speeds between 28.8 kps (kilobits per second) and 56.6 kps. Because a mps is a unit of measure 1,000 times faster than a kps, you can see that the speed at which a page downloads at a college may be significantly faster than download time for the same page at a student's home. ("Downloading" refers to getting a Web page or other data from a server to your computer. "Uploading" refers to sending something from your computer to a server.) So if it takes two seconds to download a page at a computer in a university office, it might take two minutes to download that same page at a computer in a student's home. Therefore, in developing Web pages, it is a good idea to calculate how much time they will take to download to a typical household connection used by your students. However, if most of the Web pages are going to be used by students in university dormitories or campus computer labs, speed differences will be of little concern. Internet 2 is a faster and newer version of the Internet available at larger research universities for moving vast amounts of data quickly, and Web pages on Internet 2 will load extremely fast.

Newer, higher-speed connections are becoming available for homes, and the difference may not be as great in the near future. Cable modems and Digital Service Lines (DSL) are being installed, and new technologies are increasing bandwidth all the time. Getting to know students in courses where Web pages are to be used involves *getting to know what kind of Internet connections they have.*

Similarities and Differences Between a Web Page and a Printed Paper Page

There are many differences between a Web page and a printed paper page, but there are many similarities as well. It's important to review both, but I do not want to belabor the topic. Many of the nuances of each will become apparent as we further discuss using pages for teaching and learning.

Text

The use of text on Web pages has gone from a limited set of typefaces to a fairly large family, limited only by what is available on the client computer. Unlike paper where all text printed on a piece of paper is going to be the same for all viewers, what you see on a Web page depends on everything from the font set in the client computer to what default font is set on her browser. Sticking with fairly limited sets of fonts, such as sans serif (Arial, Helvetica, Verdana, Geneva), serif (Times, New York), or mono-spaced (Courier, Monaco), you will have a better chance of having the viewer see what you intend. Figure 2-2 shows examples of sans serif (top) and serif (bottom) fonts.

Formatting text on a Web page is also more difficult than on paper. Using Cascading Style Sheets (CSS), it is possible to do a good job incorporating all of the different style conventions found on paper. Perhaps the most important is the simple *indent*. Rather than reading through blocks of squarely formatted text separated by double spaces, it is possible to include CSS instructions to use a wide variety of conventional formats. Further on in this book, we will see the different formatting options in HTML and how to incorporate them and others in making text behave.

One option some Web page designers use when a certain font is required for them to create the desired effect is the use of graphic fonts. Unlike fonts in text that depend on the client computer to have the same font set, graphics fonts are the same on all client computers. They take up more room and can slow Web page load time, so they should be used sparingly. However, graphic fonts can play important roles as display type used in headings.

Resolution

Probably the most important difference between a computer screen and a printed page is resolution. A typical typeset page will have about 2,400 dpi (dots per inch), and the typical computer screen about 72–100 dpi. Even an inexpensive laser printer has 300–600 dpi, and most inkjet printers have between 600 and 1,200 dpi. For all practical purposes, that means that text and graphics on paper have far

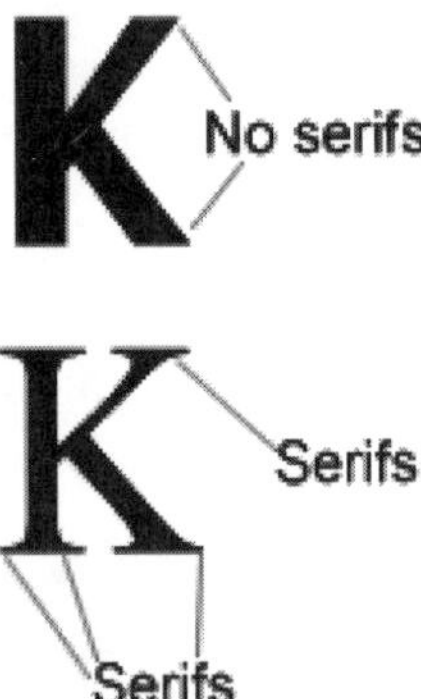

FIGURE 2-2 The little spurs on fonts are called "serifs." Fonts without serifs are sans serif fonts. With the relatively low resolution of Web pages, often sans serif fonts such as Arial or Verdana are preferable because the serifs may give the text a "dotty" appearance.

more detail and realism than on a computer screen. To be sure, the resolution on computer screens has improved and will continue to do so. Nevertheless, it is crucial to understand that text is more difficult to read and graphics have less detail on a computer screen than on paper. From my own experience with using Web pages, I have found that students wisely print out Web pages with a lot of text. It's more transportable and easier for them to read.

If high resolution is of paramount importance, such as showing fine detail in paintings and subtle differences in color, texture, and shading, paper is superior. However, if the learning goal is for students to differentiate between two schools of painting, good graphics on a computer screen have sufficient detail so that students can learn the difference between a Van Gogh and a Renoir.

> Using a combination of Web pages and paper pages can add a great deal to the utility of teaching and learning. A wise instructor will use the advantage of each so that paper and screen will work together rather than against each other.

Links

Paper documents are essentially linear. Books, articles, and papers proceed in a linear fashion by having the reader turn the page. Web pages can be either linear or nonlinear. The concept of hypertext is a nonlinear one, and the most important feature of a Web page is its ability to be linked to any other Web page in the world. However, a well-organized lesson on the Web should have features of *both* linear and nonlinear organization. In the next section, this will be discussed in more detail, but for now it is enough to understand that the ability to link directly from one page to another is a key feature of a Web page.

Articles in magazines often skip pages by having a reference to an out-of-sequence page. This is different from a Web page in that Web pages have direct *links*. The "next" page in a Web site depends on the organization of the links rather than the physical arrangement of the pages. This feature can be difficult to fully exploit initially because most professors are used to working with linear concepts and tools. Chapter 3 provides a conceptual framework for integrating a combination of linear and nonlinear features together.

Color

One of the major features of Web pages that is important for faculty creation of learning environments is the use of color. Color slides, prints, videos, and films are nothing new in teaching and learning. However, most of the time, *creating* and *duplicating* materials in color has been either prohibitively expensive or simply unavailable.

Like resolution on paper, there are far more limitations to the use of color on a video monitor than on paper. However, most of what faculty creates and prepares for a course is in black and white. Color inkjet or laser printers can do a pretty decent job of printing out single sheets of paper in color or transparencies for overhead projection. However, for providing each student a color copy of a lesson, Web pages are virtually free in their distribution. All a faculty member needs to do is to put the color components into a Web page and put the page on a server, and every student who goes to the URL will see the same lesson in color.

Color on the World Wide Web is as good as the monitors and computers processing the color. Early on, it became apparent that only certain colors were common to the browsers, operating systems, and monitors. Called "Web-safe" or "browser-safe" colors, the 216 common colors have limited what can be done safely (that is, with the secure knowledge that all the colors will look the same to all computers). However, having identified the Web-safe colors, one can forge ahead with the knowledge that the colors will be the same to all viewers.

There are a number of ways to ensure the colors you use are Web-safe. The most simple is to use Web-safe palettes when developing graphics for the Web. Most tools used for creating Web graphics will have an option for Web 216 colors. For example, Figure 2-3 shows how *Fireworks*, a Web graphic tool, provides a set of swatches clearly labeled as such.

By selecting the Web 216 Palette in *Fireworks*, your work is essentially "frozen" to those colors. This prevents accidentally using a color that will look different from the intended color.

When attempting to effect an exact match in colors, you can use the values for the RGB (red, green, blue) palettes. There are three different sets of values. First, in the native language of HTML, there are sets of six hexadecimal values. These values are expressed in terms of sixteen alphanumeric values from 0 to F. For

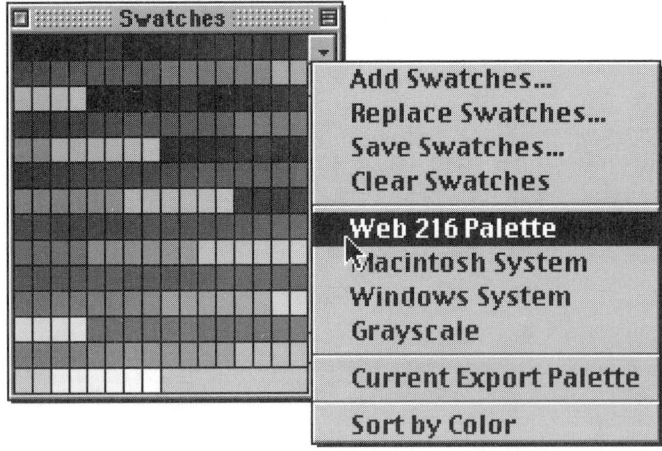

FIGURE 2-3 Most graphic applications contain a set of Web-safe colors so that the colors will appear the same on all monitors.

example, in an HTML color value, you may see the number FFCC66. That number tells your computer to create a color that has the following values:

Color	*Hex*	*Decimal*
Red	FF	255
Green	CC	204
Blue	66	102

Most Web and graphic tools do all the numeric conversion for you, and the only real knowledge you need is to be able to duplicate the value. So if you see the color value CC3399 and you use that same value in another graphic, you'll get the same color.

For example, in using the Netscape Composer, the Web page tool that is provided with Netscape Communicator, you will be given a color picker that uses several different kinds of values (see Figure 2-4). To keep your pages within the Web-safe realm, you can use the HTML picker that can lock in the 216 colors you need.

By checking "Snap to Web color" it is possible to keep colors locked into the six values for each color that guarantee Web-safe colors. The hexadecimal values are:

00 33 66 99 CC FF

Safe **hexadecimal values**

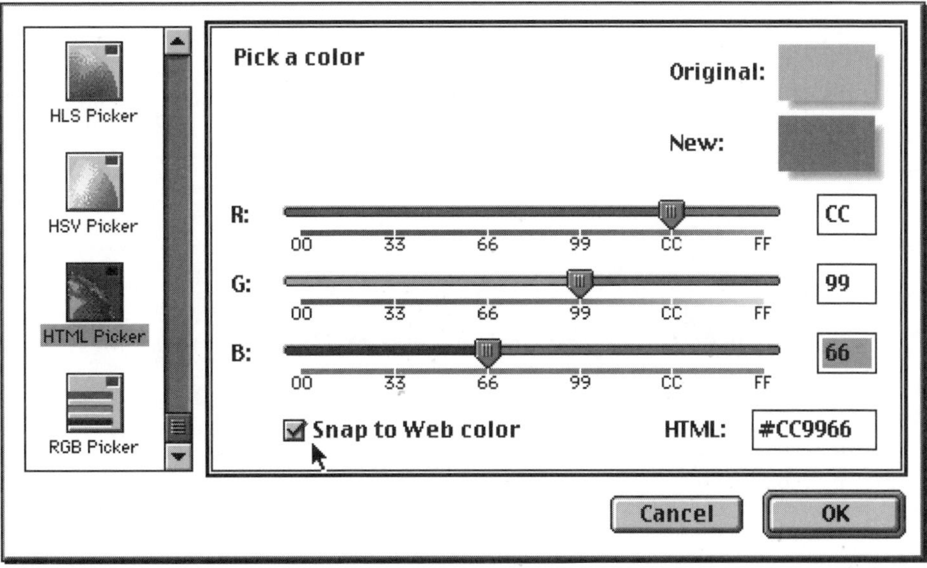

FIGURE 2-4 Web-safe values can be controlled by color pickers that limit the values to a globally accepted set that ensures the same color on different monitors.

Any RGB combination of those values will be safe on any Web browser. For example, the value 0099CC or 33FF66 would be safe, but FC42AB would not be, even though it would be accepted as a legitimate color by the browser. You just couldn't be sure how it would look on anyone else's computer screen.

Some color pickers provide values in percentages of RGB. Their safe values are:

0 20 40 60 80 100

Safe **decimal percentages**

In using percentages, just remember to count by 20, and your color will be safe. Netscape Composer's percentage color picker shows how this works in Figure 2-5.

A final way that colors are selected by RGB values is using decimal values (not percentages) instead of hexadecimal values. If a picker uses decimal values, the safe ones are:

00 51 102 153 204 255

Safe **decimal values**

For example, Figure 2-6 shows *Fireworks'* mixer in the RGB decimal color mode. Note that the colors in decimal are part of the "safe set" for decimal colors. If using commercially prepared art, or "clip art," try to get artwork that uses browser-safe colors.

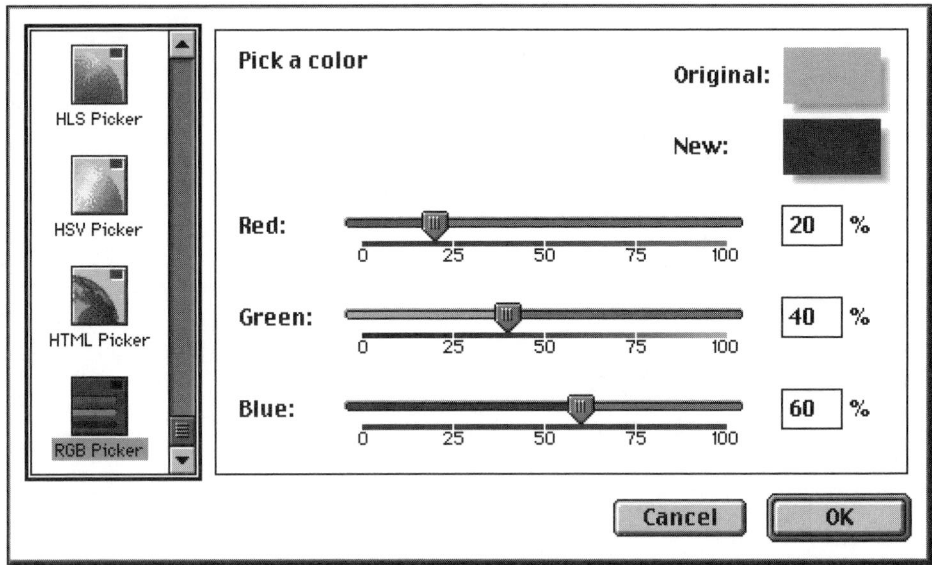

FIGURE 2-5 Using decimal percentages is easy because the Web-safe values are in counts of 20 beginning with 0 and ending with 100.

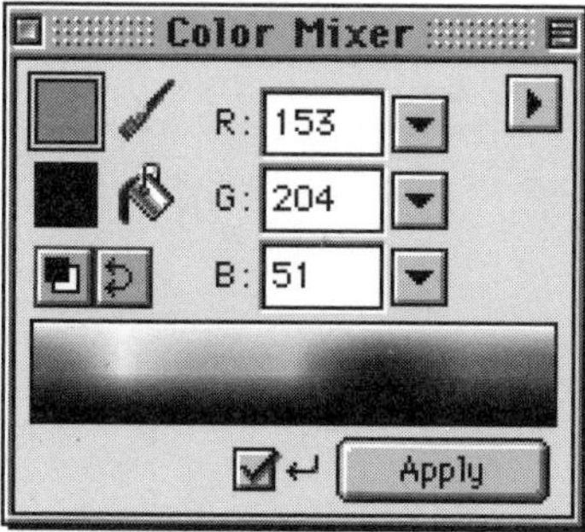

FIGURE 2-6 Remembering the RGB decimal values not represented as percentages is more difficult, but it can be useful if other methods are not available.

Animations

Another important difference between paper and Web pages is the capacity for Web pages to show animations. Like all animations, those on Web pages are a series of still images flicked in sequence to give the illusion of motion. There are several types of animation associated with Web pages.

1. **Animated GIFs**. These are the most ubiquitous types of animation found on Web pages. They are a series of GIF images that are sequenced through either a set number of loops or infinite loops. Used wisely by faculty, animated GIFs can help students understand conceptual processes, change, and other phenomenon that is subject to change. Far too often, though, animated GIFs are used in a superfluous manner that distracts from the page's focus. Designers use the term "dancing baloney" to effectively describe and discredit such usage of animated GIFs.
2. **Swapped images**. Often called "rollovers," graphic images on a Web page can be swapped, showing change and comparison. Using different buttons and pointer positions with the mouse, it is possible to swap several images in a single position.
3. **Movies.** There are several different types of movies. Some are simply digital videos translated from videotape. Others are created with special software using a plug-in so that they can be shown on a Web page. (A plug-in is a file that adds special functions to a browser—plug-ins can be downloaded from the Web.) One technology used is called Shockwave, which has the ability to run very compact movies made with programs such as Macromedia's *Flash* and *Director*. Instructors using *Flash* have produced interactive movies to help students understand relationships between dynamic concepts where a change in one dimension will lead to changes in others. Apple Computer, Inc. introduced the iMac DV in 1999 along with the iMovie editor. These movies run in

a QuickTime mode using a QuickTime plug-in that runs on both Windows and Macintosh computers. Movies in digital format that run on the Web are also called "d-films."

Interaction

A final and extremely important difference between paper and Web pages is the enhanced capacity for Web pages to be interactive—the extent to which a student gets feedback based on her actions and then can respond to the feedback. Dynamic Web pages allow students to receive feedback based on responses they generate by writing information on a Web page or using the mouse or keyboard to indicate a choice or decision. (See the Allyn and Bacon companion Web site for this book at http://vig.abacon.com/gallery/ for some examples of interactive Web pages. In later chapters there are examples as well.)

Linear and Nonlinear Organization and Learning

It would be an oversimplification to insist on an either/or classification to linear and nonlinear organization of Web pages. However, it is useful to *begin* a discussion of Web pages in terms of linear and nonlinear organization. Then we will examine the richer aspects of organizational possibilities.

Linear organization in Web site design means that each Web page is designed to follow sequentially from a previous one. If the sequence is broken, there will be skipped or missing information. On the face of it, it would seem that most learning necessarily has this kind of sequence. After all, in order to learn many concepts, it is first necessary to master prior concepts. One cannot do multiplication without understanding addition and subtraction. Figure 2-7 illustrates a linear organization.

Web pages can be organized in a linear fashion, but at the same time Web pages have other options not available with a paper page. A link on a Web page can do more than simply replace a current page with another page. It can bring up additional information in a window while the current page stays in place. In a

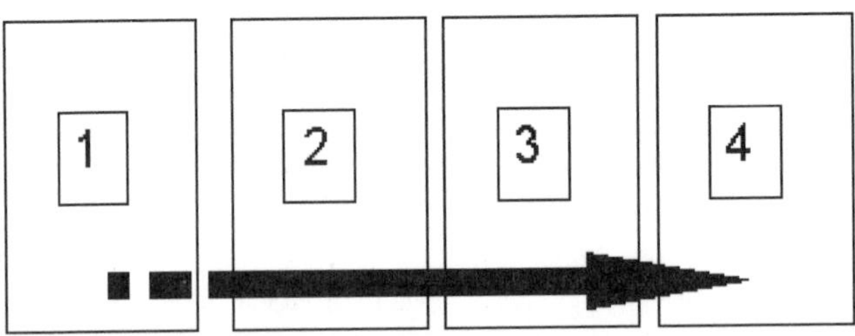

FIGURE 2-7 Linear organization expects each page to be approached in sequence.

similar manner that an annotated text has information in the margins, a Web page can have a link to an expanded annotation. However, instead of placing additional information in a margin, Web pages can bring up one or more separate windows to provide vocal, animated, graphic, or textual enhancements to what is on the page. Figure 2-8 shows how a window can be brought up to supplement a current page.

Another type of linear organization has features of both linear and nonlinear. This is a "tree organization." The Web pages are organized so that there is more than a single option of where the student will go next. This can either be a form of decision tree with feedback for an incorrect choice, or it can be used as a way to explore a subject matter that has different branches a student can visit in a number of different manners.

Another kind of Web organization is one that can go in a wide array of directions. This kind of organization can be employed to provide students with information around a central point or page. I will use the term "contextual" to describe the organization to underscore the role this organization plays in providing students with a larger context for a topic.

Contextual organization is useful when the instructor wants students to examine a topic in terms of different dimensions and to understand a topic in a fuller context. Also, the instructor can have students compare a core idea from different perspectives or fully explore a topic that is best accomplished by the student following his interest from piece to piece. One very interesting use of this

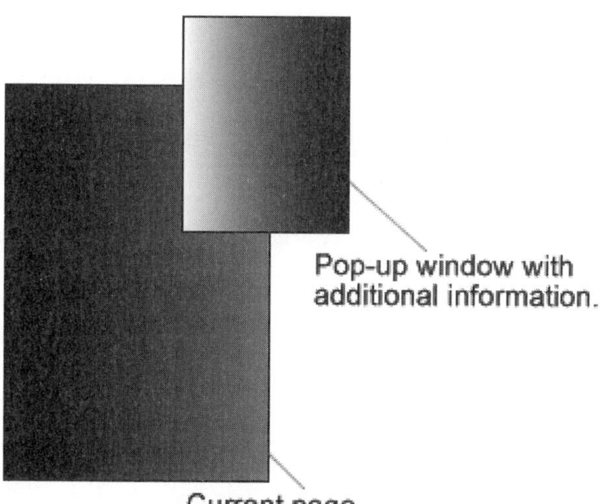

FIGURE 2-8 Several different pop-up windows can be brought up to supplement a current page. Graphics, sound, or textual materials can be brought to bear for enhancing information on a current page—not amenable to paper publications.

organization was done by an anthropology professor who showed her students the many different definitions and aspects of the concept of culture. Throughout the text, links to different definitions provide exploration paths for students to examine how different theorists conceived of culture.

Many more variations of these basic Web page organizations certainly exist, and new forms of Web page organization are likely to emerge as professors create them to meet educational needs. The main point in this section has been to show alternative forms of organization that extend beyond what is available only with traditional paper modes. Web pages should be viewed as invitations to go beyond what is possible or practical with paper-based means of communication. At the same time, Web pages can be an extension of paper materials to be used in conjunction with them. It is important to always remember that the goal is not to use one media or another, but rather use whatever best meets a pedagogical end.

Learning and Lesson Sites

Finding the right metaphor for a Web-based learning site very much depends on the nature of the course and the material the students need to learn. In Chapter 3, we will discuss Third Generation Web sites, but here, we need to look at how a Web page is to be used as part of a lesson in the context of different kinds of course uses. In that way, it is possible to better understand the use of a Web page in a teaching and learning context.

Syllabus

Probably the easiest and most useful way for faculty to begin developing Web pages for teaching and learning is with a course syllabus. The major purpose of a syllabus is to provide a means for students to quickly look up assignments, be linked to course pages, be linked to sites outside the course, and have a ready source for detailed information about the course. Another very useful purpose for an online syllabus is to link the student to the professor and to other students. Email links enable the student to quickly contact the professor or classmates.

In my own experience with online syllabi, I have also found that they are useful for adding new information once the course gets started. For example, during the crisis in Kosovo, new information about the plight of refugees became available online. It was a simple matter to add a link to sites concerning the refugees to a course that dealt with hunger, malnutrition, and disease. Likewise, online study guides can be added along with any other timely information that was not initially put in the syllabus. Finally, students never lose online syllabi.

Part of a Lesson

My first use of Web pages for a course was born of necessity, not planning. Having to go to a convention, I was unable to find someone to cover my classes. Therefore, I put together an elaborate Web lesson that did several things:

1. Sent students to obtain data available online.
2. Explained to them how to take the raw data and transform it into a rate so that they could compare unequal populations.
3. Enabled students to send the process and product of their work to the professor via email

As it turned out, the students did a much better job on that particular part of the lesson than those in the past who had taken notes from my lecture. It was *not* because the material had been on a Web page, but rather it was due to several components of the assignment. First, it included *active learning* (they had to go get the data themselves). Second, there was *good contact with the professor* (email). Third, the students were involved in *problem solving* (they had to learn a new technique to solve a problem). Finally, students received *prompt feedback* (I responded to 150 emails individually as soon as I got back).

Sometimes, there will be only a few lessons in a course for which a faculty member will feel that a Web page will be useful. Web pages can also be a supplement to a full lesson. Faculty can present material in class using a strong pedagogy and supplement that with material on a Web page that covers the same materials. Given the diverse ways of learning and understanding, such a use of a Web page acts as an additional angle, perspective, or way of looking at course material.

Part of a Schedule

Some classes would be much better for certain students if they did not have to travel to campus for every course meeting. Students who work full time, have families, or have some other responsibility or limitation that requires their off-campus attention may find it very difficult to come to classes three times a week. However, they may want or require the in-class contact and face-to-face association with both fellow students and their professor. Meeting once or twice per week and having the other "meetings" through the use of Web pages and email is one way to both help students and optimize the use of Web pages. Faculty can make adjustments both in class and on the Web based on the different kinds of feedback they get from the different sources.

Virtual Labs

Another use of Web pages in a class organization is for virtual labs. These labs can be held either in computer classrooms or at distributed sites. For example, some psychologists are experimenting with Web-based labs where students conduct traditional experiments on Web pages. One experiment asks experimental subjects to pronounce different colors based on three different conditions:

1. Viewing blocks of color
2. Reading colors
3. Reading words of colors but in a different color than indicated by the word. (For example, the word "red" is colored blue.)

The Web page has a timer, and after each experimental condition is presented, the student writes down the amount of time it takes to complete uttering all of the colors on the page. Using single or multiple trials, the student learns the rudiments of comparing experimental conditions, recording data, and comparing data with the rest of the class.

All of the fundamental conditions of experimental procedures are present, but there is more consistency in the testing because the pages and timing mechanism are identical. Other experimental conditions from natural, social, and behavioral sciences can be simulated with Web pages as well. It is simply a matter of putting some or all of the materials on a Web page and having students record the events. A lab assistant can be present both to help in working with the experimental elements and to help students with procedural, analytical, or conceptual problems they encounter. If the lab is accessed through remote sites, an online lab assistant using synchronous or asynchronous communication provides the assistance. With a remote assistant, a virtual Web lab can function in the same way that a combined on-campus and online course is organized.

Full Course

In some cases, entire courses are handled over the Web. In this arrangement, it is crucial that communication and feedback are regular. From experience, it has been found that after an initial rush of enthusiasm, there is a sharp falloff in student performance and interest. A good and easy-to-use online syllabus is the key to keeping everyone in touch. Likewise, online discussion software needs to be used to provide synchronous discussion (chat groups) or asynchronous discussion for students. Using collaborative projects will help students better master the material and help keep up interest. Students feel less isolated and often students helping each other can clarify points that the professor could not.

It is essential to have carefully scheduled assignments, regular and prompt feedback, and constant checking on students who are getting behind, even a little. This type of course requires more faculty monitoring and work than a course in a classroom. If a student has an unanswered query, she may not ask again or may end up misunderstanding whole portions of the course. It has been found that students working at their own pace can be fatal for those who procrastinate. When organizing a course that is taught entirely on the Web, there can be flexibility in the student's timing, but only up to a point. Very early on, it is important for faculty to advise students, no matter how convoluted their schedule, to make the necessary time to complete all the work, and faculty monitoring has to be rigid and constant.

Bringing All the Parts Together

This chapter provides an overview of what Web pages are, how the Internet works, and some things that can be done with Web pages to enhance the communication between professors and their students. Importantly, instructors can do things with Web pages that are not as easily or well done with paper and lectures alone. They can serve as extensions of a professor's ideas, concepts, and imagination, working to supplement both paper and spoken presentations. Web pages are relatively easy and inexpensive multimedia and so they are affordable and possible for most universities. The flexibility of hypertext allows both linear and nonlinear organization of content that best serves the nature of the content.

Most dynamic materials are presented in the static and flat environment of paper. Verbal descriptions in class accompanied by text and static graphics tell part of the story. Web pages provide animated components to bring processes and change alive in real, accelerated, or decelerated time. Presented in a classroom, a computer lab, or a student's home or dormitory computer, animated content on a Web page extends further the way in which a professor's message is communicated. It is not a matter of tossing out methods that have proved effective in the past. Rather, Web pages contain the technology to extend those methods in ways not previously possible.

Glossary of Terms

Animated GIFs Graphic files that provide animation by quickly showing a series of still images.

Associated files Any file that is called by a Web page's HTML that is to be displayed with the Web page.

Bandwidth The amount of data that can pass through a connecting line or wireless connection. The greater the bandwidth, the more data that can pass through it.

Clients Computers used to view Web pages.

Contextual organization Also called "random" organization; the user can go from any one place in a Web site to another.

d-film Digital movie that can be viewed with a Web plug-in such as RealVideo or QuickTime.

Hexadecimal A base-16 counting system used in computers for counting. Colors on the Web are read in six-digit hexadecimal values.

iMovie A software editing program for digital video from Apple Computer, Inc. It is also used to refer to "Internet movies" created in the iMovie software.

Linear organization An organization that requires that each page be viewed in a sequence with a specified page necessarily preceding another.

Links On Web pages, any area that calls the address of another page to be brought to the screen is referred to as a link. Usually a link is initiated by clicking on text or graphics that are coded to call the linked Web page.

RAM An acronym for random access memory, it refers to the amount of bits of information a computer can handle when it is turned on. Web pages are stored in RAM when they are called from a server. Parts of RAM may also store previously called Web pages, negating further calls to the server after initial access. You cannot have too much RAM, but too little RAM will slow down the time it takes to load a Web page.

Servers These are computers that store Web pages, their associated files, and other data. They send the files to client computers that request them over the Internet.

Tree organization An organization that provides two or more choices (branches). Used in problem-solving and exploration Web sites, they can serve as a useful learning environment.

URL Acronym for Uniform Resource Locator. Essentially, it refers to a unique address on the Internet where Web pages and other files are stored.

Virtual labs Rather than using physical objects, representations of the objects animated on the computer screen are virtual replacements of the physical. These labs can be created using Web pages.

W3C World Wide Web Consortium is an international group that sets the standards for Web languages and protocols to be used on the Web.

Web page A document written with HTML and accessible over the World Wide Web.

Chapter 3

Third Generation Web Sites and Learning

This chapter examines design models for communicating over the Web. When all is said and done, the purpose of a Web page is to invite learning, and to do that, there must be good communication. For good communication to exist there must be good design. In the same way that an instructor must organize a presentation or lecture, a Web site must be designed to convey the information and engage the audience—the learner, a term that focuses on the centrality of who's getting the message. If it does not communicate, we cannot expect much learning to take place. The same is true for a poor classroom learning environment.

As we saw in Chapter 2, the basic learning environment we are creating is one that uses text, graphics, and links. This simple set is expanding rapidly into full-blown multimedia where sound, video, animation, and fuller interactivity are possible. However, by getting the text, graphics, and links right first, we establish a starting point from which to move into more sophisticated multimedia and improved learning environments.

The Learning Context

In thinking about creating a Web page, it must be envisioned in a learning context. As we saw in Chapter 1, the idea of distributed learning means that learning is going to occur in more places than just the classroom. The same is true with Web pages. Students will learn from the Web page, but that will be only one of the places that will be the source of learning. Clearly it can be a central locus of learning, but it may be a sidebar—a review session, extra help, or adjunct to the book or classroom presentation. Virtual realities, such as flight simulators, have been around for a long time. However, they are only part of the learning that pilots go through. There are classroom meetings, lots of books and readings, maps, flight computers, and actual flying. The flight simulator is only part of the overall design for learning to fly. Web pages must be considered in the same light. What role are they expected to play in the overall course design? In this section, we will consider some roles that a Web page may have, and some design features of a page.

Adjunct to Reading

If a Web site is an adjunct to reading a book, the pages should do something that was not done, could not be done at all, or could not be done as well as on a printed page. For example, if the reading is about certain math problems, the Web page might be sample problems the students can solve and assess. A literature assignment in a book might be supplemented by Web pages that show maps and pictures depicting the time and place of the novel. However, if there are only to be textual comments the instructor wants students to read, a printed handout might do just as well if not better.

Adjunct to Classroom or Lab Meeting

One thing that a Web page can do that cannot be done easily in a class or lab is to be available at all times. Often students just begin to get something in class, and then the hour is up and everyone is off, sometimes in the middle of a thought. Web pages with interactive elements or with email links to the professor can help out with key points that need further explanation or student involvement not available in class. Instructors need to think of what the Web site can add, if anything, to the classroom experience. This requires global consideration for the entire course as well as for individual classes. Review sessions are great on Web sites so that students can spend more time on them than in class. Pre-class Web site reviews generate questions to be asked and answered in class.

For faculty who have large classes, email links in Web pages, either through forms or through browser email, do a lot to help shy students. Chapters 11 and 13 will show how to set up email and email forms in Web pages. This is especially true for shy students in large classes. Attempting to respond to hundreds of emails each day can be daunting, but it helps students. Some faculty overcome having to send hundreds of individual emails by grouping answers to questions using LISTSERV® or some other distributed email list.

Replacing a Classroom/Lab Meeting

The most thorough replacement demanded by Web pages is that of a traditional classroom or lab. Full distance learning occurs when electronic meetings replace all face-to-face meetings. If that is the goal, then a learning-centered approach is essential to the success of a Web-based design. As we discussed in Chapter 1, the instructors can improve their overall teaching effectiveness by taking a learning-centered approach. If a learning-centered approach is being used in the classroom, the change is a matter of transferring the learning-centered experiences from the classroom to the Web. In some cases this may be relatively easy, and in others extremely difficult or even impossible. Effective interactive Web-based biology labs have been created that simulate work in the lab. Students learn by going through the process that they would otherwise go through in an actual lab. Classroom designs involving high student-instructor interaction, immediate feedback, and abstract concept applications, on the other hand, may be more difficult. Replacing a talking head in a classroom by videotape, CD-ROM, or eventually streamed video over the Internet is very simple. However, learning is less likely to take place if a talking head in the classroom is replaced by a talking head on a Web page. Moreover, straight information that students passively receive can be handled better and more effectively with a printed page. The remainder of this chapter will present a model of a Web site to capture the essence of what best can be done with sites that fully replace the face-to-face meeting in a classroom. At the same time, it will be important to discuss design lessons, mostly applied to printed pages, which may be usefully incorporated in Web pages. This is not to suggest the student be a passive actor, but rather this chapter will explore connections between page design per se and page design on the Web.

Light and Heavy Solutions

In bringing together design and technology, especially technology on the Web, *weight* is an important consideration. By "weight" I am referring to the amount of time it takes to create a page, the size and load time of the page, and the amount of software running in your computer's memory. This is important because while the computer used to develop lessons may be fast enough and big enough to handle everything you put in a Web lesson, the learner's may not be. This is especially true in considering bandwidth and the speed of Internet service. Educational institutions, especially colleges and universities, are likely to have T1 lines or faster. These lines may be running data in the megabit (millions of bits per second) range, while the home user receiving Web pages over a modem may be getting only kilobit speeds (thousands of bits per second).

You may have seen a dazzling page with wonderful animated graphics, lots of interaction, and full sound. Such pages are likely to have been the result of several thousand dollars in investment, sophisticated development tools and developers, talented designers, and months in planning and execution. These are very *heavy* pages. Besides taking up a lot of memory resources on your computer, they take up a lot of bandwidth. On the other hand, pages with gray backgrounds and nothing but text are relatively *light* in terms of everything from development time to the amount of memory they take up. Pages that have lots of graphics, animation, and other associated files take up more memory. These are very heavy pages. Besides taking up a lot of memory on your computer, they take up a lot of bandwidth on the Internet. On the other hand, pages with gray backgrounds and nothing but text are relatively light in terms of everything from the time it takes to create them to the time it takes to load them on your computer over the Internet.

With the development of new tools, more and more can be added. Web page designers must be cognizant of a page's weight. Therefore, in discussing design, weight is a constraint in the technological context.

Fundamental Design Considerations

In 1997, David Siegel wrote *Creating Killer Web Sites: The Art of Third Generation Site Design*. At the time the book was published, the level of the design capability of HTML was relatively primitive, and by the book's second edition, Cascading Style Sheets were just becoming available. The third generation Web site is one that invites the viewer into the site with lures and metaphors. They are nonlinear and alluring. They should be attractive and interesting to get the viewer's attention. Siegel contrasted his concept with what he defined as first and second generation sites which were, at best, technologically interesting, but tended to be linear and based on simile rather than metaphor. Concepts built around similes treat Web sites *like* some other kind of communication device—such as a book or some other familiar communication source. However, a metaphor assumes that the Web site *is* a virtual representation of the metaphorical entity. For example, a cave may be a metaphor for a Web site that is to be explored. All of a cave's characteristics can be brought to bear and provide the same sense of exploration that a real cave would. (By the way, third generation design has nothing to do with the version of Web browser being used. One could use a Version 5 browser to create a first generation Web site.) What is important for Siegel and other designers is this:

> *No matter how important and content rich your message, if no one is going to look at it, they're not going to get the message.*

This message is especially important to those of us trying to generate a learning-rich environment on the Web. It's hard enough keeping a group of students in the same room interested in the class. How can we expect to do it on the Web unless we pay attention to designers who have spent a lot of time developing principles and techniques to get the viewer to do exactly that? We probably can't very well, and so we need to consider carefully what they have to say and use their wisdom where possible.

Another important designer is Edward Tufte from Yale University. In 1983, Tufte published a remarkable book entitled *The Visual Display of Quantitative Information*. This book took on the challenge of explaining how to best take rich and complex sets of data and display them in a manner that was clear. Using the history of design as a backdrop, Tufte examined and explained the nature of communicating quantitative multivariate relationships. Tufte's insights, along with those of David Siegel and other designers, are employed in this chapter to provide the larger context of what it means to design a meaningful Web page.

The Sins Are Many and Varied

Sometimes avoiding doing wrong will better inform us of how to do it right. Siegel (1997) listed "Seven Deadly Sins" of Web page design, as did interface designer Jakob Nielsen (1998, 74). However, both Nielsen and Siegel went on to describe a good deal more than seven sins. Likewise, Tufte enumerated a number of design flaws that are relevant to Web and non-Web pages. Drawing on these and other designers, this section represents my own list of sins that I have found to most get in the way of good Web page design.

All Caps: One of the best ways to call attention to one's design ineptness is to use all caps in the body text. Even headings with all caps can be difficult to read, and there are better ways to bring headings to the attention of the reader. It's best to avoid all caps until your design skills are high. Good designers know how to use all caps effectively, but they tend to use them sparingly as well.

Interference from Background Graphics: One of the fun additions to Web pages was the background graphic. Unfortunately, many who created Web pages felt obliged to include cluttered designs in their background, making it very difficult to read the text. Edward Tufte (1997, 74) talks of "chartjunk" as unnecessary graphics that get in the way of the message being delivered, and bad backgrounds certainly qualify as "chartjunk." Often one will see backgrounds causing a moiré effect—a vibration to the eye. Other times the background will effectively camouflage whatever message or other graphics are on the page. Careful use of certain backgrounds can enhance a page's appearance, but for the most part I avoid using them altogether.

The Long Load: For a Web page designer, the greatest fear is that her page will be ignored. If the page is a long time in loading, the user might hit the back button and zip off to the next page that requires a short attention span. For designing learning pages, the threat is not quite as great, but a long load time for a Web page means that it is taking up a lot of memory. By taking memory size into account, using tricks to reduce file size, and remembering that added material can be placed on another page, good and rich designs are possible without a long load.

Dancing Baloney: In an early version of HTML, the <BLINK> tag was introduced, causing text to blink incessantly. (This too can be classified as "chartjunk.") It was used to draw the viewer's attention to some aspect of the page, but its major achievement was distracting the viewer. Since then, animated GIFs and other forms of "dancing baloney" have found homes on Web pages with a similarly distracting characteristic. There are very few applications where the same jumping or blinking item on a page serves much purpose after the initial blink or bounce. Slowly moving objects and gradual changes are far more effective and less distracting.

The Long, Long Page: How long should a page be? Loading up a long page with lots of text invites the user to print out the page. Loading up a long page with lots of text, graphics, and other heavy extras invites the user to leave and jog around the block while the page gets squared away. It's better to concentrate on a good system of navigation than to have the seemingly endless scroll.

Broken and Missing Links and Graphics: Jakob Nielsen suggests hiring a "Web gardener" to keep outdated information off your page. The same gardener needs to keep a page's links current as well. In creating learning pages, instructors need to keep checking to be sure that a valuable educational link is still around when the new term begins. The target page may be long gone and the same or newer information is elsewhere. Sometimes graphics become corrupted on a server and need to be replaced so that they'll load as well.

No Real Paragraphs: David Siegel went to great lengths to lambaste those who did not use indented paragraphs on their Web pages. With CSS, this is not a difficult matter, but many page designers use either big blank lines or (worse) horizontal rules to separate paragraphs. The nonbreaking space [ ] should be used, even if it requires hand coding to create a proper indent. Using indents for paragraphs not only gives the page a better flow and unity; it follows good rules of punctuation.

Random Style: In designing a Web site, remember that a consistent style is a unifying force. Imagine reading a book with different typefaces and spacing for every page. Quickly, the attention would be drawn from the content to the design. Even a relatively bad design that is consistent is better than several different designs that keep pulling the viewer's attention away from the content.

Clutter: Edward Tufte (1990, 53) noted that "Confusion and clutter are failures of design, not attributes of information." As a designer's knowledge of Web page capability increases, she often adds all the new technology she can on a page. The content is smothered in a train wreck of techno-pieces happily added by the Web page designer. It is reminiscent of the early days of desktop publishing. The desktop publisher, in a rush to use *all* of her new fonts, ended up with a page that looked like a ransom note. A clear page does a better job.

Developing the Third Generation Learning Site

In discussing third generation sites, the concept is one that emphasizes designs that are engaging, active, interesting, and well ordered. Third generation design is not a technological development so much as taking the technology and applying good design principles to it. Wedding learning-centered educational practices to a third generation concept is a dynamic one meant to be a starting point and a point of reference. The concept is offered as a guide and not a straitjacket.

In the remainder of this chapter, I provide one of David Siegel's third generation models and transform that into a learning-centered model. Then I want to show some examples of how that model was actually applied. There are many parts to the process, and one of the most important is working with others who have talents and skills that educators may not. Most important of those skills include those of basic artistic design and the technology of page development. In working with my own pages and helping faculty work on their pages, the concentration needed to be on the content and ways that content could communicate in a pedagogically sound manner. On the following pages is the tip of the developmental iceberg.

The Basic Model

Beginning with the idea of a "core page" replacing a "home page" Siegel argues that the viewer needs to be provided a clear and intuitive yet alluring experience. Rather than beginning with a "home page" up front, the viewer begins with an "entry page" that gives a quick look at what's available and invites her to see more. The entry page is bait to attract the viewer to look beyond the entry. An "entry tunnel" pulls the viewer into the site, providing more information as she enters the tunnel. Once "inside," the viewer encounters the "core page," a menu and map that reveal and guide the viewer. Throughout, there are clearly marked exits and guidance back to the core page. Likewise, clear guideposts show the way to the exit, and like the entrance tunnel, an exit tunnel escorts the viewer out of the site.

The Third Generation Learning Site

Adopting Siegel's model to a learning-centered one is relatively straightforward. However, instead of beginning within the site, the starting point is the ***syllabus***. In one sense the syllabus is the core of the course, but in the model presented next, the syllabus is more of a launching pad—perhaps an index. Each lesson constitutes a third generation site, and so the ***lesson*** is the focal point.

Entry: Entry to the lesson is from the syllabus. The ***entry page*** is one that tells the student what the lesson is about. It begins with something interesting and appealing, and gives the student a hook of interest. Following the entry page are two ***entry tunnel pages***. The first page lays out the lesson's ***objectives.*** This page tells the student what she can expect to get from the site. Second is a ***pretest or pre-assessment page.*** A lot can be done with this page. It can be treated as a challenge, an impetus of interest, or simply a set of questions that will alert the viewer to what he can expect to learn.

Core: The ***core page*** is something like a mini-syllabus. It shows the student the title of all of the pages so that she knows where the lesson is headed. This is where contextual material needs to be included to set the stage for the entire lesson. Depending on the topic and nature of the material, linear or nonlinear courses can be charted. To some extent most material is linear, either developmentally or due to the necessity of having a sequence of topics to cover in a limited time period. However, a page within the linear series can and should have many nonlinear features.

Exit: The ***exit tunnel*** is made up of a review of key concepts and a quiz prior to the exit page itself. The ***key concept*** page is an opportunity for the student to review the essential concepts presented in the lesson. Next a ***quiz page*** gives the student immediate feedback to how well he understood the materials. Finally, the ***exit page*** offers a return to the core page or syllabus. It also is a good place to include recommended reading or off-site links for a student interested in further exploring the topic.

Permeating the site are good practices for learning-centered understanding. The design lends itself to incorporating these practices. Figure 3-1 shows one way to design a learning site using third generation design.

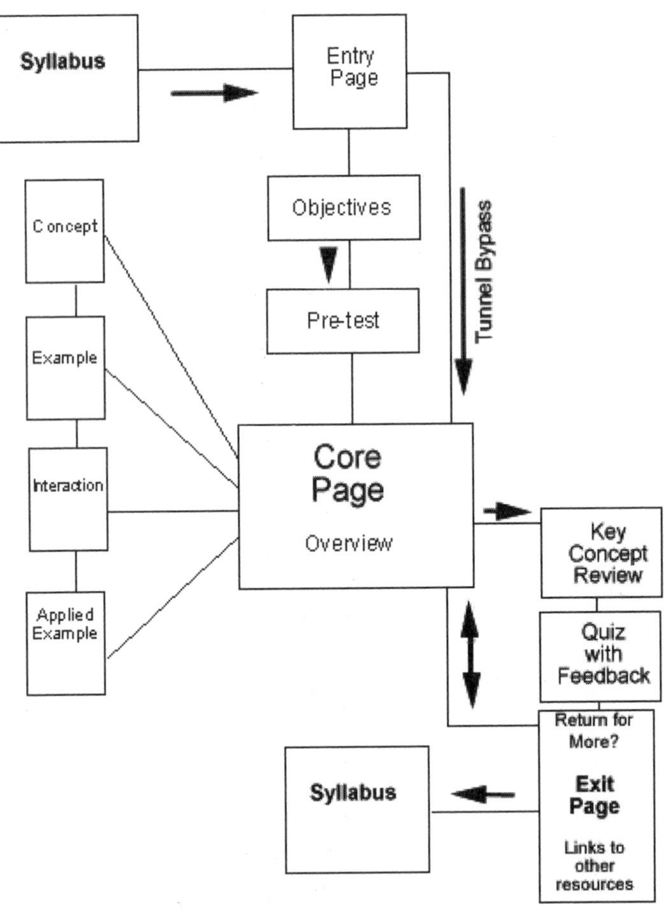

FIGURE 3-1 Third generation site developed for lessons in a course.

Syllabus and Course Content

Deciding on Content and Creating a Syllabus

This first step in developing a course is deciding on what content should be included. This is no different from deciding what material would be covered in a traditional course. The scheduling of content along with all assignments are put into a syllabus. Because the course material is online, the first Web page to be developed is an online syllabus. If the course meets in a classroom as well, the online syllabus serves as a resource for updating a syllabus, adding material, and alerting students to exams or due dates for events occurring in the classroom. An online course syllabus template should have all the materials a traditional syllabus does as well as email and URL links. For example, a faculty member may want to have an email link to herself, links to online discussion groups, and links to individual students or groups of students on a syllabus. Good navigation is essential to an online syllabus because the students will be using it often. It should be easy to update so the faculty member can add reminders, extra-credit assignments, or study guides to the syllabus. Figure 3-2 shows a syllabus with navigation and several links for increasing class communication.

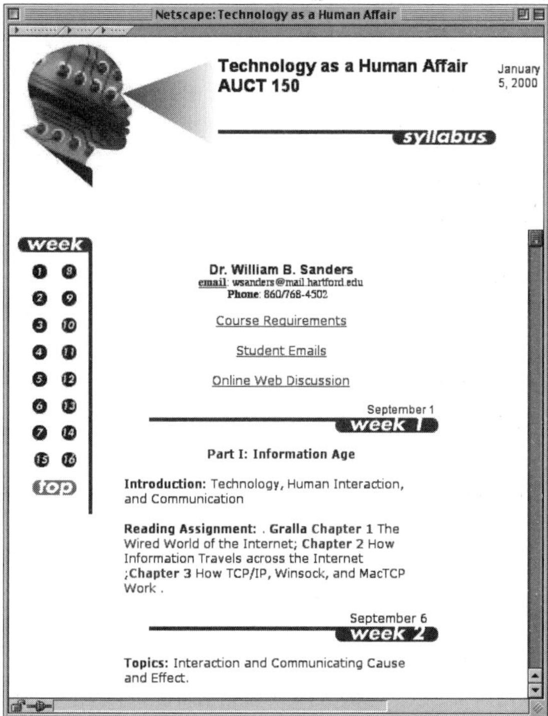

FIGURE 3-2 A good online syllabus provides more ways for students and faculty to engage one another.

Preparing Content for Transfer to Web Pages

To help faculty organize the content into the format of the Web site, a word processor template was developed. Faculty can follow the template so that each element of the lesson design is incorporated. Reminders of what should be included are built into the form. Faculty write the content and describe graphics, links, and any other instructions in arrowhead < > brackets. All phases of the course are discussed with the student assistant (if available) at different stages to ensure the pages meet faculty standards.

Template Word Processor Form

1. **Entrance Page:** Tell something interesting about material. Including a graphic is a good idea.
2. **Objectives:** List what student is expected to learn, understand, appreciate, and accomplish.
3. **Pre-Test:** Pose several questions to let student determine how much he understands. If interesting questions are posed, student will want to learn more.
4. **Core with Overview:** Provide a thesis paragraph or two to set the stage for what will come.
5. **Lesson Pages:** This is where the content goes.
   - Page 1 <Describe graphics between pointed brackets> E.g. <Create a collage of text and graphics that show different political beliefs—maybe a donkey and an elephant with words like Liberal and Conservative and issues such as taxes, abortion, education.> Text content follows . . . .
   - Page 2
   - Page 3
   - Etc.
6. **Review Key Concepts:** List all of the key concepts, ideas, and major points in lesson.
7. **Assessment:** Provide an online self-grading quiz based on material in lesson.
8. **Exit Page:** This page should be a gracious exit with appropriate links back to the core page in case the students want to review materials. This also is a good place to include links to other interesting or related sites, books, articles, or other references.

Schedule

During the initial stages of preparing materials for the Web, the faculty and student assistant need to meet and work out a schedule. Without experience, initial trial and error helps to get an idea of what it takes to get the content into the forms and from the forms into the Web pages.

Training

Depending on the skill of the student assistant, there may be need for training in working with various software tools and Web page languages. Faculty may also want to learn to work with the graphic and page-design software and languages for better understanding of what can be done with the software and hardware.

On Your Own

Many faculty will be on their own with no help from student assistants. In this case, it is even more important to get a template, a faculty-development schedule, and the organization to get everything where it belongs in a timely manner. For wholly online courses, all of this needs to be worked out ahead of time because getting a complex lesson together at the last minute and winging it is not much of an option.

Creating Lessons

Preparing Content for Web Pages

With a standard Web Site Template, the student assistant's job is much simplified. The student assistant knows what to look for, what to expect, and what needs to be done. Since the faculty member provides the content in a word-processed format, the student's main job is taking the material from the word processor and transferring it to the pages. The entry page requires a graphic along with a little textual material to interest the student in the lesson. The graphic here is important because it provides a visual context for the entire lesson. Experimentation has shown that the entry page graphic repeated on the core page provides a good link from the introduction to the heart of the lesson. Figure 3-3 shows a typical entry page.

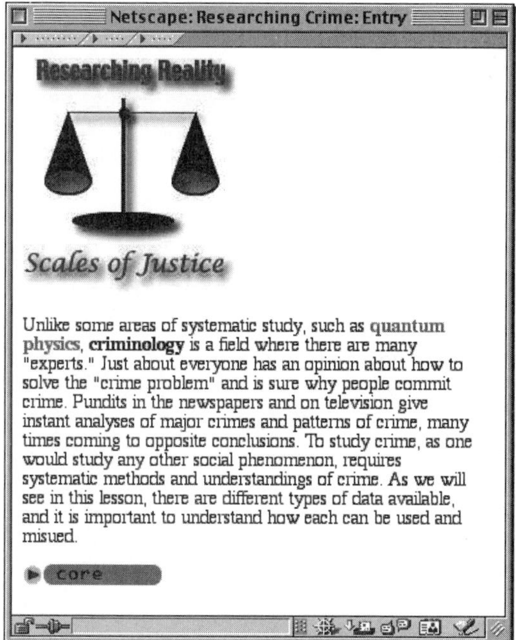

FIGURE 3-3 An entry page should have something that will pique the student's interest. The "core" page icon is a jump around the entry tunnel.

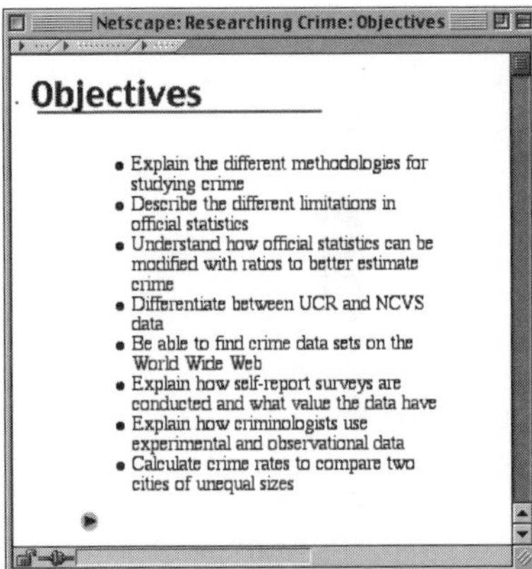

FIGURE 3-4 Objectives are part of the entry tunnel.

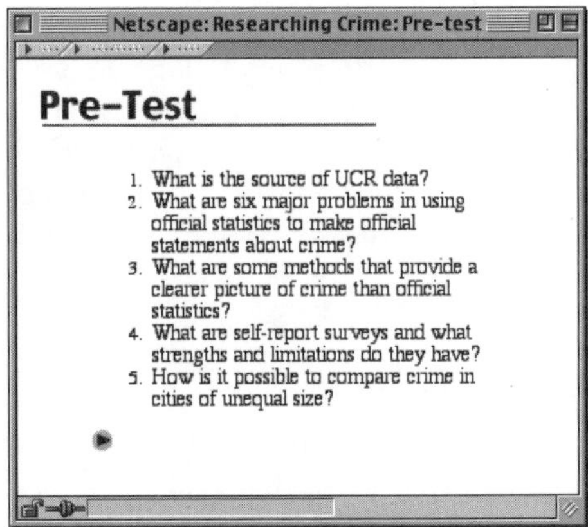

FIGURE 3-5 Pre-test questions can pique students' interest.

Consistent Elements

In setting up pages, consistent elements aid in navigation and communication. In the example, a green right-pointing arrow indicated a link to the next page and black right-pointing arrows indicated links to other forward pages. Left-pointing arrows linked to the previous pages, an "X" marked the current page relative to the other pages in the lesson, and a special core page button linked to the core page. (They were intuitive enough so that no students asked for instructions on how to use them.) By placing identical sets of navigation buttons at the top and bottom of the lesson pages, navigation was convenient as well. Figures 3-4 and 3-5 show two entry tunnel pages with objectives and a pre-test. Note the little arrow in the lower left of the page for one-way navigation through the tunnel.

Core Page

The core page sets the context for general navigation because it provides an overview of what is in store for the viewer. From the core page, students can go to any place in the lesson except back through the entry tunnel. Figure 3-6 shows a sample core page that provides links to the lesson, to the exit, or even back to the syllabus—just in case they got the wrong lesson.

Lesson Pages

General Page Elements

Most pages consist of text, the navigation buttons, and a graphic relating to the text. These pages can be very much like a book page except that the navigation

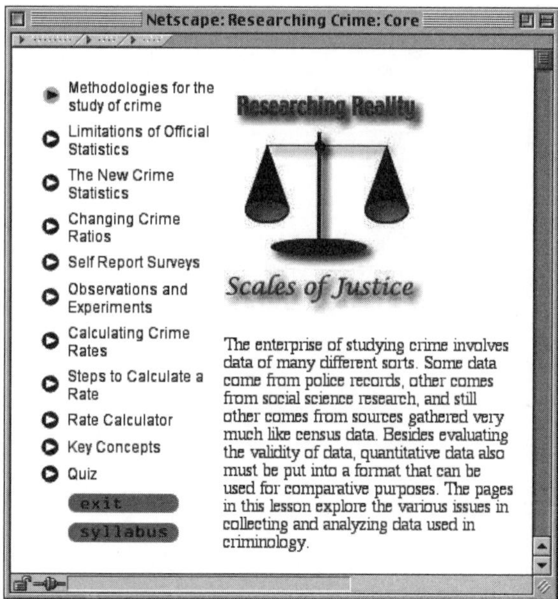

FIGURE 3-6 The core page is a center from which students can see both the sequence of the lesson and yet have the ability to jump to any part they may want to review.

system is nonlinear. It is very important that a simple, effective, and clear navigation system be used consistently throughout the lesson and the course. Haphazard or inconsistent navigation can be confusing and wastes time.

Interactive Pages

Some pages require the student to provide feedback to the professor using email links or email forms. Feedback can also be built-in using JavaScript or links to feedback pages. This may be done over several pages or on a single page. Figures 3-7 and 3-8 show a set of pages that first shows a student how to accomplish a task and then sends the student off to gather information and perform the task himself.

Test Pages

Each lesson has self-scoring quizzes in the exit tunnel once the lesson is completed. Faculty members provide quiz questions and answers, and the student assistant creates JavaScript quizzes using software designed specifically for generating short-answer and multiple-choice questions. Faculty or student assistants would most likely use a program such as *Dreamweaver Attain* so that all he would have to do is provide questions and answer selections. After completing the test, students are scored and given the list of incorrect answers.

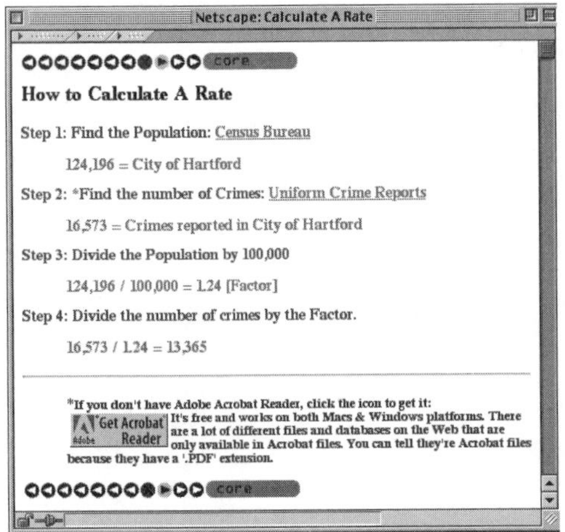

FIGURE 3-7 Links on pages provide students with sources of data.

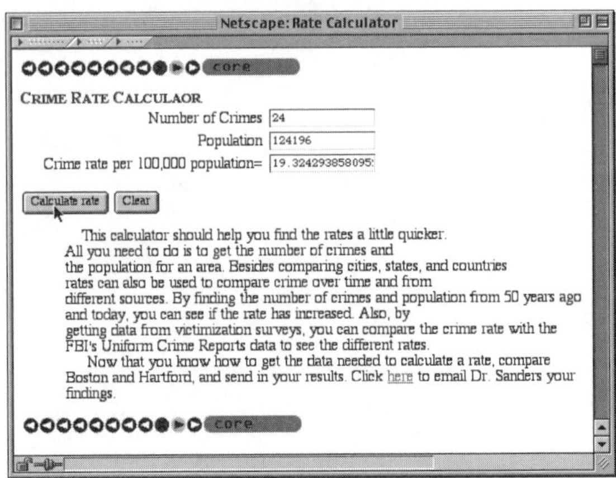

FIGURE 3-8 Web pages with forms can be used as ways to actively involve students.

Projects

Interactive projects can be handled using either email or email forms. Figure 3-7 provides the student with several links to look up information that would be calculated into a rate. The results would then be emailed to the professor.

Forms for Pages

Another way of communicating directly with students is through email forms. Essentially, the student writes the requested information in a form, then clicks a **Submit** button that sends the data to the instructor. This method can be used to direct the student to a number of more structured interactions. Using forms allows a closer connection between the task and the student's behavior. However, in creating forms, care is necessary with the coding of the HTML. Sometimes there is cross-browser incompatibility. Specifically, Netscape Navigator and Microsoft Internet Explorer sometimes behave differently with forms.

Exit Tunnel

At the end of the lesson, rather than drop the student off when the last content has been presented, several pages ease the student into several options and a review of what has passed. First, a simple listing of key concepts gives the learner a quick overview of what major points were made in the lesson. This is a simple and short page that can be reviewed in a glance. Figure 3-9 shows a Web page that begins the exit tunnel with a set of key concepts.

There are opportunities in the exit tunnel to bring in many different pages that help the learner better understand the content. For example, the instructor may

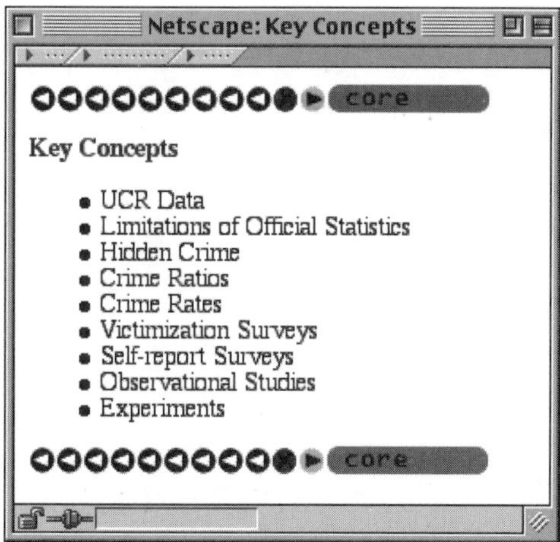

FIGURE 3-9 An exit tunnel should have a review of the key concepts the lesson covered.

wish to have pages that ask the student to apply what he has learned, solve a problem with the knowledge, or take a simple quiz. Whatever the option, though, this site design concept discourages ending when the last page of content has been offered.

Self-Assessment

One of the important principles of learning-centered education is prompt feedback. One way to achieve that feedback is through self-assessments. Figure 3-10 shows a typical online quiz students use to receive immediate feedback. A combination of multiple-choice and short-answer quizzes are self-scored by a quiz program written in JavaScript. Faculty simply enters their questions and answers and the quiz-making program does the rest.

Professor Feedback

Another type of assessment may involve the instructor responding to a student email. This helps ensure the student has covered the material and understands it and provides the instructor a chance to respond directly to the student. A good deal of clarification, explanation, and instruction takes place when professors deal directly with student queries through email.

Exit Page

The exit page serves as a capstone for an online lesson and should not be overlooked. It provides both a way back and a way out for the student. Also, the professor can use it for links to other sites or paper references the student may need to review. Figure 3-11 is a typical exit page.

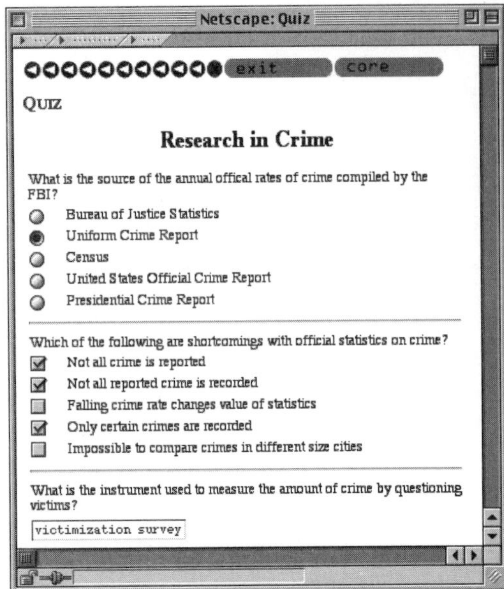

FIGURE 3-10 Online quizzes provide immediate feedback to students.

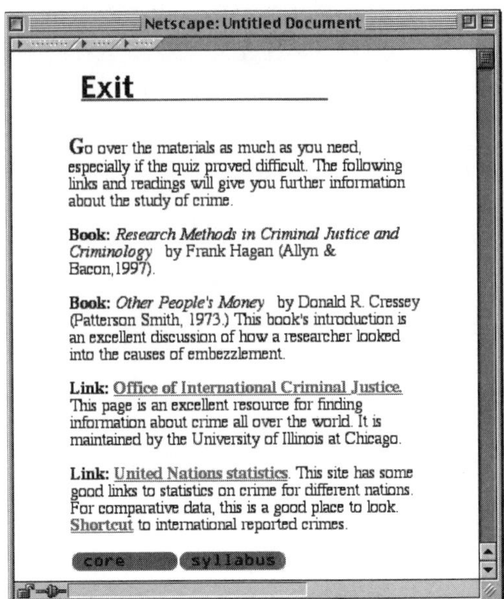

FIGURE 3-11 The exit page provides a last opportunity to provide links and references as well as a way out of the site.

Summary and Review

The most important lesson to take from this chapter is to learn something about design. If possible, use the services of a good designer. In my own experience, I hired a student with design skills and no Web technology skills at all. In a short period of time, he mastered the tools needed to create Web pages and enough HTML and JavaScript to make first-rate pages. If you cannot hire someone with designing skills, at a bare minimum, avoid the most glaring design sins. Half the battle is avoiding ugly and distracting Web pages. Better yet, read some books on design, especially those that discuss the connection between design and communication. Edward Tufte and David Siegel have excellent works cited in this chapter. Again, both are highly recommended. Another book that bears a recommendation for those who have never read a design book is *The Non-Designer's Web Book: An Easy Guide to Creating, Designing, and Posting Your Own Web Site* by Robin Williams and John Tollett.

Because learning is about paying attention, and design is about getting attention, the connection between learning and design is fundamental. This is especially true when there is no face-to-face contact between instructor and student as is the case with full distance learning. The idea behind a third generation Web site is to gain the viewer's attention and keep it. Learning basic concepts and many of the facts and figures needed to understand a course requires the learner to pay attention to what is on the Web page. Encouraging and enhancing that attention by engaging the viewer goes far to achieve the learning goal. Ignoring design altogether is both naive and counterproductive. Transferring the third generation Web site concepts to learning is a means of easing the work of creating lessons on the Web and encouraging learning there.

Glossary of Terms

Core page Different from a home page, a core page is a true overview of a Web site. It puts the viewer into a position where she can see the site, its logic, and its context.

Entry page The entry page in a Web site is an invitation to a viewer to enter the site. Often with little content and a lot of enticement, the entry page tweaks the viewer's interest.

Entry tunnel As an enticement to enter a Web site, third generation sites often employ a series of Web pages to lure the viewer into the site.

Exit page The last page in a third generation site provides an exit for the viewer along with an opportunity to return to the site. It is the door out of the site.

Exit tunnel As an aid to navigation, a clear exit, and an opportunity for the viewer to review a Web site, the exit tunnel guides a viewer through a series of pages that escort him out of a site.

Third generation Web site Web sites that employ nonlinear design and metaphor in their creation. Use of intuitive navigation and a core allow users to easily explore this kind of site.

References

Nielsen, Jakob. "Seven Deadly Sins of Web Design." *Technology Review* (Cambridge, MA: MIT Press, September/October 1998), p. 74.

Siegel, David. *Creating Killer Web Sites: The Art of Third Generation Site Design* 2nd ed. (Indianapolis, IN: Hayden Books, 1997).

Tufte, Edward. *The Visual Display of Quantitative Information* (Graphics Press: Cheshire, CT: 1983).

Tufte, Edward. *Envisioning Information* (Graphics Press: Cheshire, CT: 1990).

Tufte, Edward. *Visual Explanations* (Graphics Press: Cheshire, CT: 1997).

Williams, Robin and John Tollett. *The Non-Designer's Web Book: An Easy Guide to Creating, Designing, and Posting Your Own Web Site* (Berkeley, CA: Peachpit Press, 1997).

Chapter 4

Creating Pages: Tools and Templates

Web Page Design for Discovery, Understanding, and the Love of Learning

This chapter, while focusing on the pedagogical goals in developing Web pages, introduces several tools that function to help create Web pages. Keeping in mind the goal of creating effective third generation Web sites, even good tools can result in awful Web pages if care is not taken. Chapter 3 introduced third generation Web sites and *one suggested* adaptation of that concept to learning. The purpose of organization is to provide a general framework for integrating linear and nonlinear elements in a lesson. It emphasizes and encourages exploration, reflection, and going beyond the lesson to further discovery. Yet at the same time, the site format is organized to guide the student through information. Using the tools introduced in this chapter, other Web page arrangements for particular courses are encouraged, especially as faculty members get new ideas, inspirations, and insights that they want to try out. Likewise as new tools become available, faculty should not be wed to a single application or tool in the dynamic growth of the Internet and World Wide Web.

Ideally, faculty should have the services of artists, Web page code developers, instructional designers, and research assistants. Of these roles, the artists and Web page code developers are the most important. Artists should be able to create drawings, designs, and other artistic renderings in the computer-based tools for artwork. Web page code developers who can work with HTML, JavaScript, CGI, XML, Java, and new technologies that arise should be trained to help *meet faculty goals.* University Instructional Technology offices may have the necessary personnel, equipment, and facilities that will do just that. Rather than forcing a new technology onto a Web course, developers should listen to and work with faculty, artists, and designers to implement learning ideas, not to implement technology ideas. However, technical developers can be important and creative forces if they understand how to introduce a new technology or techniques to faculty that will help them create learning-rich Web courses. Instructional designers can save a great deal of time by helping faculty take course material and organize it for multimedia presentation on the Web.

Even with all of the ideal help possible, faculty members still need to take charge of and direct what will happen in a learning environment created with Web pages for their course. The more faculty understand design and the application of strong pedagogy in Web pages, the better the results, whether they have to do the whole thing themselves or direct a team of developers. Therefore, understanding the tools and how they apply to creating rich learning sites is important.

Web Design Tools

The *very best* tool for developing Web pages is the one faculty members can use the most effectively. For the purposes of this discussion, it will be prudent to assume that a faculty member is going to tackle a lesson without a supporting team of artists and other developers. This assumption is made with the understanding that faculty will be in all stages of development and should understand something about the tools they themselves will use or a development team needs. We will begin with the most simple and least expensive and proceed to more robust tools.

Netscape Composer

One of the most popular Web page design tools is freely available on the Web in the Netscape Communicator (http://www.netscape.com). The tool, Composer, is not very sophisticated but is easy to use and can be employed to create many simple yet effective Web pages. Available for both Macintosh and Windows versions of the popular browser package, Netscape Composer handles all of the simple tasks required in a Web page editor. Figure 4-1 shows a simple page in Netscape Composer, and Figure 4-2 shows how it looks in a browser—Microsoft Internet Explorer. One limitation of Composer is that what is viewed in the editor (Composer) may not look the same in a browser. Note in Figure 4-2 how the text and links are aligned in a parallel column next to the graphic. A good Web page editor is WYSIWYG—What You See Is What You Get.

While Composer is not a true WYSIWYG editor, it takes a lot of the guesswork out of creating a Web page. For most simple pages, Composer works fine, but with more complex Web pages, including frames, Dynamic HTML, and CSS, it will be necessary either to learn how to code HTML and JavaScript or to use a more robust Web page creation application.

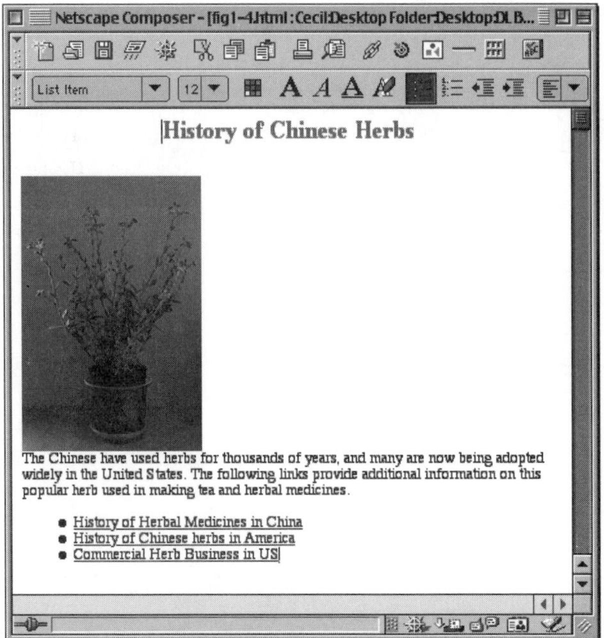

FIGURE 4-1 Text, graphic, and links in Netscape Composer.

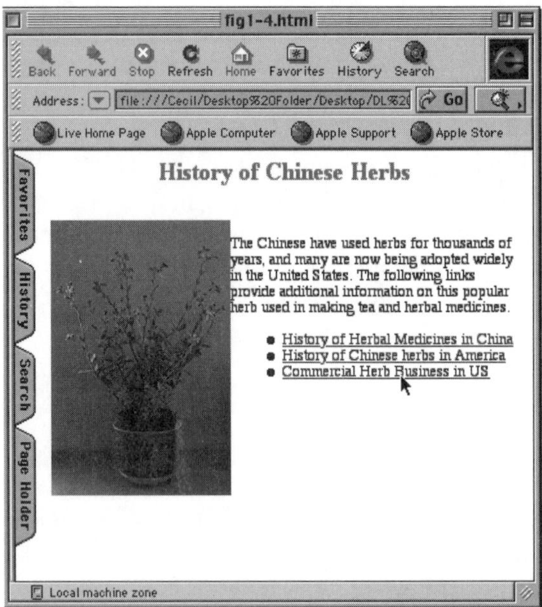

FIGURE 4-2 Web page created in Composer as seen in Microsoft Internet Explorer.

Microsoft Word

Another simple way to create Web pages is with a word processor. New versions of Microsoft Word for both Windows and Macintosh computers provide an option in the **File** menu to **Save as HTML**... Faculty who are familiar with Microsoft Word and most other contemporary word processors may feel more comfortable using the text editing and graphic tools built into or connected to their word processor. All graphics imbedded in the word processor document will be transformed into Web graphics (JPG or GIF), and the page created on the word processor will be re-created as a Web page. Because all of the graphics are renamed, there may be some initial confusion in using this feature of Word, but with practice, it can be a simple way to quickly create pages. This is especially true with existing materials saved in a word processor file.

As with using Netscape Composer, there are a number of limitations in using a word processor. Frames, Dynamic HTML, and all of the more robust and interactive features possible in a fully developed multimedia Web page are difficult using a word processor. However, with a well-thought-out use of links, graphics, and text, faculty can create excellent Web sites to help students learn.

Shareware and Freeware

Shareware and freeware are available on the Web. Freeware is software that is free to use indefinitely, while Shareware asks the user to pay a minimum fee on a voluntary basis. To find various freeware and shareware HTML editors for Windows that you can download to your computer begin with:

http://www.freewarehome.com/internet/htmled.html

For Macintosh computers, look at:

http://www.macdirectory.com/

Because all of the developmental tools are free to try, download several to see which ones you like. A popular one for Windows is **SiteAid,** available at http://www.siteaid.com/. SiteAid allows sophisticated insertion of JavaScript code but requires some time and practice to master. Although it is a powerful tool, SiteAid is not as intuitive as Composer or Word. However, when it's time to begin including more robust interaction in Web sites, this tool is a good one to learn. For the Macintosh, a popular freeware program is BBEdit Lite. This Web page editor has a more powerful commercial counterpart, but there are a number of functions available with the free version.

Text Editors

Both SiteAid and BBEdit have considerable text editing features, but if one's preference is more toward simply writing HTML tags and JavaScript, it may be just as easy to use a text editor that comes with your system. Windows includes a text editor, ***Notepad*** in the **Accessories** folder, which can be used for making simple editing changes or writing all Web pages in HTML and JavaScript tags and code. Remember, *all* Web pages are *text files*. Therefore, any text editor can be used to make changes to a Web page. ***SimpleText*** is the Macintosh text editor supplied with the system. The only advantage to using a text editor is that any kind of code can be entered and most people are familiar with their use. All that need to be remembered in creating a Web page with a text editor is to add the extension .html or .htm after the file name.

Commercial Web Editors

As there are several good commercial Web editors on the market, look for key important features when deciding on a purchase. The following list provides key elements usually not included in the freeware or shareware Web page editors.

- Has WYSIWYG. The editor should show you pretty much what the page is going to look like. Visual layout and design make it far easier to get the pages to look like what instructors want students to see. A really good WYSIWYG Web development tool shows what a page looks like on different browsers and on Windows and Macintosh computers.
- Has a Source code-editing module. The ability to edit source code for making small or large changes in HTML or JavaScript is important.
- Supports Cascading Style Sheets.
- Generates JavaScript or similar script for creating interactive pages.
- Supports Dynamic HTML. You should be able to work with and animate layers on a Web page.
- Has Web site management modules to help you organize, update, and keep track of all pages used in a site.
- Supports developing frames.
- Supports developing all types of forms.

At this writing, there are several advanced Web editors on the market. An excellent one for educators is *Coursbuilder for Dreamweaver* by Macromedia. In the *Coursbuilder* version of *Dreamweaver* is a test-making module, making it easy to include short-answer, multiple-choice, and "drag and drop" quizzes and exams. As noted in Chapter 1, one of the important practices in developing learning-centered education is *prompt feedback*, and quizzes and tests are mechanisms whereby this can be done. The "drag and drop" exams are useful for mixing graphic elements into the feedback.

Another outstanding Web site development application mentioned is Adobe *GoLive*. This program is an excellent one for faculty because it is easy to use yet extremely powerful. Its capacity to preview pages from different types of computers and browsers on a single platform makes it especially useful when there are several different unknown computers and browsers that students will be using.

Figure 4-3 shows how *GoLive* can take a sample of a graphic's color and provide a match to be used in the page color scheme.

GoLive includes support for XML and active server pages. For more advanced applications, active server pages and XML can take advantages of databases and interactive features of Web pages that use information stored in a server. *GoLive* also includes a QuickTime movie editor and some art tools. Such tools are important for some basic editing and fine-tuning graphics and movies used in Web pages.

GoLive has a great Preview mode where the user can see what his page will look like on different browsers and on Windows and Macintosh screens. When creating Web pages for a truly World Wide Web with different platforms and browsers generating different versions of the same page on a computer screen, the ability to know what the page will really look like is very valuable.

Adobe *ImageStyler* is a great tool for making complex Web pages. Beginning with a blank page, the user can put graphics anywhere on the page desired. Because Web pages are notoriously difficult to design and lay out, *ImageStyler* has to slice up a page into a complex table to get graphics and text where the user wants them, but it does get the job done.

A final Web page development tool worth noting is Microsoft's *Front Page*. This popular Web site development package is designed to be used in conjunction

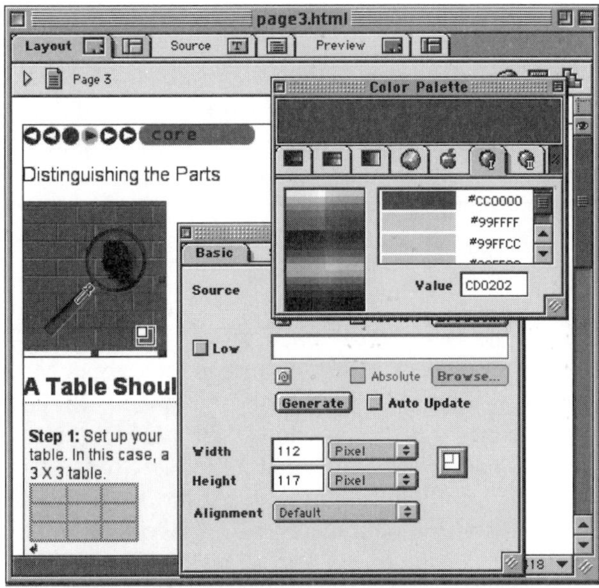

FIGURE 4-3 Adobe's *GoLive* has a color matching feature that allows taking samples from a graphic and getting a matching color that can be applied to Web elements such as text or background.

with *Microsoft Office*. Creating Web pages using *Word, Excel,* and other *Office* software, *Front Page* allows the user to easily go between the various tools for creating Web pages. It also has a complete set of design templates to give Web sites an integrated look and feel. However, do not expect *Front Page* to do everything that either *GoLive* or *Dreamweaver* can. It was created to be used by nonprofessional Web site developers who were comfortable using the popular *Microsoft Office* software. Not surprisingly, *Front Page* creates many interesting effects that work correctly only on *Internet Explorer* and not at all or in strange ways on *Netscape Navigator*.

Before buying any software, download the demo version of the software to try it out first. All of the software discussed above can be downloaded for a trial period. If after the trial expires, you decide it is what you want, then you can buy it.

Graphic Tools for the Web

A longtime favorite is Adobe's *PhotoShop*, with the latest versions having special features especially designed for enhancing Web-based graphics. Likewise, Macromedia's *Free Hand* and Adobe's *Illustrator* are standard graphic artist tools that have been adapted to save files in Web format.

Macromedia's *Fireworks* was developed particularly for working with Web graphics, including making buttons, rollovers, and other Web-related icons and pictures. One of the favorite features of *Fireworks* is the **Export Wizard**. . . option. With it, you can save graphics at the optimum size for both Web and non-Web graphics. Figure 4-4 shows a graphic in the "Wizard" comparison boxes.

Page Makeup Programs

Page makeup software such as *Adobe PageMaker* includes export functions that allow the user to export a file as an HTML page. However, there is loss of formatting and just about everything else that makes a page look good. More useful for the Web is the ability of *PageMaker* to export a set of pages in PDF (Portable Document Format). The formatted page can be viewed in a browser using the *Adobe Acrobat Reader* plug-in. If a page has been formatted already for a course, it is simpler to transform that page into PDF format than to start from scratch. However, in some cases where active and interactive pages are important, often the instructor will find it more useful to just take the textual and graphic materials from the page makeup files and transport what is needed in the Web page. Also, remember that sometimes the paper version originally developed for a course may *still be the most useful for student learning*.

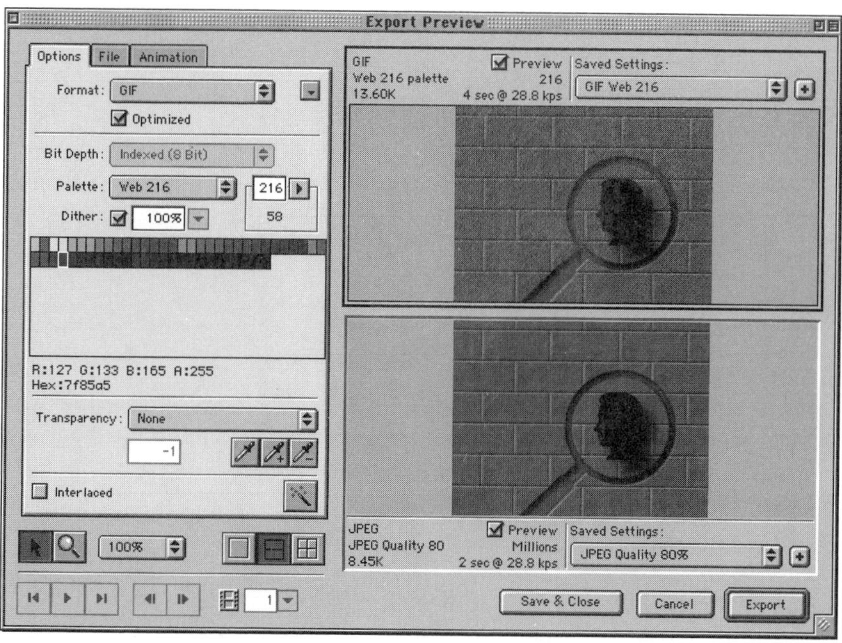

FIGURE 4-4 ***Fireworks*** **shows both the appearance and file size of a graphic. As can be seen, the top and bottom graphics look almost the same, but the top one is larger (13.60K vs. 8.45K) than the bottom one. (Note also that the load times are provided.)**

Lesson Templates

When attempting to create an entire course on the Web, it helps to have templates. A good template incorporates many features required for a Web page to serve as an effective learning tool and have a good design. That is, every new lesson is not a reinvention and rediscovery of work that has been done previously.

Chapter 3 provides an example of a template that began asking pedagogical questions and developed as a design to incorporate answers to those questions. By no means, however, is the template shown in Chapter 3 to be treated as an ideal template or even as a guide to making Web templates. Rather templates are only one application of *an idea* for creating Web lessons. In actually using a template do not hesitate to break out of it whenever a learning strategy or idea demands it. A good template allows users to do that. So while templates are valuable for guiding the user to incorporating both design and pedagogical practices, as new ideas and technology are made available, they should not be treated in a straitjacket manner. Templates are guides, not tracks.

Many templates are arranged around certain key design components to communicate a certain look and feel. The color scheme, proportions, and placement of components are based on a single design concept. As much as possible, try to keep the suggested colors and proportions consistent with the template design.

In using templates that attempt a certain look and feel, be sure that you select one that has the correct look and feel for the topic being covered. For example, an art nouveau design may be great for early twentieth-century or late nineteenth-century historical discussion of literature, but it may not fit in a lesson on contemporary biochemistry. Getting some help from an artist or designer when creating your own template is essential.

Educational Packages

To meet the demand for a simple-to-use solution to Web-based courses, a number of companies have developed "packages" that have all of the components needed for a course. By organizing software that makes it easy to create Web pages, including both chat and asynchronous online discussions, tests, and administrative materials (such as grade books), these packages make it easy to include an online component to just about any class.

Course site development tools provide an array of options for creating pages. Most of the site development is done simply by adding text or links to pre-existing materials in formats that can be read either by the interpreters embedded in the site or by materials already formatted for the Web. Different general design options provide a limited set of looks for a site, and the professor can add design elements of her own making as well.

From the Control Panel professors can select whether they want to edit pages, create exams, or perform several other course site functions. For full courses, the Site Management option provides a way to keep track of where everything belongs. This can be very important with several Web pages with information students need to find.

Another Web authoring tool developed for educators is *Web Course in a Box* (http://www.madduck.com/madduck.html). This educational package is template-based as well, and it has many features that make it easy to develop courses, including exams and quizzes. Like Blackboard's Web course development software, *Web Course in a Box* can be tested free of charge. Overall, the most useful features of both of these educational packages include the ease with which different types of assessments can be created and the site management features. There are minimal built-in design components, but what there is constitute good solid design. This is good for instructors who want to incorporate good design features in their pages and not be forced to accept a design for a particular focus.

Summary and Review

This chapter is the starting point for faculty new to the idea of creating Web pages. The tools required range from fairly simple and inexpensive ones to robust and pricey. Even the most simple Web development tool in the right hands can create an interesting and useful learning-centered lesson site. It is more important to have clear pedagogical avenues and learning goals than it is to have expensive and complex tools.

However, for faculty who want to have fewer limits on what can be accomplished with multimedia on the Web, more complex tools and support for both development and artwork are required. It is a rare faculty member who has the artistic, programming, and instructional design capabilities for some of the more complexly interesting Web pages that can be created. With the right understanding of what needs to be accomplished, though, along with the right tools and enough time, instructors can learn to create everything they need for a good lesson for helping students learn from a Web page.

Glossary of Terms

CGI (Common Gateway Interface) When a user enters information that will be stored and accessed later on a server, it uses the CGI protocol. This is important for online exams that will be graded and stored for later access. CGI programming generally requires technical help from computer services.

Java A programming language created for cross-platform development of programs that would run on the Web. This is a fully compiled program similar to C++ in many respects. Java applets (programs) are called up by HTML codes.

JavaScript Related to Java in name only, this scripting language can be placed directly into an HTML file. Like HTML it is an interpreted language that is decoded in the browser. It is widely used to add activity, feedback, and data access to Web pages.

QuickTime Digital movie format developed by Apple, Inc. for both Windows and Apple computers. Browser plug-ins allow QuickTime movies to run on the Web.

RealVideo Digital movie format developed by Real, Inc. for both Windows and Apple computers. Browser plug-ins allow RealVideo movies to run on the Web.

Rollover When the mouse pointer passes over or clicks on a graphic, it changes. Web site development tools such as *GoLive* provide built-in features to help create rollovers easily. Also, Web graphic tools like *Fireworks* and *ImageStyler* have functions for creating both the graphics and the rollover code for Web pages.

XML This markup language is used in formatting databases. It has a tag format like HTML but it is organized to generate tag names that reflect the data and objects it controls.

Chapter 5

Essential HTML

Why It's Important to Know Some HTML

In developing Web pages for your courses, most of the time you will be using a WYSIWYG tool such as Netscape *Composer*, *Dreamweaver*, *GoLive*, or *Front Page*, or converting a word processor page into a Web page. Even better, you will have a template where most of the design work has been done for you already. Using nothing but HTML code is difficult because you are unable to see what you're doing while you're doing it. Designing the look and feel of a page using nothing but code is like painting with a blindfold.

However, because HTML uses a *tag* system of encoding, it's fairly simple to learn, and there are times when it's actually easier to change a little code than it is to use tools. Other times, the tools won't do what you want them to do, and so you need to hand code some of the page. Learning HTML code is primarily for doing touch-ups on your site, not for the bulk of the work you will be doing.

Evolution of HTML

HyperText Markup Language (HTML) was designed to build pages for all sorts of different computers. What the viewer would see on her page depended on how her screen was set up, how the browser was configured, and the depth of colors being used, among other things. Naturally, this was enough to drive designers to distraction. Designers wanted to put a page together that would be seen consistently on all computers. After all, how could one design a page if it was to change with different monitors, computers, browsers, and whims of users? With the evolution of HTML, the designers would be given more of what they wanted.

At the beginning of HTML's evolution, the user could control certain aspects of text and color. As HTML evolved, the user got more and more tags with which to control more aspects of how a page looked and worked, as well as the overall sense and feeling the design gave the user. The Web browser interprets the HTML code in your computer. Currently, Netscape Navigator and Microsoft Internet Explorer are the two dominant Web browsers, and each has its own decoding device for HTML. As each new version of the browsers was released, new tags were introduced as HTML evolved from Version 1 up to Version 4. Version 4 of HTML was also called DHTML for *Dynamic* HTML. This was an important milestone for it introduced both layers and *Cascading Style Sheets* (CSS) allowing new design and interactive possibilities. Version 5 and versions beyond keep adding new features and functions as the World Wide Web, the Internet, and new technologies grow and change.

From the Basic to the Robust

Understanding the most basic aspects of HTML will help a great deal with the more complex aspects. In part, this is because you'll have the ability to better troubleshoot a Web page and make crucial changes without having to do a lot of work. Even though you may not understand all of the code, the code you do understand will help. When something goes wrong and you look at the HTML, it won't be like reading a passage written in Sanskrit. You'll understand enough to spot a problem or to make a change. In the more advanced HTML and specialized applications, there may be things your Web design tool just won't do but you can do with a little code. You will quickly find that the free or inexpensive Web development tools will not do very much at all when it comes to a really robust application. More expensive tools may do the trick, but not everyone will have those.

The Foundation Tags

To get started, we'll look at some basic foundation tags. These tags are pretty simple and straightforward and will give you an "under-the-hood" look at a Web page. Also, we'll look at a trick a lot of browsers cannot handle without your help.

Without getting too technical, the people who designed HTML were attempting to create a set of *structural* tags that would tell your text what to do. Because these people were not page designers, they did not pay attention to the same things page designers have for centuries. All of the pages in this book, your newspaper, and any magazine you read are designed by talented page designers. We look at a page and see nothing wrong with it and so don't notice all the work designers have done. That's good, actually, as people tend to overlook good design when it is done correctly. Bad page design, on the other hand, is quite noticeable and is readily available for viewing on the World Wide Web. Just look.

Generally, tags work with a beginning tag and an ending one. They were conceived of as ***containers***, and everything between the beginning and ending tag is *in the container*. A beginning tag is simply a code inside "arrow brackets." For example, the tag

```
<H3>
```

is the beginning of a container that creates a given "heading" size. The ending tag is the same thing with a slash following the first bracket, thusly,

```
</H3>
```

Before the advent of tools that automatically generated the code, all Web pages were created using this tag system. (It's little wonder that most of them looked awful.)

Administrative Tags

As we saw in Chapter 2, the basic Web page is made up of text, graphics, and links. The beginning and end of Web pages have what we might call "administrative tags," ones that have to be there but don't do anything that we can see. They tell the browser that it is now looking at a Web page. So to get started, we'll look at these administrative tags. In fact, you might want to put them in a text file for later use and then just put code in between them. On your basic page, you will always see *at least* the following tags:

```
<HTML>
This is where the bulk of your page goes . . . .
</HTML>
```

If you save the above code into a text file and give it a name with the extension ".html" it will actually work as a Web page. Using a simple text editor such as *Notepad* on a Windows computer or *SimpleText* on a Macintosh, copy in the above code, and save it as "test.html." From your browser open the page and note that all of the tags are hidden. Only the text sitting outside of the tag brackets is visible. If something is inside the "arrow brackets" your browser thinks it's a tag and won't show it on the screen. The first lesson in troubleshooting HTML code is to look for "broken" tag brackets. When you edit pages, you may sometimes clip off a leading or trailing "arrow bracket." If you do, you might encounter unexpected junk on your screen, and in most other editing you'll find that problems usually are caused by something simple like a missing bracket.

Text Tags

The basic text tags deal with relatively simple structures—structures that do not involve the use of more advanced HTML such as tables and frames. We'll look at the main ones employed and show how they appear on the screen of a Web page. First, we will look at the **BODY** tag to see what it can do to generally define global elements of the page. With the advent of Cascading Style Sheets (see Chapter 15), many of the key functions of the BODY tag have been replaced. However, the BODY tag is still widely used for assigning page characteristics. We will deal with background color of the page so that we won't have the default gray background. To get started, try the following:

```
<HTML>
<HEAD>
<TITLE>Background Color</TITLE>
</HEAD>
<BODY bgcolor="white">
The background color on this page is white.
</BODY>
</HTML>
```

The results of that little program are not dramatic, but they illustrate that you can control the page's background color. The colors available for Web pages are a very strange combination of "Web-safe" colors, an odd collection of names, and hexadecimal values. The current list of colors is in Appendix A. If you use any of the colors from the list, they are "Web safe," meaning they can be view from virtually any browser or color monitor. Most Web development tools will give you a set of colors from which to choose your background, and these too are safe.

Unfortunately for most people but happily for computers, colors also can be specified using hexadecimal values. A six-digit alphanumeric value often is displayed where the color goes. For example, instead of "white," you may see the value "#FFFFFF" with the "#" (pound sign) telling the browser that a hexadecimal value is about to follow. Caught between goofy names like "papayawhip" and hexadecimal values like "AB14CD" it's best to stick with simple colors like red, green, and blue. Better yet, just select the color you want to use in your Web development tool. However, if you see a color you really like on a Web page, and the source helpfully tells you it's "#BBC4FA," all you have to do is to use that value in specifying your color to get the desired hue.

"H" Tags

Basic text sizes are defined as "header" or H values. There are six tags to specify size from <H1>, the largest, to <H6>, the smallest. Rather than discuss them, it's better to see exactly what they look like on your computer. Create the following Web page and save it as "header.html." Then examine the results in a browser.

```
<HTML>
<HEAD>
<TITLE>Header Values</TITLE>
</HEAD>
<BODY bgcolor="papayawhip">
<H1> This is H1 </H1>
<H2> This is H2 </H2>
```

```
<H3> This is H3 </H3>
<H4> This is H4 </H4>
<H5> This is H5 </H5>
<H6> This is H6 </H6>
This is text with no header specified.
</BODY>
</HTML>
```

As you will see on your screen (see Figure 5-1), the headers are all in boldface, while the text outside of the header container is not.

Formatting Text

Without belaboring the point, let's just say that page designers had a fit when they saw what the framers of Web formatting did to paragraphs. Instead of having regular paragraphs that were separated by an indent, paragraphs were separated by a blank line and *it was impossible to indent them!* This is the work of the notorious <P> tag. In addition to the <P> tag, the <BR> tag was provided, and designers soon realized that it broke the line without inserting a blank line. However, to get an indent, some designers resorted to inserting a single pixel graphic. Fortunately, a slightly better way came for an indent, and that is using the innocuous ** **. Whenever you see an ampersand in front of a code, it means that it's a special way of getting a character not otherwise available. In this case, the code is for "non-breaking space"—in other words, a space. By lining up about four   characters, it's possible to get a simple indent. Let's see how this works. It's important because a lot of Web development tools don't know how to use .

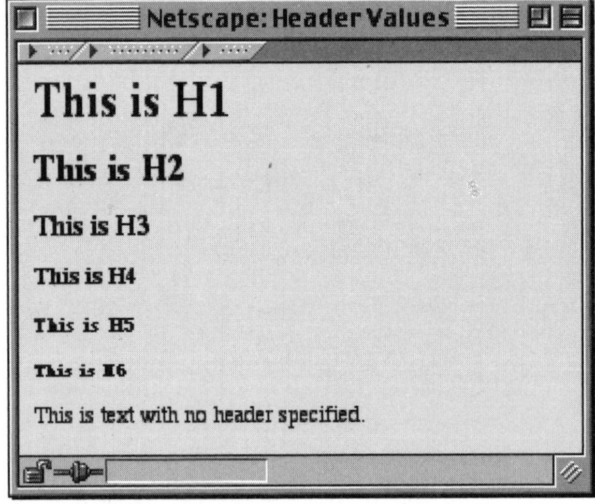

FIGURE 5-1 The H tags control text size in paragraph groups.

```
<HTML>
<HEAD>
<TITLE>Paragraphs</TITLE>
</HEAD>
<BODY bgcolor="oldlace">

The original creators of HTML decided not to let designers
have regular paragraphs. Instead, they provided the P tag
that stuck a blank line between two bodies of text. This
artificially tended to break up the flow of thought.<P>
Not only did they stick a big blank line in between the
paragraphs, they disallowed for spaces or tabs to be
inserted in front of the first word of a paragraph. How
were English instructors supposed to show students proper
grammar without a paragraph? <BR>      
  To get around this limitation, designers first used
invisible graphic blocks, but they later discovered the
non-breaking space symbol. Until CSS is widely available,
it will probably be employed.

</BODY>
</HTML>
```

Look carefully at the code and what you see on the Web page (see Figure 5-2). Be sure to look to see where the <P> and <BR> tags are placed and the effect of the line of " " characters on the indent. Note also that a semicolon separates all of the " " characters. It may seem odd that something as ubiquitous as a paragraph is so difficult to create on a Web page, but that is the case. Fortunately, CSS has provided a much more robust way of formatting pages, but Web development tools have not yet taken full advantage of its power. Additionally, earlier Web browsers cannot read CSS, so to keep on the safe side, designers are only gradually incorporating it into their designs.

> **Note**: This book is not intended to be a full resource on HTML. Rather, its purpose is to show how to design courses using tag codes only where the Web development tool won't do what you want. Also, because HTML is a dynamically changing language, learning the basics is more important than learning all of the many nuances of the language. However, for those who find HTML an interesting challenge and want to do more coding, take a look at http://www.w3.org to find the latest development in HTML. That address is the home page of the World Wide Web Consortium (W3C), the official organization for developing a common HTML protocol. Both Netscape Navigator and Microsoft Internet Explorer are supposed to follow their protocol.

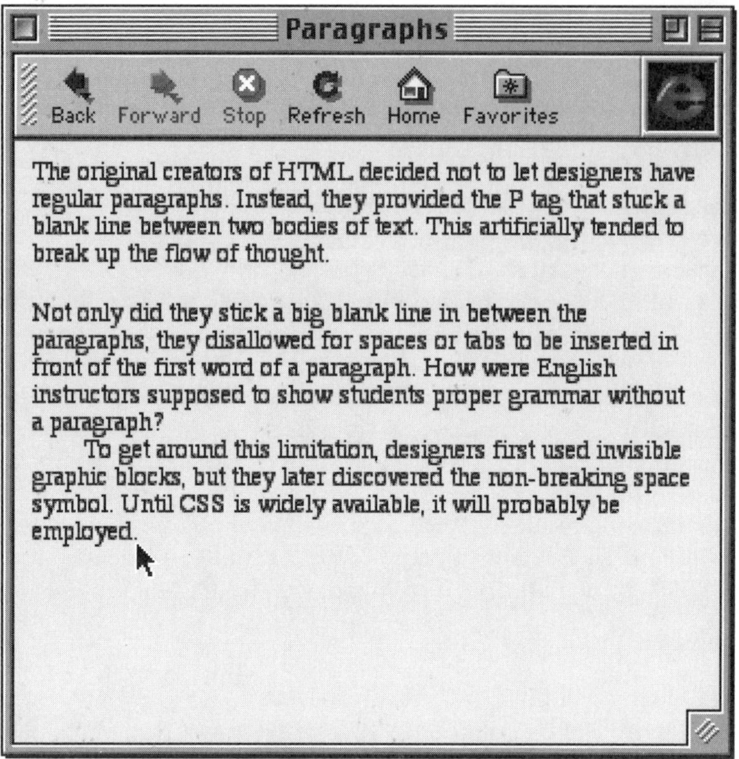

FIGURE 5-2 The paragraph tags provide no indentation, so users resort to using ampersand indents.

The other major forms of text formatting to be discussed in this chapter are lists, "blockquote," center, and character style. For the most part, your Web development tool can create text in these configurations without any hand coding at all. However, in looking at source code, you may come across these tags and knowing what they are will help both in editing the code and in making it behave.

Lists

Page designers have used the various list tags in their Web pages to provide either a straightforward list or to format text in ways that were not possible otherwise. The following set of code shows an "ordered list" **<OL>** which is also called a "numbered list." The "unordered list" **<UL>** is a bullet list, and the **<BLOCKQUOTE>** serves as a paragraph indent.

```
<HTML>
<HEAD>
<TITLE>Lists</TITLE>
</HEAD>
<BODY bgcolor="azure">
This is a numbered list. The OL stands for ordered list.
[In your Web page editor, you may see pound signs (#)
instead of numbers, but in your browser, you should see
numbers.]

<OL>
<LI>Active learning</LI>
<LI>Problem solving</LI>
<LI>Discovery</LI>
<LI>High standards</LI>
</OL>

<P><BR>This is a bulleted list with everything in the
list behaving as you see. The UL means unordered list.
<BR>
<UL>
<LI>Good faculty-student contact</LI>
<LI>Cooperation among students</LI>
<LI>Time on task</LI>
<LI>Prompt feedback</LI>
</UL>

<BLOCKQUOTE>
This is a BLOCKQUOTE. It indents the text giving it a
block appearance on the page.
</BLOCKQUOTE>

<BLOCKQUOTE>
  <BLOCKQUOTE>
If you use multiple blockquote tags, you will get more
indentation.
  </BLOCKQUOTE>
</BLOCKQUOTE>
</BODY>
</HTML>
```

Instead of getting numbers in ordered lists, some Web editors will show pound signs (#). However, in the browser itself, you should see numbers. If not, it's probably an older browser (see Figure 5-3).

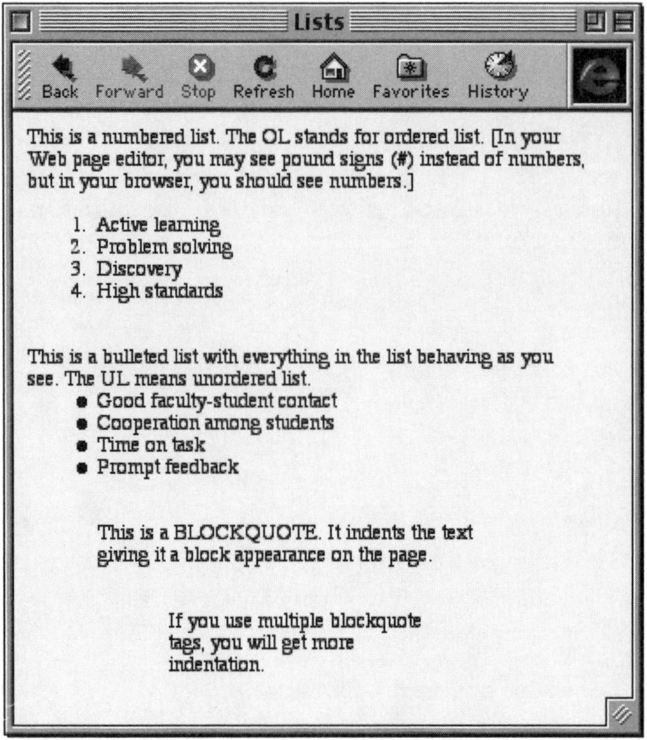

FIGURE 5-3 Lists and blockquotes are basic formatting tools in HTML.

A Little Style

Prior to CSS, all HTML could do with fonts was to provide one of three styles in addition to the default—bold, italicized, and monospaced. In looking at code regarding font style, there can be some confusion because there are *structural* and *procedural* tags. For our purposes, we will look only at the procedural tags.

<B> Bold

<I> Italicized

<TT> Monospaced (The TT is for Teletype.)

In addition, we will add the main structural formatting tag **<CENTER>**. For some strange reason, getting things centered does not always work from the coding used in Web page development tools. However, by using **<CENTER>**, all text and graphics in that container will march to the center of the page. The following code shows an example of what the code does:

```
<HTML>
<HEAD>
<TITLE>A Little Style</TITLE>
</HEAD>
<BODY bgcolor="blanchedalmond">
<Center>
<B>The Styles of HTML</B>
</Center>
Presenting the basic styles:<P>
<B>This is bold.</B><BR>
<I>This is italicized.</I><BR>
<TT>This is monospaced</TT><BR>
<B><I>What will this look like?</I></B><BR>
<TT><I>What happens with monospaced and
italicized?</I></TT>
</BODY>
</HTML>
```

There are several items you should note here (see Figure 5-4). First, when there is a structural change, there is a line break—note after the </CENTER> tag, there is no <BR>, but there is a line break before the next line. Also note that styles can be combined. Even using less sophisticated Web editing tools, it is a simple matter to combine styles.

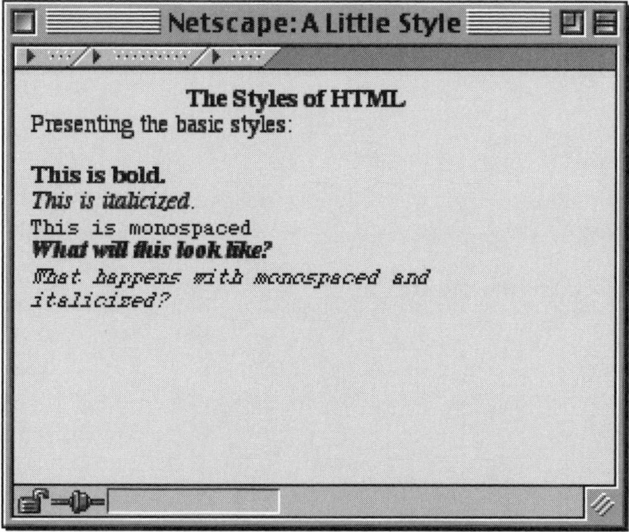

FIGURE 5-4 The styles available in basic HTML are basic indeed.

Graphic Tags

Graphic tags are quite simple in one respect, but they can be messy under certain circumstances. For the most part, let your Web editing tool do the work in filling out the information for you. The real secret to making life simple with graphics in HTML is having your graphics well organized. This means either having your graphics in the *same* folder as your HTML page or having all of the graphics in a separate folder. If all the graphic files for a Web page or even a Web site are in a single folder, there will be a direct reference to the file—just using the file name. Otherwise there is a long string of folder references that can be a headache to keep track of.

Tip: Remember that all of the Web pages and associated files, including graphic files, will be on a server—not your computer. If you put everything in a single folder for your Web site and send that folder to the server, *every associated file* is in the same relationship to your Web site on the server as on your computer. On the other hand, if you have several different folders or even different disks that are referenced for graphic files, chances are your page will not appear as you want on the Web. Keep it simple and well organized.

The HTML codes for bringing in a graphic are IMG and SRC. The tag **<IMG SRC="graphic.gif">** is the most basic for putting in a graphic. There is not a closing tag, and if there is a path to the graphic, the path must be included in the tag. (That's why it is easier to put everything in a single folder if you are writing your own HTML in a text editor like Notepad.) The following listing shows a simple example.

```
<HTML>
<HEAD>
<TITLE>Graphic Tag</TITLE>
</HEAD>
<BODY BGCOLOR="white">
```

The following code puts in a picture:

```
<BR><IMG SRC="Crim.gif">
</BODY>
</HTML>
```

Just about all browsers recognize either a GIF or JPG graphic file. New browsers will also recognize the PNG file type. In the above example, the graphic and background meld together because both the backgrounds for the graphic and for the page are white. Had we used a Web editing tool, more information about the graphic would be included. For example, had we used Microsoft Word and saved the file as an HTML one, the WIDTH and HEIGHT parameters would have been filled in automatically as shown in the following line:

```
<IMG SRC="Crim.gif" WIDTH=382 HEIGHT=112>
```

Given that information in the tag line, the browser can better load it quickly and correctly. If the WIDTH and HEIGHT values are changed proportionately, the graphic's size on the Web screen can be changed to fit virtually any page segment. Most Web editing tools can do that. For example, using Microsoft Word, the same graphic was reduced proportionately by holding down the SHIFT key and pushing in on one of the graphic's corners. Saved as HTML, the smaller version of the graphic generates the following code:

```
<IMG SRC="Image3.gif" WIDTH=217 HEIGHT=63>
```

That method is a lot easier than trying to calculate the proportional size of the WIDTH and HEIGHT by hand, and using a Web editing tool, you can see what it is going to look like on the page. (Note also that Microsoft Word's HTML editor changed the name of the graphic from "Crim.gif" to "Image3.gif." That can be a problem if you are expecting the other graphic to be located on the server. Changing the name of the graphic back to the original name will give you the correct graphic with the new correctly proportional graphic.)

A final little trick you might want to use is to provide a "load message." Using the **ALT** word, your screen will show a message about the graphics while they are loading. For example, changing the line to read

```
<IMG SRC="Crim.gif" WIDTH=382 HEIGHT=112 ALT="Criminology
Banner">
```

would show the message "Criminology Banner" while the page loads. This gives the viewer an idea of what is about to be presented. In cases where the link to the graphic is broken, it tells which graphic should load. Most Web editing and developing tools will have a way of allowing you to insert such messages without having to go directly to the code, but some do not and you may need it on occasion.

Link Tags

As pointed out in Chapter 2, the essential HTML Web page is composed of text, graphics, and links. Of these three components, the one feature that distinguishes a Web page from a book or magazine page is the link. The most basic link tag is:

```
<A HREF="http://www.mnh.si.edu/">Link Name</A>
```

The **<A HREF . . . > . . . </A>** container has the special property of making the text within the container "hot." That means when the user clicks the text, it opens the page that has been referenced. All Web editors I have seen make it easy to create a link, and so it is unlikely you will be writing your own code for links. ***However,*** when something goes wrong, you should be able to quickly check the source code and make needed changes. First, let's take a look at a quick program, and then we'll see what can go wrong.

```
<HTML>
<HEAD>
<TITLE>Basic Link</TITLE>
</HEAD>
<BODY BGCOLOR="Thistle">
Look at the text below. It is the link to the World Wide
Web.<P>
<A HREF="http://www.mnh.si.edu/">Smithsonian Institute's
Museum of Natural History</A>
<BR> Note that the link is underlined. Click the link,
and then click the <b>Back Button</b> on the browser. You
will notice that the link text changed colors. Since the
new color is close to the background color, the visited
link may be difficult to see.
</BODY>
</HTML>
```

As you can see on the next page (see Figure 5-5), the background color may interfere with the visibility of a *visited link*. However, when making a Web page for a course, it is important to use the colors best suited for the page, and so it is important to understand how to change the colors of the links and know what they look like in HTML. Like the BGCOLOR, the LINK, VLINK, and ALINK codes all belong in the BODY definition. Here's what each code stands for:

LINK: This is the color of the link before it has been visited or after it has been reset.

VLINK: This is the new color of the link once the user has visited it and before it is reset.

ALINK: This is the active link color when clicked. (It quickly blinks this color.)

In a learning situation, there may be many times when the instructor wants the link's and the visited links' colors to be the same. For example, in a multiple branch where the student must work her way through a series of problems, the student may use different colored visited links as the guide to the correct answer rather than the material she is supposed to learn. By having all links the same color this problem is avoided. Most Web page editors and development tools have a set of "Page Properties" where the colors of the links can be established.

The following listing shows how to control the link colors and to make the "hot spot" bold (see Figure 5-6).

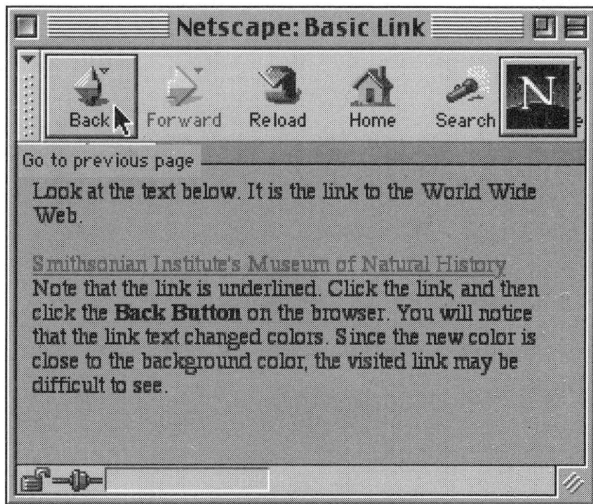

FIGURE 5-5 In using background colors with links, remember that the default link colors change after being viewed.

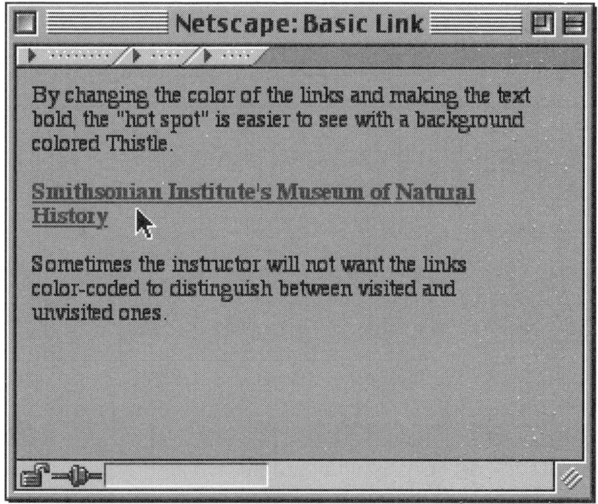

FIGURE 5-6 All aspects of a link color can be changed to conform to the overall style of the page design.

```
<HTML>
<HEAD>
<TITLE>Basic Link</TITLE>
</HEAD>
<BODY BGCOLOR="Thistle" LINK="forestgreen"
VLINK="forestgreen" ALINK="red">
By changing the color of the links and making the text
bold, the "hot spot" is easier to see with a background
colored Thistle.<P>
<B><A HREF="http://www.mnh.si.edu/">Smithsonian
Institute's Museum of Natural History</A></B><P>Sometimes
the instructor will not want the links color-coded to
distinguish between visited and unvisited ones.
</BODY>
</HTML>
```

Graphic Link Tags

Another type of link defines the graphic as the "hot spot." Instead of having text in the **<A HREF . . . > . . . </A>** container, a graphic is placed there. You need to note a couple of things in the following listing. First, unless you want the graphic to be surrounded by the LINK/VLINK colors, use the BORDER=0 code as shown. Second, having done that, be sure to instruct the user what to do. Rather than just stating "Which one represents a foundation concept?" you have to provide a statement that tells the user exactly what to do. Finally, note that the links went to addresses that simply have the name of the Web file (see Figure 5-7). In Chapter 6, we will discuss the different ways to reference links.

```
<HTML>
<HEAD>
<TITLE>Graphic Link</TITLE>
</HEAD>
<BODY BGCOLOR="white" LINK="slategray" VLINK="slategray"
ALINK="Red">
<P>
<P>Click the image that represents a foundation concept:
<CENTER>
<A HREF="correct.html"><IMG SRC="light.jpg" BORDER=0
HEIGHT=64 WIDTH=80></A>
<P><P>
<A HREF="incorrect.html"><IMG SRC="lamp.jpg" BORDER=0
HEIGHT=53 WIDTH=80></A>
</CENTER>
</BODY>
</HTML>
```

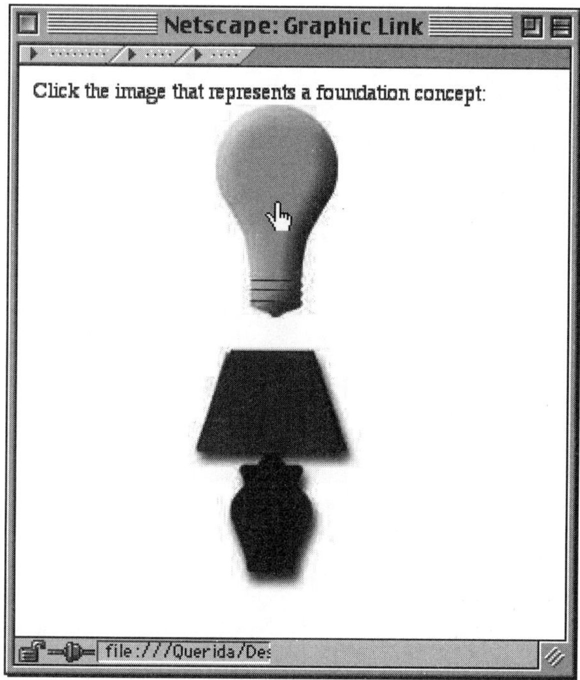

FIGURE 5-7 Graphic images, including photographs, can be clicked to aid in learning.

Administrative Tags That Help Others Locate Your Web Site

Some other administrative tags that you will find useful are ones that provide identification for your page and help others find your Web site. You will see them at the beginning of most programs, and they are handy to know—if for no other reason than not to be concerned with them right now. However, as you develop confidence and talk to Web page developers, you will want to understand how these tags can help your page.

The **HEAD** tag is a special section at the beginning of programs. Before the browser starts dealing with the rest of the page, it handles everything in the HEAD container. You will find JavaScript programs in the area bracketed by the HEAD tags along with other administrative tags and containers. The following shows typical contents in a head container:

```
<HEAD>
<TITLE>The Works of Jane Austen </TITLE>
<META NAME="keywords" CONTENT= "ENG 2210, English
literature, writing, Jane Austen, fall 2001">
```

```
<META NAME="description" CONTENT="ENG 2210 is a course in
English Literature focusing on the writings of Jane
Austen offered in the fall semester of 2001.">
<SCRIPT LANGUAGE="JavaScript">
  alert("Manners are morals.")
</SCRIPT>
</HEAD>
```

The **TITLE** tag puts the name on top of your page. It is handy to remember to use because it will tell your students what page they're on and help you organize your pages. It's not essential, but generally it's a good idea to name each page with the title tag. For example, the title

```
<TITLE> Elementary Quantum Mechanics </TITLE>
```

would inform a literature student that he's probably on the wrong page.

A **META** tag has several uses, and they are extremely important for getting noticed on the Web. These tags are found in the HEAD container to give information to Web search engines such as Yahoo!, Excite, Altavista, Lycos, and Webcrawler. For search engines, the two most important META tag names are "keywords" and "description." The META tag for "keywords" takes the following form:

```
 <META NAME="keywords" CONTENT= "ENG 2210, English
literature, writing, Jane Austen, fall 2001">
```

The keywords are the words used in matching a user's search term. A student looking for a course on Jane Austen would most likely use the search word "Jane Austen." However, a student may want any course in English literature or a course in the fall semester of 2001 and use "English literature" or "fall 2001." Having the right keywords in the META container may mean the difference between having your course found and missed.

The second META tag used for searches determines what will be said about your page when a keyword has been located. It takes a slightly different form, expecting complete sentences describing the Web site.

```
<META NAME="description" CONTENT="ENG 2210 is a course in
English Literature focusing on the writings of Jane
Austen offered in the fall semester of 2001.">
```

It is important to include both keyword and description META tags in the HEAD section of your Web site. You need not put these META tags in all of your Web sites, just on the first page of your first lesson or syllabus. Notice that the META tags do not have a closing tag. (There's no </META> tag.) You don't need one.

IMPORTANT NOTE: Many Web page development tools do not have an automatic or clear way to include keyword and description META tags. That's one reason you need to know a little HTML. Once you've got your page finished, code in the needed META tags by hand. A single course should need no more than one page with these tags, but they are important ones to have.

Finally, **comment tags** are a programmer's comments to herself or others looking at her page. The beginning of a comment is tagged with

```
<!--
and the end with
-->
```

The browser ignores all text in a comment, but when looking at the source code of a Web page, you can see the comments. These are reminders or explanations that you want included with the code. For example, the following comments may be included near a META tag.

```
<META NAME="description" CONTENT="COMM 101 covers
beginning communications for communications majors
only.">
<!-- Change the description in the spring semester to
COMM 202 for intermediate communications -->
```

Comments can be placed anywhere desired in the Web page, and good programmers usually have lots of comments to help others reading their pages. When looking at other people's pages, read the comments for some tips on what they're doing.

TIP: Reading other people's source code can help you see how they do what they do. To read any source code on the Web, simply select "Page Source" [or "Source"] from the View menu and a page with the tags will appear.

Summary and Review

The point of this chapter has *not* been to run out and spend a lot of time learning HTML. For the great bulk of work done to create Web pages, using the editing and development tools available for creating Web pages is sufficient. However, because many of the tools have quirks, and you may use different tools for different projects, it is good to know a little HTML. Ironically, you can actually save time in developing a page that's not performing as you wish using a little code rather than trying to get a Web editing tool to do it for you. In part, that is why the most powerful (and most expensive) Web editing and development tools have easy access to the page's HTML. Users often need full control over the page. Throughout the book, I will provide some little code that will help you understand how to edit and "tweak" some pages created for your classes. Because HTML is developing faster than the editing tools to handle it, knowing just a little of the right code can go a long way.

By dividing HTML into *administrative, text, graphic,* and *link* categories, I am attempting to provide a useful image of what gets done on a basic page. The framers of HTML did not intend these categories, but I believe they will help clarify a little of what the code does. Further on in the book, when we discuss tables, frames, and Dynamic HTML, we will see much more than a basic page. However, for the time being, just think of HTML code doing something in one of those four categories. It will help you get a handle on source listings and basic editing.

Glossary of Terms

Administrative tag This tag is used for a number of purposes other than defining how text and graphics such as the title appear on the page.

Comment tag This tag helps the Web page developer understand code she wrote and helps others to use the code for their own Web sites.

Foundation tag The term is used in this book to reference a tag that defines the text as code for the browser to read.

Link tag Used with text or graphics, this tag serves to call up another Web page.

Meta tag A tag used for providing information about the site that helps others find it when using search engines.

Style tag A tag used to define how the text appears on the page. Style tags include bold, italicized, Teletype (monospaced), underlined, and other effects on the text appearance.

Chapter 6

Designing for Discovery: Links to Find Knowledge

Perhaps the single most important feature of Web pages is their linking ability. Fundamentally, there are two basic types of links. First, internal links connect to other pages within the instructor's site. These pages are connected to a lesson in the context of a course and are arranged by the instructor. Professors have total control over how these pages will look, the kind of information they contain, and what the student must do to go on to the next link or go back to review other information. Second, external links take the student to the rich possibilities of the World Wide Web. These are links over which the instructor has no control and she cannot alter or change in any way. Therefore, when selecting external links the instructor needs to be sure that the links have the information required for the lesson, and equally important that they are still at the same location. (See Chapter Appendix A for an example exercise in creating a simple link.)

Internal Linking

When creating links to pages the instructor has prepared for the course, there are several different ways the pages can be arranged—the paths the student takes to learn the needed materials. Such links are referenced in this book as *internal links* even if the pages created by the professor are on more than a single server. The first consideration in setting up internal links is the use of folders or directories. To make life simple, put all files for a single lesson in the same folder. If you link to another page in a lesson in the same folder or directory, all you need to put in is the file name (for example, **socialnorms.html**). For example, an introductory course in biology may have a lesson on mammals. By creating a folder or directory named "mammals," the instructor can place all of the pages within that folder dealing with the topic on mammals. He might, for instance, have the following pages:

domestic.html

wild.html

aquatic.html

endangered.html

If all of the files are in the same folder, linking the page entitled **domestic.html** to the page entitled **aquatic.html** only requires a reference to the file itself and not the route through several subdirectories. This makes it very simple for developing lessons in a course. Although it may not be as efficient for using server space, it is a good way to get started. If several people—a team-taught course, for example—are developing parts of the lesson, knowing that all internal links for a lesson are within a single folder, everyone knows that all associated files have a direct link (see Figure 6-1).

The best place to work on a computer is in the desktop area. Create the folders in either Windows or the Macintosh on the desktop, or drag the ones to be used onto the desktop. Depending on the version of Windows, there may be slightly different ways to create new folders. In Windows, select the Start button> Programs>Windows Explorer>File>New>Folder>. However, Windows may be upgraded so that making folders and directories is even easier. On the Macintosh, selecting *New Folder* in the File menu creates the file menu in the Finder.

With more experience, and a good site management tool, it will be time to consider using more sophisticated organization of materials. For example, having

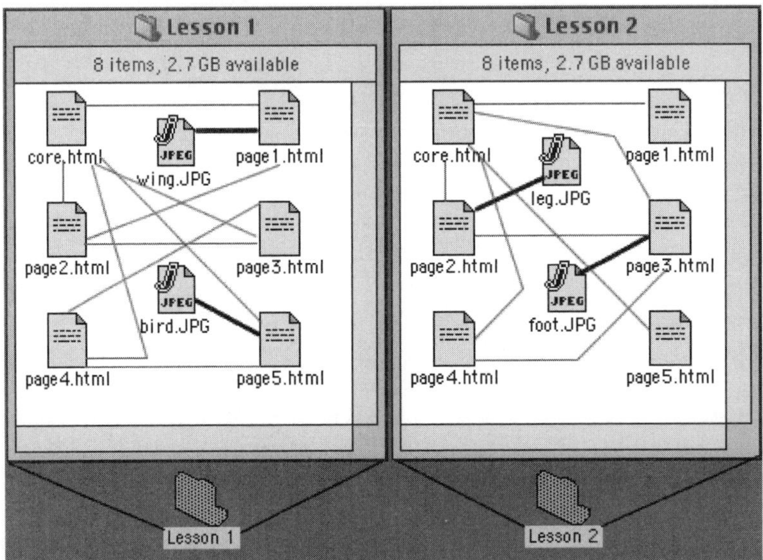

FIGURE 6-1 If all pages and associated files for a Web site are in the same folder, it is much easier to keep track of links.

all of one's graphics in a folder called **graphics** saves space on the server for graphics that are reused constantly, such as directional buttons and graphic template elements. If all lesson folders for a given course were kept in a directory called **Humanities101** and all of the graphic files for all of the lessons were kept outside of the individual lesson folders, a link something like the following would be used.

```
"... /graphics/arrow.jpg"
```

Site management is the art and science of making sure all of the links in a site are working and link to the intended Web pages. With external links, site management is a matter of periodically checking to make sure the external link is still extant. With good site management, it would not be difficult to use this more effective server organization. Figure 6-2 shows this organization with two different lessons using a common graphics folder.

It is important to note that for the student, the links and navigation should be transparent. That is, whatever organization the instructor uses internally in the server should not affect or even be considered by the student. Moreover, when planning what type of internal file and folder organization to use the look and feel of the lesson flow *as viewed by the student* are not a consideration. The way in

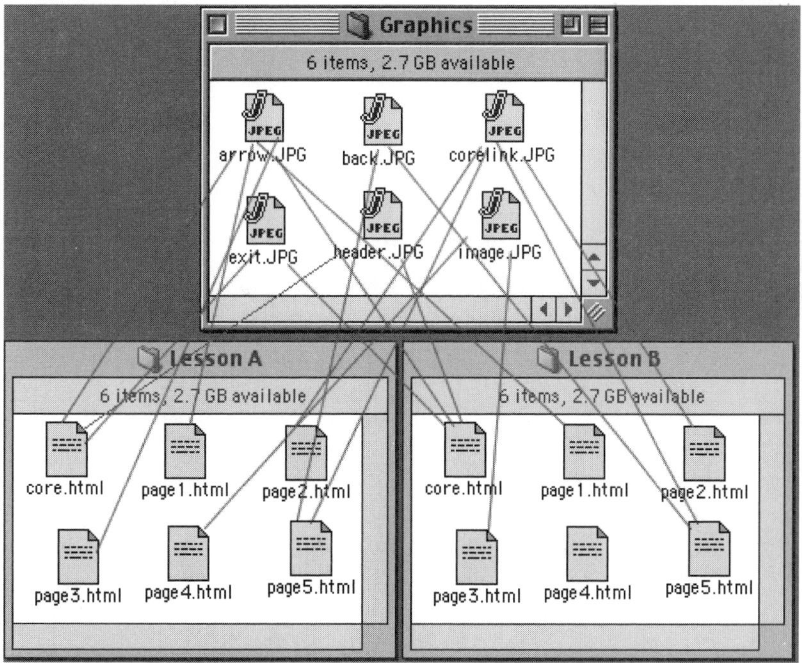

FIGURE 6-2 By organizing all graphics files into a single folder, less space is used and different pages can use all the graphics in the single central folder.

which the student encounters the materials in the lesson and how the files are organized efficiently and effectively on the server *need to be treated as two distinct areas of organization.* Computers and students have wholly different ways of encountering the world and most effectively dealing with it. If what is on the Web page is confused with the way the page is organized on the server, there is a very real possibility that the instructor will end up using a computer interface instead of a human one. (See Chapter 16 for a complete explanation of how to place files onto servers.)

Web Occasions: Cordially Inviting Students to Learn

"Human interface" is one of those terms that is an extension of computer technology that may be inappropriate in considering how to get students to click on a link. The "interface" between a computer and printer, disk drive, or the Internet is a matter of matching connective hardware and software protocol so that each can communicate with the other. The keyboard and mouse are indeed "human interfaces," but beyond that point, the interface metaphor risks thinking about students in the same way we think about computer components, and that idea strikes me as disparaging. Computers and peripherals live in an electrically charged world of relatively simple actions and reactions. Humans live in a symbolic world full of multiple meanings, nuances, gestures, and assumptions. Moreover, because we all have more experience dealing interactively with humans (for better or worse), we should use both our own personal pool of knowledge and what those who study social interaction know rather than the knowledge of those who spend most of their time getting machines to work together.

Personal knowledge about human interaction in certain very real ways tells us about who we are. In interaction with students, they learn who we are as well. Therefore, in creating a Web site for a course, an instructor is in a position to use her knowledge not only to enhance the interaction but also to present herself to students. What works and doesn't work in face-to-face interaction provide the clues of what may and may not fly on a Web page.

In planning an occasion, especially one in which people are likely to judge us, there is *rehearsal.* We think in our minds of interesting things to say or topics to raise so others sharing the occasion will become involved and participate in a pleasant experience for all. Whether that experience constitutes discovering new knowledge or is strictly a social encounter does not matter here. For the occasion to be successful, it requires some attention to what will enhance the experience and lead to *all participants' involvement in the situation.*

The role of the **link** in creating a learning-based Web site is the key to involvement. Social interaction is essentially a series of people taking turns talking. When the *next turn* is not taken, the interaction ceases, and so unless the participants wish the encounter to come to an end, they keep taking turns. The nature, amount, and quality of the talk for one side or the other vary depending on the situation, and there are many different types.

Talk is an exchange of information, and because information can be *embodied* or *disembodied* (Goffman, 1963, 14), the actual presence of those in the exchange is not required. Web interaction involves a disembodied participant—namely, the Web page developer (the professor in this discussion). Therefore, there needs to be a consideration in developing a Web page of how the other person will take a turn. Because the most common *turn* is essentially clicking somewhere on the current page, the student is severely limited in what responses he can make with links, but he can choose to be involved or not. In the same way that a lecture severely limits the role of the audience and places the onus of preparation and engagement on the lecturer, a Web occasion transfers the bulk of the responsibility and preparation to the instructor who prepares the Web page.

A lecture has been described as *an institutionalized extended holding of the floor* (Goffman, 1981, 165). In that respect, instructors who create Web pages have the same privilege. Otherwise, a lesson Web site must not be treated like a lecture. In a lecture, the speaker expects the audience to be attentive—or at least appear to be. There are strong social norms backing the dominant involvement demanded of the audience (Goffman, 1963, 43–45). These norms are on the side of the speaker, and although students may engage in subordinate involvements such as chatting during a lecture, it is well within the rights of the speaker or audience to demand the chatter cease. While a student is viewing a Web page, there are no such norms demanding attention. In settings like a library or even a campus computer lab there may be some expected decorum and attention, but in a dorm room, at home, or at work, such norms do not exist. Engaging the student must be done in other ways.

Like a book or article students are assigned to read, a Web page requires more maturity and responsibility on the part of the student to assure completion. However, Web pages should not be treated like book or paper assignments either in their creation or consideration. If there are long texts for students to read, it makes more sense to use paper. In dealing with students at remote sites, it is better to use email or downloads of text to be printed out and read than trying to put a great deal of text on a Web page. Sometimes a screenful of text is required within a lesson site, but if text is deemed the best way to communicate a lesson it is *more sensible* to use paper. In my own experience with students, long textual screens are printed out anyway. It is better to use the page formatting properties of a word processor than a Web page to prepare it for printing. It's easier and it will look better. Also, it is a very good idea to think of a Web site as part of collaboration with paper materials rather than an exclusive place for screen-only presentation.

Template Links and Navigation

The template provided in Chapter 3 shows one way of dealing with links. Think of the linking arrangement as a very formal social occasion. The student sees a clear series of steps to take to go from one page to the next. However, unlike a social occasion, where one *faux pas* is sometimes tricky to undo, the navigation and turn-taking are laid out in front of the student, and at any time she can go to the core to view the overall context. Mesher (1999, 19) talks about *passive interactivity* as the contextual background in navigation, and the need to provide the focus of the learning task. The navigation bar suggested in Chapter 3 constitutes the center of *passive interactivity*. The student is not only able to see which step to take next; she can see it in the context provided in the core. For example, in Figure 6-3, the student sees the current position as six steps into the lesson with four more to go. She also clearly sees the topic and some points emphasized with bullets. That immediately shows the student where she is now and what she can expect to see.

Like all formal social occasions, there is the risk of losing interest because of the stuffiness of and the limitations placed by the formality of the occasion. However, the advantage of such occasions lies in knowing what to do next, what is expected, and what to do and not to do. Spicing up the occasion with surprises, though, provides incentives for remaining involved. Like an engaging raconteur, a Web page can be both formally gracious as well as interesting.

In an asynchronous learning environment, student-faculty contact is mediated through the software. Mesher (1999, 16) points out that the key to online learning is *hyperlinked interactivity*. To the extent that the software becomes a stand-in for the professor, interactivity is wholly scripted, and we need to look for ways whereby students can be prompted to ask the right questions so that an appropriate response can be scripted into the model. This means leading the students to the right questions, giving them appropriate information along the way, and then providing them with answers. Goffman (1981, 53–54) notes that teachers in interaction with students attempt to find what the student has learned and then to correct and amplify from this base. Goffman (1981, 54) identifies a three-part sequence as shown on the next page.

Conflict and Death

- Sudan in the mid 19th century was in a very confused state. In the the British, invaded and unified northern Sudan (called Cush) and Egypt, then part of the Ottoman empire.
- From 1877-1880 British occupied Khartoum and suppressed slav primarily of the Arabs in the north taking slaves in the black south founded Khartoum in 1830 while under the Ottoman Empire.
- An Islamic Mahdi army defeated Lord Gordon in 1885 but Kharto was a British colony until 1956.
- The group of tribes in the south collectively known as the **Dinka** Islam, and practiced both indigenous religions and Christianity (es In the independence period, no one consulted those in the southern

FIGURE 6-3 The links in the suggested template create a formal but clear occasion.

Teacher: Query

Student: Answer

Teacher: Evaluative comment or answer

Such interchanges are simple to include in hypertext-based software where links can take the interaction in different directions. In setting up such interchanges, the instructor's query and response must be designed to react to what the student answers. If the answers are from a discrete selection, there can be a matching set of responses. Another way of putting it is that a student is guided into an interaction based on multiple choices and appropriate matching responses. The more sophisticated the forethought and feedback the professor have on hand when developing courseware, the better the response and hence the interaction. A well-planned learning-centered classroom course has the same requirements to keep focused.

Educational imperatives and sequences are only predictable insofar as students ask the right questions. For elaboration, discussion, and motivation, other means of faculty-student interaction need to be included. Email links are easy to embed, as are asynchronous discussion forums and synchronous chats. The fact that these are included is not enough, though. They must be *planned* like everything else so that they are used effectively for the learning process. Regular contact needs to be part of the design so that *both* professors and students will be prompted to use the communication technology included in the course.

Links to Elaborate

One of the nice things about Web pages is their ability to pull in added information without leaving a current position. Heavily annotated works split the viewer's attention between the main text and the annotations in the columns. William S. Baring-Gould's *The Annotated Sherlock Holmes* (1974) stands as an example of an annotated tome where the reader is given a visual and textual historical tour of Victorian England while trying to follow a Holmes' mystery. In the margins of this magnificent set are graphics and text with a rich elaboration of what the scene looked and felt like during the time Sir Arthur Conan Doyle was writing his stories about the adventures of Sherlock Holmes and Dr. Watson. However, following the stories is made far more difficult because the reader is constantly eyeing the pictures and text in the margins. With Web pages, though, it is possible to introduce informative asides and elaboration without cluttering the page or distracting students from the main flow of the lesson. Using textual or graphic links the student can easily click on a link, learn more about the topic, and then continue on with viewing the current page. Figure 6-4 shows this model of Web page elaboration or annotation.

In an interactional context, having a page pop up for elaboration is like pulling out a photograph from a wallet or purse, showing it to those at the gathering and then putting it back. Without disrupting the flow of the interaction, the interjection of annotating materials elaborates without standing as a constant

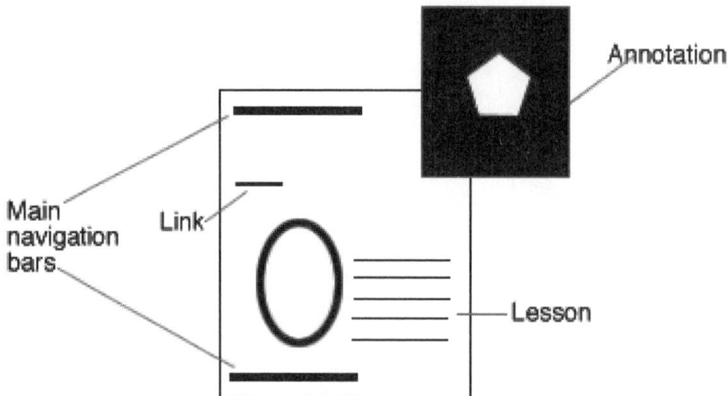

FIGURE 6-4 Annotations and elaboration can be brought out and put away using links.

distraction. Chapter 12 examines how annotation pages can be brought up and viewed while the main page dominates the real estate of the screen as illustrated in Figure 6-4. Also, Chapter 12 shows how "pop-ups" can be used for short text-only messages that serve the same purpose as additional pages providing elaboration except in much smaller clips. These activities require a little JavaScript be used.

An easy way to create elaborating pages is simply with a link to that page. For example, it is not uncommon to see educational Web pages that look something like the following:

> *Social sciences have their roots in different philosophies, and most of the fundamental differences can be traced to arguments in philosophy. In sociology, the philosophies of Hegel, Heidegger, Husserl, Dewey, and even Plato are the foundations of discourse.*

The idea is for the student to click on each philosopher (underlined) to find out how his or her work is related to sociology. If the student finds herself off the main page and suddenly reading about Edmund Husserl on a new page, even if it is only about how his works have affected certain schools of thought in sociology, the effect may be to sidetrack rather than to enlighten. There needs to be a link back to the main train of thought. Figure 6-5 shows one suggested arrangement for having a main flow assisted by links to "elaboration pages."

If the learning strategy is to have the student browse different ideas and thinking before striking off on her own, there is a need to carefully craft the Web site so that the exploration covers everything desired but does not put the student out of the learning context of the lesson. If using the contextual model (see Chapter 2) there should be a link back to the contextual core on every page as well as links that encourage exploration to other pages relevant to the core.

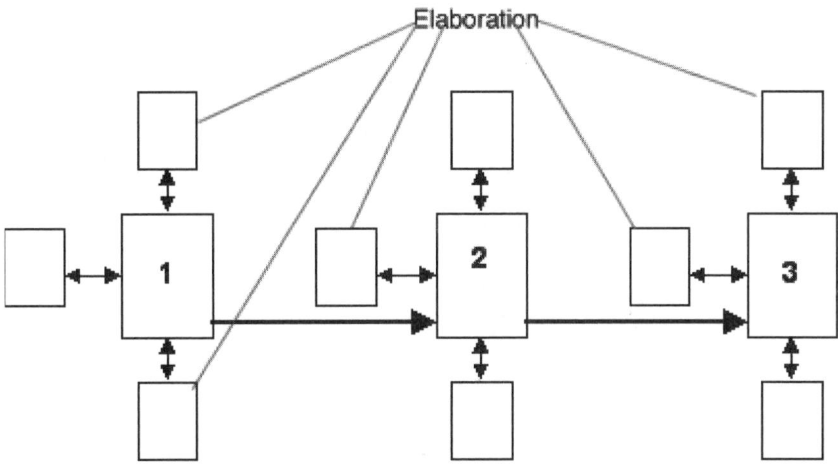

FIGURE 6-5 The main pages (1, 2, 3) have two-way links between themselves and elaboration pages. The "in-and-out" links keep students from getting sidetracked or lost.

Menus

Selection from a menu is one of the more common linking systems. Using the concept of core pages as suggested in Chapter 3, there is a place students can go to get an overview of a lesson or course. However, there are other menu systems that should be considered.

Sidebar Menus

One of the most common types of menus is one that runs along the side of the browser window. As different links are selected, different pages appear in the window to the right of the sidebar menu. In Chapter 9 frames are discussed, and there will be instructions for creating HTML tags to create frames. Here the concept is examined as a linking system. Figure 6-6 shows how the links look in a sidebar menu.

Navigation using this system is very flexible and easy for the student to know where she is and what the pertinent choices are. In many courses, the instructor has links from the menu to other elements of the course. Likewise, once this format is set up, it is easy to have a series of menus appear in the menu window as the student progresses from one lesson to the next.

Engagement Links

Using sidebar menus does not mean that all links must be connected to the menu. The lesson page may have several other links to engage the student's interest or participation. Annotations and elaboration pages expand, but other links can have the sole purpose of engagement. For example, the page in Figure 6-7 uses the

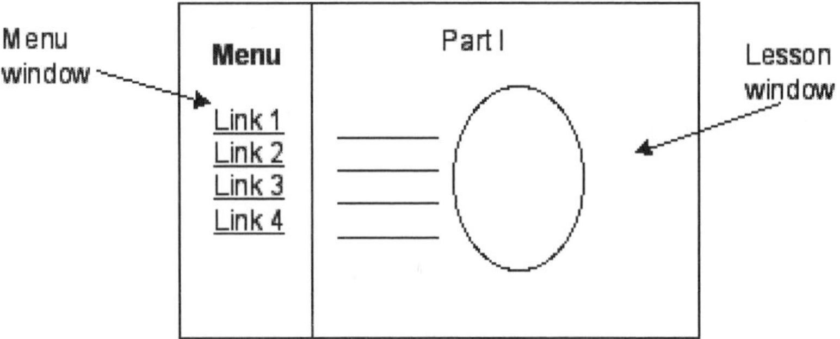

FIGURE 6-6 The links in a sidebar menu work within the context of a frame set. Each time a link is clicked the associated page of the lesson appears in the right window, but the menu remains in place throughout the lesson.

sidebar menu but has an engagement link on the lesson page. The model of interaction extends the traditional Socratic one to the following sequence:

Teacher: Engagement move

Student: Response

Teacher: Query

Student: Response

Teacher: Evaluative comment or answer

This modified sequence substitutes "response" for "answer" because what the student does can encompass a wider range of moves than an answer or even a reply implies (Goffman, 1981, 35).

As can be seen in Figure 6-7, sidebar menus can take up a lot of space on a page, but they are easy for the student to use, and some pages require relatively little space anyway. The sidebar menu model, in some respects, keeps an outline of the core page in front of the student at all times. However, it is important to remember that the convenience of Web pages means that a link to a core page makes it easy to jump back and forth between a core and a current page in a lesson. Unlike a book page, there is no fumbling back and forth between a current page and an overview page at the beginning of a chapter. Likewise, faculty may wish to include a *glossary* link on a page so that students can quickly look up the meanings of words introduced in the lesson or other lessons. The point to keep in mind is that it is easy to link the student to a contextual overview, glossary, elaboration, or engagement without getting in the way of the flow of the lesson.

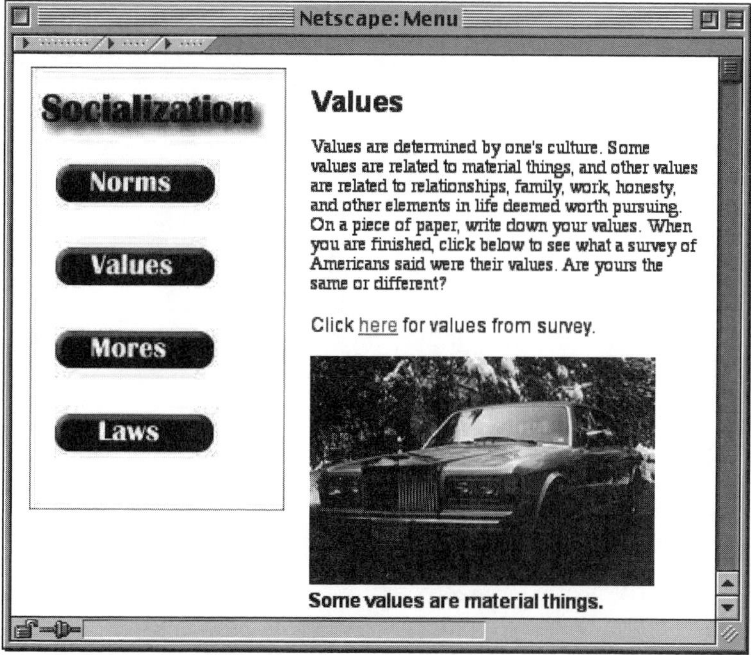

FIGURE 6-7 In this page, the menu on the side directs the student through a lesson on socialization. One of the pages on values invites the student to write a list of values and then selects a link to another page.

Small Text Menus

Another common strategy found in linking is to use small text links at the top or bottom of a page. For example a lesson on the range of English writers might have a menu that looks like the following:

Yeats | **Browning** | **Dickens** | **Shakespeare** | **Browne** | **Chaucer**

These menus are simple, yet very effective. They take up little room on the page, they are clear, and they provide their own context and overview. Each page can have copies of the menu within a current page. The lack of an underline shows that it is not linked to itself. For example, the small text menu on the Dickens page would look like the following:

Yeats | **Browning** | **Dickens** | **Shakespeare** | **Browne** | **Chaucer**

It is clear where the student is, and what other choices can be made. Sometimes the current page will have the name in a different color, make it bold, or do something else to make it stand out. However, usually it is enough to simply remove a link to itself, thereby removing the telltale underline common to most Web page links.

Small text menus can also be used in conjunction with other navigational systems, such as the one offered in Chapter 3 or sidebar menus. They are small enough to be placed throughout a page for elaboration of a point or engagement of students.

When using small text menus, use a sans serif font such as Arial or Helvetica. When smaller-size text is used, the serifs on typical body fonts such as Times Roman make the text even smaller and more difficult to read. A sans serif font calls attention to itself subtly and is slightly larger than typical serif fonts used in body text. Using size –1 (or 10 points) is quite clear and out of the way. It is even possible to go down to –2 (or about 8 points) in font size with small text menus.

Pull-Down Menus

Another type of menu that is nice to have available is the pull-down. This menu takes up little space, and gives the instructor many options in the small space available on the screen. Most Web page editors make it easy to create pull-down menus, but they do not make it easy to create links with them. Chapter 13 shows how to create linking capabilities with pull-down menus in the discussion of using forms. (Pull-down menus are a type of form.) A few JavaScript tricks are required to get these menus working as needed, but they are very handy to have available.

Basically, a pull-down menu is a form that opens up into several selections when selected—just like the pull-down menus found on most word processors and other non-Web applications. Because they take up little room, several such menus can be put on the screen at the same time. For example, Figure 6-8 shows how an exit page employs three pull-down menus that lead students to reviews, useful links, or suggested readings.

Information Is the Interface

In discussing the use of visual confections, Edward Tufte (1997, 146) notes that *"In an architecture of content, the information becomes the interface."* The information on a page tells the user what is available in text, graphics, or a combination of the two. The information is laid out spatially rather than *stacked* in multiple layers with each layer being a clue to what comes next. The conceptual framework behind the core page provides this kind of flat interface for the entire site. There is information about what is available in one place instead of arranged in a hierarchy where the student keeps clicking until he reaches the part of the lesson he needs. Consider the following outline:

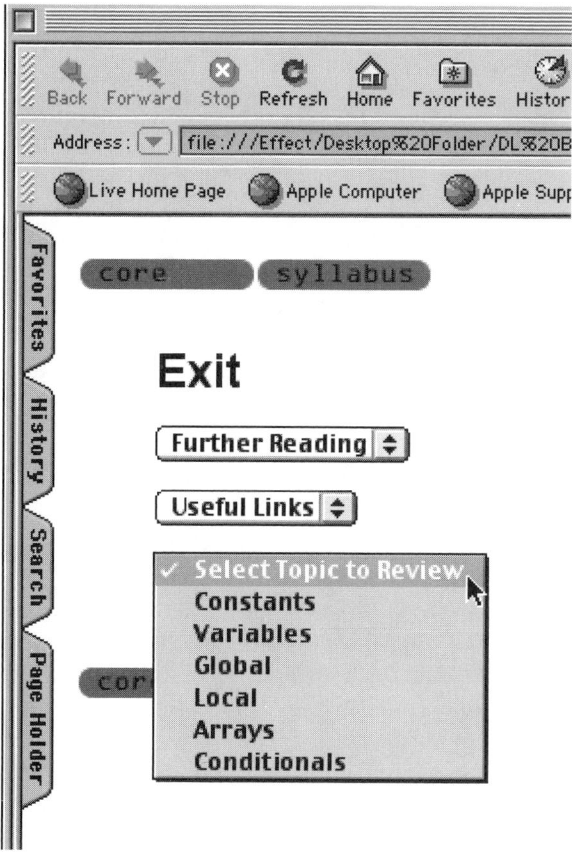

FIGURE 6-8 Pull-down menus take up very little space and can be used to offer students several options. Unfortunately, they require more sophisticated code to effect a link. (Chapter 13 shows how this is done.)

1. Law

    A. Civil

    B. Criminal

        1) Against Persons

        2) Against Property

            a. Felony

            b. Misdemeanor

                [1] Petty Theft

On a single page, it is easy to find "Petty Theft" and click and go to that page. However, some design pages with more information than is needed in the details and arrange information in a "stack" of links like the following:

Level 1

Law [Click to see next level]

Laws are formal norms that societies develop to. . .

Level 2

Civil [Click to see next level]

Civil law regulates relations between people. . . .

Criminal [Click to see next level]

Criminal law defines acts against the group as a whole. . . .

Level 3

Against Persons [Click to see next level]

Against Property [Click to see next level]

Level 4

Felony [Click to see next level]

Misdemeanor [Click to see next level]

Level 5

Petty Theft

Everything you want to know about petty theft. . . .

Such arrangements can lose the context of where the student is going. In the above example, the student has to drill down five levels before finding what she needs. By the time she gets there, she may be confused. Another arrangement of the information shows several levels as links to both higher and lower levels. Figure 6-9 shows how a menu made completely of text links provides a strong information interface.

With this arrangement, the student sees where each topic lies within a context. She can find out about the general topics (for example, Civil or Criminal) and the specific topics (for example, Robbery or Petty Theft) without having to drill down several levels. *The links themselves are part of the information.*

Graphics images can be used as well as text to provide a clear set of links to a set of information. In Figure 6-10, the menu contains the topics in a cultural

Law

Civil			**Criminal**
Family Law			**Against Persons**
Custody	Divorce	Homicide	Robbery
Business Law		Rape	Assault
Contracts	Mergers		**Against Property**
Bankruptcy	Finance	Misdemeanor	Felony
		Petty Theft	Grand Theft

FIGURE 6-9 Where information is the interface, it is important to provide both higher and lower levels of information in a single spatial plane. Each word describes its own link.

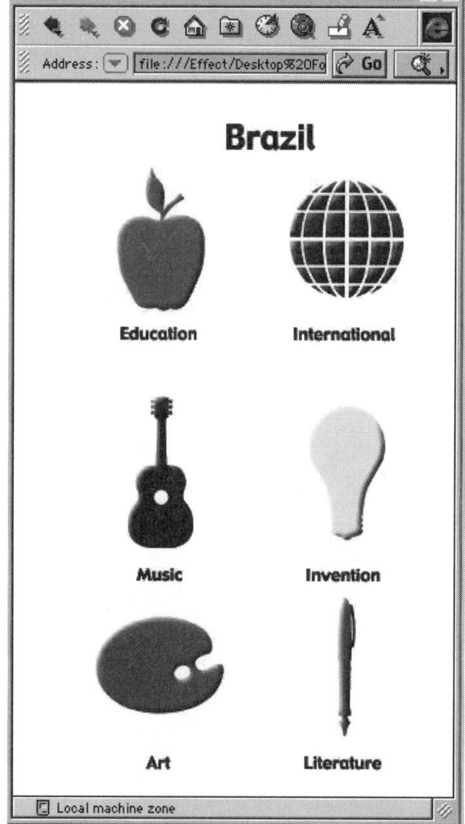

FIGURE 6-10 All of the links are shown in text and graphics, both of which are links. Using a graphic text instead of standard text, it is possible to use a wider variety of font styles that will look the same on all computers. When a text-font is used that is not in the client computer's text library, there can be unexpected results.

geography course shown with both graphics and text. The graphics and text provide quick and clear information about the topics. More elaborate and precise graphics can be used as well. For example, in a course on molecular biology, the different types of molecular structures could serve as graphic guides to topics on each structure. Similarly, an art course could have graphic paintings representing different artistic styles.

Links to Compare

A final use of internal links for a learning-centered approach to education is to bring two or more contrasting forms into juxtaposition. Tufte (1990, 67) states "[a]t the heart of quantitative reasoning is a single question: *Compared to What?*" For Tufte, *small multiples* serve as a prime design structure for bringing out comparative differences between everything from statistical diagrams to the movement of a planet. By seeing small graphical representations next to one another in a single visual plane, the viewer is better able to compare and contrast. However, a link has the property of being able to quickly switch between pages and hence images for student-involved comparison. There are a number of ways this can be accomplished. In this chapter we will examine the concepts and in Chapters 8 and 9 we will look at how this can be done using HTML frames and tables.

In order to have effective comparisons, it is necessary to have two viewable objects in the same place at the same time. Therefore, I do not recommend showing an image on one page, linking to another page, and expecting the student to usefully compare what is seen on the first page with what will come next. A more useful model is to have some way of showing an image and switching in different images to compare with the initial one. For example, an instructor might have an image on the left side of the screen showing an Impressionist painting. Then, by clicking a link other Impressionists' paintings appear in an adjacent window to show a common thread. The same technique could be used to compare anything else as well, whether plants in botany, organizational structures in sociology, or writing styles in literature. Not only can such comparative linking be managed to show the difference with movement from one image to another thereby animating the difference, but the student is forced to be involved in the process. (See Chapter 10 for a discussion of the importance of active learning.) Figure 6-11 illustrates how this model works.

Faculty may wish to have more than two frames for comparisons, and the same technique could be used with whole classes of images or forms. What is essential to grasp is that the faculty member who wants to have students understand differences through comparison can do so effectively with internal linking. The only limitation is the resolution of the screen and the materials under comparison. Keeping in mind that images on a video screen are about 72 dots per inch whereas a typical magazine image is about 24,000, subtle differences in images on a computer screen will lose their effective differences far sooner than images on paper.

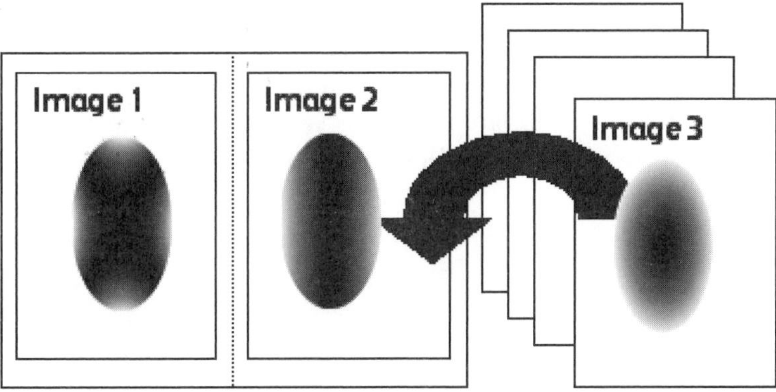

FIGURE 6-11 As a student clicks on a line, Image 1 stays in place while a series of other images are displayed for comparison.

External Linking

Linking to the World Wide Web is one of the most powerful tools ever in the hands of faculty. It is essential that faculty who guide students on the Web outside of what they have created themselves carefully review materials. Unlike most publications where there is some kind of editorial review, very little review exists on the Web. The very democracy that enriches the Web also allows just about anything passing as informed knowledge to be posted. During the bombing of Yugoslavia relating to the ethnic cleansing of Kosovo, the Serbian Ministry of Information had an excellent Web site in terms of style and presentation. However, were any students to take the information presented there as objective, they would have come away with a very one-sided and skewed view of that conflict. Likewise, an Albanian-sponsored Web site had an equally skewed interpretation of the history of the area and conveniently left out the period in World War II when the Kosovars sided with the Italian Fascists and German Nazis against the Serbs. However, given these different views and the propaganda both sides used on the Internet, they stand as excellent opportunities for faculty to provide comparisons in everything from communications to historical relativism.

To create an external link is simple. Find the URL for the link, and put it in the Web page in the same way as an internal link. The HTML code involves using the following tags:

```
<A HREF="http://www.explore.org"> Explore </A>
```

The link can go to any address on the Web, whether it is a friend's Web page or one on the other side of the world. Breaking it down, into component parts, there are three:

Beginning tag: <A HREF. . . > This is an "A" tag with a "HREF"—think of it as a Hyperlink Reference. This is where the URL is placed.

Hot spot: Whatever is placed between <A. . . > and </A> will be the hot spot on the Web page. It's where the viewer will click.

Ending tag: This turns off the hot spot and ends the link code.

Generally, Web site editors or development tools do this kind of work. However, coding with tags is relatively simple, and if the occasion arises, the only tool required is a text editor like Notepad.

Controlling External Links

It may sound like an oxymoron to discuss controlling external links. However, there are ways faculty can control returning to the lesson after guiding the student to different locations on the Web created and maintained by others over whom faculty have no control or even influence. The most basic and simple way is to have an announcement on a Web page for the student to *bookmark* the page where the link to an external site is placed. Then, when the student has viewed the external site, she can use the bookmark (or *favorite* on Internet Explorer) to return to the launching page. Figures 6-12 and 6-13 show the bookmark features of the two main browsers. Bookmarking both a current page in a lesson and an external link assist in keeping the student navigating in the relevant areas.

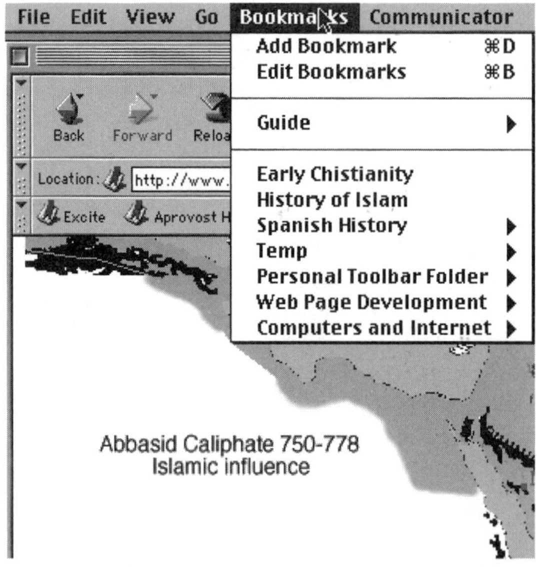

FIGURE 6-12 Bookmarks in Netscape Navigator.

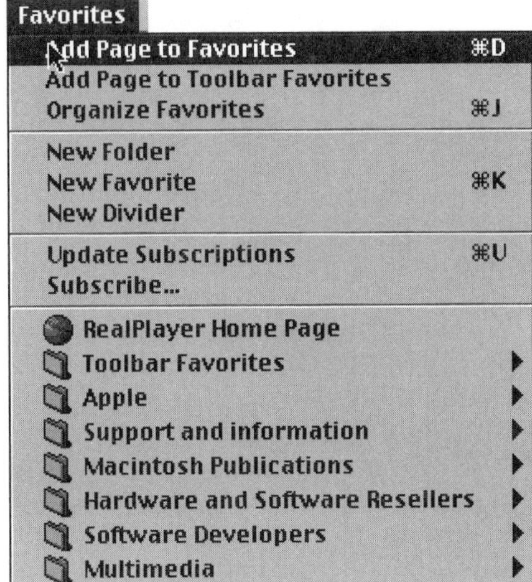

FIGURE 6-13 Favorites in Microsoft Internet Explorer.

A second way to keep external links from getting away from a lesson is to keep them within a frame set. (See Chapter 8 for the techniques used to do this.) Basically, a menu in one frame drives the lesson and the external pages appear in another frame. This is essentially the same arrangement as shown in Figure 6-6 where the menu makes up the left column and the lesson pages appear in the right column. Using external links, it is possible to pull an external Web site using frames into your own frame set resulting in a double set of frames and often a big mess as illustrated in Figure 6-14.

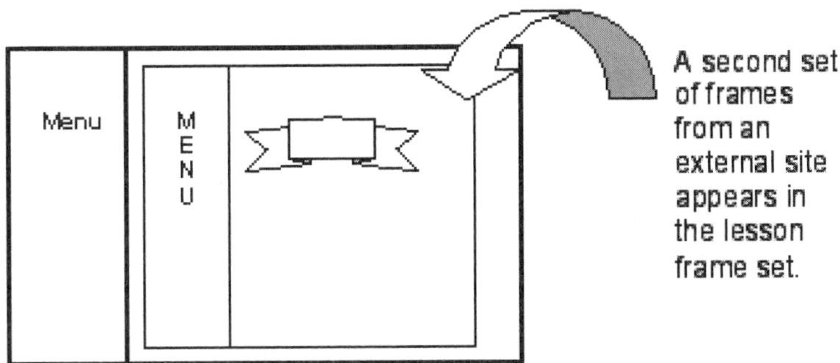

FIGURE 6-14 When an instructor attempts to keep a lesson together using external links within a frame set, he may accidentally bring a second frame set into the one created for the lesson.

If external links are to be managed using a frame set, it is very important that the professor not draw in external Web sites also using frame sets. The area for the lesson can become very small and it can be easy for the student to become lost within a maze of frames, more intent on finding his way than on learning the materials for the lesson.

Another potential problem of trying to keep external materials within your own lesson's frame set is that some Web sites are designed to open outside of any frame set. The page that opens is set to replace whatever is on the screen rather than obeying the link and opening in the lesson frame. Again, this is a matter of the instructor testing her external links to see what happens before incorporating them into a frame set.

Syllabus: Link Central

The online syllabus should be linked to all Web lessons, discussions, and email. No matter where the student is in a course, she should be able to find her way back to the syllabus. In turn, she should be able to find links to anywhere in the class.

General Course and Email Links

The first set of links in a syllabus are those dealing with general issues in a course. Included in the general course links are the following:

- Email addresses
- Online discussion
- Course information
- Quizzes and tests

For example, the syllabus segment in Figure 6-15 has several different kinds of email links along with other kinds of information for the course that makes it easy to get to any information on a single screen. The links at the top in Figure 6-15 have an email link to the professor, group email to the class, individual student email, and email links to the teams of students. Also near the top of the syllabus is a link to the course requirements and an online Web asynchronous class discussion. To the left is a 16-week graphic link to anchors on the syllabus so that the student can quickly go to any week in the semester. Anchors are targets on a page, and with long scrolling pages as might be found in a syllabus, it is a good idea to use anchors (also called targets) and make links to them. Also, when using anchors, be sure to have an anchor at the top of the page so that the student can quickly find his way back to the beginning. The "Top" icon on the numbered menu on the left takes care of this. (See Chapter Appendix C for an illustration of how to create anchors.)

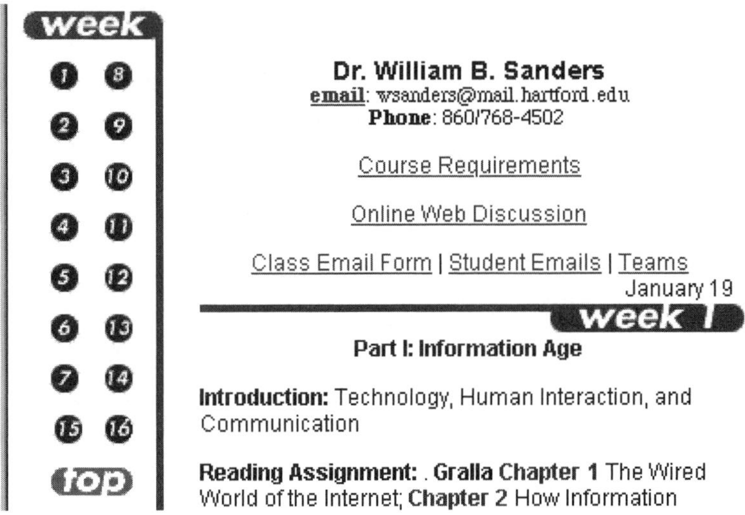

FIGURE 6-15 In a single screen, the student can quickly see several different links to needed information.

Links in Lessons and Quizzes

From the syllabus, links to online lessons fit in with the timing of the assignments. Figure 6-16 shows another segment of the syllabus with both internal and external lesson materials. Within a given lesson prepared by the professor, it is possible to build in the quizzes, as suggested in the third generation lesson site discussed in

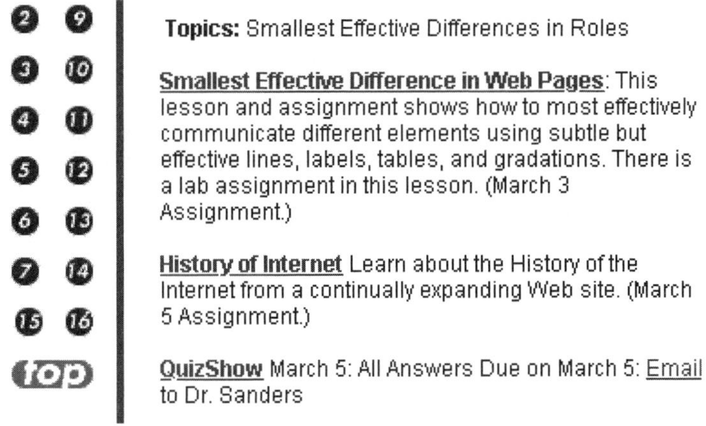

FIGURE 6-16 Links can be provided to both internal and external lesson materials on the syllabus in addition to exams.

Chapter 3. However, if the instructor wishes to quiz students about external links, she may wish to put a quiz link in the syllabus itself. Also note that a repeat of the email address of the professor is put in the same line as the quiz. This is redundant with the email at the top of the syllabus, but it makes it easier for the student to remember to email the answer to the quiz to the professor. If the focus is on *linking the student with learning,* redundancy is not a problem.

Other Syllabi Links

A final set of links is a miscellaneous one. Everything from programming examples to students' presentations can be added to a syllabus. Unlike a paper syllabus where a segment cannot be fit easily into an existing one without redoing the whole thing, an online syllabus can grow during the course's term. Figure 6-17 shows some other kinds of links possible.

In addition to those links shown in the sample syllabus, it is important to remember that links to download material are also possible. For example, if the instructor has a set of text materials she wants the student to read, it is easy to have links on the syllabus to PDF (Portable Document Format) files that will be downloaded onto the student's computer for printing. (See Chapter Appendix B for an example and further detail.) An online syllabus should be viewed the same as a paper syllabus with the ability to reach out and bring in material to the student—material she would have to find elsewhere were she not able to access it quickly from the online syllabus. This leaves more time for the student to concen-

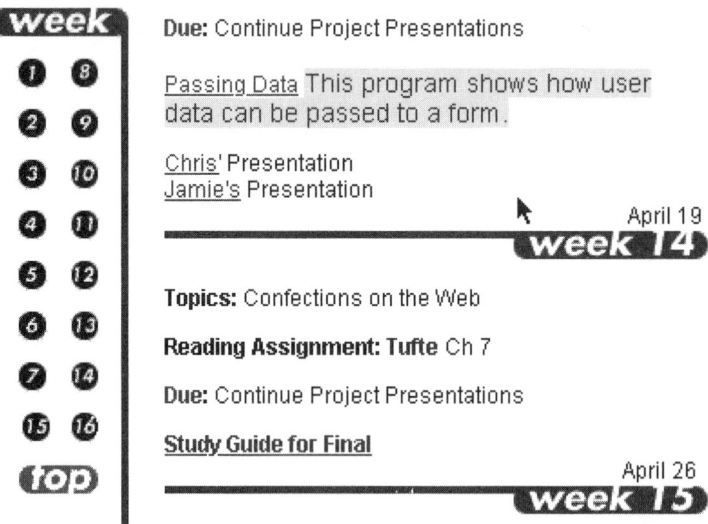

FIGURE 6-17 Anything the professor wants to be included in the course can be linked to a syllabus at any time during the term.

trate on learning the course materials rather than looking up information. (I will quickly grant the point that learning how to look things up is an important lesson that students learn in college. If a major learning goal is how to do that, then the simpler methods might be put aside until the student has learned the methodology of document research and retrieval thoroughly.)

Summary and Review

Understanding how to use links effectively is probably the single most important lesson that this book can provide. Links are the *sine qua non* of Web pages in a learning environment because they bring students and knowledge together. Using them well is critical because everything from linking the student and professor through email to connecting the student to a recent discovery in science is done with links.

For creating a learning occasion, links put the student into a context where he can see the larger picture. In part, as Tufte notes, *information is the interface,* and so while links are clearly part of a navigation system, they are also part of an information system. Setting them up establishes the *moves* the instructor makes in the learning encounter the student has with the information provided by the instructor. As such, *links are the interaction* in a well-designed Web site.

The student needs a good navigation system to focus on the learning task, the next step, and where she is in the lesson. Several have been suggested in this chapter and need to be considered in the context of the instructor's specific lesson and type of course. Whether linking to internal links created and orchestrated by the professor or external links, at all times the student needs to know where he is and how to get back to any page in the lesson. This eases learning and reduces frustration.

A center of links is the syllabus. Not only should it be the home base of all links from a lesson, it also needs to be a source where the student can find anything she needs in a course. When planning and designing a syllabus, the task is essentially one of planning links. The better this is done, the more time the student will have to spend on the content of the course.

Glossary of Terms

Anchors Targets on a page to which links can be established.

Asynchronous In the context of the Web and Internet, interaction and communications that occur at uncoordinated times are asynchronous. Two or more people need not be on the Internet at the same time. Email and online discussions are the most common types of asynchronous interaction.

Compressed file A file that is made smaller by special programs that remove elements that are then replaced when the file is expanded. On Windows computers, Zip is a popular compression program, and Stuffit on the

Macintosh is widely used. Plug-ins available for browsers automatically open compressed files sent over the Internet. The advantage of compressing files is that they take less time to send over the Internet.

Interface The term was originally used to describe the connections and communication between a computer and peripherals such as printers and disk drives. The human interface refers to the ways in which a person sends and receives information to and from a computer.

PDF Abbreviation for Portable Document Format. Standard formatted text or text and graphics can be placed into a PDF file and viewed in a formatted view over the Web. The required plug-in and PDF file reader are available from Adobe Systems at www.adobe.com.

Synchronous Two or more persons in contact and communication over the Web receiving and sending data at the same time. Chat rooms are a widely used form of synchronous interaction over the Web. Use of audio and video on the Web is increasing in synchronous communication.

Targets (see Anchors)

References

Baring-Gould, William S. (ed.). *The Annotated Sherlock Holmes: The Four Novels and Fifty-Six Short Stories Complete* (London: Clarkson Potter, 1974).

Goffman, Erving. *Forms of Talk* (Philadelphia: University of Pennsylvania Press, 1981).

Goffman, Erving. *Behavior in Public Places* (Glencoe, IL: The Free Press, 1963).

Mesher, David. "Designing Interactivities for Internet Learning." *Syllabus* 12:7 (March 1999). pp. 16-20.

Tufte, Edward. *Envisioning Information* (Graphics Press: Cheshire, CT: 1990).

Tufte, Edward. *Visual Explanations* (Graphics Press: Cheshire, CT, 1997).

Appendix

A. Basic Links

As a quick review of creating links, type in the following two little Web pages using Windows *Notepad* or Macintosh *SimpleText*. (Normally this code would be generated in your Web development tool, such as Front Page or Composer.) The first one will link to the second and so inform the viewer. The second one will show that a link has been accomplished and provide an option to return to the first page.

Save this page as Link1.HTML.

```
<HTML>
<HEAD><TITLE>A simple internal link</TITLE></HEAD>
<Body bgcolor="white">
This page is linked to another page. When you click the
underlined text below, the other page will appear. <P>
```

```
<A HREF="Link2.html"> Click here for link </A>
</BODY> </HTML>
```

Save this page as Link2.HTML.

```
<HTML>
<HEAD><TITLE>An internally linked page</TITLE></HEAD>
<Body bgcolor="lightblue">
This is an entirely different page. This shows how
internal linking works. You can also go back to the first
page by clicking the link below. <P>
<A HREF="Link1.html"> Click here to go back. </A>
</BODY> </HTML>
```

Be sure to save the two pages in the same folder, and then load the file "Link1.html" into your browser. Remember, to load a page into a browser from the desktop, simply select **Load** from the File menu. Locate your folder and file on the desktop and load the correct file.

B. Downloading Files

Instructors can get a lot of good information to students by having them download formatted files to be printed out and read on paper. For example, if the faculty member wanted students to read an article she had written and saved in Microsoft Word format, she could have the students download the file to their disks. All she would have to do is to place the file on a server (see Chapter 16) and have a link to the file name. This can be done with PDF (Portable Document Format) as well as compressed files. All that needs to be done is to create a link to the file name as you would an HTML file. For example, the tag

```
<A HREF="wittgenstein.pdf"> Ludwig </A>
```

sets up the Web page to download a PDF file named "wittgenstein.pdf" when the word Ludwig is clicked. This can be done with *Netscape Composer* or any other Web editing tool by using the file name in the same way as when making a link to another Web page. (A PDF file reader *(Adobe Acrobat Reader)* and plug-in are available at http://www.adobe.com.)

C. Creating and Linking to Anchors

To set up an anchor, first put in a tag line next to the area of the page that will be the target of a link. For example, if you want a link to the top of a page, you might want to have an anchor called "Top." Use the following code to create such an anchor:

```
<a NAME="top"></a>
```

The <A> tag is employed, but instead of HREF, there is NAME. The name is the place a link will jump to when clicked. If the anchor with the name "top" is placed at the top of the Web page, all links to the anchor will jump to the top of the page. To create a link to the anchor, use the pound symbol (#) in front of the anchor's name as shown below:

```
<a href="#top"> To the Top</a>
```

The hot spot will work the same when clicked, but instead of going to a URL and calling up a new page, the link causes the page to jump to the anchor on the page.

Chapter 7

Integrating Graphics with Text and Links: Getting the Design Right

Using Graphics for Teaching and Learning

Next to links, the most important feature of Web pages is the ease with which color graphics can be put in front of students. In many fields, color graphics greatly enhance student understanding, and the Web has provided an inexpensive way to create and display graphics in full color. Courses using color slides have been available for a long time, but the user was dependent on sets of slides being available in the configuration the professor wanted. There was not a lot that could be done *easily* to label slides or modify them for a particular use in class.

When personal computers became available along with graphic tools to create, enhance, and change graphics, a lot more could be done to enhance a class because the instructor was able to create labels and make other necessary modifications. However, when the graphics were printed, even on a laser printer, the results were in black and white. Making lots of copies of colored graphics prepared for a course was and still is expensive on a paper medium. With the Web, though, once a graphic is prepared in color, it can be re-created and distributed by the World Wide Web.

The works of Ken Burns represent one model of excellence of using still graphics and narration. His use of still photos in a Civil War series on Public Broadcasting set a standard for and an example of how to communicate both an understanding and essence of a historical phenomenon. By examining how Burns integrated still photos, sound effects, and narration, we can see the importance of melding an explanation and images so that each enhances the other. As more tools for creating low-bandwidth sound for the World Wide Web become available, creating a Burns-like production for a course becomes more of a practical reality. Instructors should look at some of Burns' works on PBS to get a sense of how he integrates graphics into the narration and how the narration provides context for the images. This chapter is only a starting point, and the "narration" is all text.

Good Design Is Not *a Common Feature of Most Web Pages*

That heading is designed to bring forth the fact that most faculty members are not artists or designers and have no training in that field. That insight took me a while to learn and being among the artistically challenged but a great admirer of art and artists, it was an important one. One only need examine just about any Web site created by a faculty member to see the truth in that assertion. Nonartist faculty can create good-looking Web sites, but just about all of them (myself included) would be a lot better off if they got help from a real artist—even an art student. In the same way that engineers, biologists, philosophers, psychologists, and historians have skills, knowledge, and practice in their respective fields, so do artists and designers. As a sociologist, I would not expect an artist to be able to perform a logistic regression on NORC data. By the same token, the inability of nonartists and nondesigners is not a matter of being inadequate. It's just that one's background has prepared one for another course in life with talents, training, and interests in other areas. So get advice from a good artist or designer and read something about design. Robin Williams' book *The Non-Designer's Design Book* and Robin Williams' and John Tollett's *The Non-Designer's Web Book* provide a good starting point.

Good use of artwork, photographs, and elements of design that go into a Web page is something that needs to be treated seriously. A good deal of what is communicated effectively occurs because a good design serves as a pathway between the information on the Web page and the student. Bad design draws attention to itself and away from the content. Using graphics and design well together means that the student will not notice the design. She will be immersed in the content. So get over the fact that you're not an artist or designer and learn from those who are. Better yet, get a real artist or designer to help you.

Graphic Formats

Three graphic formats can appear on a Web page:

1. GIF
2. JPEG
3. PNG

If you are at all experienced with graphics on computers you may be familiar with file formats such as BMP, EPS, PICT, or TIFF. None of these formats can be seen on a Web page. A PDF file can contain viewable graphics that can be seen on a Web page running *Adobe Acrobat Reader* from a plug-in. However, a PDF file per se is not a viewable graphic format on a Web page.

For the most part, graphics on the Web are either GIF or JPEG because most browsers can read either one. PNG files have not yet been fully integrated into HTML and the browsers that read HTML.

GIF

This file format was the original one for Web browsers and is widely used. The GIF (Graphic Interchange Format) file is a proprietary format of CompuServe and was developed for the Web. The GIF format uses "indexed color." The indexed-color mode uses a palette of 256 colors. Compared with the millions of colors available in RGB (red, green, blue) format, GIFs may appear to be severely limited. However, if used wisely and correctly, great-looking graphics can be created using GIFs.

On the Web, bandwidth is the key limiting factor in selecting graphics. The bigger the graphic, the longer it takes to be shipped across the Internet and load. Anyone who has waited a long time for a Web page to load most likely was waiting for a big fat graphic to trundle its way across the Internet. However, limiting the number of colors used in a GIF graphic can greatly reduce the amount of space used. For example, suppose a lesson is designed to help students learn about changes in population in a city. A bar chart incorporating different colors might be used and look something like Figure 7-1:

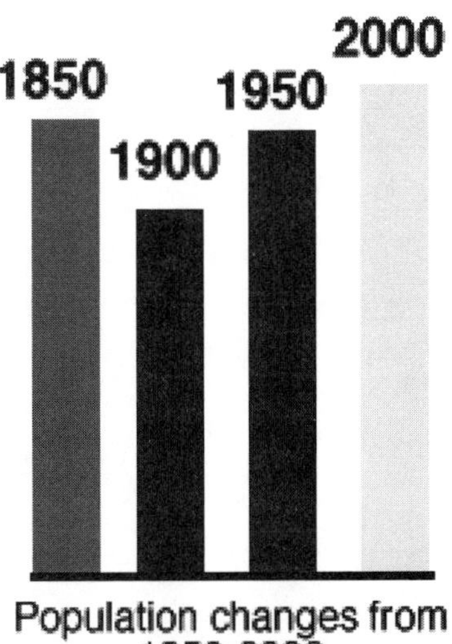

FIGURE 7-1 GIFs are good for graphics with few colors in large areas.

Shown in its actual size, this GIF graphic takes up only about 3K. The index palette (indexed color) uses only eight colors, and the actual graphic shown in Figure 7-1 uses only five. When considering the use of GIF, keep simple drawings and limited colors in mind for the best combination of small size and clear appearance.

One characteristic of GIF not found in JPG is its ability to have a transparent color. If you want the background color of a Web page to show through a graphic, one of the colors of your GIF file can be designated to be transparent. With complex drawings designed to appear as though fully integrated with a page and not within a graphic "box," using a transparent color is very useful.

A good program to use in converting graphics from one format to another for the Web is Macromedia's *Fireworks* discussed in Chapter 4. If we compare a GIF with JPG in *Fireworks*, we can see how much more effective GIF would be for the chart, as seen in Figure 7-2. It is important to note that the GIF format is not always the best one to use, and as was shown in the example in Chapter 4, a GIF took up twice the space a JPG did with another format.

JPEG

The name JPEG stands for Joint Photographic Experts Group, and in that name is the clue that will help you remember when the JPEG format is best to use—**photographs**. Complex graphics with lots of colors, shades, and gradations will either look flat in GIF format or take up a great deal of space as it attempts to use all 256 colors to paint your picture. It is far better to use JPEG because it uses a different compression algorithm that does a better job where more colors are required.

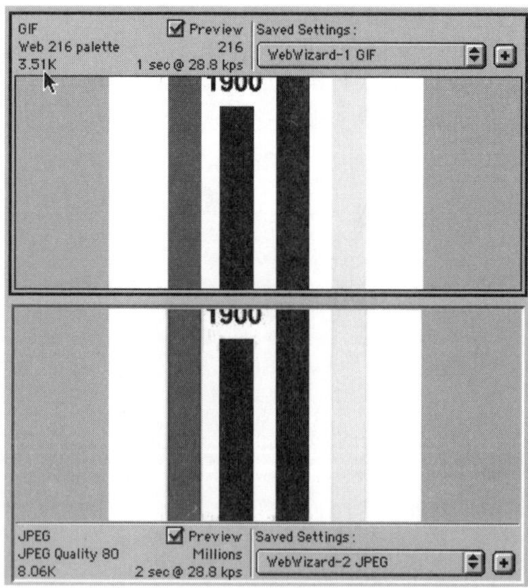

FIGURE 7-2 The JPEG file is about two and a half times larger than the GIF.

FIGURE 7-3 With scanned photographs, it is generally better to use JPEG instead of GIF.

Figure 7-3 shows two 5K graphics of a scanned photograph. It should be clear that the graphic on the left is less splotchy than the one on the right. It is sometimes difficult to see the differences on paper, but on a computer screen, the splotches turn up as oddly colored, bringing unwanted attention to them. It is most visible on the palm of the hand and forehead.

It is possible to have a better looking GIF of a photo, but to do so would require a larger file, and in creating a Web page it is very important to keep the file size small. This is especially true in teaching and learning where the goal is to have the student spend most of the time looking at the content rather than waiting for a page with a large graphic to load.

Fix Your Windows!

If your computer has a newer version of Microsoft Windows, you need to be aware of the option to hide extensions. When you are looking for a file to put into a Web page, you may need to know what kind of graphic it is, and usually the extension is either .GIF or .JPEG—or HTML for that matter. If your **View** menu in **My Computer** has the **Option** selected to hide extensions, you won't be able to determine what type of graphic you are viewing—either on the desktop or within a folder. So if your extensions are invisible, all you need to do is to change them in the Options in View of My Computer. You may also select from Start>Windows Explored>View>Options.

PNG

An acronym for Portable Network Graphics, PNG is a patent-free replacement for GIF. PNG supports indexed-color, grayscale, and true color and has an optional alpha channel for transparency. It has better compression than GIF files, and it can maintain layers and other computer graphic formats for future editing and ease of making changes. However, unlike GIF files, it cannot be animated.

PNG has three main advantages over GIF. First, PNG provides variable transparency so that the pixels can be up to 254 levels of transparency on the Web. In GIF files, transparency is either on or off. Second, gamma correction (cross-platform control of image brightness) allows for more flexibility in correcting how different monitors will interpret a color so that the color is more stable. Third, PNG provides two-dimensional interlacing, which means the viewer can see the image faster with PNG than with GIF.

Color

Color on the World Wide Web is as good as the monitors and computers processing the color. Early on, it became apparent that only certain colors were common to the browsers, operating systems, and monitors. Called "Web-safe" or "browser-safe" colors, the 216 common colors have limited what can be done safely (that is, with the secure knowledge that all the colors will look the same to all computers). However, having identified the Web-safe colors, one can forge ahead with the knowledge that the colors will be the same to all viewers. (Of course, nothing can be done for viewers who have their monitors incorrectly adjusted.)

A number of ways are available to ensure the colors used are Web safe. The most simple is to use Web-safe palettes when developing graphics for the Web. Most tools used for creating Web graphics will have an option for Web 216 colors. For example, *Fireworks*, a Web graphics tool, provides a set of Web-safe swatches clearly labeled as Web 216 Palette as shown in Figure 7-4. By selecting the Web 216 Palette in *Fireworks*, your work is essentially "frozen" to those colors. This prevents accidentally using a color that will look differently from the intended color.

When attempting to effect an exact match in colors, you can use the values for the RGB (red, green, blue) palettes. Three different sets of values are used to define Web colors. First, in the native language of HTML, are sets of six hexadecimal values. These values are expressed in terms of sixteen alphanumeric values from 0 to F. For example, in an HTML color value you may see the number FFCC66. That number tells your computer to create a color that has the following values:

Color	*Hex*	*Decimal*
Red	FF	255
Green	CC	204
Blue	66	102

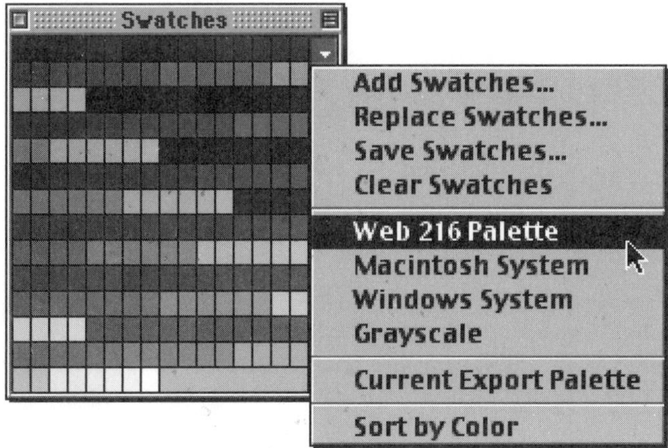

FIGURE 7-4 Web-safe palettes in swatches make it clear that what can be expected to be shown on the Web is the same way as it is on the developer's screen.

Most Web and graphic tools do all the numeric conversion for you, and the only real knowledge you need is to be able to duplicate the value. So if you see the color value CC3399 and you use that same value in another graphic, you'll get the same color.

For example, Netscape *Composer*, the Web page tool provided with Netscape *Communicator*, provides a color picker that uses several different kinds of values as shown in Figure 7-5. To keep your pages within the Web-safe realm, you can use the HTML Picker that can lock in the 216 colors you need.

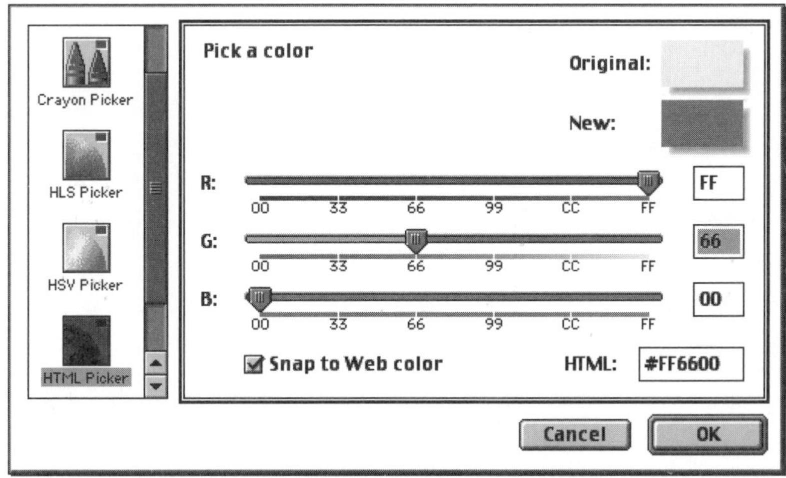

FIGURE 7-5 The HTML Picker keeps colors within the Web-safe range.

By checking "Snap to Web color" it is possible to keep them locked into the six values for each color that guarantee Web-safe colors. The hexadecimal values are:

00 33 66 99 CC FF

Safe **hexadecimal values**

Any RGB combination of those values will be safe on any Web browser. For example, the value 0099CC or 33FF66 would be safe, but FC42AB would not be, even though it would be accepted as a legitimate color by the browser. You just couldn't be sure how it would look on anyone else's computer screen.

Some color pickers provide values in percentages of RGB. Their safe values are:

0 20 40 60 80 100

Safe **decimal percentages**

In using percentages, just remember to count by 20, and your color will be safe. Netscape *Composer's* color picker is shown in Figure 7-6. In some applications, matching graphics with text and background colors may be best accomplished using decimal percentages.

A final way that colors are selected by RGB values is using decimal values (not percentages) instead of hexadecimal values. If a picker uses decimal values, the safe ones are:

00 51 102 153 204 255

Safe **decimal values**

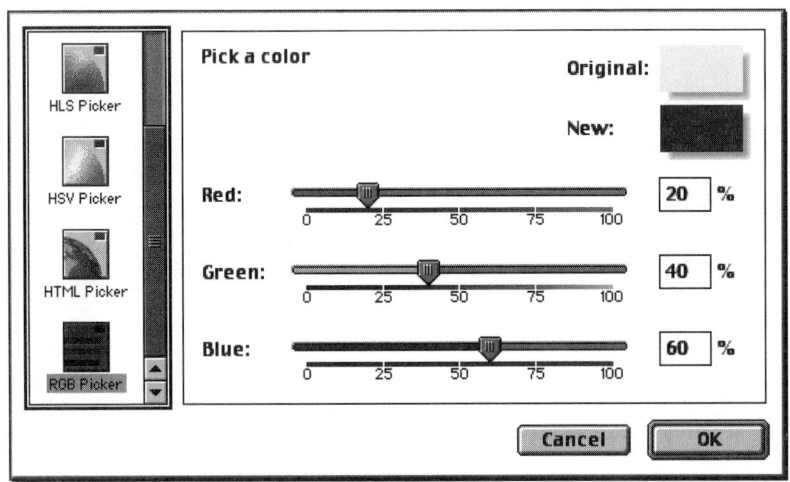

FIGURE 7-6 If using percentages of RGB, be sure to use one of the Web-safe percentage values.

FIGURE 7-7 Note that the colors in decimals are part of the "safe set" for decimal colors.

For example, Figure 7-7 shows the color mixer from *Fireworks* in the RGB decimal color mode. Be sure not to confuse decimal values with either the percentages or hexadecimal values. If using commercially prepared art, or "clip art," try to get artwork that uses browser-safe colors.

Another Web-safe palette that shows the limitations of using the color set can be seen in Adobe's *ImageStyler*. It shows a fairly blocky gradation in the color set it provides. This gives the developer a much clearer idea of what to expect when this palette is employed, as seen in Figure 7-8.

Recoloring Graphics for the Web

It is fairly simple to make adjustments to graphics in programs like *ImageStyler* and *Fireworks* so that the image colors are Web safe. However, if using a photograph or some other graphic prepared without a Web-safe palette, it is a far greater challenge. Programs like *PhotoShop* can be used gingerly to isolate and recolor portions of a photograph to a Web-safe set. Adobe *ImageReady* can maximize an existing image's color for the Web with a Web-safe palette. However,

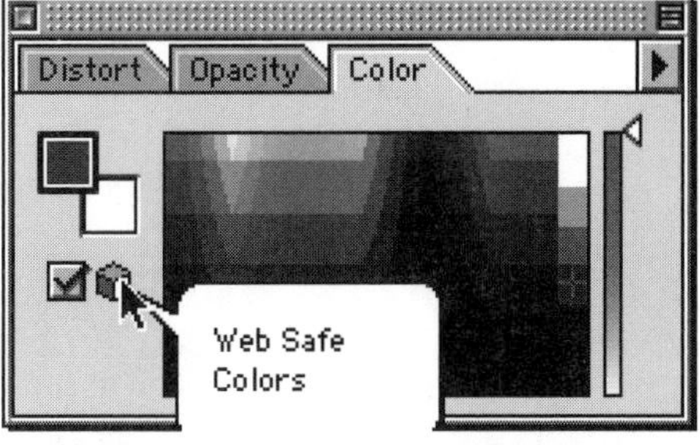

FIGURE 7-8 No matter what color area is selected when the Web Safe cube is "on" it will be Web Safe in Adobe's *ImageStyler*.

boiling down a colored graphic to 216 colors may so distort the image's appearance that it may not be worth it. A better idea is to adjust the background color, if possible, so that large areas of the image will appear the same on all computers.

Another option is to match a large area of color on a primary graphic. Using *GoLive*, it is possible to get a "color sample" of a graphic that has been inserted on the page. This color can then be used with the background and text colors to provide a good-looking page. *GoLive* can constrain the background and text colors to a Web-safe palette, but it cannot change the colors in the graphic itself.

A final way to approach the color-matching problem is to use PNG files. Although these files cannot guarantee color matching on all monitors, the gamma correction feature of PNG files is better than either JPEG or GIF in making the colors more uniform on different monitors. Ultimately, the solution is in a uniform monitor color-generation standard. Until that time, what color is viewed on one's own screen outside of the Web-safe palette may appear different on others.

Photo-Retouching, Merging, and Image Labeling on Your Computer

A major advantage of using computer graphics is that nonartists can take photographs and other existing artwork and use them effectively for a course. Getting faculty creations on a Web page is relatively simple once they have been saved as a GIF, JPEG, or PNG file. Using programs like *Photoshop* and *Fireworks*, it is possible to bring in some very creative and useful images to help students learn concepts, facts, and understandings.

Confections

Tufte (1997, 121) describes a *confection* as "an assembly of many visual events, selected . . . from various Streams of Story, then brought together and juxtaposed on the still flatland of paper." The "Streams of Story" refer to the flow of nouns and verbs over time that make up the complex of events and ideas in the world. Borrowing the idea from Salman Rushdie's *Haroun and the Sea of Stories* (1990, 71–72), Tufte shows how by bringing together a multiplicity of image-events, it is possible to "illustrate an argument, present and enforce visual comparisons, combine the real and the imagined, and tell us yet another story."

Using confections, it is possible to create *visual lists*. A series of historical events, such as key political elections, can be brought together in an imagined scene showing images of winners leading to some historical event. A graphic bringing together several different architectural styles can show similarities or differences. Likewise, a process over time can be compacted into confection *compartments* to show in one moment and place how the process works and the discrete key points in the process. Compartments are framing components that serve to order and partition the related images in a confection.

Confections done creatively and well provide faculty with a very powerful, creative, and fun tool to use in bringing out complex issues that are scattered across time and space. They serve to organize seemingly disparate items and show them together interactively. Accompanied by text and supplementing the text, relationships and connections can be shown that students may otherwise miss.

Creating a Confection

The steps in creating a confection are quite simple, but getting artistic advice and talent is very important. Using programs like *ImageStyler* makes it very easy to create confections from fairly abstract forms that can be arranged on the page. Using a combination of photos, drawn art, and even graphic text, confections require a bit more planning and talent. To create a confection:

Step 1: Clearly decide on the story the confection will tell.

Step 2: Create or gather the graphics needed in separate files.

Step 3: Using a graphic editing program such as *Photoshop* or *Fireworks* edit the images to the shape and size they will be in the confection.

Step 4: On a blank page in the graphic editing program arrange the images into the confection. This includes adding any text that will be part of the confection.

Step 5: Save (or export) the combined image as a GIF, JPEG, or PNG file and put it on the Web page.

Labeling Graphics

Another important use of photo retouching is in creating labels for images. Here again, Tufte provides some key and important insights. When labeling a graphic the attention should not be drawn to the labels, for to do so awakens the background, taking attention away from the key graphic and its importance. Tufte shows how the strategy of the *smallest effective difference* keeps attention where it belongs and not on the background. For example, Figure 7-9 shows a clock with giant arrows appearing to skewer the clock and a big display font. Attention is moved to the background noise of the labels and away from the object of the label.

Following Tufte's advice (1997, 73) it is more effective to "make all visual distinctions as subtle as possible, but still clear and effective." Using *Photoshop*, the arrows were removed, the font subdued, and the lines lightened. Figure 7-10 shows this more effective labeling.

Another helpful concept from Tufte (1997, 98–99) for labeling is *avoiding* a coded key. One may be tempted to use numbers or letters instead of words as labels. The numbers are coded in a look-up key the viewer is guided to use to decode the message. The viewer is separated from the object of the label and goes back and forth, spending as much time decoding as trying to understand the

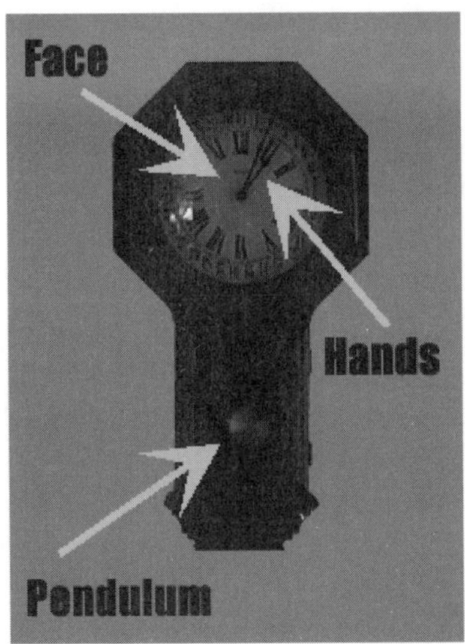

FIGURE 7-9 Large arrows used as pointers and a heavy display font bring unnecessary attention to themselves.

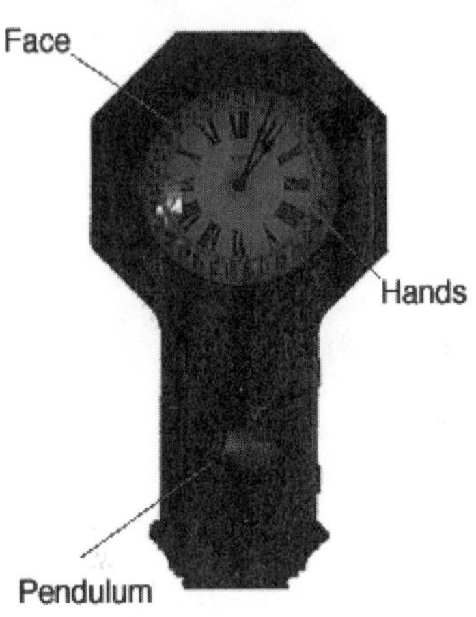

FIGURE 7-10 The labels and indicating lines are just as clear, but the clock rather than the labels is kept as the main focal point.

labeled image. Usually, this can be avoided by creating the central object large enough and the labels small enough to fit in the graphic to be placed on the Web page. For example, Figures 7-11 and 7-12 use a limited set of labels for purposes of illustration. Figure 7-11 has a code and key whereas Figure 7-12 uses the labels directly.

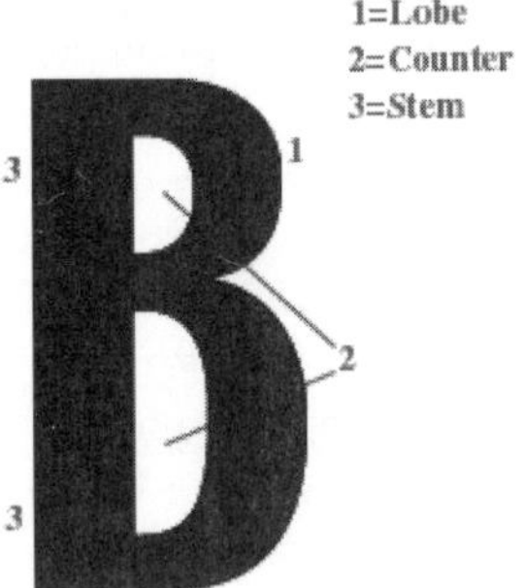

FIGURE 7-11 Bouncing back and forth between a number code and a key is usually unnecessary.

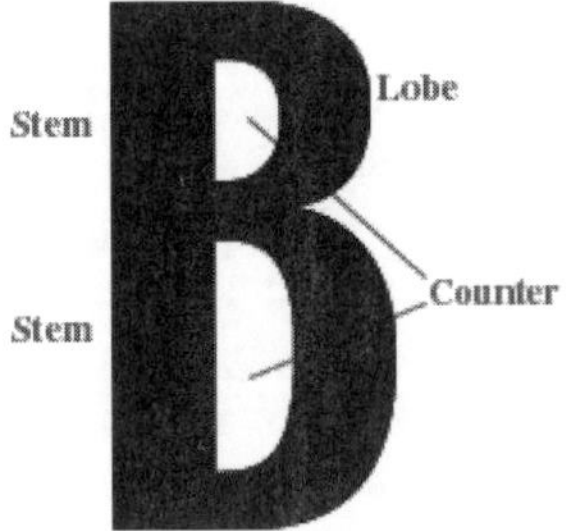

FIGURE 7-12 Labels can be placed directly on the image or with lines indicating the area for the label. It is much easier for students to learn using direct labels than codes and keys.

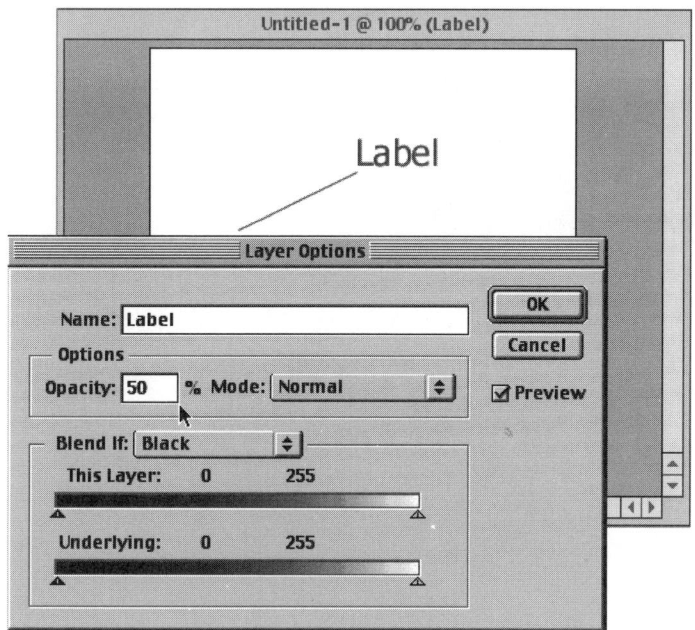

FIGURE 7-13 Creating the minimal effective difference in PhotoShop by reducing opacity.

To create the minimal effective difference with both lines and text labels in *PhotoShop*, the layer with the text is selected and in the Layer Options dialog box, the opacity is reduced. When the figure is saved as a JPEG or GIF file and the layers are flattened, the opacity effect is not lost. Figure 7-13 shows both the label and line with the Layer Options dialog box opened with the opacity reduced to 50 percent.

Drawing Original Artwork

To create your own artwork, programs like *Photoshop* and *Fireworks* are limiting because they are designed more for working with existing art than for creating new art from scratch. However, in a pinch, you can create original artwork with *Fireworks* or *Photoshop*. Newer programs for Web graphics, such as *ImageStyler*, have several tools for creating images on Web pages. Included in *ImageStyler* is a great tool for nonartists that allows one to add images (shapes), textures, and styles to a Web page. Figure 7-14 shows the texture palette and some of the shapes available. By using the art tools creatively, even a nonartist can create the images needed to help get a point across.

For those with real artistic talent, Adobe *Illustrator* and Macromedia's *FreeHand* are two favorites of artists. With these tools, it is possible to create just about any

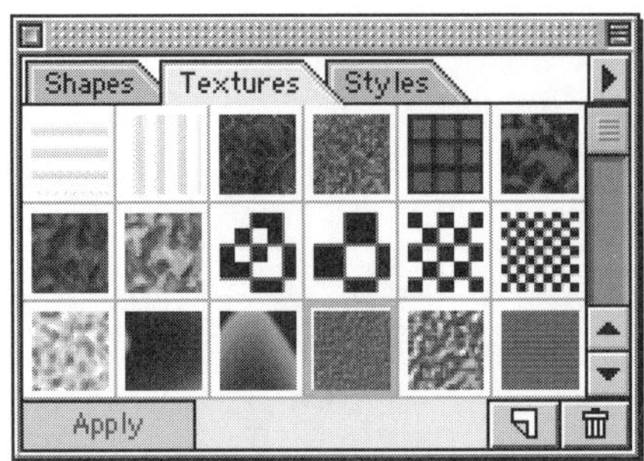

FIGURE 7-14 For the artistically challenged, *ImageStyler* provides a number of shapes, textures, and styles.

type of image you want. However, it is very important to remember that whatever graphics are created, they must eventually be saved or converted to GIF, JPEG, or PNG files that can be viewed on the Web. Also, if a palette of Web-safe colors is used, there will be assurance that all creations will appear in the intended colors.

Using Clip Art

Clip artwork purchased to be used copyright free in Web pages is called "clip art" or "click art." Several companies have artwork and photographs that can be purchased on CD-ROMs or downloaded over the Internet. Many of the images that can be downloaded from the Web can be used free of charge for limited educational purposes, such as using it for an individual class. Others require a fee or simply a permission note. For example the *Molecular Expressions Gallery* has a full set of color photos of different molecules at:

http://micro.magnet.fsu.edu/micro/gallery.html

For creating your own photos through a microscope *Magical Display: The Art of Photomicrography* (1998), is an excellent book on the topic.

Clip art for artists can be found all over the Web. One place to start is at http://www.artmuseum.net. This Web site is extremely well designed and could even be used as an art lesson in itself. A huge collection of art can be found at http://www.art.com as well. Several other Web sites contain fine art samples, and many of them allow "fair use" of them for courses that are limited to a single institution—an individual's own course but not published and sold on CD-ROM. Since Web sites change so often, I recommend using a search engine with the key words "clip art."

Commercial clip art for a wide variety of subjects is available from several sources found at http://www.getty-images.com. Getty Images, Inc. has several different image companies online that have professional photography and artwork covering a wide array of topics.

How to Download Graphics from the Web

Most of the graphics seen on the Web can be downloaded to your computer. Here's how:

Step 1: Put the mouse pointer on the graphic.

Step 2: Press down the right mouse button (Windows) or just press and hold the mouse button down (Macintosh).

Step 3: Select "Save to disk" from a menu that will appear as you hold the mouse button down.

Step 4: Provide a name and location on your computer to save the image file.

That is simple enough to do, but like everything else published on the Web or elsewhere many of the images require permission to use. Usually for use for educational purposes where the image will not be resold, there is no charge. However, it is wise to get permission to use a graphic and give proper credit to the graphic's owner.

Scanning and Digital Cameras

One of the easiest and increasingly affordable ways to create images for Web pages is with a scanner. Flatbed scanners that create good-quality graphics for the Web are available for less than $100. For a very small investment, it is possible to take virtually any picture on paper and transfer it to the Web. Faculty can create their own graphics in exactly the way they want with a regular camera.

An alternative to using a scanner is a digital camera. These cameras either record digital images directly to a floppy disk in the camera or store them to be downloaded into your computer. This is a convenient way to quickly create a set of images without having to scan in the image or draw it. However, digital cameras are significantly more expensive than regular cameras or scanners. Like everything else in high technology, the price of digital cameras keeps dropping, and they may soon approach the price of a regular camera or inexpensive scanner. The earlier digital cameras have very poor-quality output, and if the choice is between getting a used digital camera and a new inexpensive scanner, get the scanner.

Graphics and Links

In Chapter 5 we saw how to create a link using an image. As a quick refresher, the tags are:

```
<A HREF="newlink.html"><IMG SRC="graphic.jpg></A>
```

In the learning process, it helps to provide both a textual and a graphic connection to an idea, concept, or process. One way to do that is to have a graphic link go to a page with a textual description of the graphic. Depending on the learning goal, this will be done either by shifting to an entirely different page or by having a window pop up with the information in text. It is important to experiment with different ways that a graphic link can bring a student together with a better understanding of what is to be learned. In later chapters more sophisticated techniques are examined, but for now it is important to begin thinking about images as links to information and understanding.

For example, in a biology class, a professor may want her students to learn the process whereby a caterpillar becomes a butterfly. Rather than telling about the process, she may have a series of images that when clicked take the student to the next stage in the process. The links are all images that show what occurs in each stage with a text description. By clicking the image instead of a "Next" or arrow link, the student's attention is directed to the actual image of each stage in the process (see Figure 7-15).

Hot Spots

Another term used to describe text or graphics that are linked is "hot spots." To make text or graphics "hot" all one need do is to use the following tags:

```
<A HREF="#"> <IMG SRC="image.gif"> </A>
```

or for text

```
<A HREF="#"> Text </A>
```

The "#" (pound) sign is a dummy link used solely for making the link "hot." That means the computer thinks something is supposed to happen when the mouse affects the text or image.

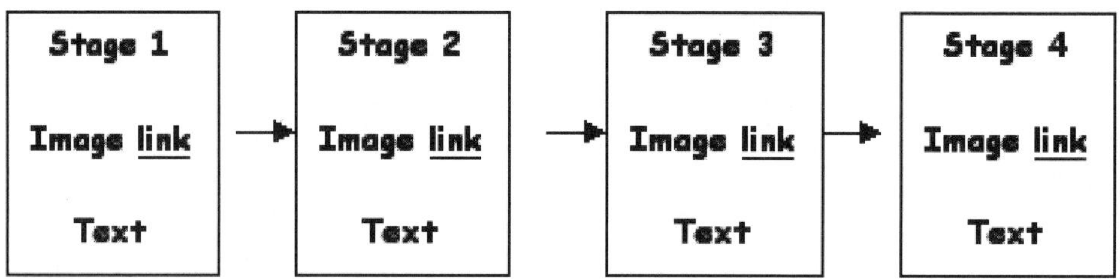

FIGURE 7-15 Images can be used as linked to create the sense of emerging stages.

It is useful to think of links as "hot spots" because more can be done with a hot spot than just linking it to another Web page. A hot spot is *active* in some way, and by thinking of images as possible hot spots, they can be used more for active learning in creating a learning-centered page.

Image Maps

One of the most interesting and useful types of graphic hot spots is an image map. An image map is a graphic with different areas being defined as hot spots. By clicking different areas of the image, different links or actions can occur. This makes image maps useful for navigation, elaboration, labeling, and other strong learning-centered activities. For example, Figure 7-16 shows a graphic of a menu bar used for navigating through a 15-week syllabus. Each number is a hot spot and when clicked, the syllabus jumps to the indicated week.

The tags and code for an image map are based on the horizontal (x) and vertical (y) coordinates of a screen. For example, the coordinates for "Week 5" are:

```
<AREA SHAPE="circle" COORDS="23,142,9" HREF="text.htm#5"
target="right">
```

Figuring out what each coordinate is for the different types of shapes is both complex and time-consuming. To create an image map, though, is very simple if the right tools are used. Commercial applications like *GoLive, Dreamweaver, Front Page,* and *Fireworks* have excellent image map creation functions. Figure 7-16 shows

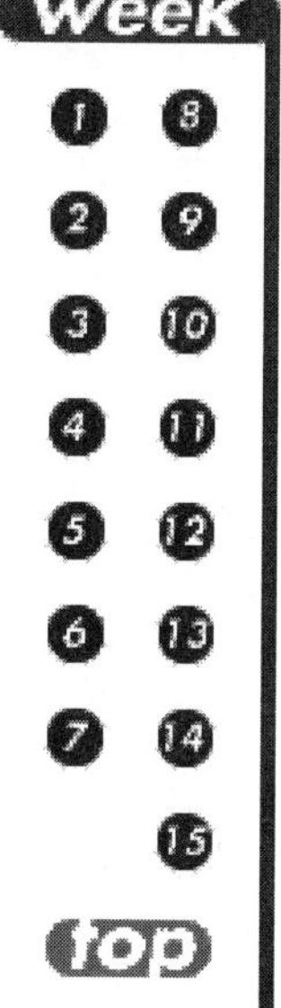

FIGURE 7-16 Each circled number is a hot spot on this image map. The rounded rectangle at the bottom is another hot spot of a very different shape than the others. Even though the images are part of a single graphic each area designated a hot spot is a unique link. A hot spot on an image can be any shape desired.

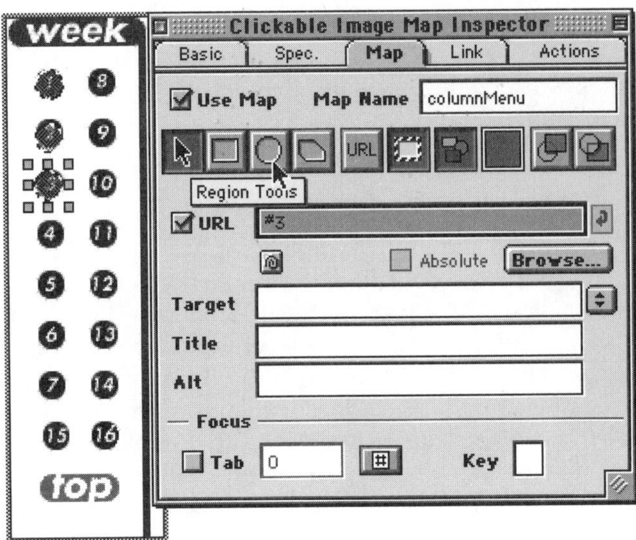

FIGURE 7-17 With the right tools, making image maps is fairly simple. Just about any shape can be made "hot" using tools like *GoLive* as shown above.

different shapes being made into hot spots in *Fireworks*. About a dozen free or shareware image map programs for Windows and the Macintosh are available at:

```
http://www.ihip.com/tools.html
```

Using the search words "image map" will return thousands of Web sites with tools and information about image maps. All that is needed to create an image map is a graphic, an image map tool, and a clear idea of what each part of the image will do (see Figure 7-17). In the remainder of the book there will be references to image maps combined with various learning goals and ways to use them effectively.

Summary and Review

The work involved in getting graphics and text or narration to work well together is the most important issue to consider in creating Web pages for learning. The technical aspects, while not trivial, are not major ones. The limitation of 216 Web-safe colors is a lot better than the two colors (black and white) that most faculty are limited to in classroom productions. All of the technical graphic savvy does little good if a Web page is poorly designed, for poor design equates poor communication and poor understanding. Therefore, it pays off to spend some time learning about graphic and page design and listening to graphic artists and designers.

Fortunately for nonartists plenty of tools and resources are available to help get the images needed to create an effective page. Using clip art or scanning in your own graphics and tools like *Photoshop* and *Fireworks* make it relatively easy to crop, enhance, collage, and label graphics for an interesting and effective page.

Using graphics as links, the page can establish a visual relationship between concepts, processes, and structures. Virtual realities can be created with image maps that act like calculators or visual directories. The opportunity for creating exciting and interesting Web pages that bring better understanding has a core in graphics and textual or vocal explanations. In the same way that Ken Burns produced television series that brought alive the past through weaving together still images, passages from diaries, military dispatches, and historical analysis, faculty who use their imaginations creatively can do the same for their courses.

Glossary of Terms

Animated GIF A series of GIF files that are shown in sequence to create an animation effect. An animated GIF contains several GIF "stills."

Clip art Professionally rendered art that can be electronically cut and pasted into a Web page.

Confection Bringing together visual events and text to tell a story by showing slices of the streams of the story.

GIF (Graphic Interchange Format) Patented compression format used most effectively with a few colors in a large area of a Web page.

JPEG (Joint Photographic Experts Group) Graphic compression format used most effectively with photographs.

Opacity Effective amount of transparency in an image.

PNG (Portable Network Graphics) Patent-free compression format developed to replace GIF.

Web-safe colors A set of 216 colors that will be displayed the same on different monitors.

References

Davidson, Michael W. *Magical Display: The Art of Photomicrography* (San Francisco: Amber-Lotus, 1998).

Rushdie, Salman. *Haroun and the Sea of Stories* (London: Viking, 1990).

Tufte, Edward. *Visual Explanations* (Graphics Press: Cheshire, CT: 1997).

Williams, Robin. *The Non-Designer's Design Book* (Berkeley, CA: Peachpit Press, 1994).

Williams, Robin and John Tollett. *The Non-Designer's Web Book: An Easy Guide to Creating, Designing and Posting Your Own Web Site* (Berkeley, CA: Peachpit Press, 1997).

Chapter 8

Designing with Tables: Organizing the Elements

For those who have designed pages using page makeup programs such as *PageMaker* or *Quark Express*, making a Web page look the way you want can be a major frustration. Web pages do not behave like a paper page. They don't even behave like a computer screen version of a paper page. Text and graphics have very few options for where they will go on a page using standard HTML formatting. Something as simple as placing text in the upper left-hand corner of a page, a graphic in the center of the page, and text along the side of the graphic requires a lot of planning and work.

One way to get a page to behave as desired is to create the page as one big graphic. Using a graphic editing or drawing software application, it is possible to simply create a graphic the size of the page using the images, fonts, and text you want and put them exactly where you want them relative to one another. Then save the image as a GIF, JPEG, or PNG file. Were it not for the extremely high cost in terms of bandwidth and computer memory, making pages from single large image files would not be a bad idea. However, bandwidth and speed are essential considerations in making a Web page. Therefore, other ways have to be found for formatting materials on a Web page.

This chapter explores the use of tables as a formatting tool. Using tables, the few formatting options in HTML can be expanded to give the instructor what is required to do a better job of placing text and graphics where they need to be.

Basic Formatting Options

The developers of HTML did consider formatting, but it was not until the introduction of Cascading Style Sheets (CSS) that there were many things that could be done with text, and mixing text and graphics together was equally limited up to that time.

Text

The formatting for text in HTML is limited to full paragraph indentations using the <BLOCKQUOTE> tag, lists of numbers, bullets, and menu items. Different size headers can be created with the <H1>, <H2>, etc. tags. To get a simple indent, several " " codes have to be inserted (" " stands for "nonbreaking space"). The text placed next to a graphic has a tendency to jump all over the place, even if the correct HTML tags are used to place text and graphics where you think they are supposed to go.

Images

Image placement is pretty much a left, right, or center option. With text, the options are top, center, and bottom relative to the image, and a word wrap option is available that puts text around the image. This allows some control over where things are going and how they're going to look on a Web page, but designers want images and text to go on the page *exactly* where they want them to be.

Getting Things Where They Belong in a Table

Even the simplest Web page editing tool can create tables and so direct HTML coding is not required. For example, using Netscape *Composer*, click on the Table icon and an Insert Table dialog box provides places to write the required number of columns and rows the table should have, as seen in Figure 8-1. Then put text

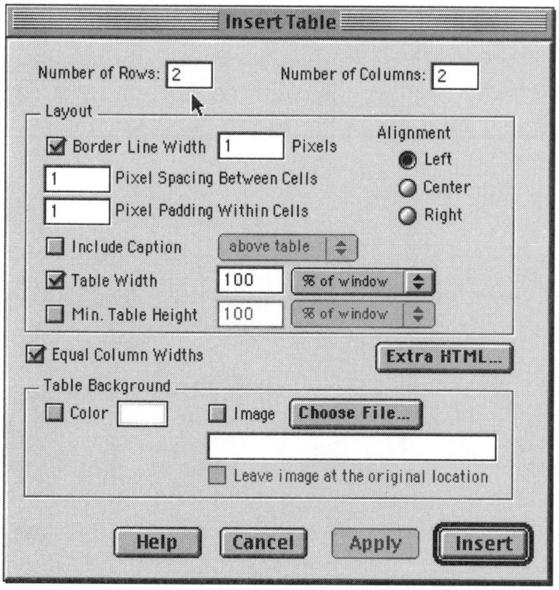

FIGURE 8-1 Creating tables is easy using Web editing tools.

and graphics into the various cells that make up the table. (Appendix A at the end of this chapter explains the HTML code for tables.)

Tables for Clarification of Complex Data

This section examines some table parameters and how they can be used to tell a story. The stories that data in tables tell can be in the form of numbers, text, or images. Or the tables can handle any combination of these elements. For example, table cells can be employed as sidebar notes. We'll start with a basic table of numbers. Figure 8-2 shows a Web page with data collected by psychology students in studying the time it takes a rat to run through a maze.

Each cell is clearly delineated by the thick border in Figure 8-2, serving to isolate each cell. Light pastel background colors have been added to each row to provide a connection between the trial times—the main variable of importance. It is not a good idea to use heavy or bright colors because they tend to emphasize themselves rather than the connection between the cells in a row or column. However, the table looks choppy because of the thick borders. To remove the borders in the table, simply insert BORDER=0 in the <TABLE> tag. The page now looks like Figure 8-3. The cells are still separated into color blocks, but less so than when the border "walls" were installed. By right justifying the student names and data, it is possible to better separate the student names from the first column. Because the first column identifies the trial numbers and the rest of the columns provide the times, such a separation will *clarify* rather than isolate. Also, by removing the space between the cells, the row trials are better integrated by the individual color for each row. Figure 8-4 shows how the table now looks with only space and color separating the labels and data.

If the columns are to be the emphasis, the same kind of arrangement could be done by unique background colors for the columns. For example, in Figure 8-5, each column has a separate color drawing the eye to the columns. In a psychology class attempting to show students the J-curve in learning, for example, this

Trial/Student	Lee	Jackson	Werner
First	4.45	4.43	3.53
Second	3.55	3.35	3.34
Third	3.45	3.00	2.58
Fourth	2.55	3.18	3.03

FIGURE 8-2 Different background colors were added to each row to emphasize the trial times.

Trial/Student	Lee	Jackson	Werner
First	4.45	4.43	3.53
Second	3.55	3.35	3.34
Third	3.45	3.00	2.58
Fourth	2.55	3.18	3.03

FIGURE 8-3 With the borders removed from the table, the cells are now separated by the cell spacing attribute—not the border.

Trial/Student	Lee	Jackson	Werner
First	4.45	4.43	3.53
Second	3.55	3.35	3.34
Third	3.45	3.00	2.58
Fourth	2.55	3.18	3.03

FIGURE 8-4 Now the cells for the table are invisible and the eye examines the rows lined up by individual background colors.

Trial/Student	Lee	Jackson	Werner
First	4.45	4.43	3.53
Second	3.55	3.35	3.34
Third	3.45	3.00	2.58
Fourth	2.55	3.18	3.03

FIGURE 8-5 Changing colors by column brings the student's eye to change in the trials rather than comparison between the time it takes for a rat to negotiate a maze.

arrangement focuses on the changes as the learning times drop and dip up slightly at the end. (In one case, the curve obviously does not take the predicted upswing, and this too will be brought to the students' attention.)

One difficulty in changing column colors compared to row colors is that a tag has to be created for each cell. The tag <TD bgcolor="azure"> will change the background color of the cell to azure. In the way HTML reads the tags, though, the next tag set it reads is for the next cell in the row, and so it will have a different color. To create a color for an entire row requires only a single color tag at the beginning of the row—<TR bgcolor="palegreen">. It will not encounter the </TR> tag until all of the row cells are placed. With more sophisticated Web page tools such as *Dreamweaver* entire columns can be colored with a single command, and using such tools is highly recommended.

Graphics in Tables

As in placing text, getting graphics or a combination of graphics and text together where you want them on a page can be a real challenge. By using a table, though, the process is much easier. As with text, all you need to do is to use the table as a layout grid and place the graphics and text where you want in the grid.

To see how this is done, consider a page where you want to show students examples with images and text. The images will be dominant, but the message and lesson need to be expressed strongly as well *and* integrated with the images. Figure 8-6 shows the table grid and how everything is placed within one of the many table cells. Note also that some of the cells are left empty. When the Web page is viewed the text and images appear to stand independent of any table as seen in Figure 8-7.

One simple but important function of tables is to label an image. A two-row table can place the label over or under an image as can be seen in Figures 8-6 and 8-7. Rather than wrestling with the limited formatting for text and graphics in HTML just to label a picture, keep in mind what can be done with a simple table.

FIGURE 8-6 A two-by-two table was created using only the two center columns. The text has been centered in each cell but the images are left justified in the cells.

FIGURE 8-7 The alternating images and text integrate the pictures and the message. In addition, each image has its individual label and the viewer sees no evidence of a table at all.

Sophisticated Table Designs

To get a better idea of what a table can do for putting text and graphics right where they need to be, consider the Web page shown in Figure 8-8. The text is floating exactly where it is intended to be, but the way in which this is accomplished is not with standard formatting. Instead a complex table has been created and each

FIGURE 8-8 An invisible table is behind the placement of the elements on this Web page.

FIGURE 8-9 ***Composer*** **reveals the complex table.**

element is in a cell in the table. The Web page editor, *Composer*, reveals the hidden table that positions the elements of the page. Figure 8-9 shows this.

To create these complex tables requires either the right tools or very good scripting skills in HTML. Adobe *ImageStyler* created the table in Figure 8-9. Even excellent scripting skills would make it difficult to create the aesthetic design. It is much easier and more effective to use a software application that allows one to concentrate on creating effective Web pages for a lesson than trying to determine the combination of tags needed to position a Web page. Knowledge of the HTML tags, though, can prove to be very useful for editing and fine-tuning a design. If the design is off a little, some knowledge of table HTML helps make needed adjustments. When adjusting HTML code in a complex table generated with a Web page tool, use a *backup copy*, and then when the copy is adjusted to satisfaction, resave it as the primary page.

Back Up or Pay Up

Remember: *You Only Lose Important Web Pages.* Computers were designed to destroy only important documents. Useless files that clutter computers are never lost or destroyed. It's only the important ones that the computer destroys, so remember to back up your Web pages once they are completed. Use a floppy disk or high-density disk such as Zip or Jaz to keep a complete set of Web pages. In this age of computer viruses, this advice is more important than ever.

Graphic Depiction of Quantitative Data Using Tables

Edward Tufte (1983, 178) notes that the "basic structures for showing data are the sentence, the table, and the graphic." (See Figures 8-10 & 8-11.) To examine Tufte's proposition an example of each structure is shown below:

Sentence

"The Democrats won with a total of 205 votes. The Republicans followed with 171 votes trailed by the Independents with 20 votes."

Table

Voting Patterns in Local Election

Republicans	171
Democrats	205
Independents	20

FIGURE 8-10 Data in table.

Chart (Graphic)

Voting Patterns in Local Election

FIGURE 8-11 Data in chart.

The graphic shows the results in a quick glance, whereas the table and sentence provide more detail. However, the sentence and table do not immediately show the pattern seen in the graphic. Adding the number of votes at the end of the graphic bars would provide the best combination of graphics and data.

With simple quantitative data as shown in the voting patterns of a local election, each method works well enough. However, as data become more complex, it is important to maintain both the clarity and integrity of the data. The clarity refers to the ability of the viewer to understand at a glance and upon closer inspection exactly what the data show. Integrity means that the graphic should accurately represent the data. Distortions in graphics that purportedly represent data can not only be misleading and confusing, but they bring the veracity of the author into question.

The clarity of a chart is a matter of simplicity and good labeling. For example, in the chart on voting patterns, each bar is clearly labeled so that the viewer quickly sees that the Republicans and Democrats were pretty close and the Independents were far behind in the race. It is clear who won, how close it was, and the gap between winner and losers.

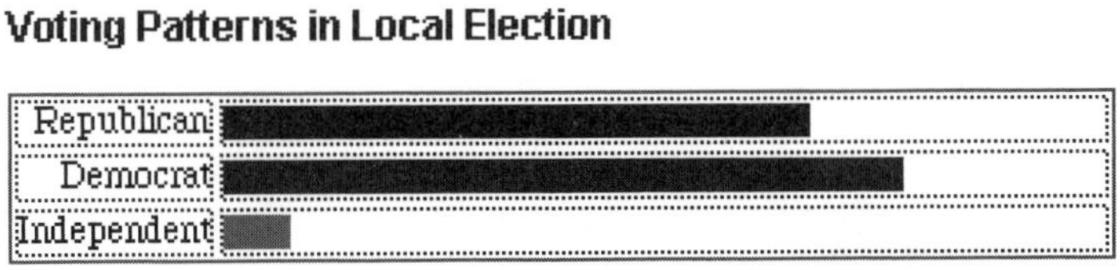

Voting Patterns in Local Election

Republican	
Democrat	
Independent	

FIGURE 8-12 Text and graphics are placed in a three-by-two table. Labels are in the left column and graphic bars are in the right column.

The integrity of the chart on voting patterns is not so clear. In fact, it is invisible, but it is very important to show that the bars in the chart do indeed accurately represent the data. Examining how the chart is built and how the length of each bar was established is crucial to understanding the integrity of the chart. Figure 8-12 shows the bar chart in Netscape *Composer.*

Tables and the Single Pixel GIF Trick

Before the introduction of CSS (Cascading Style Sheets) Web page designers desperate for such simple punctuation marks as en and em dashes (– and —) resorted to the single pixel GIF trick. Whenever a graphic is loaded in HTML, parameters can be set so that the graphic can fit the page. The "height" and "width" parameters allowed designers to load very small graphics made up of a single pixel and then change their width or height to create the marks they needed.

To create a single pixel GIF, use virtually any drawing program that creates GIF files. Using the pencil tool make a single dot on the drawing program's canvas. Select the dot, and then from the File menu select "Save Selection." Make sure the file is saved as a GIF file. Depending on the drawing program used there may be some variation in the way a GIF file is saved, but the basic process is the same. (See also www.killersites.com or David Siegel's 1997 book, *Creating Killer Web Sites.*)

For example, to achieve the horizontal bar for the Republicans' votes the following code was used:

```
<img SRC="blackdot.gif" BORDER=0 height=10 width=177>
```

The graphic file "blackdot.gif" would appear as a little black dot on the screen were it not given special instructions to be 10 pixels high and 177 pixels wide. What's more, the time it takes to load a single pixel GIF file is very fast because little bandwidth is required for the tiny file.

To make the adjustment from Netscape *Composer* change the Height and Width in the Dimensions window in the Table Info Dialog Box. Figure 8-13 shows how this appears. (Appendix B at the end of this chapter shows the HTML code generated and explains what it does.)

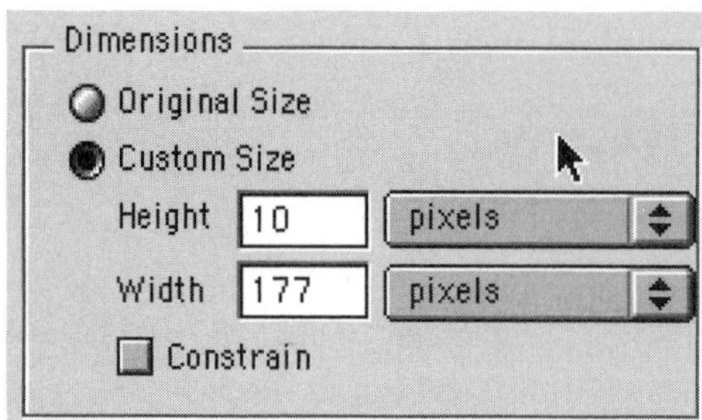

FIGURE 8-13 In Netscape *Composer* and other Web editing tools, changing the dimensions of a graphic is simple. Making chart bars with single pixel GIFs using this method keeps the size of the graphic small but creates different graphic bars with a single pixel graphic.

How to Lie with Graphics: Lack of Integrity by Design

In the example of the graphic chart depicting quantitative data, the width of the bars is exactly the number of pixels as the number of votes each party received. In working with an area of 640 by 460, what happens when the values being depicted are greater than 460? For example, suppose a professor wants to show the results of a state or national election where the values will be far greater than 460? Actually, it is quite simple. Decide on the maximum number of pixels to put in the horizontal bar. Suppose 300 pixels is all of the horizontal space to be used with the other 160 pixels to be reserved for labels and margin space. We'll say the maximum value is 24,561. Because the maximum number of pixels to be used for the horizontal chart is 300, divide 300 by 24,561 and get .01221448638. Treat that value as the "factor" for the table. If each value is multiplied by the factor, all of the bars stay within the 300-pixel boundaries and are proportional to one another. Use the following formula and steps:

Step 1. $\frac{\text{Maximum number of pixels}}{\text{Highest value in data set}} = \text{Factor}$

Step 2. Multiply each value in the table by the factor to get proportional values.

The following example shows how this works. First, get quantitative data from a reliable data source. The FBI site (http://www.fbi.gov) provides the hate crimes for 1995 in six states shown in Table 8-1.

Next, divide the maximum number of pixels to be used (300) by the highest value in the data set (1,751). Thus divide 300 by 1,751 to give a multiplying factor of .17133066819. Each value for each state is multiplied by .17133066819 to get the number of pixels for each bar. Instead of making a horizontal bar chart, the next chart uses a vertical one shown in Figure 8-14. The chart is clear, and the data

TABLE 8-1 All the data need to be examined to determine the range of values.

State	Number of Hate Crimes
Arizona	220
California	1,751
Idaho	114
Massachusetts	333
New Hampshire	24
New York	845

placed on top of the vertical bars provide an extra degree of precision. (To save some time on the calculations, use a spreadsheet.)

Going back to the issue of integrity, this chart can be said to have integrity in that the size of the bars represents the proportional number of hate crimes in the actual data. However, *the chart still lacks integrity*. Here's why. Students looking at the chart would be led to believe that California has an extremely high number of hate crimes compared to the more bucolic states like Idaho and New Hampshire. The kind of stampeding for new laws that the media generated with a series of

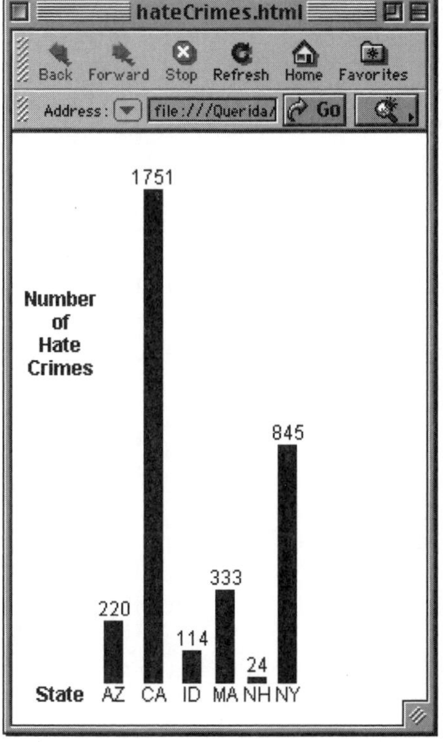

FIGURE 8-14 The data from Table 8-1 are transformed proportionately so that they fit in a window with a maximum of 300 pixels for the graphic chart bars.

well-publicized shootings in middle-class high schools, especially the killings at Columbine High School in 1999, is the kind of misinformation created by data lacking integrity. In fact, as far as juvenile homicides are concerned, schools are one of the safest places for youths to be. Had data been shown comparing where violent crimes against youth occurred over the period of time when the schools shootings occurred, this fact would be clear. In order not to make the same mistake, the data need recalculation to show the hate crimes in relationship to the populations of the states where the hate crimes occurred. As can be seen in Figure 8-15, a much different picture emerges when the crimes are linked to the number of hate crimes *per one million population.*

After recalculating the data to give the chart integrity, rather than having the fewest hate crimes, Idaho and New Hampshire have the highest based on the number of incidents for the population. Without speculating about the cause, it is clear that states like Arizona, California, and New York have a relatively low rate of such crimes when the state's population is considered.

A Note on Making Vertical Bar Charts

Making vertical bar charts uses the same single pixel GIF trick as with the horizontal bar charts. The height of the bar is the variable value and the width is the stable one. However, another important difference exists. If the vertical graphic bars are not given instructions otherwise, they will center vertically in the cell. To remedy that problem, simply align them to the bottom. This is done with the first tag in the row containing the bars—<TR VALIGN=BOTTOM>. The VALIGN parameter simply refers to "vertical alignment" and it will neatly align the vertical graphic bars on the bottom of the chart. (See Appendix C at the end of this chapter for a complete listing of the chart shown in Figure 8-15.)

Graphic Distortions

One of the most common distortions, either to falsely prove a point or by sloppy design, is to have elaborate graphics distort actual data. In discussing graphical integrity, Tufte (1983, 56) points out that a graphic should be directly proportional to the numerical quantities represented. That may be easier said than done, but the point is important. In the graphic chart in Figure 8-15, the data are proportional to the population represented and the pixels in the bars. However, when more elaborate graphics are incorporated, it is easy to create graphics that tell the wrong story—or at least misrepresent it. For example, in Figure 8-16, four cubes labeled from 15 million (15m) through 18 million represent increases in shipping. Look carefully at the size of the cubes and the differences in the data.

The raw data show a 20 percent growth. However, the cube labeled with 18m is *twice as big* as the one labeled 15m. Instead of a 20 percent growth, the graphics show a 100 percent growth. Tufte (1983, 56) notes that graphics should be clearly labeled to defeat graphical distortion and ambiguity, but in this case, the graphics defeat the data. The association between the data and the size of the cube *changes the sense of the difference.* True, a sober and careful examination of the cubes would

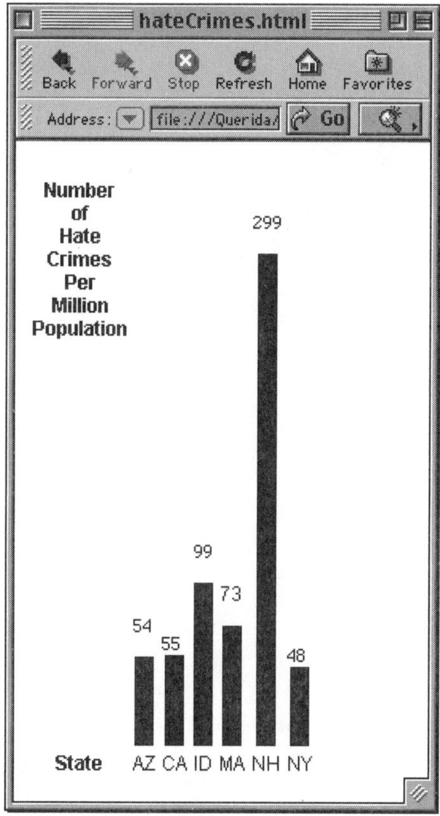

FIGURE 8-15 Once the crimes are displayed relative to the population, a much different and more accurate picture emerges.

show the distortion, but when students are learning something, they should not have to juggle two different messages on the same Web page. One might argue that if the cubes are viewed in perspective with the smaller cubes farther away and the larger ones closer, they probably do not distort the data. However, even if that is technically true, it still sends a confusing message. Two-dimensional charts

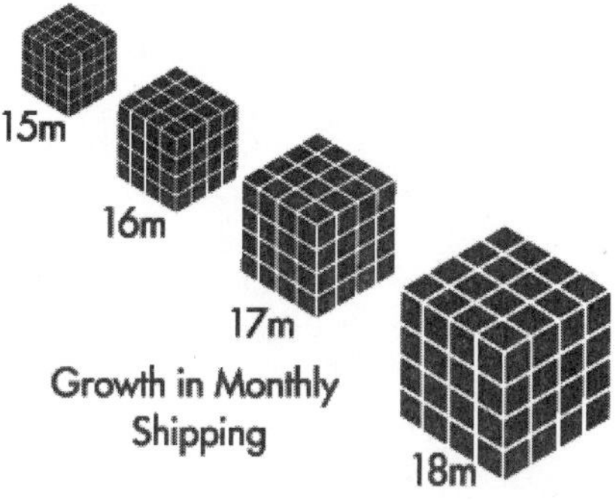

FIGURE 8-16 The graphics lack integrity because the size of the cubes distorts the data.

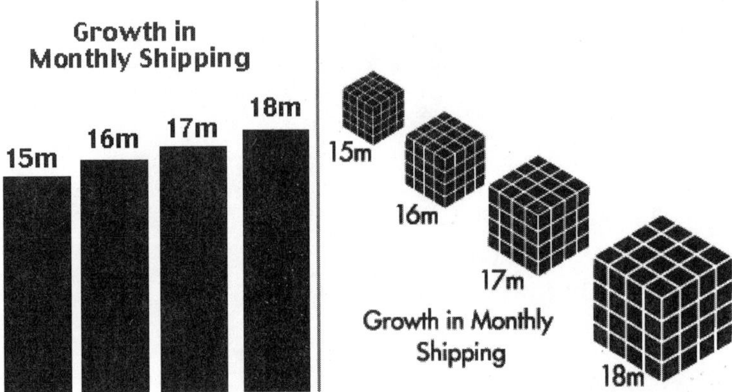

FIGURE 8-17 Comparing the two charts, the simpler one is clearer in accurately representing the actual data. Look at the difference in the 15m bar and 18m bar on the left versus the 15m cube and the 18m cube on the right to see the amount of distortion.

are clearer than three-dimensional ones, and set upon the same plane, they are far clearer. In Figure 8-17, a two-dimensional chart is set next to the three-dimensional one, and it is clear which chart better represents the reality of the data.

More interesting graphics increase student attention, but to do so at the expense of the accuracy of the content defeats the purpose. It is not a matter of substance versus style, but rather the display of clear and accurate information. Using interesting graphics that proportionately and accurately represent the data is very important. Fanciful confections discussed in Chapter 7 are designed to communicate an idea, process, or concept, and they are not expected to match a quantitative representation. However, when quantitative data are graphically represented, they should be done with clarity and integrity.

Small Multiples and Tables

Showing variation and comparisons is not only at the heart of quantitative reasoning, as Tufte (1990, 67) argues, but also at the heart of general reasoning. Comparisons of small multiples can show change, variation, and process. Tables in Web pages are the ideal vehicles for arranging small multiples.

Why small multiples instead of large comparisons, paired comparisons, or several Web pages over which comparisons can be made by clicking the mouse button? Tufte (1990, 67–79) reasons that small multiples can be viewed within a single eyespan providing uninterrupted visual reasoning. The constant design emphasizes changes in the data rather than in the design. Equal-size cells in a table with variations in each cell pull the viewer's attention to the differences in the attribute, and not to the elements surrounding it. For example, a course in communication technology may include instructions for creating animated GIFs.

Laying out the GIFs in individual cells in a table shows the changes that the GIFs go through to create the animation. A simple one would be the numbered countdown seen at the beginning of films as a rotating line whirls around the digits. Figure 8-18 shows how a simple lesson uses small multiples to show the *fourth dimension of time* in sequencing. The cell bars are intentionally left in the table to provide a slight emphasis on the uniqueness of each graphic but not so much as to undermine the connection of the graphics.

The steps for placing small multiples in a Web page depend on the organization of ideas, text, and graphics plus a clear idea of what the student needs to learn. Use the following steps:

Step 1 Outline, preferably on paper, the core idea and what the student will learn. Sketching out what the page will look like when completed will help.

Step 2 Organize the small multiples, (graphics and text) before putting them into a table.

Step 3 Depending on the size and number of the small multiples, create a table with enough cells for all of the images. Extra cells may be necessary. They can be hidden and should not be a concern.

Step 4 Place the materials into the cells based on the sketch in Step 1.

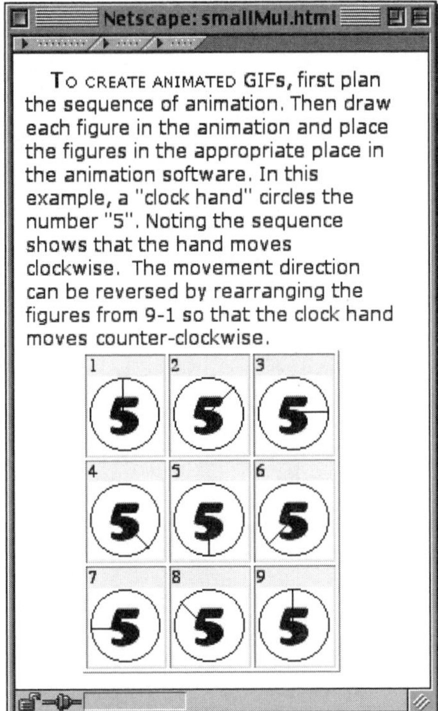

FIGURE 8-18 Numbers in the upper left-hand corner show the sequencing of the small multiples. The eye is drawn to compare the images within a single eyespan.

By using small multiples creatively, it is possible to show process, change, and comparisons. Tables lend themselves to small multiples in creating Web pages because they contain ordered cells to place images and text.

Animations and Small Multiples

One of the useful aspects of a Web page that uses and moves beyond small multiples is animation. Much of the use of small multiples is to move beyond the flat and static land of paper. For helping students learn, small multiples dissect processes and movement, freezing them in time and space so that they can be better analyzed and understood. However, although no reason exists to abandon small multiples in favor of animated sequences, incorporating animations *with* small multiples helps to clarify a process. In showing an animated thunderstorm, Tufte (1997, 20–23) explains how an animated sequence is not simply dumping data into a computer and watching it move. Rather, all of the visual elements of design need to be kept in mind and extended usefully to clarify what is occurring in the animation. For example, in compressing a two-hour thunderstorm into a five-minute movie, students can clearly see all of the phases of the storm from inception to the development of the anvil signaling the end of the storm. In and of itself, such information would be very interesting and informative, especially to student pilots who have not only conceptual but practical reasons for understanding such phenomenon. However, Tufte (1997, 21) adds another dimension to the animation—small multiples showing distinct stages of the storm beneath the moving animation. Each phase is extremely important, and the ability to recognize each phase as a separate entity in the development of such storms can have life or death consequences. Thus, as a learning tool, animations connected to small multiples and other more traditional graphic representations provide the best of both worlds. On the one hand, the process fully playing itself out, in real, accelerated, or slow-motion time, can be viewed with an animated window. On the other hand, each phase can be frozen and examined for fuller understanding and analysis of how the process works. The comparison between the fully animated phenomenon and the small multiples provides students with a greater cognitive learning experience than either alone.

Animations for the Web are increasing in sophistication and ease of use. The most stable are animated GIFs. They can be inserted into a Web page like any other graphic image. The difference is that they are animated and contain several different images that are presented in rapid succession. Table cells are crucial elements in placing animated sequences in Web pages, both as part of the design of the page and a reminder that the animations exist in a larger learning context. Other animation techniques for the Web include the following.

Flash Movies

These movies are animations requiring the *Flash Shockwave* plug-ins. Both of the major browsers have installed *Shockwave* in their newer versions of their browsers—version 5.0 and newer. However, free plug-ins are available for older versions of the browsers and are widely available on the Web. (*Shockwave* is available at http://www.macromedia.com.)

QuickTime Movies

Developed by Apple Computer for both Windows and Macintosh computers, QuickTime movies can be viewed on the Web as well as from the disk. Free QuickTime viewers are available from www.apple.com, but to create QuickTime movies requires the upgraded version of QuickTime for which there is a charge. Also, it is possible using HyperStudio from Roger Wagner Publishing to create both Web sites and QuickTime movies.

RealVideo/RealAudio

Another cross-platform video and audio programming for viewing and listening to digital media on the Web is Real Player from www.real.com. The player is free for both Windows and Macintosh computers, and there are several examples of its use in Web news programs such as www.cnn.com and similar sites. As with QuickTime, you need the upgraded version to create digital video in the Real format.

When setting up any of these animation and video programs for the Web, ideally, a strong Web editing program such as *Dreamweaver* or *GoLive* should be used to ensure a good connection between the Web page and the animated file that will either link to or download the video file. By using a table, it is easy to include all of the contextual materials around the animated segment of the Web page.

Summary and Review

This chapter has been about designing for learning, and the Web page table is a tool for formatting the desired design. In future versions of HTML, there may be simpler ways of getting images and text to the desired location on the page, but until a free-form page layout without tables is part of HTML, tables need to be used. Another way to think about tables is as sets of "placement cells." Programs like *ImageStyler* that use complex tables to put graphics and text exactly where they are needed on a page use tables seamlessly and in a way that is wholly transparent to the viewer.

Graphs and charts lend themselves to table placement as well, and using the single pixel GIF trick, it is possible to have low-bandwidth graphs. However, more important than the ability to create graphs is understanding how to do so with integrity. Using simple formulas and common sense, it is possible to not only create graphs that faithfully represent the quantitative data upon which they are based, it is also possible to do so in a way that clarifies the data.

Finally, consider the use of small multiples as a way to enhance comparative understanding for students. Because tables generate cells, they lend themselves to a hosting mechanism for small multiples whether in text, graphics, or even animations. As a tool, tables are invaluable and important, and the time spent understanding how to use them effectively will pay off in the ability to create learning-rich Web pages.

Used with live animations, small multiples can show key stages in a process that goes through rapid change. Because animations are made up of small multiples that rapidly change, adding a few small multiples in a still state provides a double comparison. They show stages in the process compared to one another, and they provide a comparative frame of reference for the fully animated image.

Glossary of Terms

Small multiples A common view with subtle or large changes displayed in several small images within a single eyespan. Small multiples enhance viewing comparison and change in objects and processes.

Single pixel GIF A GIF file made up of only a single pixel. A pixel is a dot on a computer monitor. Single pixel GIFs can be expanded vertically and horizontally but require a fraction of the bandwidth that a full graphic requires. Also, student input can change the graphic output dynamically by changing the values that expand the vertical and horizontal parameters.

References

Siegel, David. *Creating Killer Web Sites: The Art of Third Generation Site Design.* 2nd Ed. (Indianapolis, IN: Hayden Books, 1997).

Tufte, Edward. *The Visual Display of Quantitative Information* (Graphics Press: Cheshire, CT: 1983).

Tufte, Edward. *Envisioning Information* (Graphics Press: Cheshire, CT: 1990).

Tufte, Edward. *Visual Explanations* (Graphics Press: Cheshire, CT: 1997).

Appendix

For debugging and fine-tuning, it helps to know a little about HTML table code. A brief consideration of HTML tags provides an introduction how to use tables as positioning tools for designing Web pages.

A. Basic Tags

When a table is created, the first tag encountered is <TABLE> letting the HTML interpreter know that this is the beginning of a table. Other tags announce the beginning and ending of columns and rows. For example, the following code represents a simple two-by-two table:

```
<table BORDER COLS=2 WIDTH="30%" >
<tr>
<td>Row 1, Column 1</td>
```

```
<td>Row 1, Column 2</td>
</tr>
<tr>
<td>Row 2, Column 1</td>
<td>Row 2, Column 2</td>
</tr>
</table>
```

On the screen, the table looks like Figure 8-19. The text in each cell takes up two rows because the width of the table is only 30 percent of the screen. A wider table would have placed the text in each cell in a single line. As can be seen from the tags for the table there are no line breaks using <P> or <BR> tags.

In examining the tags, it is fairly clear to see that the <TR> tag initiates new rows and the <TD> tag builds new columns. The rows and columns terminate with the slash versions of the same tags—</TR> and </TD>. Instead of having text, graphics can be put into a table cell as well. In fact, a table cell is almost like a little self-contained Web page. It can have its own background color and background image. As such, there are a greater number of possibilities for designing a page to look just like you want it. In Figure 8-19, several of these options are seen as choices for configuring a table in the *Composer* dialog box.

B. Horizontal Bar Chart Table

The table shown in Figure 8-11 is a relatively simple one with the same pattern repeating itself. The main variation is the color of the single pixel GIF and the width of the graphic bar. The following listing focuses only on the table portion of the page.

```
<table BORDER=0 WIDTH="45%" >
<tr>
<td WIDTH="10%">
<div align=right>Republican</div>
</td>
<td><img SRC="blackdot.gif" BORDER=0 height=10
   width=177></td>
```

Row 1, Column 1	Row 1, Column 2
Row 2, Column 1	Row 2, Column 2

FIGURE 8-19 Basic two-by-two table.

```
</tr>
<tr>
<td>
<div align=right>Democrat</div>
</td>
<td><img SRC="bluedot.gif" BORDER=0 height=10
   width=205></td>
</tr>
<tr>
<td>
<div align=right>Independent</div>
</td>
<td><img SRC="reddot.gif" BORDER=0 height=10
   width=20></td>
</tr>
</table>
```

The <div> tag was used to align the text, but otherwise, the table is pretty straightforward.

C. Vertical Bar Chart Table

The vertical bar chart is used to display data. These tables are best created using a Web page editing tool to save time on coding (and frustration). Note where the actual proportionate values are placed in the script. The following listing shows how the chart in Figure 8-15 was created:

```
<html>
<head>
<title>Hate Crimes</title>
</head>
<body>
 
<table BORDER=0 WIDTH="30%" >
<tr ALIGN=CENTER VALIGN=BOTTOM>
<td>
<h4>
<font face="Arial,Helvetica">Number<br>
of<br>
Hate<br>
Crimes<br>
Per<br>
Million<br>
```

```
Population</font><br>
<br>
<BR></h4>
 
<p> 
<br> 
<br> 
<br> 
<br> 
<br> 
<br> 
<br> 
<br> 
<br> 
<br> 
<br> 
<p> </td>
<td>54
<br><img SRC="blackdot.gif" BORDER=0 height=54 width=12
   align=TEXTTOP></td>
<td>55
<br><img SRC="blackdot.gif" BORDER=0 height=55 width=12
   align=TEXTTOP></td>
<td>99
<br><img SRC="blackdot.gif" BORDER=0 height=99 width=12
   align=TEXTTOP></td>
<td><font face="Arial,Helvetica">73</font>
<br><img SRC="blackdot.gif" BORDER=0 height=73 width=12
   align=TEXTTOP></td>
<td>299
<br><img SRC="blackdot.gif" BORDER=0 height=299 width=12
   align=TEXTTOP></td>
<td>48
<br><img SRC="blackdot.gif" BORDER=0 height=48 width=12
   align=TEXTTOP></td>
</tr>
<tr ALIGN=CENTER>
<td><b><font face="Arial,Helvetica">State</font></b></td>
<td><font face="Arial,Helvetica">AZ</font></td>
<td><font face="Arial,Helvetica">CA</font></td>
<td><font face="Arial,Helvetica">ID</font></td>
<td><font face="Arial,Helvetica">MA</font></td>
<td><font face="Arial,Helvetica">NH</font></td>
<td><font face="Arial,Helvetica">NY</font></td>
```

```
</tr>
</table>
</body>
</html>
```

Chapter 9

Frames: Orchestrating Learning

This chapter contains a good deal of HTML tag listings. At this writing, the public domain Web page development tools such as Netscape *Composer* do not help very much in developing frame sets. Tools like *GoLive*, *Dreamweaver*, and *Front Page* all support frame development, but each has its own unique way of doing so. Rather than attempt to show tools that may not be provided at one's university, school, college, or department, this chapter uses HTML listings.

What Are Frames?

Frames are groups of Web pages that are viewed in a single window. They are invaluable for teaching and learning because they allow students to bring up different pages within the same context or "frame set." Frames are handy for creating menus, orchestrating a series of Web pages within a lesson, providing question/answer pages, making comparisons, and creating other important interactive learning experiences for students. To understand frames in Web pages first requires understanding the concept of a frame set and its relationship to all of the pages that come into the set. In order to understand frames and frame sets fully, this chapter spends a considerable amount of time on the HTML tags used to create frames. At the end of this chapter there is a brief discussion about using Web editors, and if you have an editor that can handle frame sets, by all means use it. This will allow more focus on the teaching and learning applications of frames rather than the code. However, even using a Web editor, knowing something about the HTML tags will help in fine-tuning a set of lessons.

Frame Set

Like cells in tables, frames can be treated as individual elements within a Web window. However, each frame is actually an individual Web page placed on the screen relative to other pages in the group of pages by a special page called a "frame set." The frame set is invisible to the viewer, and its purpose is to place other pages in a frame, determine the size of the frame to be displayed in, provide a name for each frame, and make up rows and columns in the frame set. Figure 9-1 shows the relationship between a frame set page and other Web pages.

In addition to organizing the *initial set of pages* the frame set provides guides for other pages linked into the frame set. For example, if there is a set of pages covering the works of Chaucer at Oxford University a professor would like her students to view, the Chaucer pages could be directed to appear in any frame the professor chooses. Thus, in addition to orchestrating pages an instructor has developed for his class, he can orchestrate pages from anywhere on the World Wide Web. To understand how this works, we will begin with a simple frame set that creates a "menu" frame and a "lesson" frame organized into two columns (see Figure 9-2). (See Appendix A at the end of this chapter for a listing of the next set of pages using frames.) When students select the link to Lesson 2, the page stays in place but the lesson frame is changed as shown in Figure 9-3.

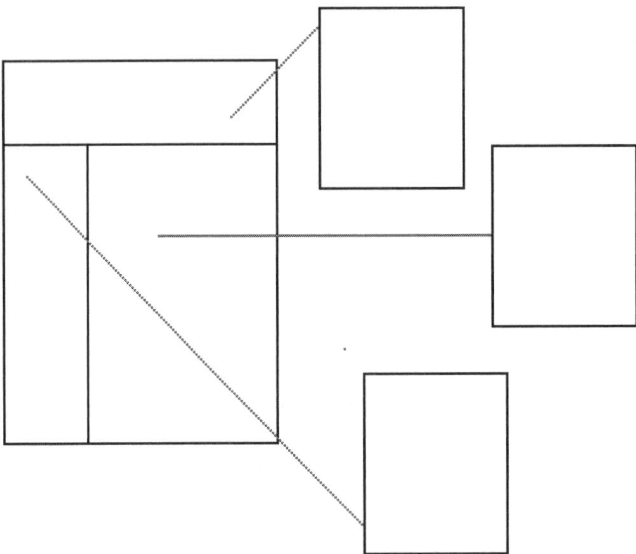

FIGURE 9-1 The frame set page is the invisible "orchestra leader" that organizes the pages in the set.

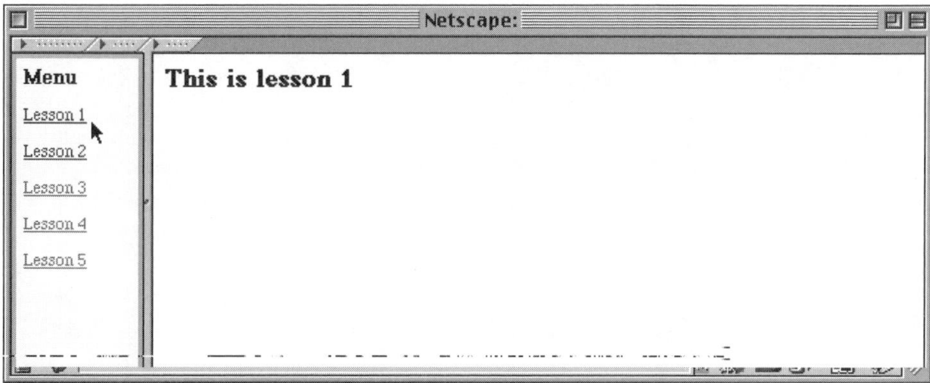

FIGURE 9-2 The menu frame takes up 15 percent of the window and the lesson takes up 85 percent. If the browser window is reduced or expanded, the proportions remain the same.

Extending the Learning-Centered Model with Frames

Working with frame sets is an essential skill that needs practice for making effective learning-centered Web pages. Therefore, this section will delve into more features of frame sets and how they might be usefully incorporated into Web pages for teaching and learning.

The initial frame set intentionally included a fat border between the two frames so that each frame could be seen as clearly separate parts of the frame set. Also, it is important to understand that each page viewed in a frame is actually a separate Web page. However, it is possible to have seamless frames that appear to be one big page with no frames at all. The first example (Figure 9-2) is restructured using instructions to erase the borders. It works very much like the borders in

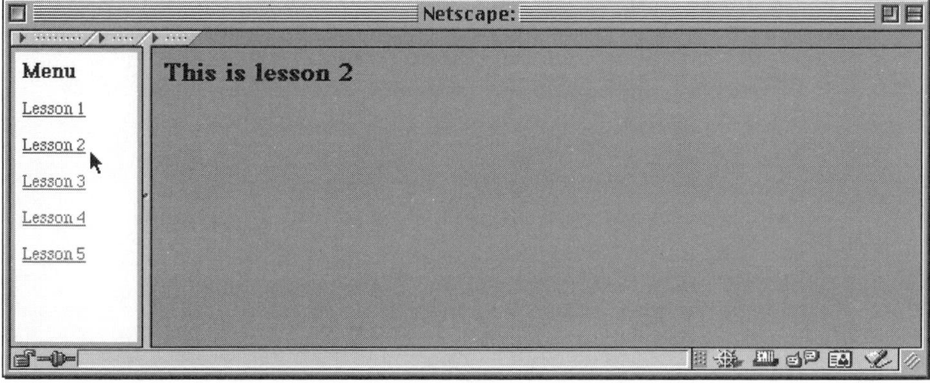

FIGURE 9-3 Only the file in the right frame is changed. Moving different pages through the right frame can create an entire lesson.

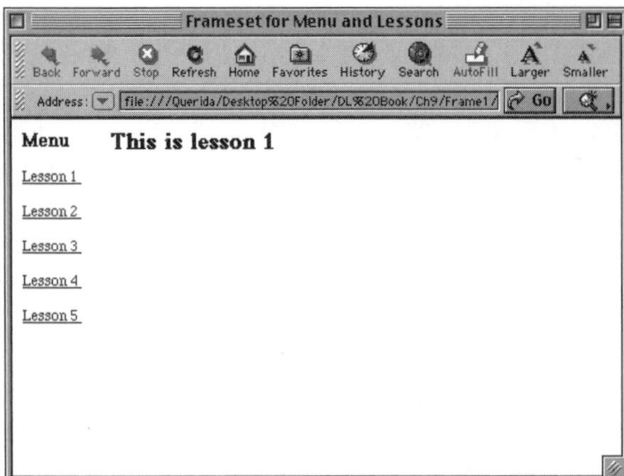

FIGURE 9-4 By making all frame borders and spaces zero, it is possible to have seamless frame sets. When a lesson requires a change in state to show a transition, without separating the pages, use seamless borders.

tables—they may be given a value of zero. Figure 9-4 shows the same set of frames without a border. (See Chapter Appendix B for an HTML listing.)

Add a title bar to the page by inserting another row in the frame set. When a title bar serves as a legend or specifies some class of objects, the bar serves to maintain and change contexts. Once the new frame set is loaded, it should look like Figure 9-5. (See Chapter Appendix C for the HTML listing.)

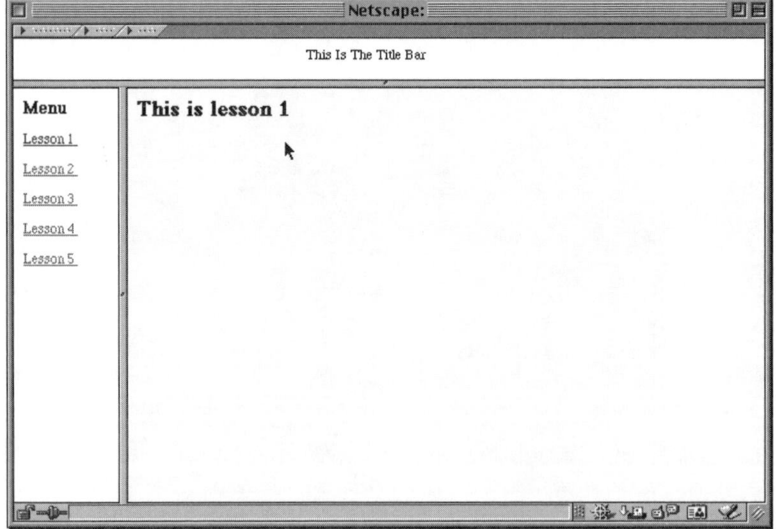

FIGURE 9-5 The new row adds another dimension to the page.

To see the real potential of using multiple frames, Figure 9-6 shows an online syllabus using three frames—a top bar, a menu column, and the syllabus area for material the professor wants the students to see. There are no borders, but the areas are defined by background patterns, giving it some separation. However, the top row, while appearing to be defined by the background pattern, is not. Actually the area where the three professors teaching the course are listed is the bottom of the top frame.

This page also shows the value of good design and artwork. Laura Spitz, a professional graphic artist and Web page designer, designed the page. (See http://www.lauraspitz.com for other examples of well-designed Web sites.) The entire layout and design are addressed to making it clear, simple, and interesting for students to see. More pedestrian efforts can be accomplished by professors on their own or by faculty with artistic skills. However, although it is essential for instructors to create the content of a Web page and orchestrate its order and manner of presentation, rarely can they do this in a way that does not require the aid of a good graphic artist.

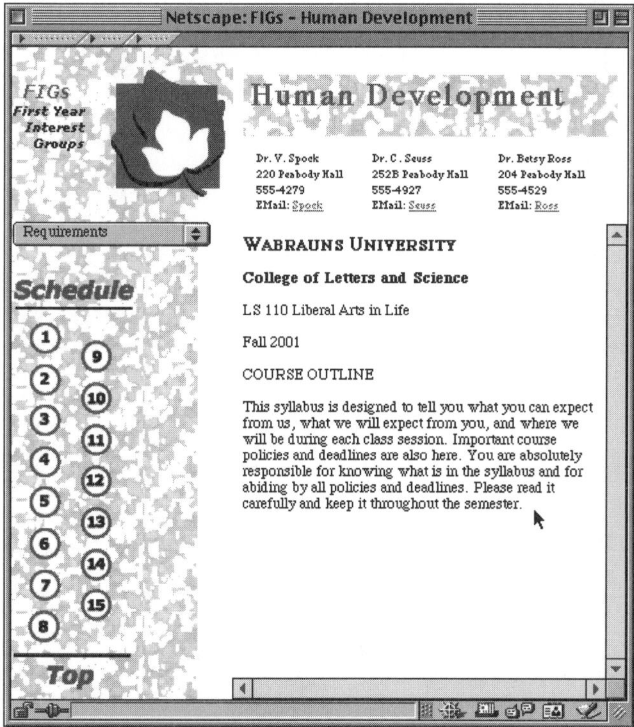

FIGURE 9-6 Three frames make up this syllabus Web page. The top frame includes the title and faculty information, the left column contains the menu, and the right column the information.

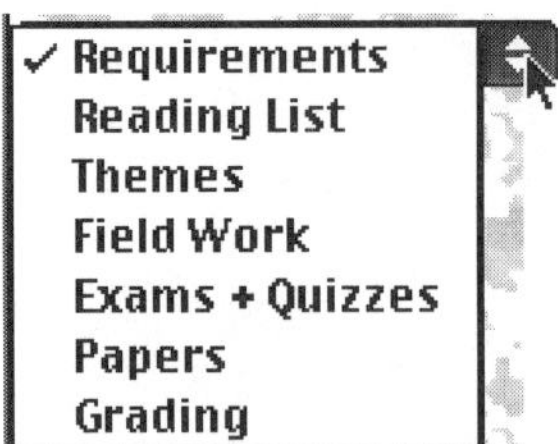

FIGURE 9-7 Several different choices are available in a pull-down menu on the navigation frame.

The frame set organizes the page into three parts. The top row is the title of the course and links to the three professors involved in teaching it. The left column is the navigation frame. In addition to having a 15-week set of buttons for students to jump to different parts of the syllabus, it also has a pull-down menu that provides different types of information that will appear in the syllabus frame that makes up the second column. Figure 9-7 shows the selections students can make from the pull-down menu. Whichever selection is made will open that material in the second column frame. Once any one is open, students then click on the week they wish to see, and the page jumps to the selected week in any of the fields.

It is important to understand that the organization of the information on the page brings together many different elements of a class. Normally, this information would be spread over several pages; however, by using frames the faculty is able to bring it together in an integrated place where students can view everything on a single screen. The design, while pleasing, is not overwhelming. This follows Tufte's point that data graphics should be designed to draw attention to the substance of the data and not the design (1983, 91). By having a well-organized frame set, the student's concentration is on what is in front of him, and not the surrounding packaging. Spending time searching through a binder of paper or a poorly organized Web site is time not spent on the content of the course.

Changing Pages in the Same Frame

A simple menu and lesson frame set can have multiple navigators. One of the cardinal rules of creating a Web site is that no single page should scroll much beyond two screens. (Imagine a book with pages that rolled off onto the floor and under the desk.) Simply adding another page can reduce this problem. However, another strategy is required when using a long menu. A current menu page can be replaced by another menu page with a simple link. Instead of calling up a page to be viewed in another frame, the menu brings up a page to replace itself. Using the example of frames in Figure 9-2, the menu will be changed to include a second menu.

There is almost an infinite combination of lessons and menus that can be generated from the simple organization using a menu frame and a lesson frame.

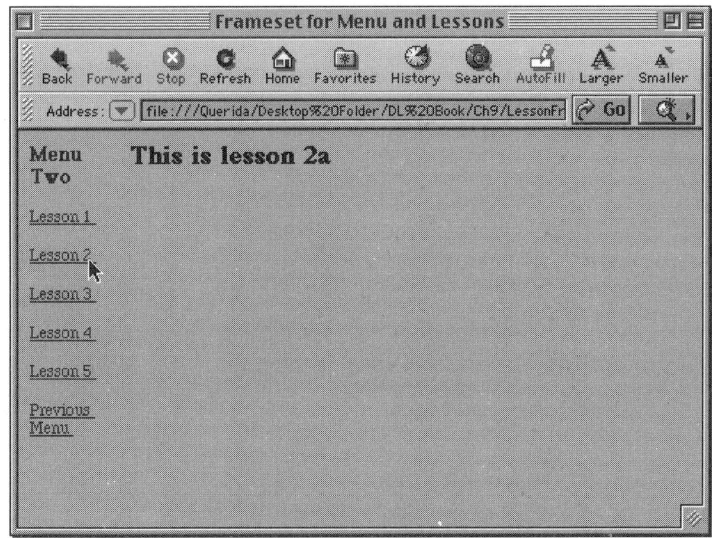

FIGURE 9-8 The added link at the bottom of the menu frame provides a means of greatly expanding the functionality of this frame set. An infinite combination of lessons can be organized and accessed this way.

When a new lesson set is required, another menu can be added into the *same* frame set. Figure 9-8 shows what it will look like on the screen. Note that "Menu Two" and "lesson 2a" are shown, and while appearing the same as in Figure 9-2, the menu frame has a link to the first menu at the bottom. Even though the organization is very simple, it is extendable. The value for students in having a consistent navigation system is that once they are used to it, they can get the information they need very quickly. (See Chapter Appendix D for an HTML listing.)

Keeping Links in the Lesson with Frames

An important feature of the World Wide Web is that it allows the instructor to organize both lesson materials she has developed as well as to link to other sites with information for students. External links take the student outside of the lesson context unless it can be controlled within a frame set.

As we have seen in this chapter, the frame set structures the positioning of Web pages. The Web browser does not differentiate between Web pages within the same folder or ones from the other side of the world. Likewise, the frame set does not treat external pages any different from internal ones—ones from the same folder on the same server. Therefore, organizing internal and external Web pages in a frame set is nothing more than the different URLs used. For example, the following tags show an external and internal page reference to the same frame from a menu frame:

Internal Link in Frame Set

```
<a href="ottoman1.html" target="lesson">Introduction to
the Ottoman Empire </a><p>
```

See Figure 9-9.

External Link in Frame Set

```
<a ref="http://www.friesian.com/turkia.htm"
target="lesson">The Ottoman Sultans and Caliphs </a><p>
```

The student only sees the link on the page indicated usually by underlined text. In the menu frame the student only sees:

Introduction to the Ottoman Empire
The Ottoman Sultans and Caliphs

And in the lesson frame, they will see the contents of the lesson on each of these pages. For example, students may see the professor's overview and explanation of what other pages from external sources make up the lesson, something about their source, and an overall summary at the end of the lesson. The styles may be very

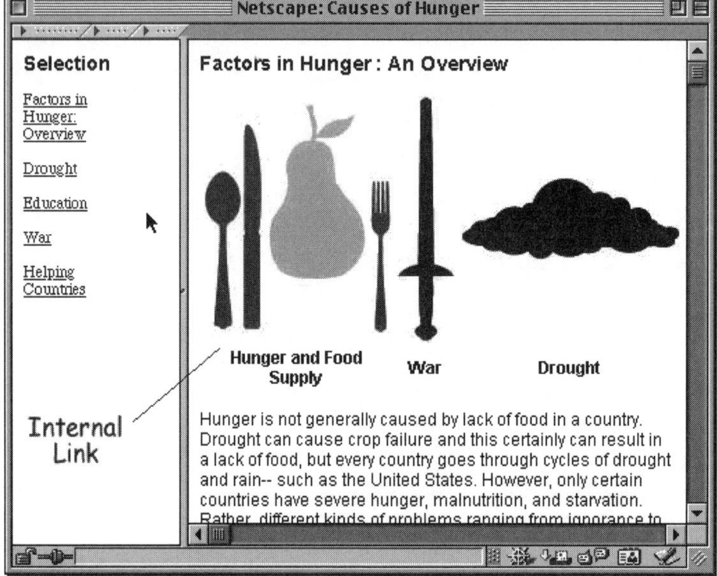

FIGURE 9-9 Using internal links in a frameset help organize materials.

different because the instructor has no control over the makeup or style of the external pages. The borders can be left in the frame set to better see the fact that the page is made up of frames and separate navigation buttons or text from external pages. If the instructor is going to use several links to the same external site, she might want to consider creating a style that reflects the external site. With multiple external sites, the more generic and plain the navigation pages, the less chance that the frames used for navigation will have a design conflict with the external pages.

Comparisons with Frames

One of the important features of Web pages using links is to provide students with comparative information. As noted in Chapter 8 the juxtaposition of two or more images or sets of text in a table provides students with comparative elements within a single eyespan. With frames, comparisons can be more dynamic as one or more frames are compared with others. Students can bring up different sets of data and images provided by the professor to actively make the comparisons. Figure 9-10 shows the general model of comparisons with frames. The "key elements" are those concepts, ideas, theories, designs, formulas, or any other kind of information the instructor wishes to be the basis of comparison, and the "comparative elements" are those to be brought up next to the key elements. This is just like a table except the student can actively engage the process by introducing new comparative sets using the provided navigation frame.

In this next example, the comparisons are not based solely on text descriptions of theoretical concepts. Although most of the materials in this book have emphasized the integration of graphic images and text, Web pages can enhance text-only materials, especially comparisons. By setting them side-by-side rather than strung out over several pages, frame sets can enhance conceptual comparisons. Figure 9-11 shows how this might be done using the model in Figure 9-10.

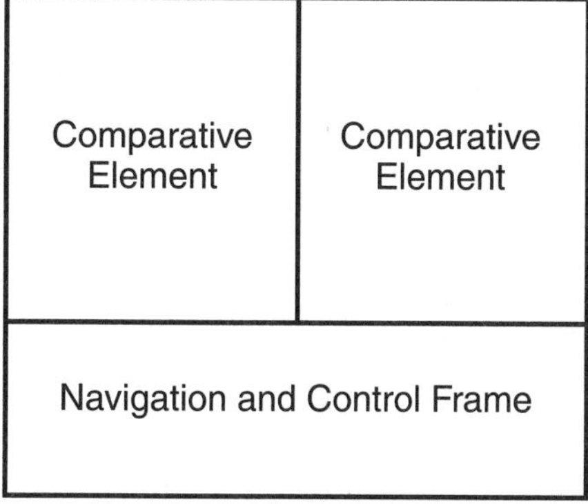

FIGURE 9-10 Frames can be used to actively involve students in making comparisons by providing the comparative frames and a navigation frame to bring in the comparative elements.

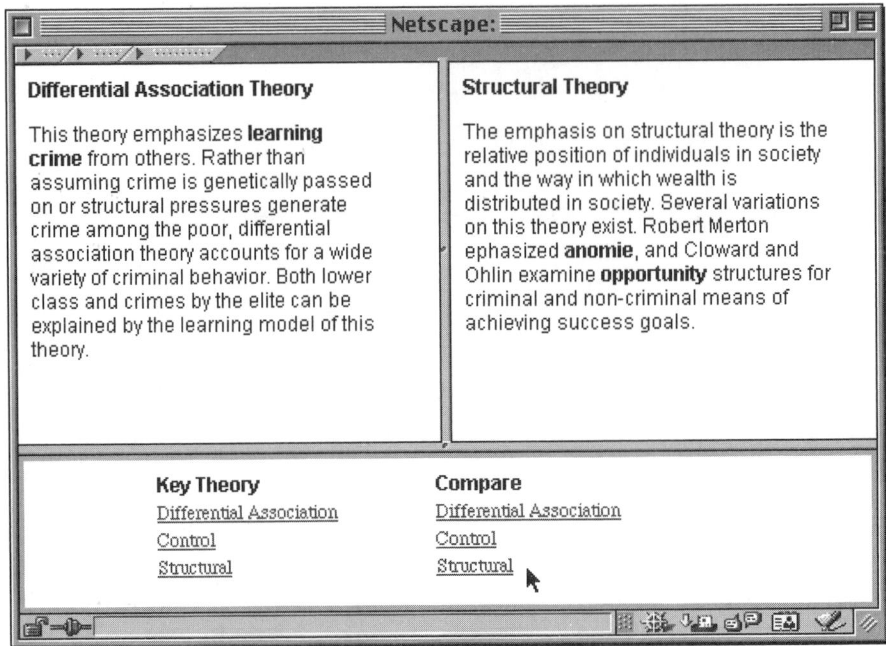

FIGURE 9-11 Using frames for dynamic comparison provides students with an active component to comparative learning.

The navigation menu at the bottom of the window simply links the pages with the information into adjacent frames for comparisons. However, when using a full row at the bottom of a page with no columns, the frame set tags are slightly different from when the row is at the top. (Chapter Appendix E shows the HTML tags used.)

Navigating Frame Targets

There is more to the "target" attribute than just guiding pages to frames created by the instructor. In addition to telling the pages which frame to enter, it is also necessary to get out of a frame set and bring up another frame set. For example, in the syllabi examined in this book, frames are an essential part. Also in the sets of lessons, frames are useful. What happens when professors want the student to fully leave the syllabus frame set and open a new lesson frame set? Several special values for the target attribute are available to help navigating into and out of frame sets. Each value is examined with an accompanying example.

_blank—Opens a new window, leaving the current window open.

Example:

```
<a href="art101.html" target="_blank"> Art 101 </a>
```

Opens up the page "art101.html" in a new window, but leaves the referencing window (the one with the link) in place.

_self—Opens the page in the frame with the link. This can be handy for switching menus in a menu frame or for links within a lesson page that will open the next page in the same frame.

Example:

```
<a href="menu3.html" target="_self"> Zoology Menu </a>
```

This would replace whatever is in the frame with "menu3.html," with the link name "Zoology Menu."

_parent—The page is loaded into the parent frame set. This means that the frame set being used is loaded with the linked page or frame set. When moving from one frame set to another, this is an important value to include. It would be the target value if moving from a syllabus made of frames to lessons made of frames.

Example:

```
<a href="VanGoghSet.html" target="_parent"> Van Gogh </a>
```

This would open up the frame set "VanGoghSet.html" in the current parent frame.

_top—The entire frame set is discarded and the new page is brought up in a new window. This seems to work exactly like "_parent" except in cases where nested frame sets are employed. In a nested frame set "_parent" will replace only one of the frame sets and leave the others. "_top" will discard all frame sets and bring up a new window. For the most part, "_parent" and "_top" will work the same.

Example:

```
<a href="MultiSetB.html" target="_top"> Bridge Structures
</a>
```

This would discard the current frame set and open "MultiSetB.html" in a whole new frame set.

One of the worst experiences instructors (and students) encounter is where one frame set is opened in another. Multiple frame sets can each open, crowding more and more into the space for the lesson. For example, Figure 9-12 shows how one frame set is loaded into the lesson frame of another because _parent or _top was not a value of the target attribute. It severely cuts into the space allotted for the lesson materials.

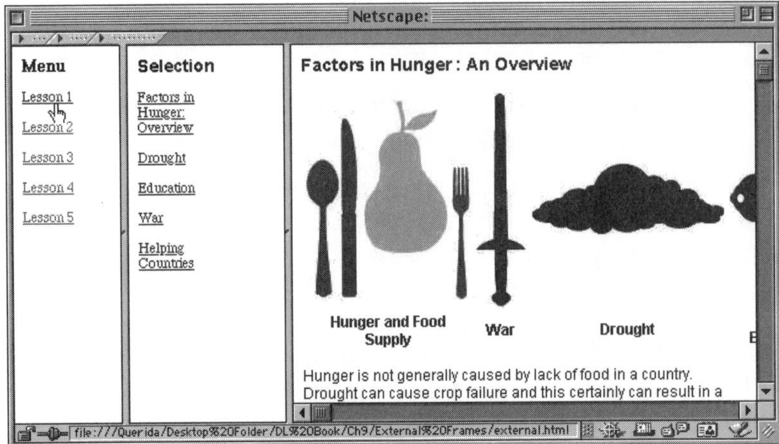

FIGURE 9-12 When one frame set is loaded into another, the area for content is severely limited. Using _parent and _top values controls this problem.

Using Web Editors and Frames

A good deal of tag code has been introduced in this chapter to show how frame sets work and what they do. However, it is very important for faculty who are going to be spending time creating syllabi and lessons with frames to use a good Web page editor. Microsoft's *Front Page,* Adobe's *GoLive,* and Macromedia's *Dreamweaver* are all candidates for creating pages with frames. Figure 9-13 shows

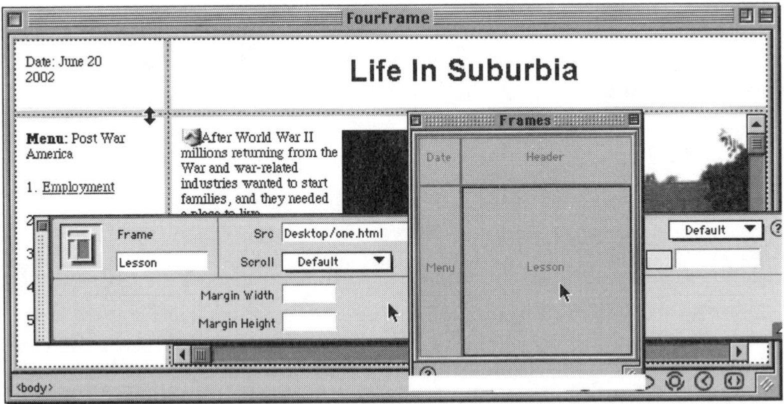

FIGURE 9-13 When creating educational Web pages using frames, it is far easier to use a Web editor than to key in all the code yourself. Many tools make it more effective, efficient, and coherent than attempting to do everything with a text editor and coded tags.

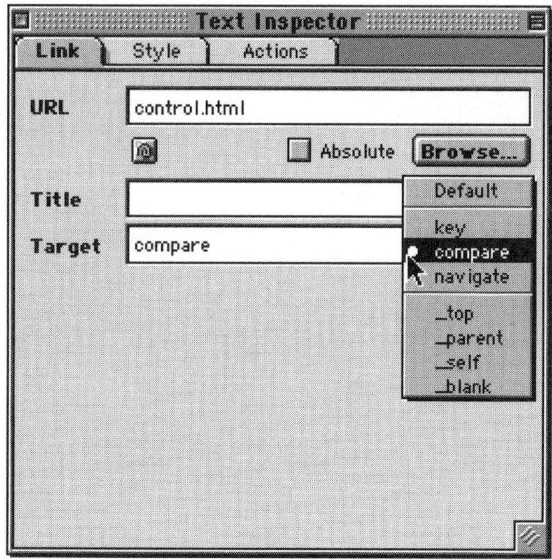

FIGURE 9-14 ***GoLive* provides multiple views for coordinating work on frames, frame sets, and associated pages. Frames titled "key," "compare," and "navigate" are examined in the Text Inspector.**

how *Dreamweaver* allows the user to work on each page while in the frame set. This is much easier than trying to imagine how everything will look once the whole has been put together.

As noted at the beginning of the chapter, it is very helpful to know something about the tags and structure of HTML frames. Powerful applications like *Dreamweaver* and *GoLive* add the capacity for writing JavaScript into the frames giving the potential for even more interactivity in learning-centered pages. Most of the Web page editors that handle frames do most of the pages that you will need for a good learning-centered educational site. Because energy and focus should be on what the student will learn and not a gaggle of HTML tags, investing in a good Web page editor is well worth the expense. Figure 9-14 shows how Adobe *GoLive* can have different aspects of a frame set open at the same time.

Summary and Review

Frames can be one of the most important tools for creating learning-centered Web pages. This is because many different elements can be brought up, changed, compared, and used to learn material. Unlike a book where each page is static, a Web page with frames provides the opportunity to bring in different information in the form of text and images dynamically. Frames are especially good for drawing comparisons and showing contrasts. Faculty can orchestrate a learning site that students can navigate in ways that enhance their involvement and activity in the learning process. Rather than flipping from one Web page to another or even one

Web site to another, frames provide an infinite variety of combinations to present materials for students to learn.

Beginning with a frame set to define the areas in a browser, instructors can place different elements of a lesson into frames within a single eyespan for students to use in seeing processes and structures develop. Students can compare and contrast ideas and concepts, and interact with the learning process by controlling what the instructor has organized. Using external links need not require the student to leave the learning site, but instead faculty can mix in externally developed Web pages with their own to give students an integrated whole rather than disconnected parts. Menus or third generation navigational tools readily lend themselves to frames.

Glossary of Terms

Frame A single window in a frame set. Each frame has an individual name used as a reference for a target to place a page in the frame set.

Frame Set An HTML page that sets the parameters for all of the pages in the frame and specifies the URLs of the initial pages to appear when the frame set is loaded into the browser.

Target The name of the frame in which a linked page is to appear. When a link in a frame set is established, it is important to name the target of the frame. Generic targets include _self, _parent, _blank, and _top.

Reference

Tufte, Edward. *The Visual Display of Quantitative Information* (Graphics Press: Cheshire, CT: 1983).

Appendix

A. Creating Lessons with Frames

Save all the files using the names shown in boldface at the beginning of the listing.

lessonset.html

```
<html>
<frameset cols="15%,*" >
<frame src="menu.html" name="menu">
<frame src="lesson1.html" name="lesson">
</frameset>
</html>
```

Notice that there is no <BODY> tag. That is because there is no text, graphics, or anything else that the frame set page shows on the screen. Its sole job is to set up the framework for the pages that will be viewed on the screen. Let's take the program line by line.

```
1. <frameset cols="15%,*" >
```

After the <HTML> tag, the <frameset> tag includes a statement to instruct the frames to be divided into two columns [cols=. . .]. Using "15%,*" tells the frame set that 15 percent of the window will be the first page (or frame) and the rest "*" will be the second frame. We could have put "15%, 85%" but used the "*" to fill in automatically what the remainder would be. Also, instead of using percentages, we could have used raw numbers to indicate the number of pixels for each column. However, it is easier to envision the proportion of a page than the number of pixels, so percentages were used.

Finally, instead of using "cols=15%. . . " we could have used "rows=15%. . . " to stack the pages on top of one another rather than side by side. Further on we will see how to mix rows and columns to make interesting and useful learning pages with frames. When combinations of rows and columns are used, there will be more than a single <frameset> tag. For now, though, seeing how the columns work with frames is sufficient for understanding the generic elements of a frame set.

```
2. <frame src="menu.html" name="menu">
```

Next, the frame set indicates the Web page name and the frame name. The Web page is either the name of a page the professor created or a URL. However, the frame name is a specific name that indicates the "target" for any Web page that happens to be resident in that frame. In this case the Web page is named "menu.html" and the name of the frame is simply "menu." Because this is the first frame in the script, it will be the leftmost column in the window.

```
3. <frame src="lesson1.html" name="lesson">
```

The third line specifies the second column. It is identical to the second line except that a different page is indicated to be loaded and the frame has a different target name. As can be seen from the name, this column will be used to show different lesson pages.

```
4. </frameset>
```

Finally, the frame set is terminated. In more complex frame sets, there will be multiple </frameset> tags, one for each set of rows or columns created—a corresponding one for each <frameset> tag.

The *minimum* number of files for a frame set is three—the frame set page, and a page for each frame. The frame set identifies the pages to be brought into the frame set, but it does not create them. The following HTML code shows the menu page:

menu.html

```
<html>
<head><title>Menu</title> </head>
<body bgcolor="lightblue">
<h3>Menu</h3>
<a href="lesson1.html" target="lesson">Lesson 1 </a><p>
<a href="lesson2.html" target="lesson">Lesson 2 </a><p>
<a href="lesson3.html" target="lesson">Lesson 3 </a><p>
<a href="lesson4.html" target="lesson">Lesson 4 </a><p>
<a href="lesson5.html" target="lesson">Lesson 5 </a><p>
</body> </html>
```

The menu page is the navigation page for this frame set. It will appear in the left column taking up exactly 15 percent of the horizontal window in the browser. It is simply a list of links to various lessons. When the frame set is launched in the browser, the student sees the menu page on the left, and on the right the page indicated in the frame set—lesson1.html. This page also appears as a link in the menu page. That is because, after viewing the initial lesson page, the student may want to come back to it. Therefore, it should be part of the links in the menu. We will examine one of the lines with a link to see what's going on within the frame set.

```
<a href="lesson3.html" target="lesson">Lesson 3 </a><p>
```

This link is just like the other links in HTML with one significant difference. This one has a "target" statement. The target refers to the frame the page will be placed in, and it is extremely important. If no target is specified, it defaults to the current page where the link has been clicked. Because you want your lessons in the lesson frame and the menu in the menu frame, keep the target in mind.

Making a Base

To save a little time in writing HTML tags, you can put in a <BASE> tag in the menu page. Just type in <Base Target="lesson"> or whatever you want for the default target in the <HEAD> area of your page. The default target would be that frame where the lesson pages go. That way you won't forget and have the lessons appearing in the menu frame.

Now, the only thing left is a couple of lesson pages to see how this works. For purposes of understanding how frames can be used, put in the following two pages. Save the first one as "lesson1.html" and the second as "lesson2.html" and be sure to put them into the same folder or directory as the other pages for the frame set. Two different background colors are used in the lesson pages to show that even though they are part of a frame set, they are essentially independent pages placed into a frame. (Type in the HTML and save it using the name in bold.)

lesson1.html

```
<html><head><title>Lesson 1</title></head>
<body bgcolor="lightyellow">
<h2>This is lesson 1</h2>
</body></html>
```

lesson2.html

```
<html><head><title>Lesson 1</title></head>
<body bgcolor="lightskyblue">
h2>This is lesson 2</h2>
</body></html>
```

Be sure that all of the four Web pages are in the *same folder*. They should be named the following:

lessonset.html
menu.html
lesson1.html
lesson2.html

When you load the file "lessonset.html" you should see a page resembling Figure 9-2.

B. Reducing Frame Borders

Change the code in the first frame set to the following:

```
<html>
     <frameset cols="15%,*" border="0" framespacing="0"
     frameborder="no" >
     <frame src="menu.html" name="menu">
     <frame src="lesson1.html" name="lesson">
     </frameset>
</html>
```

The only change that was made was to the <frameset> tag. By reducing all frame spacing and borders to zero, the only way to tell there is more than a single page or frame on the screen is by the different background colors. Change the background colors of "menu.html" and "lesson1.html" to *white* and there is no way to tell the demarcation between frames as can be seen in Figure 9-4.

C. Creating a Title Bar

```
<html>
     <frameset rows="10%,*" >
     <frame src="title.html" name="title">
          <frameset cols="15%,*" >
          <frame src="menu.html" name="menu">
          <frame src="lesson1.html" name="lesson">
          </frameset>
     </frameset>
 </html>
```

The new <FRAMESET> tag used 10 percent of the vertical space in the window. Then, the following frame provided the new name "title" for that area of the frame set. Notice also there is a new Web page required—title.html. So the next thing to be done is to provide one.

```
<html>
     <head><title>Title Bar</title></head>
     <body bgcolor="white">
     <center>
     This Is The Title Bar
     </center></body>
</html>
```

The title is centered on the horizontal plane of the frame with the <CENTER> tag, and if a longer title were used, it would span over both columns. Be sure to save the script as "title.html" in the same folder as the other pages. When creating frame sets, one of the most common "bugs" in the program is having part of the set outside of the folder where the pages are being developed. If a path to the page has been established, there will be no problem, but to save time and headaches, be sure to use a single folder for all of the Web pages you plan to put into your frame set. External pages are simply linked using the full URL as would be done with a regular link.

D. Multiple Menus

Add the following and there will be two menu sets and lesson sets.

Menu 1: menu.html

```
<html><head><title>Menu</title></head>
<body bgcolor="lightblue" link="darkgreen"
   vlink="darkgreen">
```

```
<h3><font color="darkgreen">Menu One</font></h3>
<a href="lesson1.html" target="lesson">Lesson 1 </a><p>
<a href="lesson2.html" target="lesson">Lesson 2 </a><p>
<a href="lesson3.html" target="lesson">Lesson 3 </a><p>
<a href="lesson4.html" target="lesson">Lesson 4 </a><p>
<a href="lesson5.html" target="lesson">Lesson 5 </a><p>
<p><a href="menu2.html" target="menu">Next Menu </a>
</body></html>
```

Menu 2: menu2.html

```
<html><head><title>Menu Two</title></head>
<body bgcolor="lightblue" link="darkgreen"
   vlink="darkgreen">
<h3><font color="indianred" >Menu Two</font></h3>
<a href="lesson1a.html" target="lesson">Lesson 1 </a><p>
<a href="lesson2a.html" target="lesson">Lesson 2 </a><p>
<a href="lesson3a.html" target="lesson">Lesson 3 </a><p>
<a href="lesson4a.html" target="lesson">Lesson 4 </a><p>
<a href="lesson5a.html" target="lesson">Lesson 5 </a><p>
<p><a href="menu.html" target="menu">Previous Menu </a>
</body></html>
```

Lessons:

lesson1.html

```
<html><head><title>Lesson 1</title></head>
<body bgcolor="lightyellow">
<h2>This is lesson 1</h2>
</body></html>
```

lesson2.html

```
<html><head><title>Lesson 2</title></head>
<body bgcolor="lightskyblue">
<h2>This is lesson 2</h2>
</body></html>
```

lesson1a.html

```
<html><head><title>Lesson 1a</title></head>
<body bgcolor="paleturquoise">
<h2>This is lesson 1a</h2>
</body>
</html>
```

lesson2a.html

```
<html><head><title>Lesson 2a</title></head>
     <body bgcolor="lightpink">
     <h2>This is lesson 2a</h2>
</body></html>
```

E. Comparative Frames

The following tags show how this was done:

```
<html>
     <frameset rows="70%,*">
          <frameset cols="50%,*">
          <frame src="dat.html" name ="key">
          <frame src="control.html" name="compare">
          </frameset>
     <frame src="nav.html" name="navigate">
     </frameset>
</html>
```

Notice that a </FRAMESET> tag is placed before the bottom row tags. In the other frame sets, there has been a set of adjacent </FRAMESET> tags when both rows and columns are used. However, in this arrangement, the column frame set is separated from the next row by a </FRAMESET> tag inserted between the column frames and the second row. This is because the two columns were to be inserted before the second row.

Chapter 10

Active Learning with Links and Frames

In a wonderful study of face-to-face interaction, Erving Goffman (1961) considers the *involvements* in an encounter. Social situations, including those in the classroom, are made up of foci to which participants are supposed to pay attention. These Goffman calls *dominant involvements*. However, in class or in front of a computer screen, students often have their attention elsewhere than on the lesson. Rather than listening to lectures, students often interact with one another on wholly irrelevant matters, doodle in their notebooks, or simply daydream of what they'd rather be doing. Likewise, students in a computer classroom will often be playing computer games, writing notes to friends on email, or be involved in a chat room devoted to a recent movie—not the Web pages the instructor has so painstakingly prepared. If a student's engrossment is in another place than the materials she is supposed to be learning, she is not going to learn very much. These distracting *subordinate involvements* (Goffman, 1963) are often the bane of creating an effective learning environment, whether in class or on the Web.

Samuel Johnson aptly noted, ". . . when a man knows he is to be hanged in a fortnight, it concentrates his mind wonderfully." Although not suggesting a hanging to rally student engrossment with the topic at hand, a need often exists to do something to bring students' attention to the content. *Active learning* is one way to help students pay enough attention to learn something, and while it is only one part of an overall strategy, it is a crucial and important one. Combined with motivations to learn something important, not to flunk the class, and to be a better person, active learning *engages* attention.

Active Learning with Web Pages

Requiring the student to do something other than simply look at a page or go to the next page by clicking on a link is the crux of the issue faced in designing active learning. Most active learning requires information gathering by reading or listening prior to activity. However, at the root of active learning is *feedback* or some kind of trial and error. That means when a student does something, she should get some kind of response, and the feedback should tell her whether she is on the right or wrong track—or if no right or wrong track exists, *which* track she's on. Furthermore, this implies some kind of choice. If students have only a single choice, *active* learning is not possible. For example, when a student encounters a "click here" to continue selections, there's not much action and little choice. (The situation is analogous to turning the page in a book.) Likewise, a Web menu is usually a sequence of Web pages and not a choice in the sense that the student can choose another sequence. So the student must encounter:

1. Choice (alternatives)
2. Consequences of the choice (feedback)

Learning is knowing what choice to make for the desired outcome. By providing choices and feedback, the student comes to learn what will happen with a choice. Essentially then, active learning is a process of *informed* decision making with the student involved in making a decision. He is informed by either reading or listening or *doing*. By leading a student through the process of choices, he learns from the effect of his choices, and the feedback is either immediate or delayed until his professor provides it with comments on the work. The extent to which the student knows why a choice is the right or wrong one, we say that the student *understands*. For instance, studying history is essentially the study of choices made and the consequences of those choices. The idea is that if confronted with the same choices, we would do better by understanding the historical consequences of choices in the past. By throwing a student into the process of making choices, he better understands everything from the process to the structure surrounding the decision to select one action over another.

Some kinds of learning may not *seem* to involve making choices. For example, teaching a student how to paint would appear to be a skill that is based on *practice* and guidance by a professor. Doing a painting is certainly an active process involving the student—immersing the student actually. It is just the kind of activity being promoted in this chapter. However, some key parts of becoming a good painter involve a lot of decisions. What media should be used? What type of paint, brush, stroke, and technique are the best to employ? The action of creating a painting involves a good many choices and the guidance by a professor is feedback to the sum of those choices. This is not to argue that Web pages are to be designed like some behaviorist's maze independent of the symbolic reality of humanity. Rather, it is to emphasize *the role of students making choices* in the context of understanding a subject matter. If nothing else it is a heuristic device for guiding us in thinking about how to get students involved *actively* in learning what we want them to learn.

So, how can Web pages assist in this process? Because Web pages are based on hypertext, it means they are essentially nonlinear—remember, HTML stands for *Hypertext* Markup Language. Because of that fundamental structure, Web pages provide alternative routes. Building a route where the student makes decisions and receives feedback concerning those decisions is a fundamental element of active learning. Using the following logical steps, it is relatively simple to incorporate active learning with Web pages:

- The student encounters a Web page with a request for the student to make a choice. The choice can be a single one or involve a series of choices.
- More than one outcome is based on the choices.
- The student receives feedback based on her decisions.

Those three steps are at the core of active decision making and active learning based on feedback concerning the decisions.

Besides decision making, active learning can involve carrying out a number of steps learned from information provided on the Web or another source. For example, students often need to learn a set of steps to accomplish a task. A marketing student may need to know all of the steps to take in creating a marketing plan, or a chemistry student may need to know the steps in an experiment. The steps in a given sequence constitute a pattern of decided actions. However, not to overdo the concept of decision making, we can talk about certain steps involved in understanding a process as active learning without having to refer to decisions. It is enough to guide the student through a number of steps to achieve a goal in order to effect active learning.

Learning Through Feedback without Instruction: Pure Experiential Learning

Imagine a situation in which the only way it would be possible to teach a student a process was through trial and error. You were not allowed to explain the process or tell the student what to do next. The student must take an action and decide from the consequences (feedback) whether or not she is on the right track. After enough trial and error, the student learns the process. This is learning through experience or *experiential learning*. By examining such a way of learning, we will see how feedback and decisions are set up.

As an example subject matter, we will take bomb defusing. The students in the class must learn how to open a vault using trial and error only. The example is trivial only insofar as it is quite simple; however, it serves to focus on the *process* of active learning with no communication other than trying different combinations. Table 10-1 shows the pages in sequence.

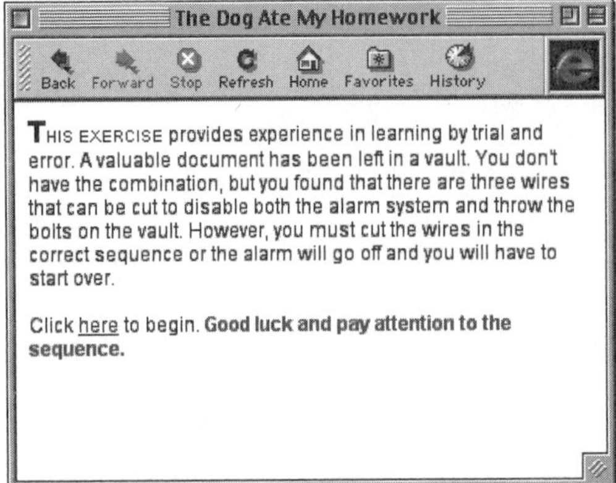

Page 1: Brief introduction.

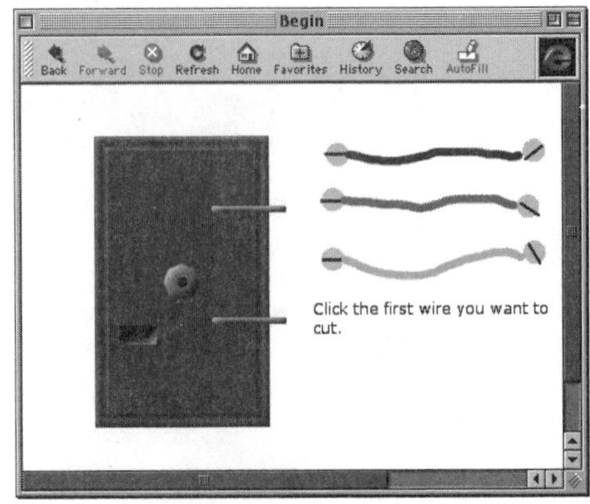

Page 2: Prompt to decide.

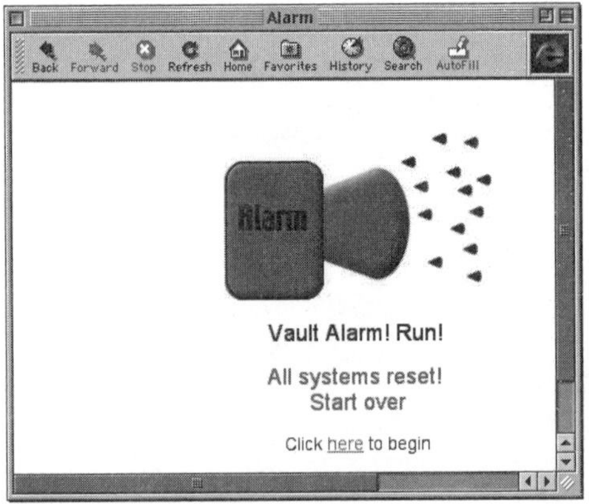

Alarm Page: Feedback.

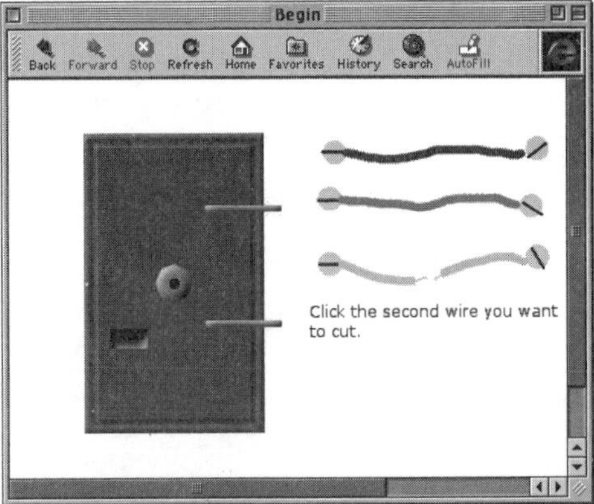

Page 3: Feedback of correct path.

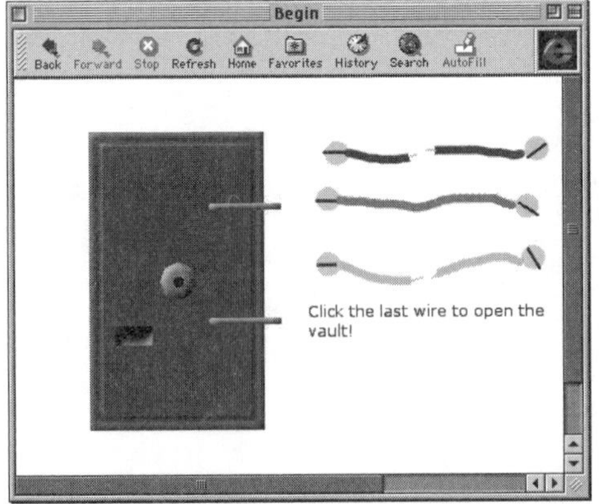

Page 4: Last decision.

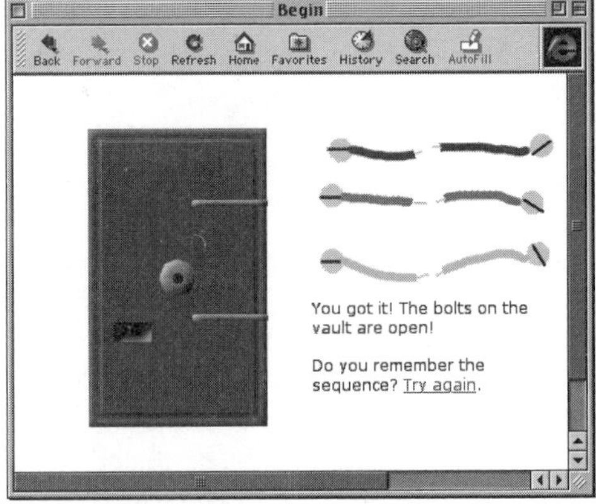

Page 5: Problem solved.

TABLE 10-1 A set of active learning pages with only feedback and no explanations or instructions. The emphasis is on the student working out the problem herself.

In the locked vault example, six pages are used to create the active learning site. They guide the student to make decisions, take actions, and make adjustments in her behavior.

Page 1	This page has minimal instructions on what to do.
Page 2	Here is the first encounter with the problem. Each "wire" is a separate graphic linked either to the next safe page in the sequence of opening the vault or to the alarm. Figure 10-1 shows how the graphics are in a table—each one a separate entity.
Explosion Page	Feedback is a simple graphic. It has a link back to the first page to start over and try again.
Page 3	At this page, the student is encouraged. She has selected the right wire. The "cut wire" graphic has no links now. It does nothing. If the student selects the correct wire, she goes on to the next page. Otherwise, she gets the alarm and must start over.
Page 4	At this point, only a single selection remains—the red wire. The student clicks it and goes to the last page.
Page 5	The final page is a "goal page." The student sees the vault door with the bolts thrown back and is asked whether she can remember the sequence that she has learned and is invited to try again.

In the vault example students could have been instructed to follow the sequence *green-blue-red* to unlock the vault. However, doing so would mean little active trial and error could take place. With more complex materials to learn, more instructions will save more time, but it is still important to help the student to see if he can do it on his own and learn from actions and adjustments.

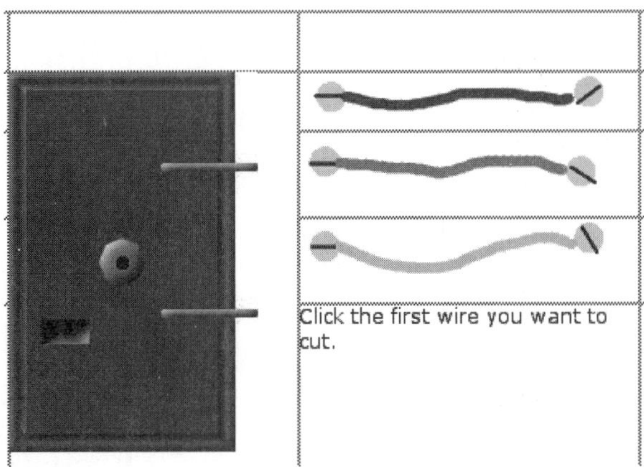

FIGURE 10-1 In a Web editor, the images of wires show separate graphics in a table. Each has a link to the next appropriate page.

Active Data Gathering and Analysis

Providing a problem, then explaining a solution in terms of a set of steps or formulas can generate another type of active learning. First, the student is provided with a general problem. Second, he is given a solution to the problem along with an explanation of why the solution works. Third, he is given a sample problem requiring actions on his part to solve the problem.

For example, a simple yet important concept in the sociology of crime is that of *crime rates*. Students learn that in order to compare crimes in cities, states, and countries of different sizes, it is necessary to first convert the data to rates. The student first encounters a real-world problem she must solve. Next, she is shown the steps to solve the problem. Then she is provided with another problem to solve. In Table 10-2, the three-page exercise shows each of these steps. Page 3 is illustrated in two different ways. First, it is shown as a traditional problem to solve using the statistical procedures for calculating rates. Using a calculator, a computer, or handwritten calculations, the student determines the rate and emails the results to her professor. In the second illustration of Page 3, a rate calculator has been built into the Web page using HTML forms and JavaScript (see Chapters 12 and 13 for explanations of using JavaScript and forms). This was done to show an alternative way to help students *focus on the data* required to calculate a rate (population and number of cases) and not the calculation itself. The instructor should determine when the student should use the Web pages or other forms of actively solving problems and the focus of the problem to be addressed.

Active Learning and the Virtual Laboratory

Active learning has generally been a key element of most science labs. In a physics lab, for example, students first learn formulas, and then they are given practical exercises to carry out to see how well the formulas predict some actual event. Likewise in chemistry, biology, and engineering, the labs bring together the actions with understandings of underlying causes. Because of a history of active learning in actual science labs, it has been a small conceptual leap to generate virtual labs using formulas to simulate what happens in physical labs.

Active learning using the lab model has another component that cannot be done practically in a classroom and involves students in understanding general concepts more thoroughly. Students have used rats and pigeons in psychology labs to learn about certain basic concepts in learning. For example, psychologists have found that rats will learn a maze in the form of a "J-curve." The learning curve goes down rapidly with each trial, but then it goes up again slightly after the learning has leveled off. Shown in a scatter or vertical bar chart, the results resemble the letter "J."

Learning a maze is the rat's job, but learning *about learning* is the student's. Using a virtual maze, the student can go through it until she learns the path to the

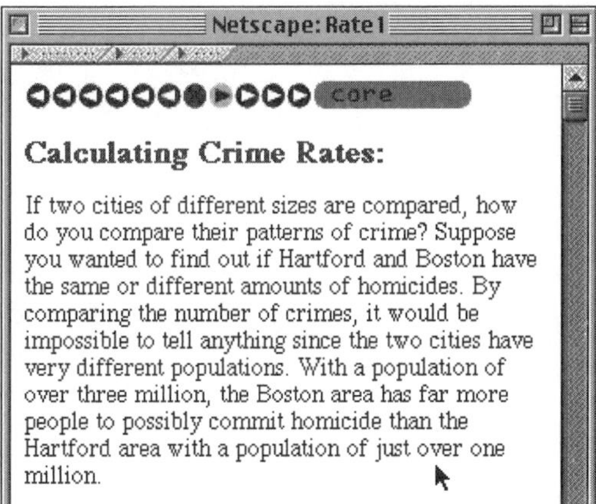

Page 1: Explain the problem.

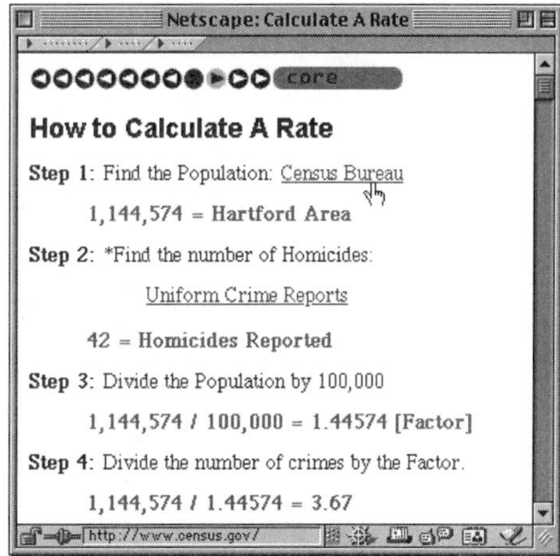

Page 2: Show the steps. In this case links to data are included.

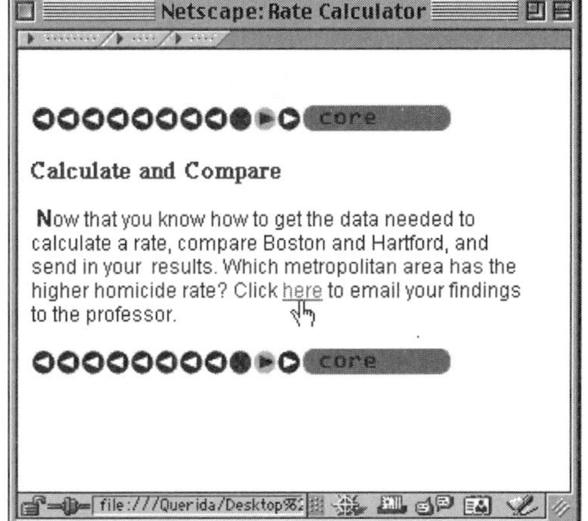

Page 3: Provide a problem to solve.

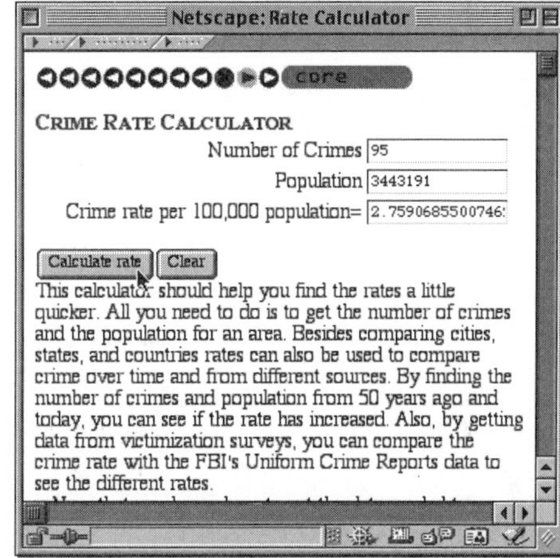

Page 3: (Alternative) Include online calculation so that student will focus on data gathering rather than calculation.

TABLE 10-2 Active learning here requires a good deal more than explanation and instruction. Two different ways of handling Page 3 are provided to show the flexibility of this arrangement.

goal. The computer can time all of this, and once the student has successfully completed the maze, she records her time. The student trials could be recorded on the computer if the professor wants. If the student records the time on a piece of paper, though, she will be more *actively* involved in the process of data collection and learn more about that process. Because pen and paper are more effective in helping the student learn the data collection process, they are more appropriate tools in this case and part of what needs to be understood in psychology experiments. In other research contexts, it may make perfect sense for the student to have the computer record data automatically, but for learning, the more involved the student is in the process, the better.

Table 10-3 shows a virtual maze, but instead of running a rat through it, the student negotiates it. As soon as the student starts, a timer begins. When the goal of

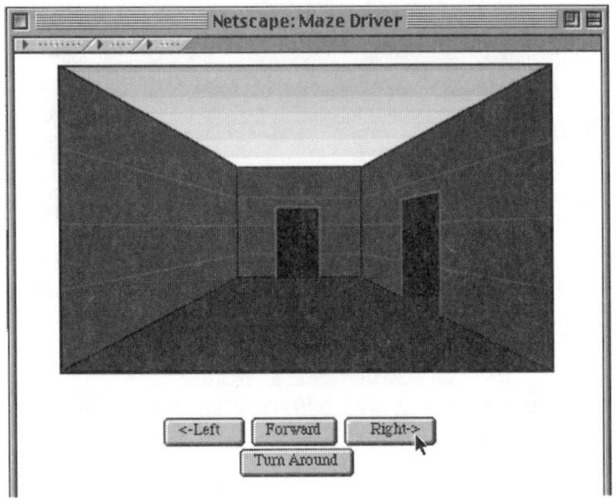

Initial Page: On the initial view, the student chooses to go forward, go right, or turn around. The left wall has no door and nothing happens if students select the left button.

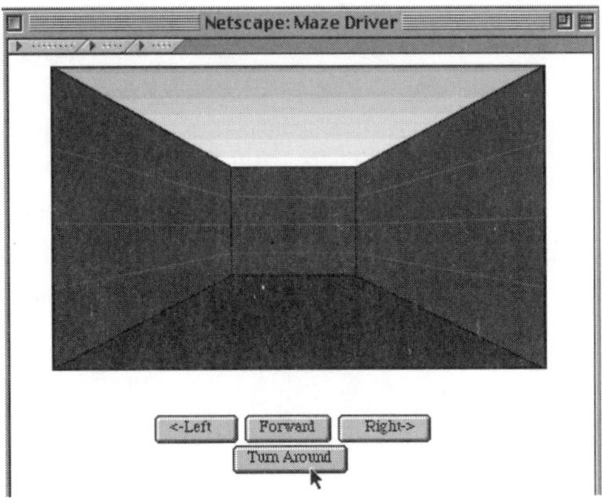

Dead End: Views can be one of several positions. If the students run into a dead end, they click the "Turn Around" option.

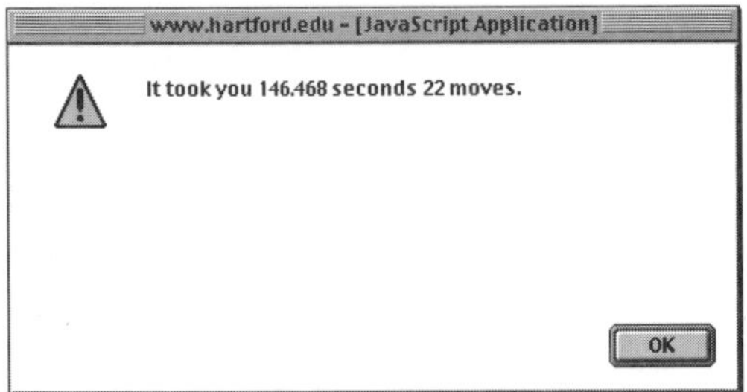

Goal Notice: When the student enters the last room, she is given a time in seconds and the number of moves she took.

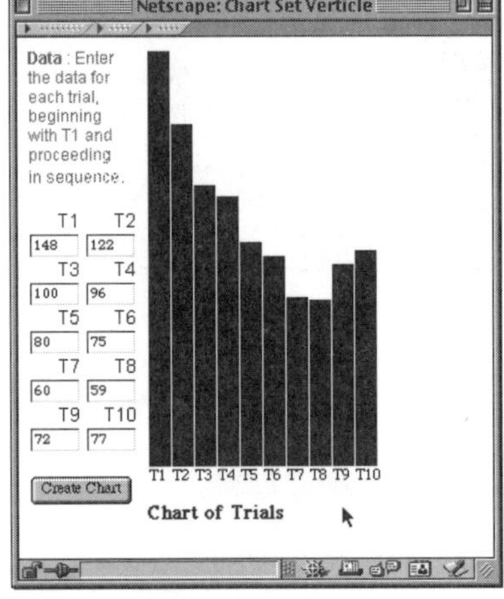

Graphic Chart: After completing the maze, the student enters her data in a chart. She can enter either the times it took or the number of moves.

TABLE 10-3 A virtual maze actively involves students in the learning process, collecting and recording data, and charting data.

the maze is reached, a pop-up message tells the student the amount of time it took as well as the number of moves. The maze is an example of active learning in which the student learns about a process by example. Explaining why a "J-curve" exists in learning requires a conceptual framework provided in class, in a book, or on other Web pages. But if a student can see that her own actions are subject to a general learning curve, she is more likely to want to understand and comprehend the underlying psychology involved. This is true for physical and biological sciences as well. The *active learning* immerses the student in a way to enhance the learning.

Students go through the virtual maze ten times or any number of times the professor decides is required. At the end of the ten trials, students are given a page where they enter their data. Having written down the times each trial took, the student now enters the data into a Web page that will graphically show the results. If their times follow the "J-curve" they can then see it appear before them. If not, they are in a position to further discuss it with their professor, compare it with other students, and generally seek more understanding of the process.

Creating this maze or another set of Web pages where data need to be continually updated requires a few tricks. This particular maze incorporated frames. The bottom frame of the frame set is a page with navigation buttons. Each button is a link to bring in a new top frame with a different view of the maze depending on which link is selected. Table 10-4 shows the two frames with the forms in the top frame visible. The frame set is designed so that the bottom frame overlaps and hides the forms in the top frame. (Using a hidden form in the top frame page is an even better idea.) The navigation buttons in the page in the bottom frame use the

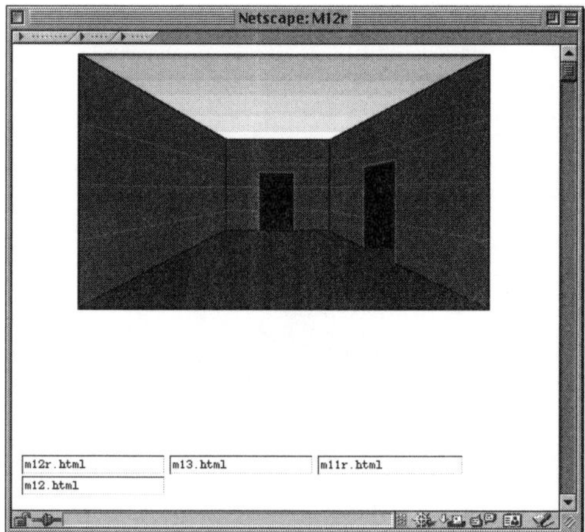

Top Frame: Besides having a graphic showing a position in the maze, the top frames have the names of the links held in forms. This data is passed to the bottom frame.

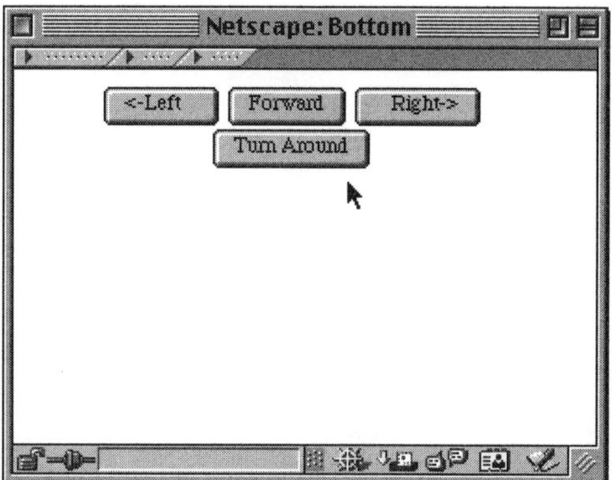

Bottom Frame: Each button on the bottom frame initiates a JavaScript function that reads the data in the forms in the top frame. The bottom frame never changes; it just calls in new top frames to change what the student sees on the screen.

TABLE 10-4 Two frames make up each page in the maze. Data are passed between the frames with forms and JavaScript.

information in the page's forms in the top frame. However, the page in the bottom frame never leaves the window. Instead it keeps track of time and the number of moves, and reads data from the top frame to use in navigation.

Chapter 13 shows how the forms and JavaScript work together, and how data from one Web page or frame can be passed to another. Here the emphasis is not the code but the possibilities and general concept of active learning. Any virtual laboratory experiment could be conducted by showing the student different conditions depending on what action he takes. By arranging the Web pages to reflect actual laboratory outcomes, the process of active learning is simply a matter of getting the student involved in and engrossed with the experiment. Using *actual data* and *actual formulas* there is no loss of reality. The tactile experience of handling plants, animals, and other physical objects with varying levels of moisture is lost, but only when the *tactile experience* is the focus of learning is that important. Furthermore, as more experiments can be accurately simulated with Web pages for research, knowing how to work with computers and experimental data comes to replace much of what was done with handling the data itself.

Simplifying the Maze and Generic Exploration in Learning

Now that there is an example of a robust active learning experiment, it is necessary to provide a much simpler way to create a virtual reality in space and time. Also, the maze is a generic example of using the Web for creating virtual reality and seeing certain basic concepts underlying what was done. First, Figure 10-2 shows a revised maze page using text links on a single page with no frame. Each link simply goes to another page with the appropriate view.

Instead of being a maze, there are many other uses of a maze-like virtual reality using Web pages in active learning. Art history students could go from room to room in a virtual museum, or political science students could be led through the various decision-making points as a bill becomes a law, visiting everything from encounters with lobbyists to committee hearings. Sociology students could tour a labeled bureaucracy to understand organizational behavior, or communication stu-

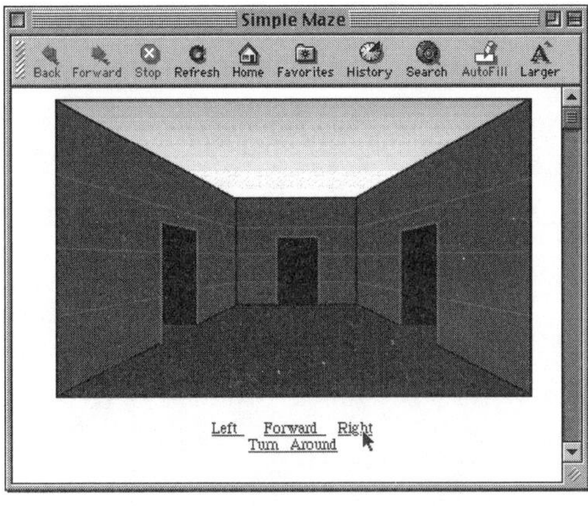

FIGURE 10-2 A maze or other virtual room can be created without using frames. Some of the data collection is lost, but it is much easier to develop for faculty.

dents could gather different materials to put together an advertising campaign. In all of these applications, students are actively involved, and they can make mistakes and receive feedback about how to understand materials in a lesson. A good book or other reading assignment can be dynamically linked to the learning experience with the Web pages to add depth and conceptual richness to the active aspect of learning.

The way in which the maze was planned can be instructive for a general plan for making virtual realities using Web pages. First, the professor needs an overall plan of the maze. The plan provides an overview of the paths the student can take, points where decisions are made, and options available to the student. It is important to emphasize that the maze is only a generic model and many other analogous virtual realities can be developed as well. When looking at the plan for the maze, try to envision other models where students can be led on an exploration. Figure 10-3 shows a part of the maze and how the Web pages were organized to create the virtual reality of running the maze.

To create a virtual reality, it was necessary to provide a number of views relative to the position in the maze, and have links to the other possible *next* positions the students could find themselves in. Beginning with a drawing of the maze, each point in the maze where a decision could be made was provided a view. It was assumed that all views would be forward looking. The views had the following logical outcomes:

- Forward, left, and right passageways
- Forward and right passageways
- Forward and left passageways
- Forward passageway
- No passageway
- Left and right passageways
- Left passageway
- Right passageway

Given the combinations of views, an artist drew the eight perspectives to be placed into HTML files. The sole remaining task was to create the individual Web pages based on the maze outline (Figure 10-3) and put in the appropriate GIF and links for each of the Web pages. Table 10-5 shows the eight GIF files that make up

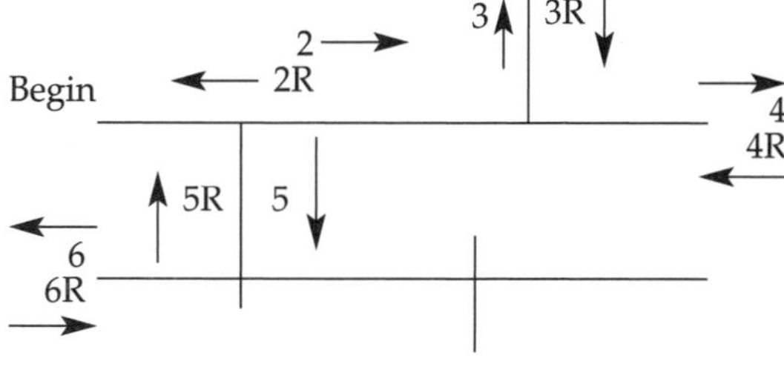

FIGURE 10-3 Partial maze with "view labels." Each label shows a position and its view and reverse (R) view as well as a directional arrow showing which direction the viewer is facing.

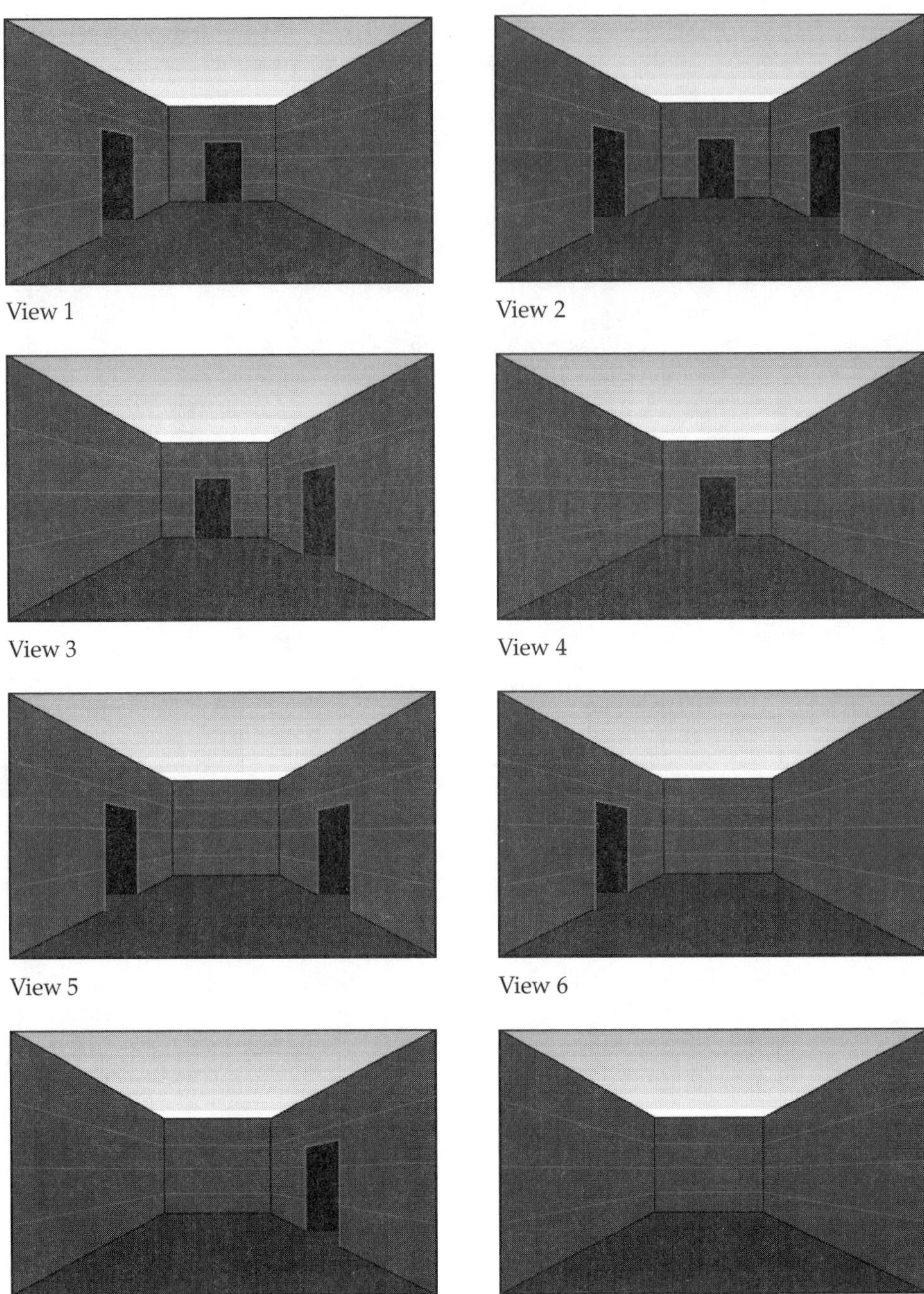

View 7 View 8

TABLE 10-5 An artist prepared eight views. From any place in the maze, one of these views would be able to describe what a student would see from that position looking forward.

the views used in the maze. Using standard image placement procedures for HTML, they are placed in Web pages.

In order to see how the rest of a maze can be created, an example would be instructive. Look at positions "3" and "3R" in Figure 10-3. In position "3," the student will only see three walls, so View 8 in Table 10-5 was used. The only "move" the student can make is to turn around. This would then put the student in "3R" view. From "3R" the student sees passageways leading to the left and right, so View 5 was used in the Web page representing "3R." Positions "3" and "3R" are shown in Table 10-6.

Once each view is established, the move to the next position needs to be determined. Using the outline of positions (Figure 10-3), the logical possibilities are established and used as link information. In the case of position 3, the only operable link is to turn around and view the position from position 3R—the reverse of view. From Position 3R are three "moves." The student can go left to position 4, go right to position 2R, or turn around to position 3 again. Therefore, the links for Web page "pos3R.html" would be:

Left = pos4.html

Right = pos2R.html

Turn Around = pos3.html

Forward = #—nothing happens.

The techniques are fairly generic. In fact, they could be used for all-text pages. The main idea is to map out the route for the student to take, what information will be given at each point, and what decisions can be made.

Many enhancements and improvements are possible for maze-like active learning designs. For example, rather than having buttons or text links, the instructor could use image mapping with hot spots right on the graphic. Each passageway could be a hot spot taking the student in through the passageway when she clicks it. Rich textual content could provide student information for decision making as she moves through the labyrinth. By learning the content, the task could be completed effectively and efficiently. In fact, virtually every other technique for learning with

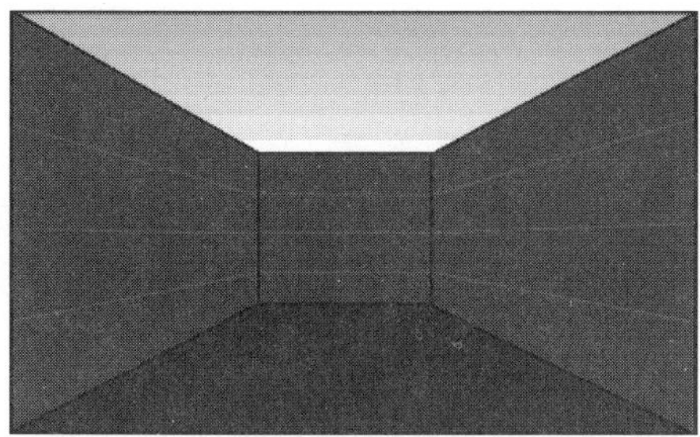

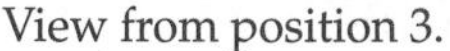

View from position 3.

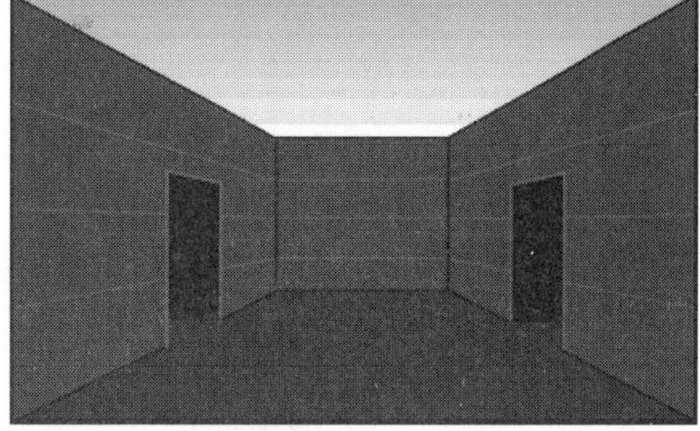

View from position 3R.

TABLE 10–6 Each position has a forward and a reverse view.

Web pages could be used in different parts of a virtual journey. What has been presented here has been only a generic concept, and expanding it can provide a much more robust, dynamic, and richer active learning experience in any virtual reality the professor wishes to create.

Interactive Link Pages

When does a link path become *interactive*? This chapter has examined *active* learning with an emphasis on active student learning—giving the student something to do. Erving Goffman (1981) points out that the *essence* of interaction is people taking turns talking. In the absence of a professor responding individually, personally, and actually, it is important to fully consider what the professor wants to communicate were she talking directly with the student. If students are provided with a number of options, instructors need to consider what a student needs to know when a given option is selected. This means that a professor needs to think through an entire lesson, as though she were there to interact in person.

At first blush, such a scheme may seem unrealistic because university students may come up with a seemingly infinite number of responses and ways of understanding and misunderstanding. However, experienced professors usually encounter a common set of misunderstandings and questions students have for a course. In turn, they prepare a general set of responses to deal with misconceptions. When students are given a set of options from which to choose in a Web page, including common misunderstandings, a follow-up link to an incorrect page provides an explanation of why the choice was incorrect. At the same time, a link to a correct page is an opportunity for elaboration and explanation as well. When the path is correct, giving students a pat on the head like a lab rat receiving a food pellet is less effective than a more subtle reward in the form of explaining why the selection was the correct one. This is what a professor might do in a class interacting with students. Sometimes students are going to guess a correct option and never learn why their action was a good one, and an interactive page with an explanation for making a correct choice provides a much more substantive learning experience. Figure 10-4 shows how this sequence of links and explanations works:

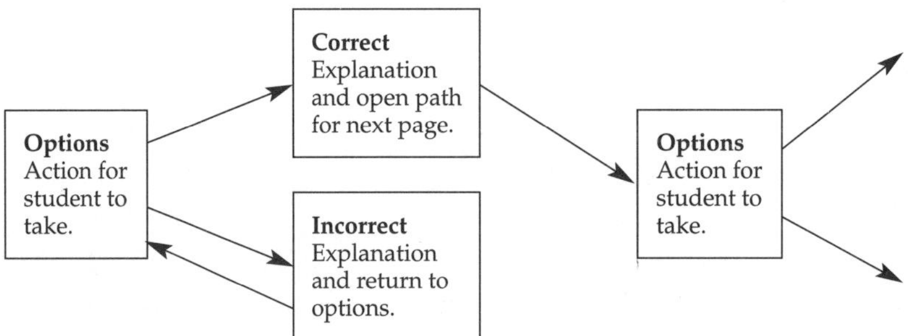

FIGURE 10-4 Interactive Web pages represent what would happen in an interactive classroom.

The entire process in this kind of interaction is relatively simple as far as making Web pages is concerned. All that is required are links and pages with text and graphics. Video and audio could be added as well, but even these enhancements change nothing conceptually with the model. The possibilities in making more elaborate and sophisticated interactive pages with these concepts are infinite. However, there are only so much time and consideration that can be given in working out the interactive possibilities. But that is not the point. The point is that students being actively involved in an interactive framework, no matter how simple and constrained, enhances learning over Web sites that do not consider the interactive possibilities. Chapter 11 examines the simple solution of creating interactive Web pages using embedded email. Although email certainly expands the possibilities of what students may ask or give their professors, it lacks the immediacy of interactive Web sites where the response is immediate. In Chapter 1, immediate feedback was noted as an effective practice for learning, and interactive Web pages do a good job of that. However, appropriate and individualized feedback is also important, and although interactive sites as modeled in Figure 10-4 are effective, the less immediate interaction using email plays another role with interactive Web pages.

Active Learning and Frames

In Chapter 9, frames provided a means to help students navigate through coursework without getting lost or sidetracked. Frames also can be used in active learning so that a student can select options within a single window, helping him keep a sense of unity within a lesson. This section examines using active learning with frame sets.

A fundamental form of active learning used in the classroom has been questions and answers. Used as a Socratic method, the question-answer sequence draws in students to actively participate in the learning process. Entire pages disappearing after the student has made a choice to answer a question may not best serve all lessons. With frames one window can be used for questions, and another for answers and explanations. Table 10-7 shows a simple example of how this might be used.

Everything is together in the window. The lesson tells about a unit of measurement, the question asks about the lesson, and there are an illustration and a statement in the correct answer. Incorrect responses keep the same window and inform the student about the width of the other objects. No matter what the student selects, he will learn something.

There is far more that can be done with frames and active learning. Chapter 12 includes a discussion of how to dynamically change a frame's content using JavaScript integrated into HTML. This provides instructors with a greater range of flexibility of what can be included in a lesson and the complexity of what actions a student can take and receive feedback. Frames and links provide an open model for creating active learning, and if planned carefully, many interesting and robust

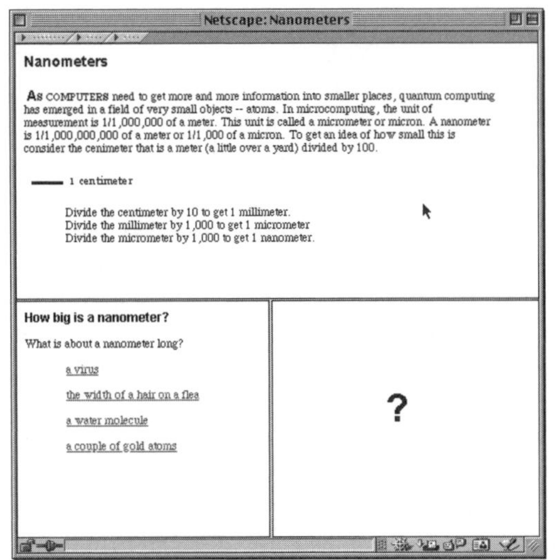

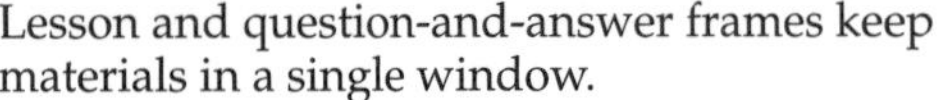
Lesson and question-and-answer frames keep materials in a single window.

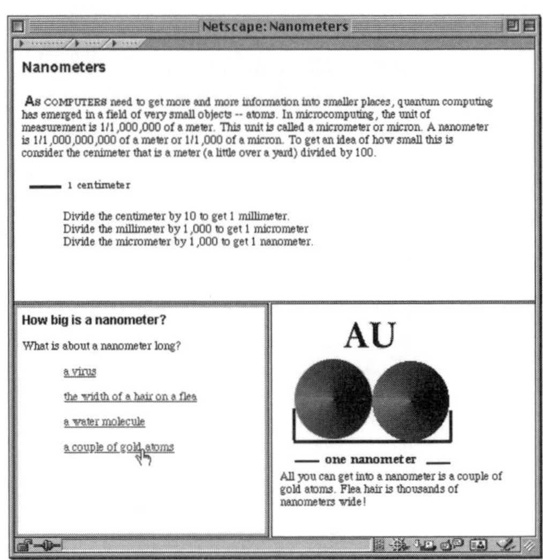

Answer frame can provide additional content with correct or incorrect answer.

TABLE 10-7 Keeping the content of the lesson in the same window with many different outcomes and further elaboration of a lesson enhances active learning with frames. The question-answer format is used to engage the student and provide additional content.

Web sites are possible. Knowing what can be done with Web pages is simply the underlying software technology. The real challenge is to envision an active learning scenario for students to follow. Once that is done, the technical part is relatively simple.

Summary and Review

It is more important to conceive of a way to engage students in learning than it is to do just about anything else in a learning-centered model of education. Engrossment with and involvement in learning can be prompted by anything from a personal motivation to succeed and learn to a structure that actively includes the student in the process. Moreover, the student must take responsibility for her learning—not the instructor. This model reverses the polarity of teaching being an active process and learning a passive one. Now, learning is active, and teaching is relatively passive. However, *passivity* is more a matter of planning and structuring than it is a retreat. A professor who writes a textbook or other work of scholarship is *passive* in this sense. When she writes a book for students to read and study, the learning is wholly dependent on the student doing the reading and spending the time to learn the content. In other words the book is a passive instrument, and the active agent must be the student.

Active learning using Web pages follows the same set of assumptions. A student is required to do something that actively involves himself in the process. The instructor can design actions for students to take beyond reading or taking notes. This does not reduce the amount of content introduced, but rather it involves and engrosses the student in the content by giving him something to do with it to help in comprehension and understanding. The more complex the materials, the more it is important to involve the student. This is because the more difficult content in a lesson requires more focus and attention to grasp.

As shown with sample Web pages, active learning can be anything from simple virtual experiences and feedback to relatively complex conceptual problems and determining solutions. Leading students step by step through materials and then giving them an opportunity to actively work with the materials keep attention and focus. The simple expedient of using links to provide paths and feedback works to create an activity that requires the student to consider alternatives and take an action. Because learning, understanding, and applying the lesson's content are the overriding goals of the educational process, getting students involved by active inclusion is part of the method. Web pages and hypertext options can easily be an integral part of that method.

Glossary of Terms

Active learning A set of learning activities where a student makes a choice, encounters feedback, makes adjustments, and takes another action ultimately leading to a goal. The learning process involves the student in taking an action by making decisions.

Dominate involvement The normatively expected attention in a given situation. What one is supposed to attend to on an occasion.

Experiential learning Some kind of experience engineered so that a student will learn a given point, concept, or process by engagement in the experience. It is a form of active learning.

Involvement Human engrossment in events. The amount of attention given to situations, occasions, and points of focus.

Subordinate involvement What one can be involved in while the dominant involvement is not commanding attention. Talking with colleagues prior to a lecture is a subordinate involvement.

References

Goffman, Erving. *Encounters* (Indianapolis, IN: Bobbs-Merrill, 1961).

Goffman, Erving. *Behavior in Public Places* (Glencoe, IL: The Free Press, 1963).

Goffman, Erving. *Forms of Talk* (Philadelphia: University of Pennsylvania Press, 1981).

Chapter 11

Communicating on the Web: Email and Wired Discussions

Chapter 10 noted that feedback to students in the form of pre-established comments on Web pages was not too flexible. A lot of questions students need answered cannot be answered if the questions are not anticipated ahead of time. Additionally, students will sometimes misunderstand a topic to the extent that the questions they want to ask are wholly irrelevant and indicate that the student is on the wrong track. In both cases, an instructor needs to help the students individually or as a whole—exactly as he would do in a classroom. If a student has either a complex assignment to complete or one that requires a good deal of writing, there is no simple and automatic way to provide feedback. Rather, the instructor needs to evaluate what the student has prepared, make comments, and communicate those comments to the student.

Because one of the key good practices in a learning-centered model of education is good faculty-student communication, the ability to communicate with students is essential to using Web pages effectively. Email has the capacity to provide one aspect of this communication, but online discussions in the form of both threaded discussions and chat (synchronous discussion) are other Web tools to consider as well. All of these need to be integrated into the course material for them to be most effective. This chapter examines both the issues involved in online communication and the mechanics of how to get it done.

Face-to-Face and Internet-Mediated Interaction

George Herbert Mead (1967), in a critique of behaviorism, noted that people do not respond to a stimulus directly, but rather interaction is *self-mediated*. By that he meant that people interacting with one another filter and interpret talk and action through a *self*. The self is the sum total of one's experience, family, culture, language, and society. The interaction is through symbols and the shared meanings these symbols have between those interacting.

Face-to-face interaction is rich in many symbols from the inflection of a phrase to a gesture, not to mention the words in the talk. The context of the interaction and the normative structure of the situation all add to what is meant, understood, assumed—in a word, *communicated*. Much of the concern faculty have about Internet-mediated interaction is that the whole host of meanings available in face-to-face interaction will be lost. That is true. It will be lost. Therefore, it is necessary to consider how the written word in interaction without visible gestures is constructed and used.

In examining email, discussion forums, and chat rooms, there is a wide range of what is communicated. Certain keyboard gesture replacements such as a symbolic happy face [:-)] or a wink [;-)] are in common use. Likewise gesture codes, such as "lol" for "laughing out loud," seem to have crept permanently into the lexicon of electronic communication. These arrays of keyboard gestures and codes give a general idea of the sender's state of mind, but there is little subtlety or range in these replacement gestures.

A more distressing problem (and perhaps opportunity) in much of the electronic communication among students is the absence of good grammar, spelling, and punctuation. Online talk has much of the fragmented character of actual talk. In the field of conversation analysis, transcribed talk from recorded verbal interaction is full of bits, pieces, and fragments rather than full sentences with clear beginnings and ends. Also, there are a lot of "ahh," "uhm," and "ooh" grunts along with a distressing number of "you knows."

The opportunity in this state of affairs is to require students to communicate in clear and correct expository English. Professors can communicate warmth, concern, dismay, elation, and all the other prodding and props used to move students to a state of understanding using the correct words and sentence structures. Students should be able to do the same. The long history of elegant letter writing as a form of communication has shown people's ability to express thoughts and emotions. Records of these letters, supplanted first by the telephone and more recently by email, showed a remarkable ability to get across most of the expressions of face-to-face interaction—sometimes better because they were unconstrained by immediate reaction or interruption. Hence, online communication need be no less personal or caring than in either a classroom or an office visit, and students learn to use English, Spanish, French, Japanese, or Russian more effectively. Furthermore, email communication represents a good opportunity to use online communication to teach English across the curriculum.

In my own experiences as a professor at institutions where large classes were a norm—especially for the survey courses—there was little communication on an individual basis in or out of the classroom. A well-planned lecture before classes of 100, 200, and more than 300 students provided little opportunity for student-professor give-and-take except on the most superficial basis. Besides, many students were inhibited by the large gathering to say anything or even visit their professor during office hours. However, as noted earlier in this book, when students began communicating by email, both the amount and quality of the communication increased. Not only were students very willing to commit to writing the questions and concerns they had in class, once an email link was made with their professor, they were more willing to meet face to face.

Embedding Email in Web Pages

One of the simplest devices in creating Web pages is embedding email into a page. The email can be to the instructor, other students, or groups. In fact, the email link can go to anyone with an email address, including someone on the other side of the planet. This section examines how to set up individual and group links.

Individual Email Links

Fortunately the major browsers, Netscape Navigator and Internet Explorer, have built-in email. Also, they both use the same HTML code for creating an automatic call to the browser's email. The code is just like a link to another page except the "link" is preceded by the keyword "MAILTO:" inside the "A HREF" tag. For example, the following line of HTML shows how a professor named Dr. Patricia Kelenbarker would embed an email link in a Web page:

```
<a href="mailto:kelenbarker@stateu.edu">Email Dr.
Kelenbarker </a>
```

The Web page itself would simply show Email Dr. Kelenbarker. Using a Web editor such as *Composer*, the email address can be added by entering "mailto:kelenbarker@stateu.edu" where the information for URLs is generally placed. When a student clicks the email, the browser's email pops up with the email address all set, and all the student needs to do is to supply the topic and type in the text.

In Chapter 6, it was noted that email links should be placed in the syllabus near the top so students can have ready access to instructors and other students. These links need to be where they are easily accessed, and so the top of the syllabus is a good place. However, email links should be placed throughout lessons as well. Two key places are:

- Exercises to be sent by email to the professor
- Points where students may have trouble with difficult concepts

When a professor has an exercise, she might simply explain materials and require the students to respond by email. For example, in an English literature class, students may be asked to interpret a poem using the *Oxford English Dictionary*, and

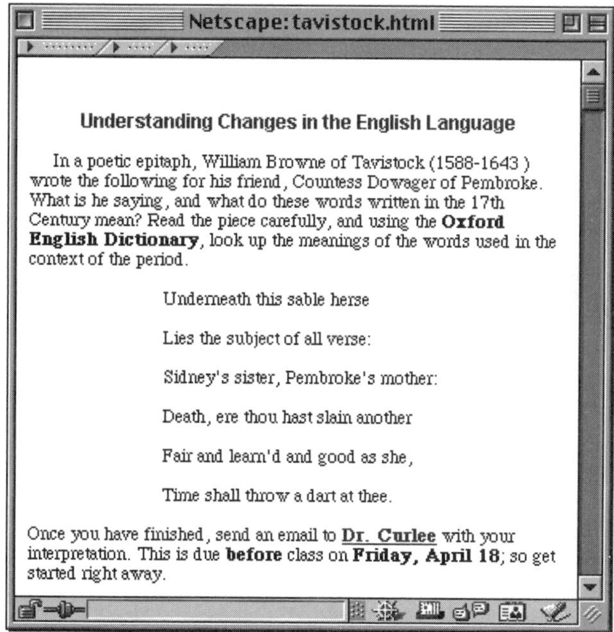

FIGURE 11-1 Email links *within* a lesson provide simple ways for professors to receive assignments from students.

send the results to the professor. This allows the professor to provide feedback to the student and check on his progress in the course. Figure 11-1 shows how such a page may look. It is simple, but shows how within a lesson, an email link makes a direct connection with the student.

Additionally, having an email link with materials that a student may have problems comprehending establishes both a connection to get help and a tacit understanding that the material may give the student a problem. For example, Figure 11-2 shows a page where a student may want to contact his professor for more information. Note that the page has a reference to a book chapter as well, and there is an opportunity to have links to other resources, but the example page was kept intentionally simple to emphasize the role of the email link.

Having redundant email links in a lesson or course serves as a constant reminder to the student that she can connect with help if need be. A single embedded email in the syllabus is usually not enough. Virtually every lesson probably needs one or more to keep good faculty-student connections while the student is trying to learn materials. This does not mean that the student is not responsible for using all resources at hand to learn the content, and an email from a professor may indeed remind the student of that. Rather, where active learning assignments and extra help are required, an embedded email link to the instructor is another link to the process of learning.

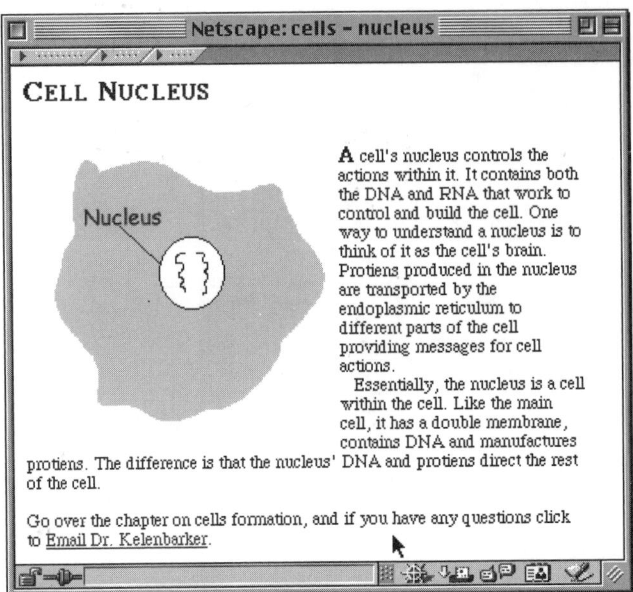

FIGURE 11-2 An embedded email link in a Web page provides an immediate connection with the professor.

Cooperative Learning and Group Email

Americans as a culture tend to put more emphasis on the individual than on groups. Individual initiative and hard work are at the core of the American psyche. However, Americans are also great joiners of organizations and great believers in teams and teamwork. In education, though, there seems to have been too much emphasis on individualized success, competition, and ingrained intelligence. As a result, many professors still believe in grading on an artificial curve. There is an almost puritanical belief that God (or Someone) endowed each student with only so much brainpower, and He did this on a bell-shaped curve for the convenience of statisticians. If the professor's students are graded on the curve, the professor guarantees he is doing God's will and betters his odds against going straight to hell for all the articles he failed to publish when he shuffles off this mortal coil for the final post-tenure review.

An alternative view is that students would rather spend more time with one another than in isolated contemplation and study. If they are encouraged to help one another and are not penalized for doing so, they will spend more of their time together studying rather than merely socializing. The question simply becomes, "How can students be encouraged to cooperate in study?"

Cooperative assignments are ones that can be completed most efficiently and effectively if students work together. Breaking up a whole assignment into component parts and parceling those parts out to different students in a group or team give the students something to do cooperatively with others, and it gives students a reason to get together. Besides learning how to complete the assignment, students learn something about cooperative efforts—a highly valued skill on the job market. For example, a research project in behavioral or social science may include the following parts:

- Literature review
- Theoretical framework(s) selection
- Methodology selection
- Data resources location
- Data collection
- Data analysis
- Interpretation and presentation of research

Not only can the students who are given the assignment learn about the particular task they are given, they can be responsible for explaining it to the rest of their team and ultimately the rest of the class and their instructor. Thus, they learn their own part and how it fits in with the overall project from direct experience and from other students. The more interesting, creative, and thought-provoking the assignment, the more enthusiasm and work the students will put into it. *That is the key.* No matter how inherently interesting a subject matter, to really understand course material takes time and effort on the student's part. It does not matter whether that time is spent with other students or alone—the time must be taken.

One of the more daunting problems found in cooperative learning and assignments requiring cooperation was resistance by students to accepting a part of their grade based on a cooperative project. They liked the idea that there would be less for them to do by taking a project apart, and they liked the concept of working together with other students. However, they believed that they should not be penalized by a lower grade if some members of their team slacked off in the group effort. Because students are less forgiving than their professors when it comes to understanding why a student's performance is less than sterling, certain adjustments are usually necessary to reward both individual and group efforts. However, emergent norms regarding getting team members to hold up their end of a cooperative effort did motivate certain lackadaisical students to put more effort into their work.

In order to engender a spirit of group effort and team building, students were immediately put together in groups. Each group was provided a name and a team email. The team email allowed students to make a single click on a Web page link to address an email to the entire team. On some assignments, the individual team members were given part of an assignment, and they had to communicate with one another to understand the entire assignment. Using their team email, it was simple to reach each other quickly. Figure 11-3 shows a typical team page.

Creating group email links is fairly simple. The technique is essentially the same as for making individual email links using the MAILTO: statements within a link tag. All that needs to be done is to add additional email addresses separated by a comma. For example, the code for the TCP Team in Figure 11-3 might look like the following:

```
<a href="mailto:christopher@stateu.edu, jaime@usa.net,
mi@aol.com, ryan@stateu.edu"><\a>
```

Note that different ISPs (Internet service providers) are used. In addition to the fictional "stateu.edu" server, commercial ones such as AOL and USA are in the same email link. Figure 11-4 shows how the email address window appears in Netscape Communicator when the student clicks the team link. In addition to team links, each student's individual email address could be included to enhance individual contact with class members.

Besides having group and individual email links in a centralized location such as the online syllabus, links from lessons can also be connected to group and individual student emails. Rather than having to grapple with an entire class's email addresses, it is far easier to have a link to a page with all of the email addresses

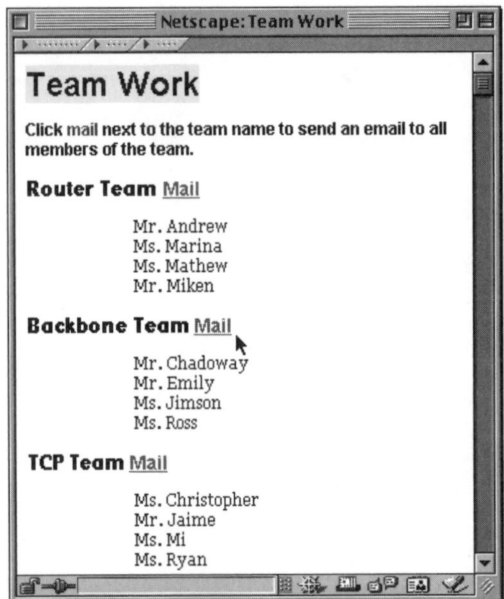

FIGURE 11-3 Team email encourages cooperative learning by making it very simple for students to contact one another.

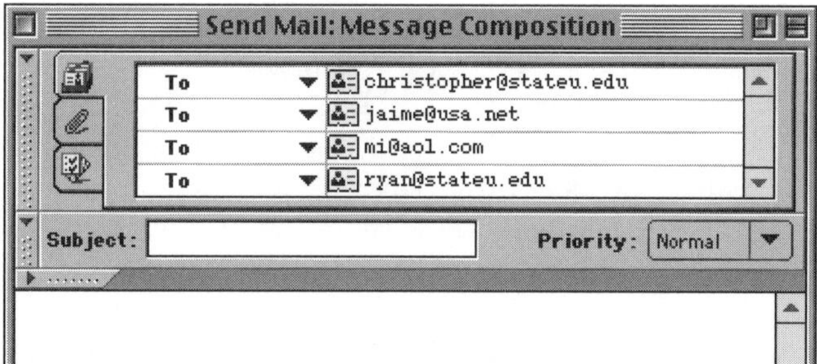

FIGURE 11-4 When a group link is selected, all of the individual email addresses appear ready for email.

already set up as shown in Figure 11-3. The student email pages are simply Web pages, and whether connected to the syllabus Web page or a lesson Web page does not make any difference except where the page will appear. If a frame set is used in a syllabus, but not in a lesson, the student email page will replace the current page. It is better to keep the lesson page on the screen and bring up the email page as a separate page. In that way, the students can use the email page in relationship to the lesson. After they use the email page and send emails to their group or an individual student, they can close the email page and still have the lesson in front of them. Figure 11-5 illustrates this use.

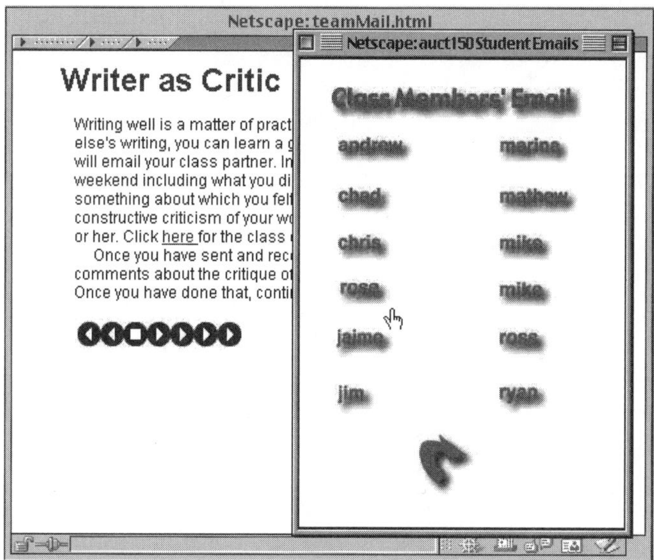

FIGURE 11-5 The Web page with class members' individual emails is loaded as part of an assignment in the middle of a lesson. After the student completes the email, she continues with the lesson.

Keeping students connected to one another as well as to their instructor is an important part of embedding emails in lessons. Cooperative learning both enhances the learning milieu of the class and helps the student learn the material. The extent to which cooperation is built into a lesson and is easily incorporated by the student helps ensure that cooperative learning will occur.

When making a link to a page with the intention of keeping the current page on the screen, it is necessary to remember the target name to use. Where the intention is to bring up a page with email addresses while keeping the current page in place, use the "blank" target. For example, the following tag line brings up a file named "stumail.html" while keeping the current page in place:

```
<a href = "stumail.html" target="blank"><\a>
```

The only problem is that the linked page is the same size as the page that called it. Chapter 12 provides instructions on how to control the size of the window of a page that is opened with a JavaScript function. However, in the meantime, it is useful to open a second window using the "blank" target designation.

Some Considerations for Using Web Email at University Computer Labs

In practice, there can sometimes be problems with Web email, but they tend to be administrative rather than technical. University computer labs may restrict email access in the labs because of the difficulty in identifying the user. This can usually be overcome by having students use their university accounts along with their passwords. However, to use either the built-in email of either Microsoft Internet Explorer or Netscape Communicator, students must reconfigure the browser to their email identification before using it. Sometimes students do not know how to do this, and so they need to be shown how if students as a primary source of Internet access regularly use a lab at the college. Otherwise, students will quickly become frustrated and spend more time berating the browser than learning anything new.

If there is a lab assistant available to help this is very valuable and saves time. However, if there are persistent problems in students having access to email from the computer lab, it is important to have a talk with the director of computer services. Sometimes there are good reasons that email from labs is restricted, and if the instructor knows about them, she can better plan. For example, in computer labs where classified materials are being developed for the government, there may be severe restrictions on who can use email and for what purposes. This happened after the Chinese were accused of stealing sensitive materials on atomic weapons at Los Alamos Labs. In a different case at one university, a student was able to obtain another student's email password. As a joke he used it to log on in a university computer lab and send a threatening email to the President of the United

States. Shortly thereafter the FBI became involved and located and arrested the student who pulled the prank. Needless to say, incidents of this type lead to very real problems and must be addressed. However, some technology administrators are unrealistic about the degree of security required and can effectively prevent many learning activities in the name of security. A compromise between reasonable security and learning requires good communication between university information technology services and the faculty. Otherwise, neither will be able to reasonably get their job done.

Online Discussions

Technologically, the Internet has two basic kinds of online group interaction. Asynchronous discussion, or just "discussion," refers to a system where messages are left, then read, and replies made without temporal coordination. Synchronous discussion, more commonly referred to as "chat," occurs when two or more people are sending and receiving messages at the same time. Other ways students and professors communicate over the Web, such as email and email through a listserv, have some of the characteristics of both online discussions and chats. However, many key features of online Web discussions and chats are unique and very useful for online learning, and the focus here is on how to set up and use these Web-connected tools in teaching and learning.

Asynchronous discussions are the most flexible because they do not require scheduling, and whenever students want, they can join in a discussion. Such discussions were found to be very helpful for extending the classroom discussion beyond the classroom and for incorporating discussions in distance learning courses where there are no face-to-face meetings. Most of the software for asynchronous discussions is set up for "threaded discussions." That means the students can reply to the topic the professor puts up or to another topic. The "thread" that is followed refers to the key item or topic to which a reply was made. A threaded discussion has the following structure:

Thread 1 Key topic

Thread 1 Reply to key topic

- **Thread 2** Reply to reply (Subtopic 1)
  - **Thread 3** Reply to subtopic (Subtopic 2)

Thread 1 Reply to key topic

One ideal learning strategy is for the professor to set up the key topic, usually in the form of a question, and then invite students to make comments to both the key topic and the comments of other students. The involvement in the discussion not only brings in new ideas and perspectives while engrossing the students in the topic of study, it also generates new information as the students and professor add data and references to the discussion. Ideally the discussion brings in materials from the assigned readings, supplementary reading, class lectures, personal experiences, and other sources of information gathered by students. However, most faculty report that although many students are less shy to respond to online discussions, they generally do not involve themselves in online discussions except with inducement—extra class credit or part of a graded assignment.

Also, some students bully and berate other students online. The bully is often a student who studies the most, is most interested in the course materials, and truly wants a lively discussion about a given topic. The irony is that it has the opposite effect. Students avoided the online discussion altogether when intellectual bullies appeared and complained to the professor that they were afraid to make comments lest the class bully make verbal attacks against them. This was not too difficult to control by establishing a set of norms ahead of time—an online discussion etiquette. Students were told to respect the views of others, keep on the topic, and make their arguments based on objective facts and not prejudice, biases, and rudeness. Ground rules for discussions are key to their success, and while students can have lively disagreements, it can be done without personal attacks and rancor.

There are many different types of software used for asynchronous discussions. Both of the major browsers have built-in discussion or newsgroup modules that can be employed for class. Asynchronous discussion groups have to be set up on a server, and faculty using them need to get in touch with their technical support department to have the discussion software installed. Besides the free newsgroup software on the browsers that can be a little awkward for both faculty and students, several commercial packages are available and easy to set up and use.

One of the best places to try out sophisticated but simple-to-use asynchronous discussion boards is at http://www.nicenet.org/. NiceNet's Internet Classroom Assistant provides free access for setting up a class for online threaded conferencing. NiceNet is a nonprofit organization, and it has been the starting point for many faculty members who want to try out online discussions prior to an economic commitment. About the only problem experienced with NiceNet is the slow speed of the system due to heavy use.

Another excellent source of both information and experience with asynchronous discussion groups is the Asynchronous Learning Network (ALN). Sponsored by the Sloan Foundation, ALN not only is an excellent source of information, it is possible to see the flow of a threaded discussion. Using *Allaire Forums* software hosted at Vanderbilt University, many different topics relate to setting up and using asynchronous discussion in the classroom. A visit to http://www.aln.org and participation in one of their discussions will reap a wealth of information.

For purposes of illustration this book uses *WebBoard*. It was found to be simple for both students and professors, and the computer network administrators found that once a class was set up, it required almost no monitoring. The first connection with *WebBoard* is to link it to the syllabus. Because *WebBoard* is set up on a

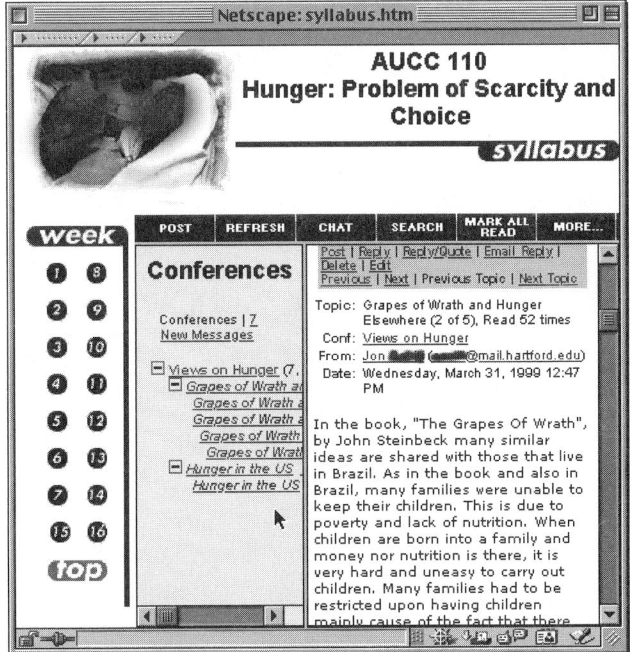

FIGURE 11-6 Links to discussions can be placed right in the syllabus with a simple link. Also, links to discussion groups can be placed in individual lessons to direct students' attention to certain collaborative elements of the lesson.

server with a unique URL, it only requires that the link be established. Figure 11-6 shows how the link was established on the syllabus and the view of the *WebBoard* within the syllabus frames. This was a case where the frames that make up *WebBoard* were within the frames of the syllabus. However, it worked fine because the windows for typing in discussion comments fit within the double frame set easily.

The threaded discussion is in the Conferences column of Figure 11-6. A *conference* is simply a topic to be discussed. Each indent is a thread as students respond to one another or to the primary topic. Getting students involved in these online discussions can help them learn not only the basics of the course material but also how to deal collaboratively with other students to understand the topic.

To initiate a discussion, it is important to spell out exactly what students need to think about and discuss. Sometimes a very general "What do you think about . . . ?" discussion topic can be used to find an opinion or perception, but more often it is important to have a clear focus initially. The threads of the discussion may go in many different directions in the back and forth of the forum, but unless the instructor is willing to let the discussion wander far afield, it is

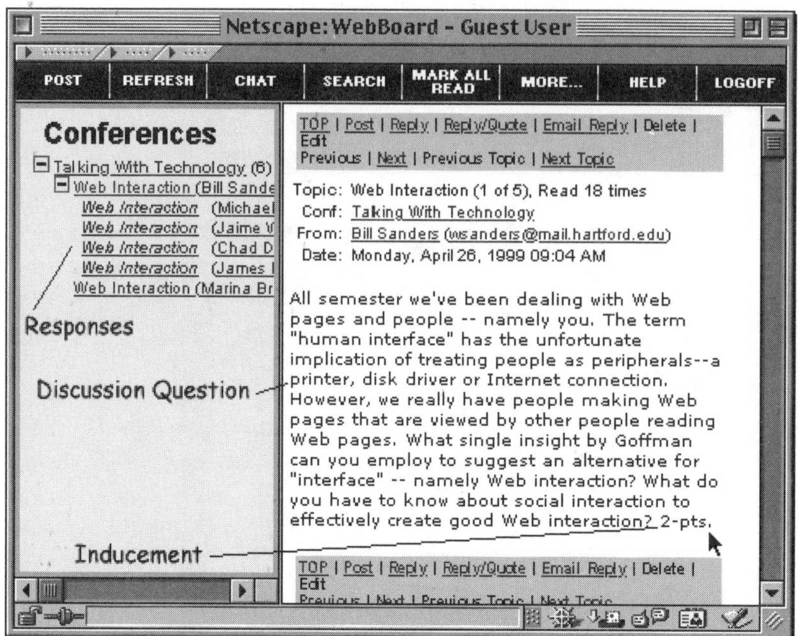

FIGURE 11-7 The discussion question in this example directs students' attention to materials they may have to spend some time working on prior to a response.

important to clarify what the students need to think about and include in their comments. Unlike during a live classroom discussion, students can pull out their books and other resources and craft a far more informed and thoughtful response. Figure 11-7 shows an example of how a discussion question is set up.

The discussion question includes a reference to a student reading providing the student with a focus and place to look up material for formulating a response. Also an inducement (2 points of extra credit) is used to prompt the students to take advantage of the forum. After an initial interest in online discussions because of their uniqueness, students often ignore them unless there is a reward structure. In some respects this reward system makes sense in that traditional sources of grades, such as examinations and papers, can be very isolated, and rewarding participation in a collaborative effort to learn is in line with good practices in learning. In the same way that students are induced to study by the reward of passing an exam or receiving a good grade on a paper, they can be induced to participate in an online discussion by points that count toward a grade. All instances of inducement contribute to the goal of fostering the learning process. So although some may feel uneasy about giving points for discussion participation, if the discussion is set up right, it can reflect learning and help students to learn.

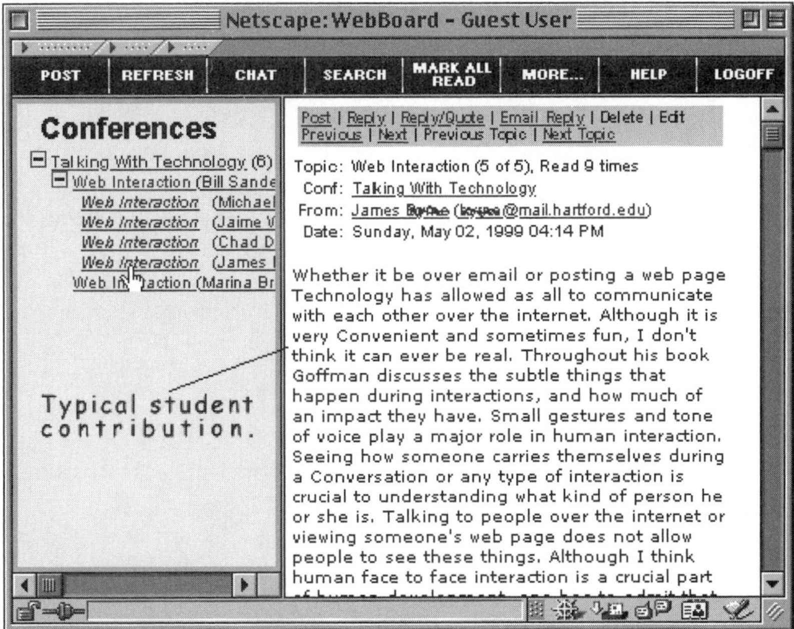

FIGURE 11-8 Students responded directly to a discussion topic or to the message itself.

Figure 11-8 shows a typical student response. Initially, students did not use punctuation in their online messages. However, after clear instructions to the effect that the online world of written communication followed the same grammatical rules as the paper world, student responses were no longer all lowercase or uppercase words lacking all punctuation. Even though most had more mistakes in their email discussion responses than in their papers, there were far fewer than initially.

An important feature of discussion software is "Email Reply" (see Figure 11-8). If a student comment is particularly off the topic or incorrect, the professor can click "Email Reply" and send comments directly to the student. These privately communicated messages can correct and redirect the student while not discouraging her from further participation in the discussion. By selecting "Reply" all comments are available to the rest of the class, and in some cases a student may be too embarrassed to post anything further if there is a public rebuke. Also, students can privately reply to one another for a comment using Email Reply and not be accused of "talking in class." This is very important, for what may be perceived as an unpopular thought may be privately held by many other students who wish not to air their views to the forum. As long as there is relevance to the class topic, all of these ways of communicating can be a source of enhanced learning.

Web Chats

Synchronous discussion (chat) over the Internet is widely used outside of the classroom, and many students may be familiar with it. Most use of online chat appears to be purely for *sociability* in the sense used by Georg Simmel (1950). The online sociability serves the primary purpose of being in touch with other human beings. As such, it is loosely structured and full of gesture replacements noted elsewhere in this chapter (for example, "lol"). Because chat occurs in real time and is "live," there is less time for reflection and study. However, like discussions in classrooms where students can voice their opinions and express their feelings, online chat can be very useful in class.

Online chats can be kicked off with a topical question from current class materials or events in the world. The point of the chat topic is to involve students in the discussion. Figure 11-9 shows the outline of a "chat room." The concept of a virtual room is widely used in chat, and you will note one of the lines announced the "entry" of a participant into the room. This feature is nice for the professor to see who's there. Sometimes professors allow students to use aliases so that a student can express himself fully without fear of reprisal or embarrassment. Reports of anonymous chats often cite irrelevant and irreverent remarks by students, and chat should be carefully planned and implemented before using it with hopes of

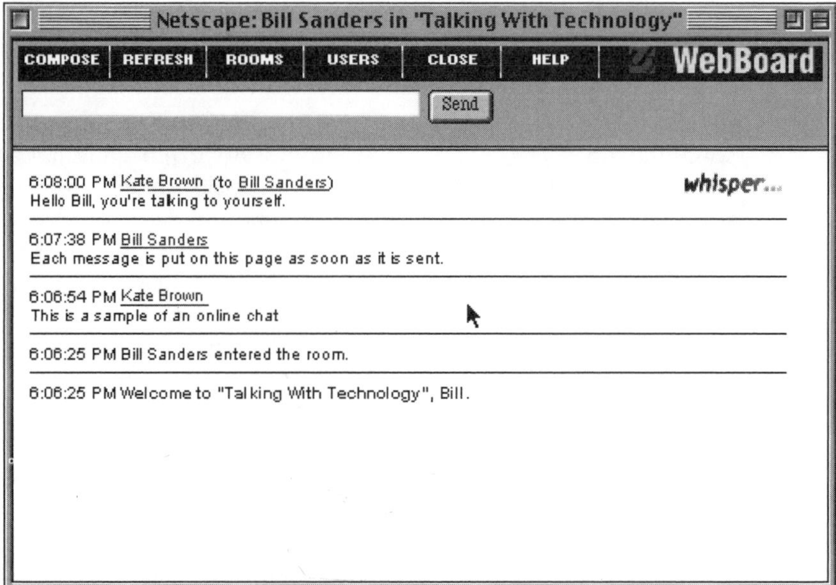

FIGURE 11-9 Online chat occurs in real time. On *WebBoard*, the time of the comment and entry is publicly logged.

helping students learn. One possible effective use would be to give students roles to play relative to the topic of study. The point would be to help engross students more into the topic at hand and help them better understand the characters they play. Using this technique for history and literature, for example, may prove to provide both involvement and anonymity for students.

Most chat software is fairly simple to use. Students and instructors enter their comments and click the "Send" button. In Figure 11-9, the comment window to the left of the "Send" button provides space for a message to be crafted. Usually a single chat comment is limited to about 250 characters or less. This limits the amount of thought and reflection that can be put into a chat comment, but it also keeps a single long-winded message from being posted.

Another interesting feature of chat software is "whisper." A whisper message sends the comments to a selected member or group in the chat room. For collaborative team interaction, simulation of negotiation and other discussions where a subset needs to communicate without the rest of the group knowing about it, this feature is very useful. It is something like an Email Reply in asynchronous discussions. Chat has many possibilities. For those teaching distance learning courses, it is a key method to foster the equivalent of a classroom discussion. For large classes where students feel estranged, small chat groups can be established online when getting small classrooms for discussions is impossible or where student scheduling is problematic.

Internet Videoconferencing

Internet videoconferencing is essentially an online chat with video. As bandwidth increases, this technology is becoming increasingly popular. Cornell University developed videoconferencing software called *CU-SeeMe*. This software was licensed to White Pine Software (http://www.wpine.com), which distributes it commercially. Combined with inexpensive video cameras that plug into USB (universal serial bus), video cards, and serial ports, there has been a great deal of this technology.

Some educational institutions have used Internet videoconferencing as well for courses, but there are many hurdles to overcome in bandwidth. With low traffic on the Internet, students connected to a T1 line or other fast connection can get very good interactive video. If they use a modem or there is heavy Internet traffic, the quality drops off very quickly. The quality of the inexpensive cameras also is relatively low, but like most other hardware in high technology, its quality is increasing rapidly. The big advantage of videoconferencing on the Internet is that it is possible to show or demonstrate a process, concept, or structure visually. For example, with one video in a chemistry lab, videoconferencing could be used to show and discuss chemical compounds. It lets students see one another's and the professor's face, and it is a clear gauge of student involvement in the discussion. Besides distance education, it is a good way to bring in people from all over the world.

Summary and Review

This chapter has been about student-professor interaction. Internet-mediated student-professor communication is new, but written communication between people is not. Rather than shutting off face-to-face interaction, the Web and Internet can be used to extend and even create interaction networks and avenues. With email embedded in Web lessons, students can contact their instructors while they are attempting to understand a problem and not wait until the next day or week when they can have a phone or face-to-face encounter. Because student-professor contact and communication are so important to the process of learning, all means possible should be employed.

Besides using Web-based email to enhance communication between students and faculty, it can be used to ease and enhance the process of communications between students. By designing courses so that students are encouraged to cooperate in the learning process, students will spend more time and learn more effectively than if they are not. Both enhanced individual contact and team contact can be implemented and assisted with Web-embedded email.

Finally, the many faces of Internet and Web discussion were examined. By linking online discussion and chat software directly to a syllabus or lesson, it is simple to establish online discussions as part of the class. The Web serves a further mechanism in that it provides a way for students to collaborate outside of the classroom. For the urban university made up largely of commuter students, this has a decided advantage over the limited time students may get to spend together on campus. Additionally, it can be used in scheduling and making contact for face-to-face student encounters as well. The video versions of online conferencing provide the added capabilities of sight and sound. The goal is not to incorporate the latest computer technology gadgets. Rather by starting with clear learning practices and the goal of creating an environment where students can discuss and communicate to help them understand what they need to learn, the technology simply becomes a tool to use effectively rather than a currently fashionable trend.

Glossary of Terms

Asynchronous discussion A messaging system where a discussion topic is placed online and others can respond to a series of messages without having to synchronize their communication in time. The form of computer-mediated discussion is usually referenced as "online discussions."

Chat See Synchronous discussion.

Online discussion See Asynchronous discussion.

Synchronous discussion When two or more people synchronize their activities so that they can discuss a topic in real time over the Internet. Special chat software is used so that several can participate simultaneously.

Videoconferencing Internet videoconferencing requires broadband communication for synchronous discussion with a video camera, microphone, and speaker used to have two-way online interaction. This type of online interaction is valuable for including visual and audio cues in instructor-student online interaction.

References

Mead, George Herbert. *Mind, Self and Society* (Chicago: University of Chicago Press, 1967).

Simmel, Georg. *The Sociology of Georg Simmel.* Ed. Kurt H. Wolff (New York: The Free Press, 1950).

Chapter 12

Active Learning with Alert Boxes, Prompts, and Controlled Windows

Throughout the body of this chapter, you will find JavaScript listings integrated with suggested uses in learning. Most of the scripts are short and provide instructors with a good deal of power to control the behavior of a Web page. Had the listings been placed in end-of-chapter appendices as has been the practice in previous chapters, too much of the discussion would have made little sense. (Chapter 13 follows the same practice.)

Increasing Interaction

Up to this point two basic types of interactivity with Web pages have been discussed. One type has been in feedback from a Web page based on the selection of links, and the other has been an email from faculty or collaborative students. Using frames, it is possible to keep materials on the screen and let the student bring up an array of choices for comparisons.

This chapter introduces a way to significantly increase active learning and interactivity on Web pages. One of the most powerful tools available for use with HTML is a scripting language called JavaScript. It can be used to make things happen based on a student's action and written as part of an HTML file. JavaScript is relatively simple to use employing little programs without having to learn the whole language. However, JavaScript can be harnessed to create very sophisticated object-oriented databases and full-scale programs for very complex learning sites if the professor has the interest in spending time learning the language (Nakhimovsky and Myers, 1998). This chapter focuses on two key aspects of JavaScript, "alerts" and "prompts." Another section shows how to better control windows using JavaScript employed to provide quick feedback. The scripts presented in this chapter just scratch the surface of JavaScript, but they should be interesting and very useful.

A Little JavaScript

JavaScript is a scripting language that is interpreted by the browser. Just like HTML, JavaScript will run on any computer over the Internet with a Netscape or Microsoft browser. JavaScript *is not related to Java*. Java is a compiled language, and only the word "Java" is the common element. No background in computer science is required to work with JavaScript, and knowing a little code will go a long way. Essentially, if you can write HTML, you can write JavaScript—or at least what we will cover in this book.

Briefly, JavaScript is able to detect far more *events* on a Web page than is HTML by itself. An *event* is an action taken that can be read by the computer, such as a mouse movement, a click, or a mouse pointer in a certain position on the screen. The single event that we have discussed is *point and click*. An *event* occurs when the student points the mouse arrow at a link and clicks the mouse button. The event is handled by HTML. JavaScript, on the other hand, can recognize and handle far more events, including point and click. The following are just a few JavaScript event handlers:

Event Handler Name	***Event***
onClick	Points and clicks mouse on hot spot
onMouseOver	Pointer is over hot spot
onMouseOut	Pointer leaves hot spot
onLoad	HTML program is loaded
onUnload	Another Web page replaces current one

JavaScript has more than 20 event handlers, and so for those interested in spending some time with the language, many different possibilities are available for active learning. However, with just the ones listed a lot can be done and done simply.

When an event is encountered, the event handler triggers an *action*. The actions are contained in *functions*. JavaScript has built-in functions and functions created by the designer. The built-in *alert function* is a good place to start. The function does something in response to a student's action that is not possible by HTML alone.

The Alert Function

The alert function sends a message once the event handler has detected an event—like a mouse click. A short message appears, and when the student clicks "OK" or presses the return or enter key, the message disappears. The Web page stays the same as it was, and so this allows the instructor to have a page with many different messages. The best way to see how to create a simple alert message is to do one. The following script will bring up a message when the student clicks the mouse on the hot spot. (Remember that a *hot spot* is any part of the Web page that responds to a user's action such as links indicated by underlined text.)

```
<html>
<head>
<title>Alert Box</title>
</head>
<body bgcolor="white">
<a href="#" onClick="JavaScript:alert('Something!')">
Learn Something</a>
</body>
</html>
```

Figure 12-1 shows how the page looks after the student has clicked the text Learn Something. The JavaScript used to make everything happen is in the code:

```
onClick="JavaScript:alert('Something!')"
```

Pay special attention to how the double quotes (") and single quotes (') are employed in the script. The entire JavaScript element after the event handler is between double quotes. Messages are between single quotes.

The event handler is the word "onClick." If "onMouseOver" or one of the other event handler words replaces onClick, the hot spot will wait until the new event occurs. For example, substitute onClick with onMouseOver and try it out. You will see that as soon as the mouse pointer passes over any place on the hot spot, the alert box appears.

Two of the event handlers, onLoad and onUnload, cannot be used with a hot spot. They are activated as soon as the page is loaded or is about to be changed—the student clicks a link to another page. Both of these event handlers *must* be embedded in the <BODY> tag. For example, consider the following script that brings up an alert box as soon as the student clicks a link to another page:

```
<html>
<head>
<title>OnUnload Alert Box</title>
</head>
<body onUnload="javascript: alert('Adios—come again.')">
```

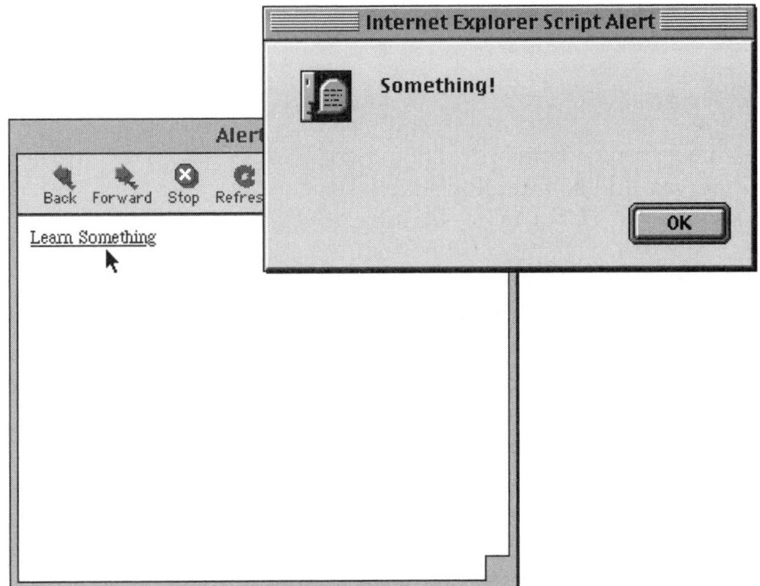

FIGURE 12-1 When the hot spot is clicked, the alert box appears with a message.

```
Once you learn how to use alert, you can put messages
everywhere.
<P>
<a href="Alert1.html">Go somewhere else.</a>
</body>
</html>
```

The link script has no event handler. At the very beginning of the script where the <BODY> tag resides, the onUnload event handler fires the event, and it will not cause an action—an alert box—until the page changes. Try out the script and be sure to include a file named *Alert1.html* so that there can be an actual target page.

Building Functions with Alert

The JavaScript examples above are based on immediate implementation of event handlers linked to built-in functions. However, to make the most out of JavaScript, it is important to learn how to create functions. Because the alert function is built in, it is relatively simple to create functions using *alert*.

To write a JavaScript function, all that needs to be done is to designate an area of the HTML script for JavaScript functions. This is done with the following tags:

```
<script language="JavaScript">
—-JavaScript code goes here
</script>
```

If all of the JavaScript is put between the <HEAD> and </HEAD> tags, all of the JavaScript will be loaded first prior to the rest of the HTML tags. This is a good place to create JavaScript functions. A function has a name and a set of instructions that will take place when the function is called—usually by an event handler. Roughly, it has the following format:

```
FunctionName () {
...instructions for what to do...
}
```

The work for a function is between the curly braces({ }), and in more complex functions curly braces are found within curly braces. Using the built-in alert function, the following script creates a little quiz with immediate feedback to the student. The name of the function is "feedBack," and rather than writing the message when the alert is launched, variables are used. They can be recognized by the word "var." One variable is named "correct" and the other "incorrect."

```
<html>
<head>
<title>Alert Quiz</title>
     <script language="JavaScript">
     function feedBack(comment) {
               alert(comment);
     }
     var correct="That's right! Good going."
     var incorrect="That's not quite it. Try again."
     </script>
</head>
<body bgcolor="white">
Which empire first brought Islam to the Balkan states?<P>
<Blockquote>
<a href="#"
onClick="feedBack(incorrect)">Hapsburg</a><br>
<a href="#" onClick="feedBack(correct)">Ottoman </a><br>
<a href="#" onClick="feedBack(incorrect)">Ming </a><br>
<a href="#" onClick="feedBack(incorrect)">Albanian
</a><br>
<a href="#" onClick="feedBack(incorrect)">Croatian </a>
</Blockquote>
</body>
<html>
```

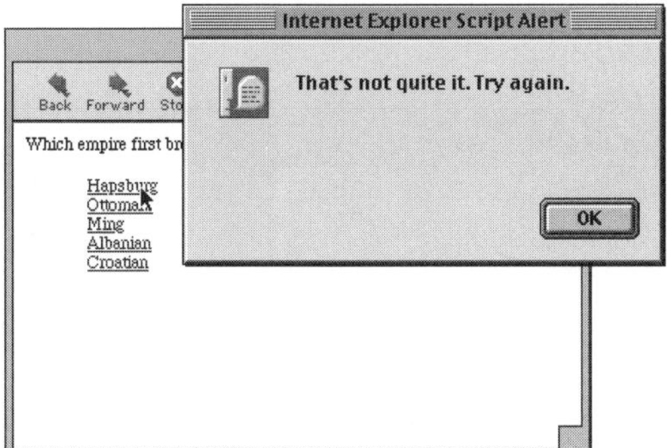

All incorrect selections come up with the same message. More elaborate and directed comments could be made for each choice.

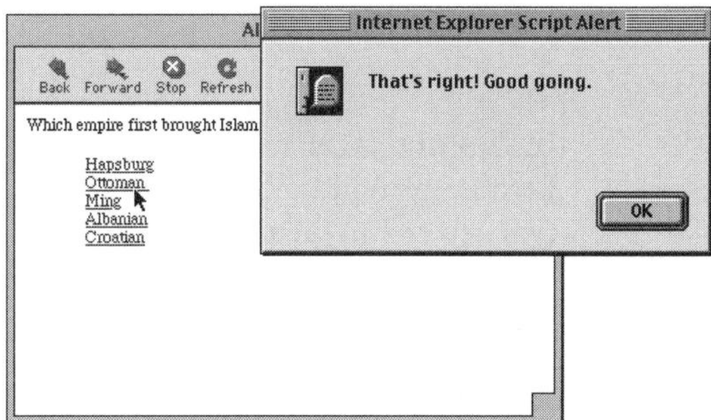

Because only one correct answer is available in this example, a single message suffices. With multiple correct answers, each correct answer could suggest the student seek more correct answers.

TABLE 12-1 JavaScript alert box provides different feedback based on student selections.

Notice how much less JavaScript code is used where the student clicks for the answer. It is far cleaner and clearer for the instructor to include the alert for the right and wrong answers using the variable names "correct" and "incorrect." Thus, instead of writing the text for the alert several times, it is written only once in the variables, and these variables are used instead of the full text. Notice also that when using variables, single quotes are not required around the variable names when an event handler launches the function. Table 12-1 shows what the student sees when he selects the incorrect or correct answer.

Guiding and Informing Student Actions with Alerts

Another use for the alert windows with JavaScript is to provide an active map of a process for students to follow. As they follow the map, made up of hot spots, new information comes up along the way. For example, in a criminology class, the professor was explaining how drug cartels work. On the first page, he put a graphic outline of a hypothetical drug cartel and provided a link to show how the cartel worked as an interdependent group of semi-autonomous organizations. Using the *onMouseOver* event handler, when the mouse moves over the hot spot on the map, the alert box pops up. In this way the student can see the information change as he moves the mouse pointer across the map.

Alert boxes have many advantages. They engage the student by responding to her actions, and they allow the professor to keep all the relevant material on a single page while additional information is brought to the student's attention. Alert boxes come to the screen faster than links to another page, and they take up less space in memory in the computer. Importantly, they add to the array of tools available to the instructor for creating active, engaging, and engrossing learning environments.

Prompting Input from Students

Up to now, all of the input from students has been to select from a finite list. Can original information originating with the student's understanding of a lesson be evaluated in a Web page? Can the student be asked to type in information, have the information evaluated, and receive a response to that information? The answer is a qualified "Yes."

If a complex question is put to a student along with a number of different possible ways of expressing an answer, it is very difficult to include all of the possible correct answers. When such questions are required, email is much easier to use and allows far wider latitude in what the student can say and the detail and sophistication of a response. However, when a simple phrase or a keyword is required in a response from a student, then using the *prompt* function in JavaScript can provide enhanced interactivity. Besides answers to questions, simple information can be entered and used to personalize the Web page using JavaScript prompts.

The most important thing to learn is how to use the information the student entered. On a very simple level, the information can be written to the Web page. To begin seeing how the *prompt* function works, the following program provides a simple use for the student input:

```
<html>
<head>
<title>prompt</title> </head>
<body bgcolor="white">
     <script language="javascript">
     var yourname;
     yourname=prompt("Enter your name:","name");
     document.write("Welcome to Biology 101 <b> "+
          yourname +"</b>");
     </script>
<p><b>Y</b>ou don't have to worry about dissecting frogs.
We use virtual animals and humans for all of our
dissections.<br>
<img src="frog.jpg">
</body></html>
```

When the page loads, a prompt asks for the student's name. Once his name has been entered, it is passed to a variable. Then, using the `document.write()` expression, the script writes a message to the page including the student's name that has been passed to the variable called "yourname." Notice how regular HTML tags have been added to make the student's name appear in boldface using the <b> tag. JavaScript can be used to write HTML scripts using standard HTML tags. Table 12-2 shows the sequence the student sees:

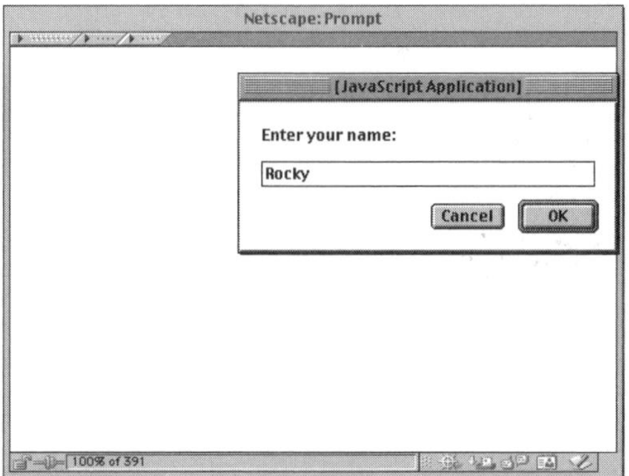

The student is prompted for a name. He enters his name and clicks OK.

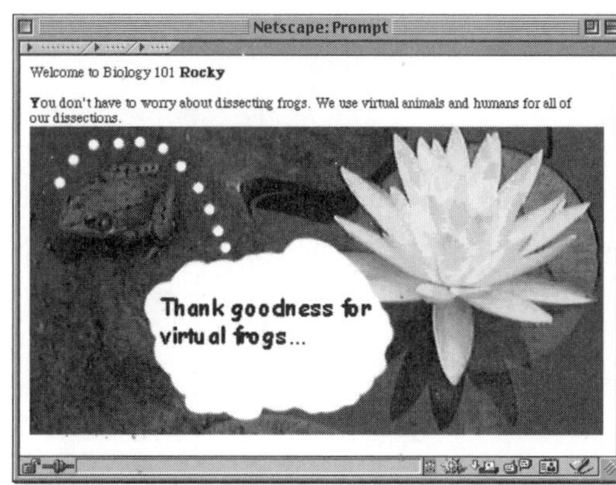

The name is printed on the page along with other HTML text and graphics.

TABLE 12-2 Data from the prompt can be passed to the Web page.

Also note how JavaScript is used in the body of the HTML. Rather than placing the script in the head area, the JavaScript was placed after the <BODY> tag. If needed, further JavaScript entries could be made elsewhere on the page simply by including the <SCRIPT. . . > and </SCRIPT> tags to indicate the text is to be interpreted by the browser as JavaScript.

Evaluating Student Responses

A far more important and flexible use of the JavaScript prompt function is to take the information the student entered and provide some kind of feedback. To do this, some way of evaluating the student's response is needed. JavaScript has statements called "conditionals" that examine information and can be used to evaluate information from students. They compare the information entered with information provided by the instructor, and depending on what she typed in, different responses are possible. For example, the following script shows how a simple question uses both alert and prompt functions to have appropriate replies to what the student enters:

```
<html>
<head>
<title>Evaluate Prompt</title> </head>
<body bgcolor="white">
<script language="JavaScript">
var answer;
```

```
answer=prompt("Who commanded the British forces at the
Battle of Waterloo?","");
if(answer=="Wellington") {
          alert("That's right. Lord Wellington led the
British and Allies at the Battle of Waterloo.")
}
else
{
     alert ("No "+ answer +" was not the British
commander. Go over the material again and see if you can
find out who it was.")
}
</script>
</body>
</html>
```

When the page opens, the student sees the question, and depending on her response, she will get an alert message either congratulating her or suggesting she go over the material again. Table 12-3 shows this sequence with both a correct and incorrect answer:

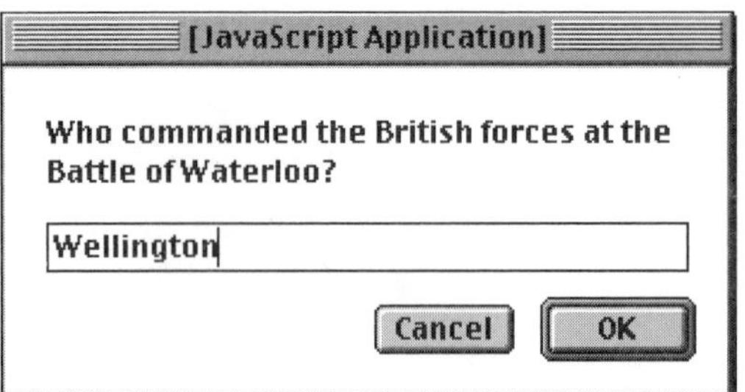

Student is presented with a question (a prompt) for which she supplies an answer.

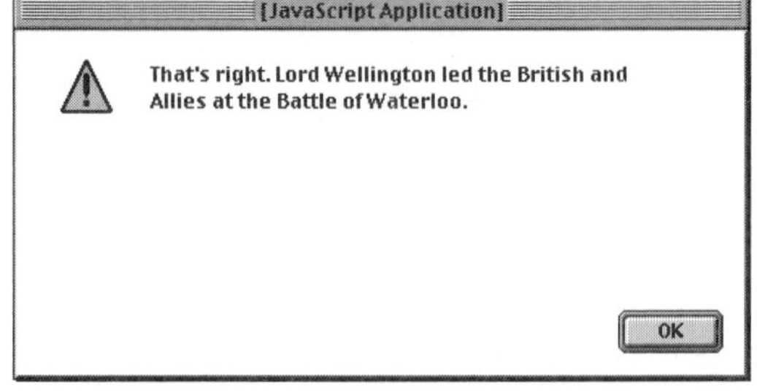

The correct answer lets her know she has done well.

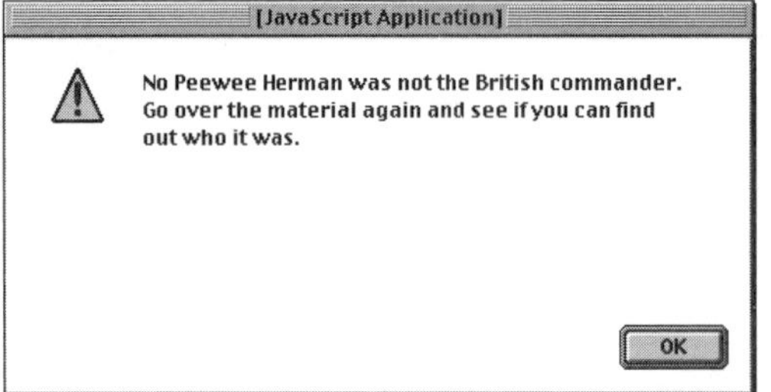

An incorrect answer uses the actual incorrect answer in the message and suggests more study.

TABLE 12-3 Prompts can get responses of slightly more than 250 characters, including spaces.

The example is fairly crude, and if the student misspells Wellington (for example, Welington or Wellingten) the answer is considered wrong, and the student may think she has the wrong person and not a spelling error. Also, the student and professor seem to have little control over when and how the question comes up in its current form. To solve this problem, the JavaScript code can be written as a function and when the student clicks a hot spot, the question will appear. This next little program shows how prompts can be written as functions. First, though, operators used in conditional statements need to be examined.

Conditional Operators

A conditional statement used in JavaScript requires a *conditional operator*. In the example illustrated in Table 12-3, the prompt response was examined to see if it equaled the word "Wellington." This was expressed as:

```
if(answer=="Wellington")
```

Notice that double equal signs (==) were used instead of single equal signs (=). This is how JavaScript distinguishes between operators used to define variables (answer=prompt(. . .) and operators that evaluate conditionals. Besides equal, several other conditional operators are provided as well. The following list shows the main conditional operators commonly used in JavaScript.

Operator — *Meaning*

- == — Equal to
- != — Not equal to
- > — Greater than
- < — Less than
- >= — Greater than or equal to
- <= — Less than or equal to
- && — Logical AND—e.g., if(a==b) && (c!=d)
- || — Logical OR—e.g., if(k<l) || (f>=n)

All of the conditional operators use the same format as was seen in Table 12-3, and so by substituting != for ==, it would have tested for the two being *not* equal instead of equal.

The Ternary Conditional Shortcut

To save some time and simplify writing questions and answers, conditional statements can be written as ternary conditionals. Most conditionals have this format:

```
If (this happens) {
    Then use Plan A
}
```

```
else {
    Use Plan B
}
```

The ternary conditional does the same thing with the format:

```
Announce=(this happens) ? Plan A : Plan B
```

It simply puts everything into the variable "Announce." If the conditions are *true*, then Announce equals Plan A; otherwise, Announce equals Plan B. The following shows how this works:

```
<html>
<head>
<title>Ternary Conditional</title> </head>
<body bgcolor="azure">
<script language="JavaScript">
var answer;
var correct="That's it exactly. The Bard would be proud
  of you.";
var incorrect="Those are not the words of the dismal Dane
  on contemplating his demise.";
answer=prompt("What famous phrase did Hamlet use to
  question suicide?","");
response=(answer=="to be or not to be") ? correct :
  incorrect;
alert(response);
</script>
</body>
</html>
```

It is clear how much simpler it is to use the ternary conditional. In a single line, all of the "if" and "else" statements are eliminated. The responses to the student are placed into variables (correct and incorrect), and the rest is all placed in a single line. It would be very simple to add a few more elements to the line to help assure that a correct answer would not be ignored. Suppose, for example, a student put, "To be or not to be." That would be considered incorrect because the match is looking for a lowercase "t" and no period at the end of the line. Using the logical OR (||), the line could be rewritten to read:

```
response=(answer=="To be or not to be.") || (answer=="to
   be or not to be") ? correct : incorrect;
```

By using substrings and transforming cases (from upper to lower or vice versa) in JavaScript you can overcome the program rejecting correct answers. Get a good

JavaScript book and spend time experimenting, and find someone at your university who can help you. The purpose of this book is to show ways it can be done, and so that faculty seeking help will have some understanding of the type of help they need plus evidence that what they want can be done on the Web.

Get Help: If some of the code here is more than your cup of java, do not feel intimidated or despair. Often the problem in developing good learning-centered Web pages is the lack of communication between faculty and Instructional Technology Services or other campus branch that provides faculty with assistance in educational technology. By learning what is possible and being armed with examples, even ones where the technology is not fully understood, faculty can better communicate with the technologists, programmers, and others who may help them. All of the examples in this book have been created to be relatively simple, but as we get into more complex scripts, even the simple ones may seem difficult to fully understand. Also, using tools like Adobe's *GoLive* and Macromedia's *Dreamweaver*, the JavaScript code will all be written for you without you having to know how to write the script.

Putting Prompts in Functions

In order to see how questions can be put into functions to be initiated by clicking a hot spot, two simple questions are created as individual functions. Then, event handlers in hot spots on the Web page launch the functions. Like all JavaScript functions, it makes more sense to place them in the head of the HTML script. In this way, they will be all loaded and ready to go as soon as the student sees the page. Otherwise, all that really needs to be done is to use a function name and put all of the script for the prompt between the curly braces. The following script shows how this is done:

```
<html>
<head>
<title>Prompt Functions</title>
<script language="JavaScript">
var answer;
var correct="That's it exactly ";
var incorrect="That's not quite it, try again.";
function question1() {
answer=prompt("On a color wheel, what color is opposite
of green?","");
response=(answer=="red") ? correct : incorrect;
alert(response);
```

```
}
function question2() {
answer=prompt("On a color wheel, what color is opposite
of orange?","");
response=(answer=="blue") ? correct : incorrect;
alert(response);
}
</script></head>
<body bgcolor = "white">
<h3>Complementary Color Quiz</h3>
Below are two questions about the color wheel. Opposite
colors on the wheel are considered complementary. By
knowing the opposites, you will also know which colors
are complementary.<p>
<a href="#" onClick="question1()";>Question 1 </a> <p>
<a href="#" onClick="question2()";>Question 2 </a>
</body>
</html>
```

Several important elements have been introduced in the above script. First, the questions were turned into functions called "question1()" and "question2()" to make them easy to identify. Second, the same variables—"answer," "correct," and "incorrect"—are used in both functions. This considerably simplifies things because separate variables do not have to be declared for each function. All of the variables are declared outside of both functions and so can be incorporated in both. When the page is loaded, instead of having the questions automatically jump onto the screen, the student waits until she is ready. Also, if she gets the wrong answer, she can try again until she gets the right one. Table 12-4 shows how the screen and alerts appear to the student. The same alert responses are given for each question.

Controlling Windows

In Chapters 10 and 11, there were examples of bringing up new windows. The problem with opening a new window in a lesson is that it covers up the lesson. However, with JavaScript, it is possible to open one or several small windows to bring more material to a student's attention, or as seen in Chapter 11 to bring up a page with the students' email addresses. Small windows would also be useful for opening up definitions, references, footnotes, and anything else a professor may find useful without destroying the flow of the lesson. With an image-mapped graphic, an instructor could have small windows appear with a magnified image of the portion of the graphic selected. Several small windows could be opened simultaneously on a page for comparison and elaboration of course material. Beginning with a simple example, this next section shows how this can be done.

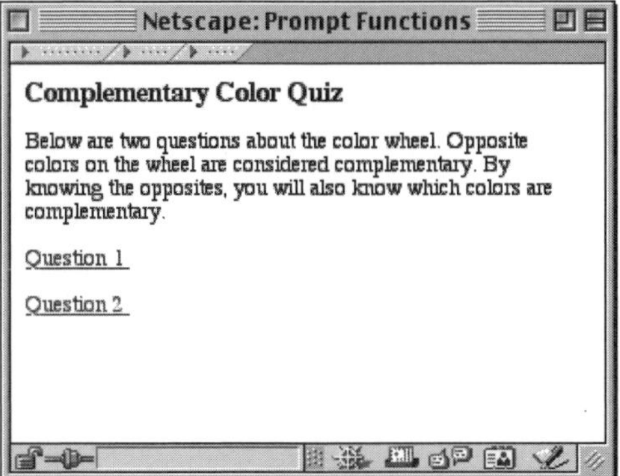

Clicking on the hot spot launches questions. Event handlers activate functions.

[JavaScript Application]

On a color wheel, what color is opposite of green?

Cancel OK

Questions appear as prompts. Each question is separately launched by a function. This can be brought up as many times as the student wishes until he gets it right.

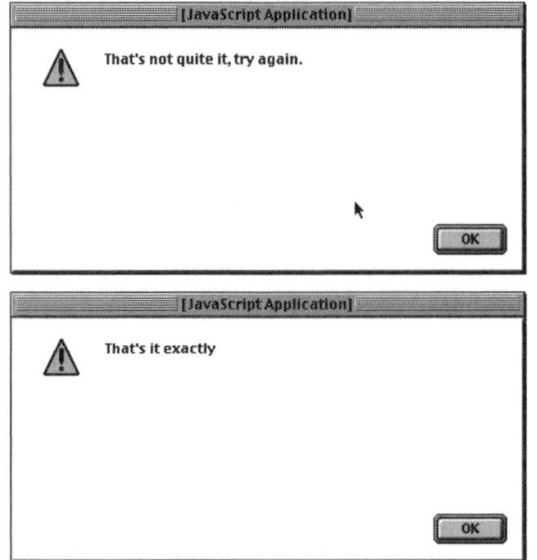

Both questions use the same responses.

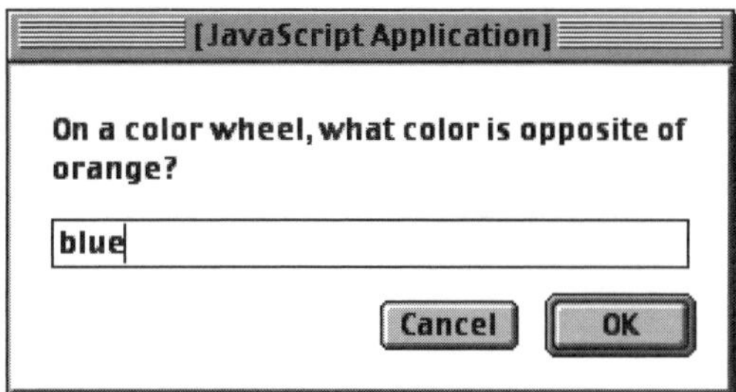

More questions (functions) can be added to the script using the same variables.

TABLE 12-4 Any number of prompts can be placed on a Web page by writing the prompts and alerts as functions and launching them with event handlers.

```
<html>
<head>
<title>Open and Configure Window</title>
<script language="JavaScript">
function seeComment() {
open("comment1.html","Comment1","toolbar=no,width=250,
height=100");
}
</script>
```

```
</head>
<body bgcolor = "white">
By having small windows open during a lesson, students
can easily get further information without having to
either cover their current lesson or link to an entirely
different page. Controlling the size of the page is just
the first step. Also, notice that the tool bar and other
navigational information are not on the little window.
Click <a href ="#"
onClick="seeComment()"> here</a> to see the little window.
</body>
</html>
```

The key to opening and controlling the size of the window is in the "open()" method. Extracting it from the script, each part is described separately as follows:

```
open("comment1.html","Comment1","toolbar=no,width=250,
height=100");
```

The first parameter states a URL or file name. Usually when faculty develops Web pages with comments, they will have their own page to bring up. However, it is possible to use a full URL (for example, http://www.Sandlight.com/comment1.html) and open it in a small separate window. The second parameter is the name of the window and may be needed in a frame set or when referencing the window as a JavaScript object. Be sure to put some kind of name or a pair of quotation marks ("") in the space for the name. Several window features can be adjusted, but the most important are ridding the window of a toolbar and specifying the dimensions. Various parts of the toolbar can be added to or subtracted from a little window, but the toolbar takes up space on the screen, and unless you see a good reason to have it, it can be removed by indicating "toolbar=no." If no attributes are listed for any of the window features, all of them will appear on the new window. Most important are the height and width of the window. To bring up a secondary window for elaboration and not detract from the main lesson, all the space it takes up on the screen should be no more than the size of the message or graphic. Both width and height are expressed in pixel values with about 75-100 pixels equaling one inch. Figure 12-2 shows how the main and secondary windows appear when the secondary window is called up.

By using several different small secondary windows, students are given some activity and a simple way to bring up different topical information about the topic under study. The following shows how to create multiple functions to bring up several different windows on the same lesson page. Note the similarities and differences between this and the previous script.

```
<html>
<head>
```

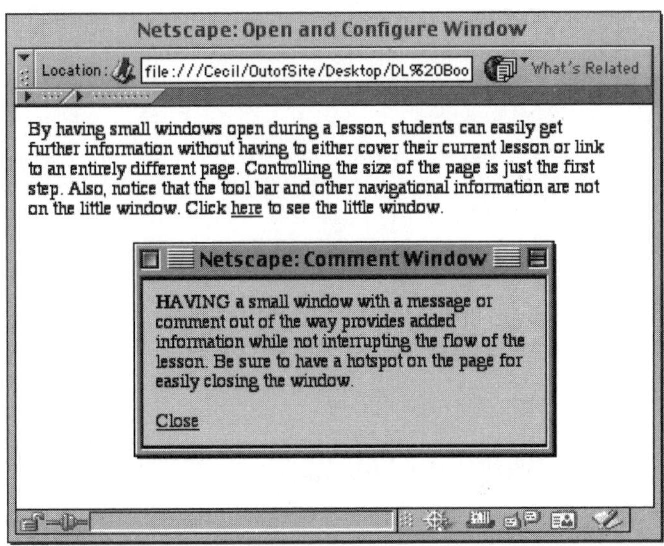

FIGURE 12-2 Controlling the size of a secondary window allows the primary window to be fully visible.

```
<title>Open and Configure Window</title>
<script language="JavaScript">
function seeComment1() {
open("pop1.html","","toolbar=no,width=300,height=160");
}
function seeComment2() {
open("pop2.html","","toolbar=no,width=300,height=160");
}
function seeComment3() {
open("pop3.html","","toolbar=no,width=300,height=160");
}
</script>
</head>
<body bgcolor = "white">
<b>T</b>he American Revolution was more than a desperate
struggle for democracy. Besides an <a href="#"
onclick="seeComment2()">international</a> cast of
nations, it was done with poor <a href="#"
onclick="seeComment1()"> communication</a> and <a
href="#"onclick="seeComment3()"> transportation</a>
systems. Often both sides were fighting without knowing
where their forces were or what the political situation
was.<br>
```

```
<img src="fig12_v16.jpg">
</body>
</html>
```

Each of the windows that the page opens when the various hot spots are clicked can remain open and be compared with the other secondary windows or be closed. Figure 12-3 shows how the page would look with all of its secondary windows opened at the same time. In Figure 12-3, the instructor has used icons to bring out certain thematic issues. Notice that the primary page is relatively simple in its basic background. A few lines of text with several hot spots provide students a rich graphic and textual page that actively engages them. Also note that each secondary page uses a common arrow icon to close the window. A student *could* click the upper left-hand corner to close the secondary windows, but a student may not think she is supposed to, and by placing a common icon at the bottom of each page, it provides a place at the *end* of the page to do so.

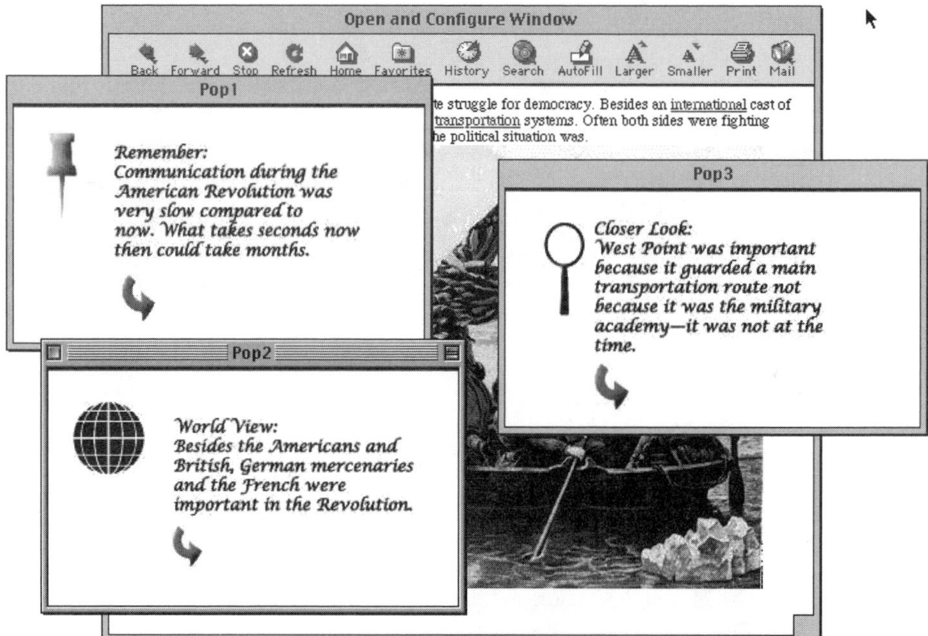

FIGURE 12-3 The secondary windows are employed with icons to focus on different important elements the professor wants the students to learn.

Summary and Review

This chapter has provided ways to increase student activity and create interactive pages. Using scripting language like JavaScript can be intimidating, but taken slowly and learning just what is required to create activity and interactivity in Web pages, it becomes just another tool to use. Many of the Web development tools such as *GoLive* and *Dreamweaver* provide relatively simple ways to get alerts without having to learn any JavaScript at all. However, learning a little will help understand what is possible. Working with support staff in instructional technology, far more interactivity and robust active learning is possible.

However, using the simple alert and prompt tools described in this chapter will increase the ability of students to actively engage in the learning process. Because most learning outside of a classroom occurs by reading books, articles, and papers, it is important to consider connecting active learning with Web pages and other reading. For the most part, reading a Web page is far more difficult than reading a book. This point has been made before, but it is worth repeating because the purpose of using Web pages is to increase many of the activities and interactions not possible in class. Rather than thinking of Web pages as a reading source, they are better conceived of as a multimedia source, with reading being secondary. The more the engagement, and the more variety of engagement tools in a Web-based lesson, the more effective it will be.

Finally, using small secondary windows, it is possible to expand basic and fundamental concepts with supportive and comparative materials in the same visual space. In most respects, the small secondary windows work exactly like alert dialog boxes, *except* with the secondary windows it is possible to have text, graphics, *and* links, whereas with alert boxes, only text is used. Secondary windows give students something to do, they provide a wider experience, and they can add supplementary information to a primary lesson page.

Glossary of Terms

Alerts Pop-up (JavaScript) messages fired when the mouse is moved or clicked on a Web page. They can be used effectively in the creation of active learning.

Prompts Pop-up requests for input from the users. Information placed in prompts can be employed in active learning to engage the student.

JavaScript A scripted language embedded in HTML and interpreted in the Web browser. The language adds considerable functionality to Web pages.

Scripts A scripted language is one considered to be fairly permissive and loose in the world of programming. The programs written with scripted languages are called scripts.

Reference

Nakhimovsky, Alexander, and Tom Myers. *JavaScript Objects: Object Use and Data Manipulation with JavaScript* (Birmingham, UK: Wroz, 1998).

Chapter 13

Using Forms: Interactive Feedback

In most of the previous chapters HTML and JavaScript listings have been assigned to an appendix at the end of the chapter. This practice reflects the contention that good practices are the focal point and the technology is merely a means to an end. However, forms constitute a unique case in developing Web pages. Creating forms with programs like Adobe *GoLive* and Macromedia *Dreamweaver* is easy enough to do, but getting forms to *do something* usually requires some knowledge of JavaScript. Once students enter data into the forms, a process evaluates their entries and provides feedback. That process is the crux of the key issue raised—providing prompt feedback. Therefore, this chapter integrates the listings and the discussion of the technology element along with the educational practices that employ the technology. The references at the end of the chapter provide a number of books found useful for learning JavaScript.

Feedback

Learning *activity* is limited in Web pages by what actions a student can take. As more robust browsers develop, bandwidth increases, and technology expands students will be able to get feedback from the spoken words and facial expressions from a Web page. Likewise, in problem solving, cooperation and coordination, assessment, and data entry, students need to exchange information with professors and other students in as many ways as possible. Also the near future promises more built-in multimedia to render rich automatic feedback on Web pages.

The issue of *prompt feedback* in learning-based education is a crucial one. The notion of "promptness" can be anywhere from a week or so to a few seconds. Students who receive a term paper back with extensive comments within two weeks of turning it in with are probably getting fairly prompt feedback considering the task of grading papers and writing helpful and pertinent comments. The feedback can be in the form of spoken or written information to the student, and to be useful it must provide specific information about the direction that student takes. Incorrect calculations, reasoning, and information need to be corrected in order to help the student. She must be guided to understand why something is wrong and how to do it correctly—or where and how to go in order to get it right. For example, a student interpreting a sixteenth-century poem may be told that to fully understand the poem, she must go to the *Oxford English Dictionary* and look up how the words in the poem were used during the period it was written. This is the kind of information that would be written in the margins of a paper, sent in an email, or discussed in a meeting with the student. The time between determining the message the student needs to read or hear and grading a hundred other papers, professor paper fatigue (they all start looking alike), and getting the message back to the student may be considerable. With the number of students who turn in their papers at the very end of the term before bolting for home being a considerable portion of a class, the student may get the feedback very late or never.

However, feedback can also be in smaller and quicker doses. Big complex structures broken into smaller parts foster better analytical thinking and understanding. Many and varied quizzes appearing anywhere in a Web-based lesson with the click of a mouse button provide another avenue for prompt feedback. As feedback, small quizzes are little signposts guiding the way and helping students make adjustments along the way. However, to be useful, they must be structured in meaningful ways. Examining many of the questions prepared for textbooks by people other than the book authors often reveals that the questions and the crucial points in the text do not jibe and are wholly unrelated to the conceptual framework of the book. The questions are often trivial, covering minor and unimportant *words* that the test-maker stumbled across after a quick read instead of *key concepts*.

Therefore, when creating feedback, especially prompt feedback incorporated into a Web page, both the questions and possible responses need to be thought out fully. The feedback may be an alert message, a message in a form, or simply a signal that a question was incorrectly answered and needs to be reconsidered. Send the student back to the book, lecture notes, or Web page where the material was introduced. This can be done with a short message as well as a long explanation. What is important is that the feedback be pertinent to both the questions and the material the professor wants the student to learn. This process is time-consuming, but once incorporated into a Web page, *it is prompt*. The hard part is deciding what to ask and how to respond. The computer does the rest. Using forms, this chapter examines the whole feedback process carefully.

Forms are very easy to create using standard HTML, and most Web editing tools make it even easier. Microsoft's *FrontPage*, Adobe's *GoLive*, and Macromedia's *Dreamweaver* all include point-and-click methods to put different types of forms on a Web page. The tricky part is taking the information the student puts into a form and doing something useful for the student and/or the professor with it. Most Web sites that incorporate forms professionally use CGI (Common Gateway Interface) to send the form information to a server. However, that process is far beyond the ambition of this book. (Chapter 16 provides a discussion of CGI so that in working with a college's computer center it will be possible to understand what can be done using information with CGI.) What this chapter will do, however, is show how data entered by the student is used to provide the student feedback and understanding using forms.

Having noted these issues and complexities, these differences should not scare one away from learning about forms and how to use them. They are critically important. This chapter will take small steps along the way so that the technical side is clear. The pedagogical use of forms involves the interaction between what the student is attempting to learn, what she puts into a form, and the different kinds of feedback she can get. Data entered into forms can be manipulated and calculated to provide students with a dynamic presentation of processes and structures faculty want them to learn. It can also be sent directly to the professor for evaluation.

Forms and Buttons

To get started it is important to examine several different types of forms. One type of form is a box or area on the screen where students can type in information. This is different from a prompt dialog box discussed in Chapter 12 because the form window is directly on the Web page and does not pop up like a prompt box. Buttons of various types constitute the other kind of forms. The buttons can be used to enter information as well or trigger an action or JavaScript function like a hot spot. Before getting into the relationship between forms and good practices in learning and teaching, each type of form will be explained along with a simple example so that each one's use can be appreciated.

Every form begins with the tag <FORM>. A single <FORM> tag can spawn many different forms of different types—text forms or buttons. Therefore, before any other kind of HTML tag that makes up the several versions of forms there must first be the <FORM> tag. This is important because it is often overlooked when the focus is on the kind of form being created. It is also important because of the structure of forms as *objects* in a Web page. As will be seen in this chapter, each form is part of a *document* that makes up the Web page. When using JavaScript to reference a particular form element, it looks for the form first and then the element of the form and its value. The value is what the student or computer enters into a form or does to it (for example, clicks it, loads it). In the discussion that follows there will be several types of forms, but be sure to notice that all are between the <FORM> and </FORM> tags.

Types of Forms

This section simply provides a brief explanation and example of each form type presented. Once each can be understood in its basic form, further discussion shows how to use the data students put into them. Try out each example on a browser to see how it works. Figure 13-1 provides a visual aid of the different forms as they appear in a browser. (Hidden forms are not displayed because they are invisible on the Web page.)

Text Box

The text box is used for entering small bits of text, much like a prompt dialog box. For short bits of text or numbers, this is the form to use.

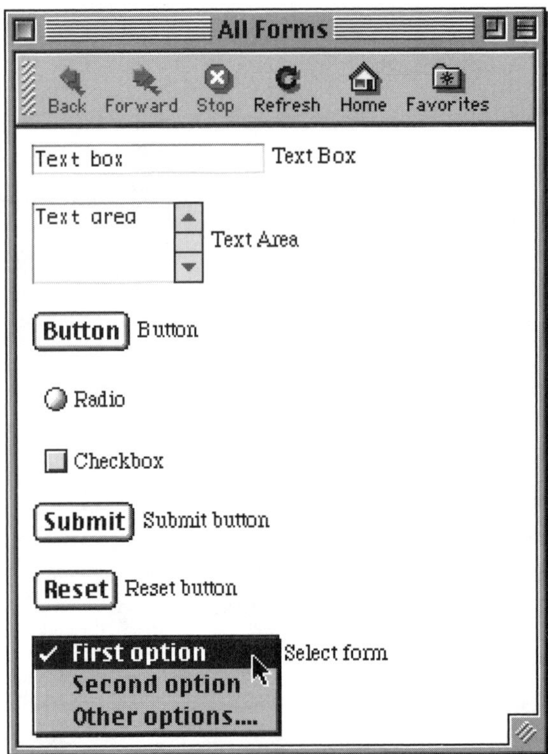

FIGURE 13-1 All types of forms reside between <FORM> and </FORM> tags.

```
<html><body bgcolor="white">
<form>
Students can write words or numbers in this window right
   on the Web page.
<input type ="text" name="studentcomment" length=12>
</form></body></html>
```

Text Area

The text area is used for entering a lot of text or comments. Notice that the format for naming a text area is different in two key ways. First, it does not have "input type" and second, the <TEXTAREA> tag requires a </TEXTAREA> tag.

```
<html><body bgcolor="white">
<form>
The size of the text area is expressed in rows and
   columns. For longer messages, text areas will
   scroll.<p>
<textarea name="studentessay" rows=7 cols=80></textarea>
</form></body></html>
```

Button

The standard button (not a radio button or checkbox) is a pill-shaped affair. Buttons are used with a single event handler, "onClick." The following example brings up an alert dialog box.

```
<html><body bgcolor="white">
<form>
Click this button for a proper introduction.
<input type="Button" name="Fred" value="Click Me"
   onClick="alert('My name is Fred.')">
</form></body></html>
```

Notice that the attributes include a name (Fred) and a value. The value is the name that appears on the button on the Web page.

Radio Button

This type of button is often used for online student surveys or multiple-choice quizzes when only a single correct selection exists. The button is either "clicked" or "unclicked." Once the button is clicked, it remains in that state until it is reset by clicking either a reset button (see next page) or another radio button with the same name. Using JavaScript it is possible to read the state of the button as clicked or not.

```
<HTML>
<title>Radio Button</title>
<body bgcolor="white">
<form>
<br><input type="radio" name="Intro" >Introduction to
  Marketing
<br><input type="radio" name="Manage">Management
<br><input type="radio" name="Finance">Finance
<br><input type="radio" name="Finance">Creative Finance
</form>
</body></html>
```

Try out the above script and try clicking the different buttons. On the first two, once they are clicked, they cannot be changed, but if one of the second two buttons is clicked, it can be unclicked by selecting the other of the two. However, both cannot be "on" at the same time. That is because they have the same name—both are named "Finance."

Checkbox

The checkbox is like the radio button, but it is different in two essential ways. Two checkboxes with the same name can both be checked at the same time, and on the second click of any checkbox, it becomes unchecked. Using the same script as was used with the radio button except substituting "checkbox" for "radio," two very different outcomes result.

```
<HTML>
<title>Checkbox Button</title>
<body bgcolor="white">
<form>
<br><input type="checkbox" name="Intro" >Introduction to
  Marketing
<br><input type="checkbox" name="Manage">Management
<br><input type="checkbox" name="Finance" >Finance
<br><input type="checkbox" name="Finance">Creative
  Finance
</form>
</body></html>
```

It is important to try this script in a browser to compare its behavior with the previous script using radio buttons. Table 13-1 shows how they appear on the screen.

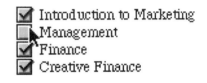

Introduction to Marketing Management Finance Creative Finance	Introduction to Marketing Management Finance Creative Finance
Radio buttons stay "clicked" unless a button with the same name is clicked. (The labels are different, but each of the last two buttons is named "Finance" in the script.)	Checkboxes can be checked and unchecked with a mouse click. Two checkboxes with the same name can be clicked at the same time.

TABLE 13-1 The different behaviors of radio buttons and checkboxes are subtle but consequential.

Submit Button

When clicked, the submit button sends all the values of the forms to a designated URL or (in Netscape *Communicator* only) an email address. The URL is established in the initial <FORM> tag. The basic script for the form is very straightforward. The value appears on the button itself.

```
<input type="submit" value="Click here to send data">
```

A later section in this chapter fully explains how this works.

Reset Button

This type of button is great for clearing all the data in a form. When a form has been filled out, the student may wish to make wholesale changes—such as changing answers on a test or essay. A single click of the reset button clears everything. Insert the following line into the checkbox script above. Put it right after the last checkbox *but* before the </FORM> tag. Check all of the boxes, and then click reset to see what happens.

```
<br><input type="reset">
```

Even the name "Reset" is put on the button. It is a simple line of script, but it is one that can prove very handy.

Hidden

Hidden forms may seem to be an oxymoron because forms are designed for the user to put in information. However, because forms can hold information, some of which an instructor may not want the student to see initially, they can be very useful for creating lessons. Hidden forms can be used to store data that will be used later or when the student takes certain actions. The values placed into the hidden forms may contain responses from students as well. So although there may not be an obvious need for such forms, they will be found to be very useful.

```
<input type="hidden" name="Q12" value="Yalta Conference">
```

Passing data to and from a hidden form can also be used for creating databases.

Select List

The select list is different from a button or text form. Students can be presented with a pull-down menu from which they may choose one of several options. This might be used as a mini-menu, a submenu, or selections for different links to pages. The big advantage of a select list is that it takes up very little room on a Web page, but it can contain a long list of options. The basic format is as follows:

```
<html><body>
<form>
<select name="Sciences" >
<option> Biology
<option> Physics
<option> Chemistry
<option> Biochemistry
<option> Quantum Mechanics
</select> Select One
</form>
</body></html>
```

Between the <SELECT> and </SELECT> tags are all of the options for the selection list. All that will be visible on the page is the first option. If the first option is a message to make a selection (for example, Select One), the default view of the selection list tells the student what to do.

Reading Form Data

In order to make forms useful at all, there needs to be a way to gather the data in the form. The data may be all the text in a text area or it may be where a radio button is "on" or "off." For example, in conducting a survey of student interests, an instructor may use checkboxes or radio buttons to see whether the student has had various types of background courses for a class. If the boxes are checked or the buttons are "on," that means they do. Otherwise, it means they do not. To create a Web page asking the pertinent questions is simply a matter of having a set of checkboxes and radio buttons with the appropriate text. Beginning with a simple example, we will see how to set up the forms to indicate whether they have been turned on or not. Checkboxes are used in the following script to show how a professor may create a simple survey to learn something about students' backgrounds in an English Literature class. The script is for illustrative purposes only with a focus on reading the state of the checkboxes to determine whether one has been checked or not. If the box has been checked, an alert dialog box appears.

```
<HTML>
<head> <title>Read Data</title>
<script language="JavaScript">
function ReadJane() {
if (document.ReadData.Austen.checked==true) {
alert("So you have read Jane Austen....");
}
}
</script>
</head>
<body bgcolor="white">
<form name="ReadData" >
<p>Select all of the writers you have studied:
<p><input type="checkbox" name="Chaucer"
  value="Chaucer"> Chaucer
<br><input type="checkbox" name="Johnson"
  value="Johnson"> Samuel Johnson
<br><input type="checkbox" name="Shakespeare"
  value="Shakespeare"> Shakespeare
<br><input type="checkbox" name="Austen"
  value="Austen"> Jane Austen
<br><input type="checkbox" name="Other"
  value="Other"> Other
<p><input type="button" value="Click Here"
  onClick="ReadJane()">
</form>
</body>
</html>
```

The key to reading data in forms is understanding a little about *objects* and *properties*. A Web page is an object as are forms. The objects have different properties such as a value, a length, and whether or not it has been checked. An object can be a property of another object, such as a form being a property of a Web page. In order to find out something about an object of interest, we need to read its properties. For example, if we want to find out about a house, we would want to know how many bedrooms it has, whether it has a gas or an electric oven, the number and kinds of bathrooms (showers or tubs?), the size of the garage, and the square footage. The object is the house and the properties are the elements that make up the house.

To read data in forms, it is necessary to understand exactly what needs to be read and how to use it. For example, the line

```
(document.ReadData.Austen.checked==true)
```

is broken into the Web page [document], the form [ReadData], the checkbox [Austen], checkbox checked status [checked], and the value [true].

The main object in a Web page is the Web page itself. Referring to it as *document* means that it is the current Web page in the current window. Using frames it would be necessary to specify the window and frame as well. Once *document* has been specified, it is necessary to indicate which properties (which may be other objects) are referenced. In this case, the name of the form is ReadData, and the checkbox of interest is named Austen. The property of interest is whether or not it is checked, and fortunately the checkbox and radio button objects have a property called *checked*. If the checkbox is checked, it returns a *true*. The *true* is a Boolean variable that has only two values—true or false. As seen in Chapter 12, the process requires a conditional statement with a conditional operator. In this case the double equal (==) was used to test for the value of the Boolean variable. If Jane Austen is checked, an alert box pops up when the function is launched. If Jane Austen is not checked, nothing happens. Experiment with the script and page to see what else can be done with reading checkboxes.

Passing Data from Forms

Now that it is possible to read data, it is important to understand how to pass data from one place to another and use it. This next script takes the data entered into a text box and passes it to the alert box. It does this by first placing the value of the text box into a variable named "who." Then, "who" is put into the alert message. It is a simple script, and the focus is on the form objects used and the *value* property. Whatever is in a text box form or text area form is the form's value.

```
<html><head>
<title>Pass form data</title>
<script language="JavaScript">
function passItOn() {
var who= document.StudentResponse.firstName.value
     alert(who)
}
</script></head>
<body bgcolor = "white">
<form Name="StudentResponse">
```

```
<input type="text" name="firstName" length=12>Enter your
   first name <BR>
<input type="button" value="Click here to transfer data:"
   onClick="passItOn()">
</form>
</body> </html>
```

The easiest way to keep track of everything is to place the data into a variable early on in the script. Rather than having to type the long document name for a Web page and its objects and their properties every time its value is used, it is much easier to use a clearly defined variable.

Data Entry and Calculations

The next step is to see how something can be done with the data entered by students. Understanding how to do something with values entered into a text box is crucial to creating feedback in the form of a calculated outcome the student sees on the Web page. It requires no pre-packaged response, but rather a script to calculate a "response."

A simple example that calculates the cost of an item after adding sales tax shows how the information in forms can be entered, calculated, and written into a text form the student will see on the page. The page uses three text forms and two buttons :

- Enter the amount (text box)
- Enter the tax rate (text box)
- Show the full amount (text box)
- Fire up the calculation and pass the data (button)
- Clear forms (reset button)

Notice how the information entered by the student in the forms is passed to variables. The calculation uses the data from the forms that has been passed to the variables. To pass the calculated data into the **Total** text box the value of that text box is simply defined to equal the calculated sum. The tax was assumed to be entered as a whole number rather than a decimal fraction; therefore, whatever was entered was divided by 100.

```
<html>
<head> <title>Simple Calculation</title>
<script language="JavaScript">
function calculate() {
     var amount=document.addTax.price.value
     var tax=document.addTax.rate.value/100
```

```
        var sum=amount*(1+tax)
        document.addTax.total.value="$"+sum
}
</script>
</head>
<body bgcolor="white">
<form name="addTax" >
<input type="text" name="price" size=8> Enter price of
  item or service.<br>
<input type="text" name="rate" size=8> Enter tax
  rate.<br>
<input type="text" name="total" size=8><b>Total</b>
<p><input type="button" value="Click Here for Total"
  onClick="calculate()">
<input type="reset" value="Clear Forms">
</form>
</body></html>
```

Now that we have seen how students can enter data into a form on a Web page and how that data can be put into a variable and passed elsewhere, it is time to see how to provide feedback to the student using Web pages and active learning. A simple project for a student might be to find the ethnic makeup of his hometown. Using census data available on the Web, the student will find the raw numbers in the population of white, African American, Hispanic, Native American, and Asian American in his hometown, and the computer will compute the percentage for each group.

Breaking down the project to create a Web page to do that, it will be necessary to have the following:

- Five text box forms to enter the numbers—one for each ethnic group.
- Five text box forms for the computer to write the percentages in.
- A function that will add up all of the values and calculate a percentage for each of the five groups.

Once it is complete, it should look like Figure 13-2. After the student enters the data and clicks the button, she will see the percentage breakdown of the different ethnic groups as illustrated. The HTML code is fairly straightforward, but the JavaScript is a bit more complex. One of the nice features about getting data from forms using JavaScript is that all form objects are part of an array. That means each element of the form can be addressed sequentially by a number instead of a name using the format

```
document.hometown.elements[0].value
document.hometown.elements[1].value
document.hometown.elements[2].value
...
```

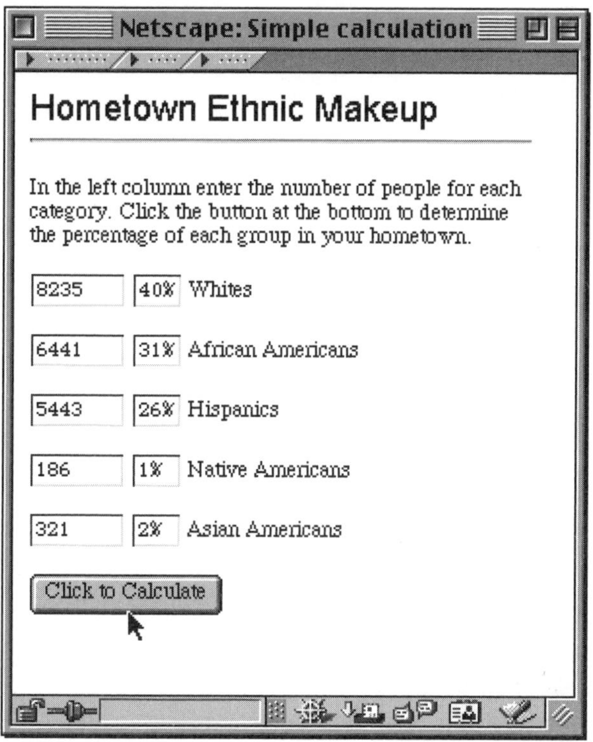

FIGURE 13-2 There are ten text boxes and a single button in a form named "hometown."

Arrays begin with zero (0) instead of one (1). The first element in the form "hometown" is named "white" and the second element is named "whitep." The "p" indicates the text box will contain a *percent* instead of a number. Using the array values, "white" would be element[0] and "whitep" would be element[1]. The last element in the form is actually the button, and the last text box named "asap" would be element[9].

Knowing that form elements are numbered sequentially, it is possible to use a loop to automatically read the data in each text box. The one used in the example is a "FOR" loop. It increments the loop variables "i" and "t" as long as the value is less than 9. The parameters of the FOR loop are bounded by the curly braces. The loop variable is incremented by two (i=i+2) because only every other text box would be used for data entry—elements 0, 2, 4, 6 and 8. The other ones, the odd-numbered elements, would be used for putting in the percentage values calculated from the values entered by the students. The values were rounded off to the nearest whole using the "Math.round" method.

```
<html>
<head>
<title>Simple calculation</title>
<script language="JavaScript">
function popCalc() {
var total=0
for (var i=0; i< 9; i=i+2) {
total=total+(document.hometown.elements[i].value*1);
}
for (var t=0; t< 9; t=t+2) {
var convert=
  Math.round((document.hometown.elements[t].value/total)
  *100);
document.hometown.elements[t+1].value=convert+"%";
}
}
</script></head>
<body bgcolor="white">
<font size="+2" face="Arial, Helvetica, sans-
  serif">Hometown Ethnic Makeup</font>
<hr>
<form name="hometown">
In the left column enter the number of people for each
  category. Click the button at the bottom to determine
  the percentage of each group in your hometown.<p>
<input type="text" name="white" size="7">
<input type="text" name="whitep" size="3">
Whites<p>
<input type="text" name="aa" size="7">
<input type="text" name="aap" size="3">
African Americans<p>
<input type="text" name="hispan" size="7">
<input type="text" name="hispanp" size="3">
Hispanics <p>
<input type="text" name="na" size="7">
<input type="text" name="nap" size="3">
Native Americans<p>
<input type="text" name="asa" size="7">
<input type="text" name="asap" size="3">
Asian Americans<p>
<input type="button" name="button" value="Click to
  Calculate" onClick="popCalc()">
</form>
</body></html>
```

Although the JavaScript may appear to be formidable in the above script, most of the page can be developed using a Web editing tool that does the entire layout and labeling of the forms. Once that part is done, the JavaScript provides the program to make the forms perform as desired.

Netscape Communicator Email Forms

A very useful communication feature of Netscape Communicator (but not Internet Explorer) is the ability to have information in a Web page form emailed. The email can go to individuals or groups—the professor or students. Special script is put into the <FORM> tag and a *submit* button is included in the script. When the submit button is clicked, all data in all of the forms is emailed to the recipients indicated in the <FORM> tag. Everything from comments to exam results can be emailed in this manner. Figure 13-3 shows how a Web page can be used to elicit student opinion on a reading assignment.

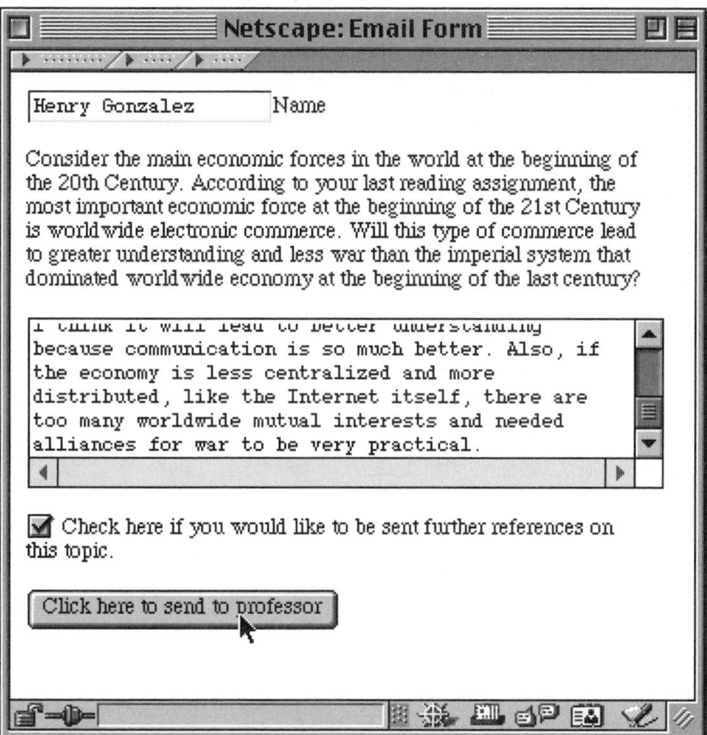

FIGURE 13-3 Built-in email makes it easy for students to send information to the professor.

The submit button is more specific than the default "Submit" by providing text for the VALUE= parameter of the button. The checkbox makes it simple for the student to get additional material from his professor.

The email recipient gets a fairly jumbled message, but it is clear enough to read. By adding extra form elements, it would be possible to add spaces between main topics. The following text would be received from the Web page shown in Figure 13-3:

```
student=Henry Gonzalez
opinion=I think it will lead to better understanding
because communication is so much better. Also, if
the economy is less centralized and more distributed,
like the Internet itself, there are too many worldwide
mutual interests and needed alliances for war to be very
practical.
sendme=yes
```

The script for the page in Figure 13-3 is all HTML. No JavaScript functions had to be written, and what little JavaScript is used is embedded in the tags. Pay close attention to the expanded <FORM> tag. All of the code for sending emails in a Web page is in that tag. For sending the data to multiple recipients, simply add additional addresses separated by commas within the same set of quote marks.

```
<HTML>
<title>Email Form</title>
<body bgcolor="white">
<form name="opinion" action ="mailto:prof@stateu.edu"
  method="post" enctype="text/plain">
<p><input type="text" NAME="student" length=14>Name<p>
Consider the main economic forces in the world at the
  beginning of the 20th Century. According to your last
  reading assignment, the most important economic force
  at the beginning of the 21st Century is worldwide
  electronic commerce. Will this type of commerce lead
  to greater understanding and less war than the
  imperial system that dominated worldwide economy at
  the beginning of the last century?
<p><textarea rows=5 cols=50 name="opinion"></textarea>
<p><Input type="checkbox" name="sendme" onClick=
  sendme.value="yes"> Check here if you would like to be
  sent further references on this topic.
<p><input type="submit" value="Click here to send to
  professor">
</form>
</body>
</html>
```

If the email information is included in the <FORM> tag of any HTML script, all of the form information is sent. However, each form with information to be emailed needs to be named. That is, the NAME= parameter needs to be completed in each text and button form.

Online Quizzes

Near the beginning of the book the concept of a *third generation learning Web site* was introduced. An important part of the *exit pages* is the use of some type of online quiz to give the student prompt feedback about his understanding of the material covered. Web editors like *DreamweaverAttain* or *Attain* objects used with *Dreamweaver* will automatically create quizzes—writing them in JavaScript. That is the smart way to create online quizzes because it is far quicker and simpler. However, if for some reason such tools are unavailable, it is possible to write relatively simple quizzes using forms and JavaScript.

The basic technique for creating quizzes involves having students put answers to questions in forms—text boxes, radio buttons, or checkboxes. The student responses are compared with the correct answers and the student gets feedback on her accuracy. Simply by adding more questions and answers, the quiz can be adapted for longer quizzes or exams. The double slash marks (//) indicate comments in the script to provide more information.

```
<html>
<head> <title>Two question & Five Choice Quiz</title>
<script language="JavaScript">
function score() {
var ql=document.quiz.length-3 //Checks the size of the
  form.
var correct=0 //Keeps track of the number correct
var k=0 //Keeps track of answer number
var qn=0 //Keeps track of question number
//Answers go here. Use array size to match number of
  questions.
//Add more questions and put answers in array
//in sequential order an[3], an[4], etc.
var an=new Array(2)
an[0]="b"
an[1]="d"
//Calculates the number correct.
   for (var i=0; i < ql; i++) {
     if(document.quiz.elements[i].checked==true &&
  document.quiz.elements[i].value==an[k])
       {
                   correct=correct+1;
          }
```

```
            qn++; //The ++ increments by 1
            if(qn>4) {
               k++;
               qn=0; }
      }
         document.quiz.myscore.value=correct;
  }
  </script>
  </head>
  <body bgcolor="white">
  <form name="quiz" >
  <p>1. If a person does not identify with his or her role
    but must play it anyway, what concept refers to the
    disidentification with the role?
  <p><input type="radio" name="a1" value="a" >Role conflict
  <br><input type="radio" name="a1" value="b">Role distance
  <br><input type="radio" name="a1" value="c" >Role segment
  <br><input type="radio" name="a1" value="d" >Role set
  <br><input type="radio" name="a1" value="e" >Role
    performance
  <p>2. Each role has a position that it accompanies. What
    do sociologists call this position?
  <p><input type="radio" name="b2" value="a" >A job
  <br><input type="radio" name="b2" value="b" >Work
  <br><input type="radio" name="b2" value="c" >Situs
  <br><input type="radio" name="b2" value="d" >Status
  <br><input type="radio" name="b2" value="e">Place
  <p><input type="button" value="Score Quiz"
    onClick="score()">
  <input type="reset" value="Clear Quiz">
  <p>Your score=<input type="text" name="myscore" size=6>
  </form>
  </body></html>
```

Figure 13-4 shows how the quiz appears on a Web page. With a few adjustments, the percent score and a list of correct answers could be provided as well. Also, JavaScript can evaluate very short answers and multiple-choice questions with more than a single correct answer. Faculty who are willing to learn more or who have access to staff who will help them write these quizzes and exams can do far more with them. Likewise, certain services and packages have built-in quiz and test-making software. All they require is that the faculty enter the questions and correct answers. Other types of test formats such as "drag and drop" are available as well, and having variety is more interesting for both the professor and students. All such test and quiz software provide additional ways to give student feedback.

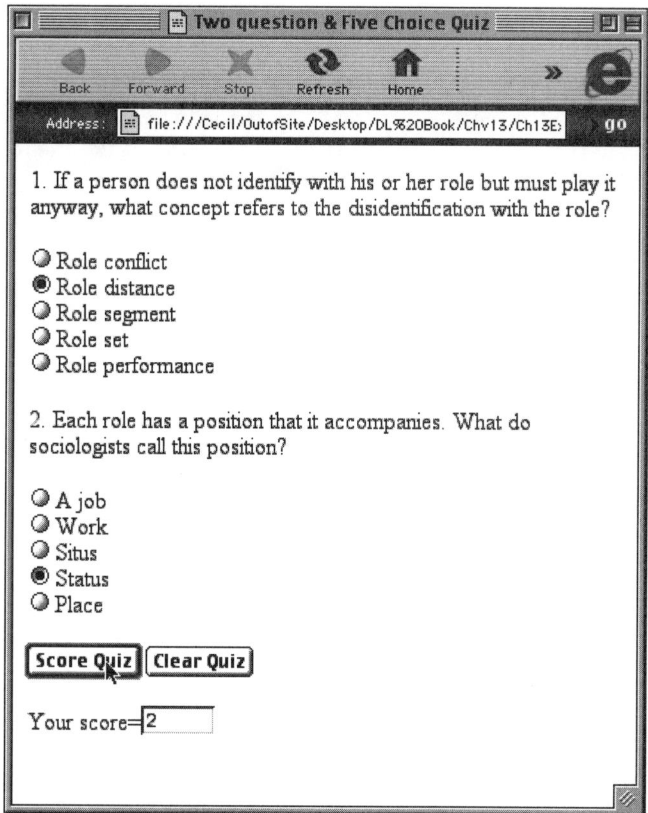

FIGURE 13-4 Online quizzes are one method of providing prompt feedback to students.

Security and Quizzes

With a learning-based model of education, student cheating is less of a concern because of the emphasis on providing feedback to the student, not on catching her cheating. However, if online exams are going to be used where student learning is measured, and the instructor does not want students looking at the source of answers on a Web page, it is relatively simple to hide the answers. Instead of putting the JavaScript function on the same page as the quiz, it can be placed on a separate page. All of the script between <script language="JavaScript"> and </script> can be saved as a separate text file with the extension ".js." For example, all of the code might be saved in a file called "quiz.js." Then, to use the code in the "quiz.js" file, put in the following line:

```
<script src='quiz.js'></script>
```

Do not put the <SCRIPT> tags in the .js file, put only the script between the <SCRIPT> and </SCRIPT> tags. Then use the above new script to call it in. (Actually, the file with the script in it can be called by any name, but the extension ".js" helps to differentiate it from other types of files that can be called into a Web page and used with HTML). The top of the quiz would now look like the following.

```
<html>
<head> <title>Two question & Five Choice Quiz</title>
<script src='quiz.js'></script></head>
<body bgcolor="white">
...rest of program...
```

As can be seen, there's nothing to provide even a hint of the correct answer in the script. More elaborate file filtering can be used to keep students out of "quiz.js" without a lot of difficulty. If "quiz.js" is put into a separate folder along with a file named "index.html" (or whatever default name a server uses) only the index file appears if the folder is accessed (for example, stateu.edu/answers/ . . .). If "index.html" is a lecture on ethics, not only will the student learn something about ethics, he will probably realize that there's a security system in place and put his time to better use prior to the next exam.

Mini-Menus and Pop Quizzes: Getting More on the Screen with Pull-Down Selections

The final type of form object this chapter covers is the select form. This works very much like pull-down menus on just about every application used in Windows or on a Macintosh. They can be used to save space but put information where students need to see it. Two examples are provided. The first uses a select form to serve as a menu that saves space but does everything a large menu would do. Figure 13-5 shows this menu on a small Web page. Having several pull-down menus on a larger menu page would be useful for guiding a student through a complex lesson. Alternatively, these little menus could be put on lesson pages for students to bring in additional material outside of the main flow of the lesson.

The format of the select form is unique in that it has both a <SELECT> tag and <OPTION> tags. All of the <OPTION> tags are placed between the <SELECT> and </SELECT> tags and the labels between the <OPTION> and </OPTION> tags. The only trick is to determine when a student has selected one of the options. In the examples, the "onChange" event handler is used, and when one of the options is selected, something *changes* and so the "onChange" event handler can be employed. Using a conditional statement to determine whether an option is selected with the "selectedIndex" property provides a way to set up an action for any number of options. The following script shows how the Web page in Figure 13-5 is created.

```
<html>
<head><title>Select Menu</title>
<script language="JavaScript">
```

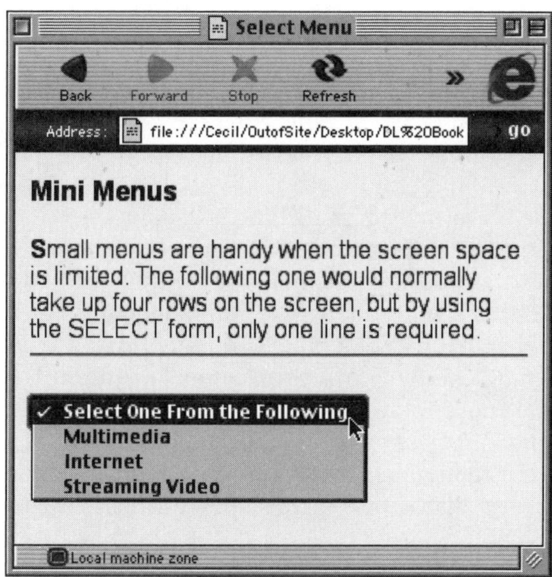

FIGURE 13-5 Select forms can be placed in a single row, but they provide several rows of selections when opened.

```
function LinkTo(form) {
var goTo
if(form.miniMenu.selectedIndex==0) goTo="#"
if(form.miniMenu.selectedIndex==1) goTo="media.html"
if(form.miniMenu.selectedIndex==2) goTo="internet.html"
if(form.miniMenu.selectedIndex==3)
  goTo="http://www.real.com"
parent.location.href=goTo;
}
</script>
</head>
<body bgcolor="ghostwhite">
<h3><font face="Arial,Helvetica">Mini Menus</font></h3>
<font face="Arial,Helvetica"><b>S</b>mall menus are handy
  when the screen space is limited. The following one
  would normally take up four rows on the screen, but by
  using the SELECT form, only one line is
  required.</font>
<br><hr>
<form>
<select name="miniMenu" onChange="LinkTo(this.form)">
<option>Select One From the Following</option>
<option>Multimedia</option>
```

```
<option>Internet</option>
<option>Streaming Video</option>
</select>
</form>
</body></html>
```

Another use for the select form is to create little pop-up quizzes. These quizzes are for the student to quickly get feedback on material and actively involve the student in the lesson. Figure 13-6 shows a small pop-up quiz using a select form. These quizzes are perfect for little, unobtrusive reminders and benchmarks for student learning. Rather than having a lot of text and scrolling on Web pages, it is better to connect the learning closely with a book or even a lecture. The point is to involve the student in the learning process, and little pop-up quizzes are simple ways to prompt a student along a learning path.

Notice how similar the following script is to the last one. Instead of having URLs selected, different alert dialog boxes are selected in this next script for the quiz in Figure 13-6.

```
<html>
<head><title>Pop-up Quiz</title>
<script language="JavaScript">
function QuizTime(form) {
if(form.popQuiz.selectedIndex==1) alert("No it was not
   that big.")
```

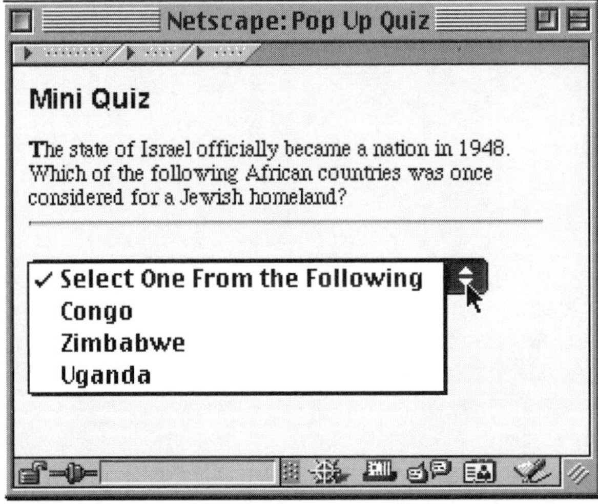

FIGURE 13-6 Small pop-up quizzes can give students quick and involving feedback. Alert boxes are used to give the feedback.

```
if(form.popQuiz.selectedIndex==2) alert("No—further
   north.")
if(form.popQuiz.selectedIndex==3) alert("That's the right
   answer. Before Amin, Israel had close ties with
   Uganda.")
}
</script>
</head>
<body bgcolor="lemonchiffon">
<h3><font face="Arial,Helvetica">Mini Quiz</font></h3>
<b>T</b>he state of Israel officially became a nation in
   1948. Which of the following African countries was
   once considered for a Jewish homeland?
<br><hr>
<form>
<select name="popQuiz" onChange="QuizTime(this.form)">
<option> Select One From the Following</option>
<option>Congo</option>
<option>Zimbabwe</option>
<option>Uganda</option>
</select>
</form>
</body></html>
```

As more college and university faculty use Web pages as one source of communication with students, better utilities and applications will be available for faculty to create Web pages without having to write a lot of code. The code is included here to provide a resource for faculty or support staff. It is also provided to show what can be demonstrated as possible connections between good practices in teaching and learning and Web pages. The inventiveness of faculty should take it much further.

Summary and Review

This chapter has been about interactive learning. The Web page and connected technologies are enablers to enhance both learning and faculty imagination. By having a response to an action, students can be better drawn into the process of learning. A primary feature of Web pages and HTML are forms. They provide not only a way to get information *from* students, they are used to provide *prompt feedback.* Forms provide a mechanism for several strategies for interactive Web pages.

By understanding how to put forms into a Web page and read the data from the forms, professors can use the data for different kinds of feedback. Passing the data into variables and performing calculations with the stored data allow the instructor to create information that shows the student new information. Because the student is involved by providing the initial data, she is part of the process that will help her learn a concept, formula, idea, structure, process, or some other instructive fact.

Online quizzes using the different buttons and select forms are a more traditional type of feedback. Using the third generation Web site model introduced at the beginning of the book, some type of self-assessment lets the student see how well he understands the material. Little pop-up quizzes give the student prompts and feedback within a lesson and keep students involved. Combined with books and lecture materials, all such feedback does what cannot be done by a book alone or very quickly in a large lecture class. As a supplement to either, however, this type of feedback moves everyone along more effectively.

Glossary of Terms

Button forms Several different button forms serve to record a state (for example, checked or unchecked) or perform a specific function (for example, reset or submit.) Buttons are useful for multiple-choice selections and firing other functions.

Forms On Web pages forms are objects that store values. The values can be defined in forms (in the tags), entered by the user, or sent to the form by external sources such as servers.

Objects Any element on a Web page is an object. In HTML and JavaScript, objects exist in a hierarchy with the window "owning" the document, forms, the forms "owning" certain elements, and the elements, owning different values.

Pull-down menu A form used to list several options opening up from a small area on the Web page. These are useful for both navigation and selection segments.

Text forms Forms that allow the user to enter text in either a window or an area.

Variables In the context of forms, the variables are the changing content of the forms. Text in a text form changes for conditions of radio buttons, menus, checkboxes, and other form objects.

References

Goodman, Danny, and Brendan Eich. *JavaScript Bible*, 3rd ed. (Indianapolis, IN: IDG Books, 1998). With the included CD-ROM, *JavaScript Bible* doesn't leave much to chance. This book is regularly updated to include changes in the browsers and JavaScript. It also shows the differences in JavaScript applications in the major browsers.

Kent, Peter, and John Kent. *Official Netscape JavaScript 1.2 Book: The Nonprogrammer's Guide to Creating Interactive Web Pages* (New York: Top Floor Publishing, 1997). Perhaps a little dated, but the authors are patient and unravel JavaScript step by step with good examples.

Negrino, Tom and Dori Smith. *JavaScript for the World Wide Web* (Visual Quickstart Guide) (Berkeley, CA: Peachpit Press, 1999). This book is one of my favorites. It is short but effective with good examples.

Chapter 14

Dynamic HTML: Layers and Interactive Learning

What is Dynamic HTML? For faculty developing Web pages it is a blessing and a curse. It is a blessing because DHTML can build robust, interactive, learning-centered Web pages. Students can make changes interactively on the page. It is a curse because there is not a common standard that has been adopted at this writing between the two major browsers—Netscape Communicator and Internet Explorer. An organization called W3C is responsible for generating standards for HTML, JavaScript, and other elements of a common language structure for the World Wide Web, but Microsoft and Netscape have different versions of the standard. Hence, there is *no actual common standard* denying the important criteria of universal access. Beginning with the Version 4 series of both browsers, there was some overlap in the way the browsers handled DHTML, and it is possible to write that both browsers present in similar manners. However, use care and test multiple browsers prior to putting any DHTML on a server.

As much as possible this chapter will deal with common elements of both browsers so that any of the examples and attending code can be used for both Netscape Communicator and Internet Explorer. However, on some critically important characteristics, JavaScript determines which browser is being used and uses different code. The Dynamic HTML Object Model will probably be more fully adopted in future versions of the browsers, and so the current problems may soon be moot. Internet Explorer introduced fuller implementation of the model since Microsoft had proposed the standard initially to W3C. However, because Microsoft proposed it did not mean that W3C would accept it. In the meantime, Netscape had its own version of DHTML, and many developers found features in the Netscape version they preferred over the Microsoft version and believe *it should* be a standard. By Version 6 or so perhaps all browsers will adhere to a common standard, and it will no longer be necessary to use only a subset of DHTML for one browser or another.

Whatever version is ultimately adopted, some common dynamic object model will be adopted, and although at this writing Internet Explorer has more fully implemented an object-oriented model, many features exist in Netscape Communicator. Here is a brief review of the main characteristics of such a model, some of which have been discussed in previous chapters.

Objects. Anything described in the code of an HTML file (a Web page) is an object. A graphic, the body of text, a layer (DHTML feature), or a form are all objects. Objects are represented in a hierarchy. Each has a level relative to another level above or below it in the hierarchy. For example, a *form* is "owned" by a *document*, and in turn the form "owns" an *element*, such as a text box or radio button. The window object is at the top, and is considered a *parent* to all other objects in the window, and each lower object is a *child* of the parent. A name or a built-in array element references objects. For example, as seen in Chapter 13 a form's value can be called from "document.Info.Name.value" or "document.forms[0].elements[1].value."

Properties. The attributes of an object are its properties. An *input* can have at least three properties, a TYPE, a NAME, and a SIZE (for example, input type="text" name="answer" size=16). The ability to change these properties *dynamically* is an important and key feature of DHTML.

Events. Anything that happens on a Web page is an event. Most of the events are initiated by something a student does with the mouse, but it can also be a key press, a page being loaded or changed, and other actions with the mouse or keyboard. When an event occurs—it is *fired*—it can be trapped or handled by event handlers. Event handlers are simply script words like "onMouseOver" and "onLoad."

Methods. The actions taken by an object are called methods. The *alert* method puts a message up on the screen, and the *close* method closes a window. Like language, methods occur in a certain context of a Web page and have both general and unique applications.

The object model applies to both DHTML and to JavaScript. In fact, JavaScript is the main "engine" behind DHTML. It makes more happen because with JavaScript, it is possible to create functions to be used for complex calculations and for problem solving. Most important, though, JavaScript can create functions to respond to student actions.

Multivariate Dynamic Pages

In discussing good design, Tufte (1983, 177) notes two key elements—simplicity of design and complexity of data. By examining a well-designed Web page, students should be guided to all of the connections between the different variables present. As an example—virtually a model—of what constitutes this type of design, Tufte (1983, 40, 176) shows a graphic drawn by Charles Joseph Minard in 1861 depicting Napoleon's Russian campaign. Graphically, Minard brings together six variables—the size of the army, the direction of the march, the dates, the temperature, and the location in width and point. In examining the chart, one is struck by the fact that of 442,000 troops crossing the Niemen River from Poland to Russia only

10,000 returned. This fact is dramatically illustrated by the width of the graphic depicting the size of Napoleon's army. However, what is most dramatic is that although Napoleon's army shrunk from 100,000 to 10,000 on the retreat from Moscow in the terrible Russian winter of 1812–1813, the great majority of the losses occurred on the *way to Moscow*. The summer of 1812 was extremely hot and rainy, making progress difficult. The retreating Russians threw dead animals into the wells to pollute and poison them and destroyed anything the French could use to feed the soldiers and animals. Likewise the battles of Smolensk and Borodino were very expensive victories for the French. However, the student can see none of this from the chart itself, and so although a student can see the army shrink, he does not know what causes it.

Using Dynamic HTML and redrawing Minard's chart, it was possible to both use multivariate (showing more than a single variable—time, direction, temperature, and so forth) design and increase the amount of information on the page available to the student. When the Web page appears, the student sees an explanation of what the graphic represents and instructions to trace the route of the march with the mouse pointer. At different key intervals different layers with information appear explaining what has happened on the march. A temperature text box shows that most of the losses occurred during warm or hot weather. Because the chart was fairly long and there was no desire to make it smaller, it scrolled horizontally across the screen as the student moved the pointer. Figure 14-1 shows a layer appearing at the bottom of the screen explaining what happened to the French in Smolensk. Other layers appear with text and graphics

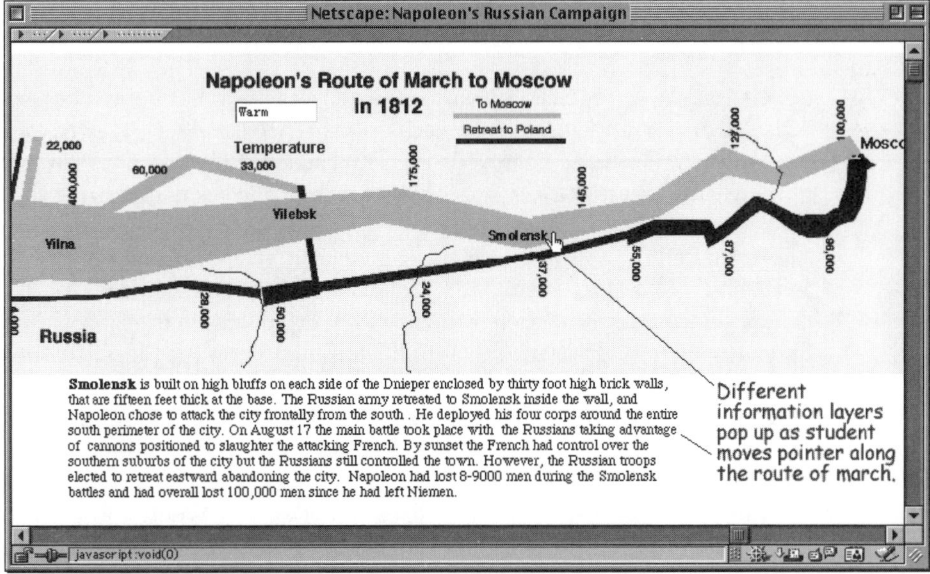

FIGURE 14-1 Different layers provide additional information as the student guides the mouse pointer over the map. An image map with hot spots was used to trigger the different layers.

providing additional textual and graphic information about the course of the campaign while not losing the simplicity and elegance of Minard's design.

A text box showing the temperature replaces the dates and temperatures that originally graced the bottom of the chart. More text boxes could have been added for other variables such as dates and other weather conditions. The main advantage of Dynamic HTML in this case is that it allows both detailed text and graphics to be turned on and off by what a student does. The next section shows how layers work and can be used for active and interactive learning.

Dynamic HTML

All of the examples used in this chapter are relatively simple ones because the HTML and JavaScript used to create DHTML need to be understood. However, to get the most out of DHTML, very complex scripts are required. Fortunately, good Web page development applications such as *Dreamweaver* and *GoLive* will do all of the scripting work required. In fact, the Web editors can write JavaScript and DHTML so that *both* browsers can read it. So while it is possible to do some very useful learning-centered Web pages with the scripts shown in this chapter, a lot more can be done with a Web page editor that can handle DHTML. To understand DHTML requires understanding layers and the use of JavaScript to dynamically change the attributes of the layers.

Layers and Divisions

Layers on a Web page can be envisioned as overlays that have most of the characteristics of a Web page. They can be shown or hidden, moved and changed dynamically. Figure 14-2 provides a visual sense of layers on a Web page.

Creating layers is fairly straightforward, but once created, they can be a handful to control. Therefore, it is best to begin with fairly simple examples. The tag for a layer is <DIV> with the contents between it and </DIV>. For example, Figure 14-3 shows two layers with different background colors placed on the screen in different locations. Notice that the layers overlap text on the underlying page, and they are positioned without being affected by text on the page. The position, size, background color, and other attributes of the layer are controlled from within the <DIV> tags. (See Chapter Appendix A.) In order to understand the style attributes of a layer, the first layer's style is broken down into its component parts:

Position: absolute	Places layer exactly where the attribute indicates. *Relative* and *static* are other attributes used when the objects (text, images, forms) in the layer or page are to be positioned relative to

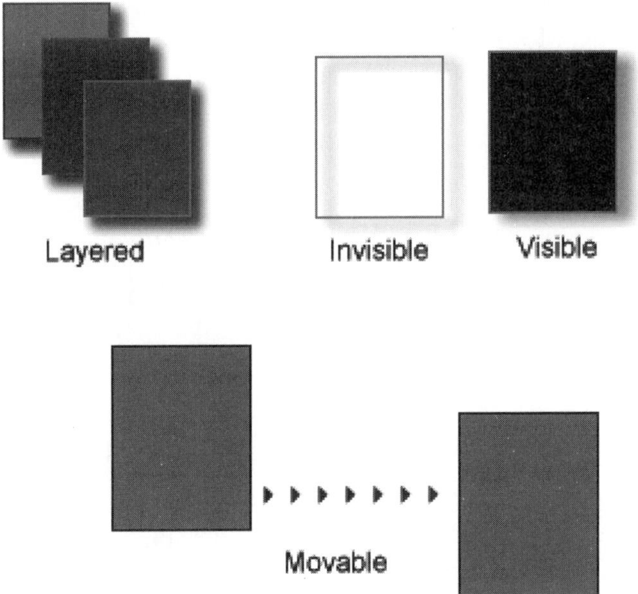

FIGURE 14-2 Layers can be changed dynamically on a Web page.

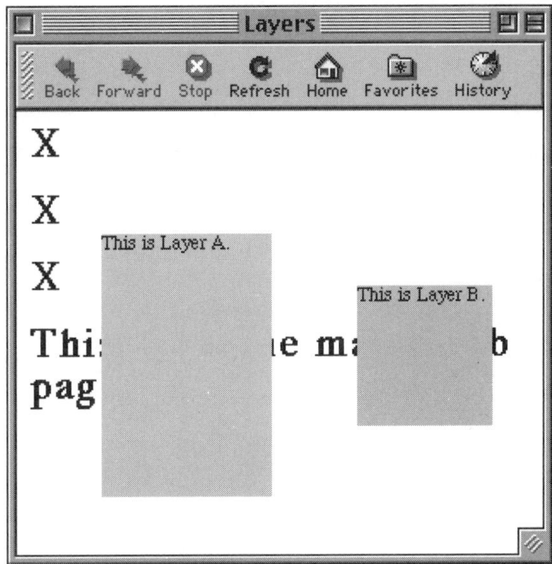

FIGURE 14-3 Layers can be placed anywhere on a page.

	other objects or when the layers follow the same positioning rules as the Web page.
Left: 50px	The upper left corner of the layer is 50 pixels from the left side of the screen. Some other units of measurement include **em** (point size of current font), **in** (one inch), **cc/mm** (1 centimeter/ millimeter) and **pt** (1 point or 1⁄72 of an inch, depending on the monitor). Usually, it's easiest to use **px** because it is a unit of measurement used on computer monitors.
top: 70px	The upper left corner of the layer is 70 pixels from the top of the screen.
width: 100px	The layer is 100 pixels wide.
height: 150px	The layer is 150 pixels high.
z-index: 1	The z-index is the depth of the layer relative to other layers. If two layers overlap, the one with the higher value will appear on top. The lowest level is 0.
background-color: yellow	The background color of the layer only. This does not affect the background color of the page or other layers not embedded in the defining layer.

The z-index is an important part of understanding and using layers. Table 14-1 shows two pages. The layers contain JPEG images to help show what happens when layers overlap and when one gets in front of the other. (Both JPEG images

TABLE 14-1 The z-index controls on which level relative to other layers a given layer appears.

have white backgrounds that contrast with the color of the layers. Using GIFs with transparent backgrounds would solve this problem.) The page on the left has defined the layer with the coffee mug as 1 (z-index: 1) and the wineglass layer as 2 (z-index: 2). By swapping the z-index values, the page on the right shows the layer with the cup covering most of the layer with the wineglass.

Controls on a Layer

For the most part, a layer is like a mini-Web page. Within the <DIV> tags, anything placed there becomes the property of the layer. Table 14-1 shows how graphics placed on layers are independent of the page. However, so too are other controls, such as event handlers. Table 14-2 shows a layer with a button bringing up an alert box in the left cell. The right cell shows the same two layers except now one layer is on top of the one with the button. The user cannot click the button because the second layer hides it. If even a portion of the button on the bottom layer shows, it could be clicked. Also, if the button were on the page, if a layer covers it, it could not be used to trigger an action. Just as one Web page window covering another would prevent access to any actions contained in the covered page, elements of a layer must be seen to be used.

Placing a form on a layer follows the identical rules that forms follow on Web pages. The only difference is that the form script is placed between the <DIV> and </DIV> tags.

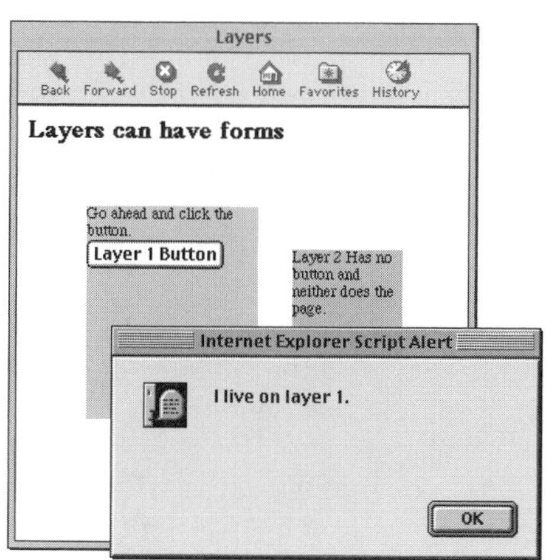

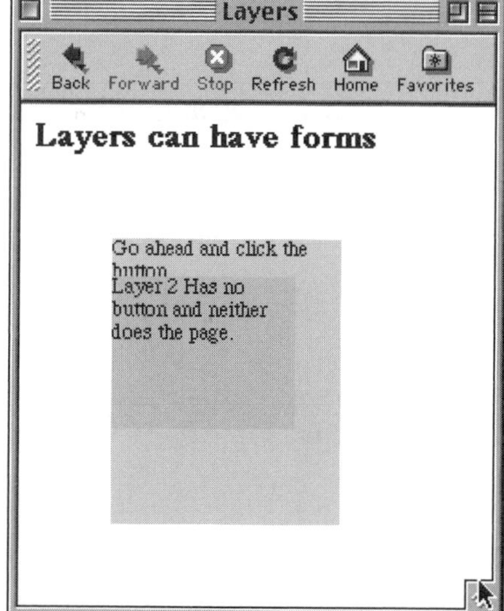

TABLE 14-2 A layer can have buttons just like a Web page, but when a layer is hidden or covered, only what can be seen can be used.

Dynamically Changing Layer Attributes

The most important feature of layers for building a learning-centered Web page is the ability for students to dynamically change the attributes of a layer by taking some kind of action. Some attributes are treated the same by both browsers and some are treated differently. Certain key attributes can be used for dynamic interaction with students. The best advice at this stage is to get a good Web page editor that can handle JavaScript and will create cross-browser applications, such as Adobe *GoLive* or Macromedia *Dreamweaver.* However, to understand more about the nature of this particular beast, sample scripts in Appendix B at the end of this chapter demonstrate how each browser treats changing attributes.

More Interactive Learning

To a great extent, having layers appear and disappear depending on what a student does works almost the same as do pop-up alert messages. However, with layers, the Web page designer can include graphics and text along with everything else found on a Web page. Because layers are loaded with a Web page, there is no waiting while a new window opens, and it is easier to have a quick response to a student's action. For example, a biology professor might want a student to move a mouse over an image of a leaf. As different parts come into contact with the pointer, a microscopic view of the part could appear on the screen. When the mouse leaves one portion of the leaf, the microscope view would disappear and a different view would appear as the student moves the mouse around. The advantage is that far more information can be placed on a Web page and the student can interact with it to bring up different materials he is attempting to understand.

Layer Movement

In addition to being able to change the visibility of a layer, a JavaScript function can make layers change position. All that needs to be changed is the "top" and "left" properties of a layer's style. Again, the two browsers handle layer movement differently, and it is best to use a good cross-browser Web page editor to create movement. Movement can be initiated by clicks and having the mouse pass over a hot spot, but the most interesting way to move layers is with what is called "drag and drop." (Tools like *Dreamweaver* generate complex JavaScript to initiate drag and drop.) This allows students to point to a layer on the screen, hold down the mouse button, move it anywhere on the screen, and release the mouse button. The layer stays where the layer is "dropped." One application for drag and drop is for self-evaluation. For example, the following sequence illustrates what can be done:

1. The student is presented with a page of graphic picture frames each containing an artist's name.

2. Using the mouse, she drags the images embedded in layers into the frames attempting to match paintings with artists.
3. The student clicks the Evaluate button, and instead of getting a score, the pictures automatically arrange themselves in the correct frames.
4. Clicking the Scatter button, the pictures are randomly scattered around the screen so that the student can try again to get it right.

Moving layers can help a learning process in several ways. Moving related examples to concepts helps students see connections between the abstract and the concrete. For example, a sociologist might show a number of different role concepts aligned with graphic elements representing the concepts such as a photo of an expensive automobile with the abstraction of *status symbol*. Moreover, often the static written page is a substitute for elements in the real world that do move. Moving different components of a static experiment into a correct sequence better helps students visualize a process.

The script for moving layers is similar to that for showing and hiding layers. Also, because the two major browsers treat layers differently, there needs to be separate script for each. We will begin with a key function of the script, and then look at an example.

```
function moveDown(){
tp=tp+12;
if (navigator.appName == 'Netscape')
   {document.layers.moveThis.top=tp; }
else
   {moveThis.style.top=tp; }
}
```

The variable named "tp" is a global variable incremented by 12 each time the function is executed. Basically, all that happens is that the value of the *top position* is changed by 12 and so the layer has a new position. As the *distance from the top* is increased, the layer moves farther from the top. That is, it moves down—hence the name of the function, *moveDown*(). By incrementing the value of the left property of the layer, it will move to the right. As will be seen, a variable named "lp" handles the horizontal movement. By decreasing the value of the *top* property the layer will move up, and by decreasing the value of the *left* property, the layer will move to the left.

Because variables are being used to move the layer, it is relatively easy to find a position on the screen. The position of the layer can be evaluated by the values of the vertical and horizontal variables, *tp* and *lp*. If the position is within the correct vertical and horizontal axes, the student is informed she got the right answer. Otherwise, nothing happens. The following segment of script shows how this is done, and because the same two variables are used for both browsers, no additional filtering is required.

```
if(tp >70 && tp < 90 &&
 lp > 245) {alert("Very good. Price fixing is the
  violation.")}
```

However, all functions need the conditional statement because there is no way of knowing which direction button will be pressed to arrive at the right answer. More script could be added to inform the student she has an incorrect answer if any of the other selections are made. Table 14-3 shows the Web page at the outset and when the student has moved the image (handcuffs) to the correct answer.

Although the following script may appear to be complex, all it does is change the values "top" and "left" of the layer until the variables with the values fall between certain parameters. The answer choices are placed into layers so that they can be placed in a specific location on the page that can be "found" by the student moving the layer using buttons. Note there are four key functions that make the layer go up, down, left, and right. Each function either increments or decrements a value defining the horizontal and vertical axes of the layer and is fired by the student clicking a button. Each function also looks to see if the layer is over the layer of the correct answer. If it is, it simply sends up an alert box. (See Appendix C at the end of this chapter for a script listing for the materials in Table 14-3 of how to move layers.)

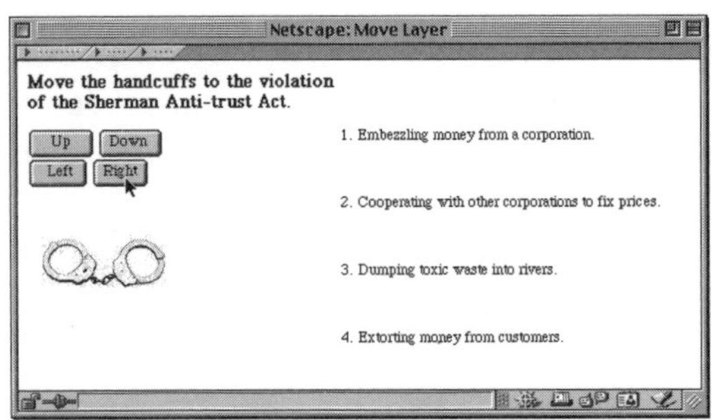

1. Student moves a layer (handcuffs) to the correct answer by clicking direction buttons. Each button fires a function to change the value of "top" or "left" in the layer.

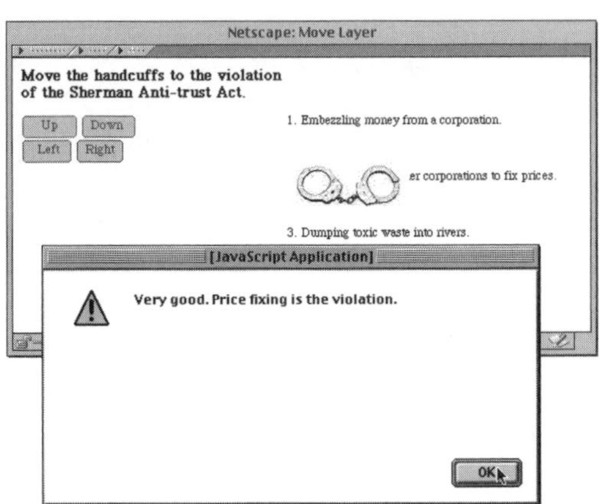

2. When layer is detected over correct answer, an alert box appears.

TABLE 14-3 Providing movable layers lets instructors use a number of different ways of helping students become actively involved in the learning process.

Summary and Review

University faculties have been limited in either resources, tradition, or invention in how they could or wanted to teach students. Most faculty became aware early on that if students did not study, they would not do well, and collectively concluded that students are adults and it was up to them to act in a mature way and do the work to pass a course. Holding office hours is a way to provide additional help to students who need it and perhaps suggest ways to better study and *learn* what is required of them. Otherwise learning is reading, attending lectures, participating in discussions, and doing lab work.

With newer tools and ideas about how to better make a connection between what students need to learn and the ways in which the materials are presented, university professors are beginning to take advantage of some of the newer tools such as Web technology. Dynamic HTML is important because it provides for far more interactivity between the student and what he is required to learn. There are more ways to involve students in the process, and whenever instructors take advantage of this technology to create interactive lessons, new ideas and ways of teaching emerge. The technology in and of itself will never make students better learners or scholars. However, when faculty understand what can be done by combining their own inventiveness with the capacity of the technology, new ways of learning will emerge.

As DHTML and other fully interactive technologies become available on the Web along with the support staff and tools to develop complex scripts for courses, there are opportunities to open up whole new ways of thinking about what it takes to communicate and involve students in materials they need to understand and learn. On the one hand, the new ways of thinking include integrating good practices into Web-based learning. On the other hand, there *must* be an openness to whole new ideas about how students might better learn and understand. Exploring and experimenting with these new technologies is a key part of the equation. Most of the really good development in instructional technology will probably come from looking at the good practices and seeing how they can be implemented. However, with the power of full multimedia, we need also to seriously consider what can be done with this media that introduces new practices that were impossible prior to the technology itself. Exploring DHTML is a step in that direction.

Glossary of Terms

DHTML Dynamic HTML refers to a combination of traditional HTML combined with layers and JavaScript routines to provide actions relative to the layers.

Events Events are actions taken by the user that can be read by the Web page. A mouse click, a pointer's position, or a page loading or closing are all events. Event handlers in

JavaScript read the events and respond to events as determined by the designer.

Layer A layer is part of a Web page that can change several attributes independent of the page itself. In effect it has most of the attributes of a Web page but is "owned" by the page.

Methods Actions that objects can take. For example, write() is a method that places text on a page, and alert() is a method that generates a pop-up box.

Objects All of the parts of a Web page are objects. In HTML and other object-oriented programs, the objects exist in a hierarchy. The page (window) is at the highest level and the value (current state) of an object is at the lowest.

Properties The attributes of objects are called properties. For example, one property of a layer is its visibility. The value of the property is a variable or condition.

Reference

Tufte, Edward. *The Visual Display of Quantitative Information* (Graphics Press: Cheshire, CT: 1983).

Appendix

A. Layers on a Web Page

Key attributes for Figure 14-3 are illustrated in the following script.

```
<html>
<head><title>Layers</title></head>
<body bgcolor="white">
<h1><P>X<P>X<P>X<P>This is on the main Web page.</h1>
<div id="Layer1" style="position:absolute; left:50px;
  top:70px; width:100px; height:150px; z-index:1;
  background-color: yellow">This is Layer A.</div>
<div id="Layer2" style="position:absolute; left:200px;
  top:100px; width:80px; height:80px; z-index:2;
  background-color: powderblue">This is Layer B.</div>
</body>
</html>
```

B. Layers and Browsers

An important feature of using layers is the ability of students to control their visibility from a running Web page. However, Internet Explorer (IE) and Netscape Communicator (NC) handle a layer's visibility differently. As a result, to dynamically change the visibility of a layer, two different kinds of scripts have to be used.

IE handles the visibility as a *style* attribute, and NC handles it as a *layer* property. Two different scripts illustrate how to write functions separately for each browser. Notice that the layers are set up identically, but the JavaScript functions are slightly different. The style attribute for IE is *visibility* and it can have a value of *visible* or *hidden*. For NC the visibility attributes are called *show* and *hide*.

Netscape Communicator Show and Hide

```
<html>
<head><title>Show Hide NC</title>
<script language="JavaScript">
function showIt(){
   document.layers.switchMe.visibility='show';
}
function hideIt() {
        document.layers.switchMe.visibility='hide';
}
</script>
</head>
<body bgcolor="white">
<div id="switchMe" style="position: absolute; top: 50px;
   left: 50px">
This message will be toggled. </div>
<form><input type="button" value="Hide"
   onClick="hideIt()">
<input type="button" value="Show" onClick="showIt()">
</form>
</body></html>
```

Internet Explorer Show and Hide

```
<html><head>
<title>Show Hide IE</title>
<script language="JavaScript">
function showIt(){
            switchMe.style.visibility="visible"
}
function hideIt() {
            switchMe.style.visibility="hidden"
}
</script>
</head>
<body bgcolor="white">
<div id="switchMe" style="position: absolute; top: 50px;
   left: 50px">
This message will be toggled. </div>
```

```
<form><input type="button" value="Hide"
  onClick="hideIt()">
<input type="button" value="Show" onClick="showIt()">
</form>
</body></html>
```

Because the only difference in the two scripts is in the JavaScript, key lines from each are compared. Using the script segments that hide the layers, we can see these differences and a way to rewrite the script so that both browsers can read it.

Netscape has a <LAYERS> tag not recognized by IE that works virtually the same as <DIV>. In part, that explains why Netscape Communicator uses *layers* as an object and Internet Explorer does not. When there are basic differences between the two browsers, either avoid the tags or write special scripts that resolve the differences.

A simple technique to make sure that no matter what type of browser the student uses, she will see the same thing is to add a line in JavaScript to check to see which browser is being used. Because there are only two main ones, it is possible to check for one, and if it is not being used, the script assumes the other one is. This requires writing a double function, but it is very important to have Web pages that work with either major browser. The following script changes the last two scripts to show how this can be done.

```
<html>
<head><title>Show Hide Both</title>
<script language="JavaScript">
function showIt(){
if (navigator.appName == 'Netscape')
{
document.layers.switchMe.visibility='show';
}
else
{
switchMe.style.visibility="visible";
}
}
function hideIt() {
if (navigator.appName == 'Netscape')
{
document.layers.switchMe.visibility='hide';
}
else
{switchMe.style.visibility="hidden";
}
}
```

```
</script>
</head>
<body bgcolor="white">
<div id="switchMe" style="position: absolute; top: 50px;
  left: 50px">
This message will be toggled. </div>
<form><input type="button" value="Hide"
  onClick="hideIt()">
<input type="button" value="Show" onClick="showIt()">
</form>
</body></html>
```

That is a lot of script work because two major corporations will not adopt the same standard. A simple version of the same "fix" could be written as

```
function hideIt() { navigator.appName == 'Netscape' ?
document.layers.switchMe.visibility='hide' :
  switchMe.style.visibility="hidden"}
```

This type of conditional is more economic in terms of generating script, but it can be more difficult to understand. The importance of creating clear script lies in the ability to use it in many different applications, and so having a good idea of what the script does will save a lot of time when used again. Even better, when developing several lessons and courses with a Web page component, put often-used scripts into a separate file that can be called up using the <SCRIPT> tag as shown in Chapter 13 (for example., <SCRIPT SRC = 'showhide.js'>).

C. Moving Layers

The following script illustrates one way to move layers on a page as shown in Table 14-3. More intuitive and powerful ways are available for students to move layers. The following script, though, is relatively simple and can be done by those without powerful Web development tools.

```
<html>
<head><title>Move Layer</title>
<script language="JavaScript">
var tp=120;
var lp=10;
function moveDown(){ //Move 12 pixels down
tp=tp+12;
if (navigator.appName == 'Netscape')
{document.layers.moveThis.top=tp; }
else
```

```
{moveThis.style.top=tp; }
if(tp >70 && tp < 90 && lp > 245) {alert("Very good.
  Price fixing is the violation.")}
}
function moveRight(){ //Move 12 pixels right
lp=lp+12;
if (navigator.appName == 'Netscape')
{document.layers.moveThis.left=lp; }
else
{moveThis.style.left=lp; }
if(tp >70 && tp < 90 && lp > 245) {alert("Very good.
  Price fixing is the violation.")}
}
function moveUp(){ //Move 12 pixels up
tp=tp-12;
if (navigator.appName == 'Netscape')
{document.layers.moveThis.top=tp; }
else
{moveThis.style.top=tp; }
if(tp >70 && tp < 90 && lp > 245) {alert("Very good.
  Price fixing is the violation.")}
}
function moveLeft(){ //Move 12 pixels left
lp=lp-12;
if (navigator.appName == 'Netscape')
{document.layers.moveThis.left=lp; }
else
{moveThis.style.left=lp; }
if(tp >70 && tp < 90 && lp > 245) {alert("Very good.
  Price fixing is the violation.")}
}
</script>
</head>
<body bgcolor="white"> //Answers are separate layers
<div id="embezzle" style="position: absolute; top: 50px;
  left: 250px">1. Embezzling money from a corporation.
  </div>
<div id="priceFix" style="position: absolute; top: 100px;
  left: 250px">2. Cooperating with other corporations to
  fix prices. </div>
<div id="pollute" style="position: absolute; top: 150px;
  left: 250px">3. Dumping toxic waste into rivers.
  </div>
<div id="extort" style="position: absolute; top: 200px;
  left: 250px">4. Extorting money from customers. </div>
```

```
<div id="moveThis" style="position: absolute; top: 120px;
   left: 10px">
<img src="cuffs.jpg"></div>
<h3>Move the handcuffs to the violation<br> of the
   Sherman Anti-trust Act.</h3>
<form><input type="button" value=" Up "
   onClick="moveUp();">
<input type="button" value="Down " onClick="moveDown();">
   <br>
<input type="button" value=" Left "
   onClick="moveLeft();">
<input type="button" value="Right"
   onClick="moveRight();"><br>
</form>
</body></html>
```

By adding spaces before and after the values (labels) of the four buttons it is possible to make them closer to the same size. Otherwise the "Up" button would be much smaller than the "Right" button.

Chapter 15

Rollovers and Cascading Style Sheets: Controlling the Page

Rollovers deal with images and Cascading Style Sheets (CSS) are part of Dynamic HTML. However, both topics deal with controlling what the student sees on a page. Rollovers are seen everywhere on Web pages and provide a dynamic, interactive element for learning-centered pages. However, equally important, they provide insight into how images can be manipulated on a page to respond to a student's action. Cascading Style Sheets are a style control feature of DHTML, and for easing the formatting problems inherent in HTML, Cascading Style Sheets are a welcome feature to Web page design.

An important part of Web pages that often is glaringly lacking from university Web pages created by faculty is *style*. For the most part, this is a matter of not having any background in style and design, and the result is poor communication. Another problem is that HTML was not originally designed to handle very many different style elements. This has changed with CSS. Not only has style become an important feature to consider in a page, there is script to allow good page design and formatting. What's more, with CSS, once a style has been developed, it can be saved as a separate style sheet and used for subsequent Web pages. It can serve as a template, and so once it has been created properly, that work will not have to be repeated. However, getting it done right is a lot of work, and this chapter examines some key elements of style that can make a page look better and better communicate content to students.

Rollovers

The term "rollover" refers to a very specific action on Web pages. Basically, it means that if a mouse passes over an image, the image will change. Actually, one image is swapped with another. The same effect can occur on a page when the mouse pointer moves over a hot spot of text and the text or something else on the page changes. In one creative example, the professor placed the Periodic Table of Elements on a Web page and when the student passed the mouse over each element, information about the element appeared in text boxes.

However, this discussion focuses solely on the conventional meaning of *rollovers* on a Web page. Furthermore, the focus will be on the concept of *image* on a Web page and how it can be manipulated to bring about a very active learning environment. Up to now, inserting images has been fairly simple because they can be easily placed with Web editing tools. By the same token, there are excellent tools available for creating rollovers with graphics. Premier among the tools for creating rollovers are Adobe *ImageStyler* and Macromedia *Fireworks*. They have special tools for making rollovers. Likewise, using Web page editors such as *Dreamweaver* and *GoLive* as well as graphic editing programs like *PhotoShop* makes creating rollovers a simple affair.

At one time while looking at an online news story about chemical warfare plants in Iraq, CNN news showed maps of Iraq with the names of various cities where suspected chemical warfare development was taking place. By rolling over the various named cities, more detailed information about the nature of the chemicals being produced appeared. I found that I wanted to look at all the cities to reveal this additional information, and by doing so I learned an effective use of rollovers in learning. The CNN site, and others like it, provides ideas and even models for involving the viewer in the site and to provide more information in a given space than is possible on paper. Most importantly, rollovers provide a mechanism to get the viewer to explore more, and by revealing surprises in the form of additional information, they are instructional as well.

The scripts for making rollovers are relatively easy, and the same script can be used with both major browsers. Using a simple script we will examine the usefulness of rollovers for learning and see how to create them for students. The example comes from pilot education in meteorology. Part of the learning includes avoiding thunderstorms and the turbulence these storms generate. The major clue to a cloud formation being a thunderstorm is the presence of lightning that can be seen from several miles away. However, in only rare occasions is lightning a threat to aircraft, and so what needs to be understood is the *relationship between lightning and the turbulence* and not the threat of lightning itself. Using a rollover, the student is presented with an aircraft in proximity to a graphic lightning bolt. When the mouse is passed over the lightning bolt, the thundercloud appears explaining *and showing* the relationship the instructor hopes the student will see and learn. The

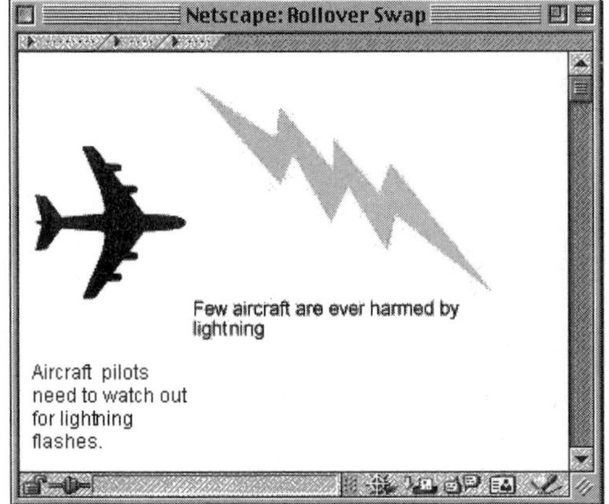

Before and after the mouse is passed over the image on the right, a lightning bolt appears.

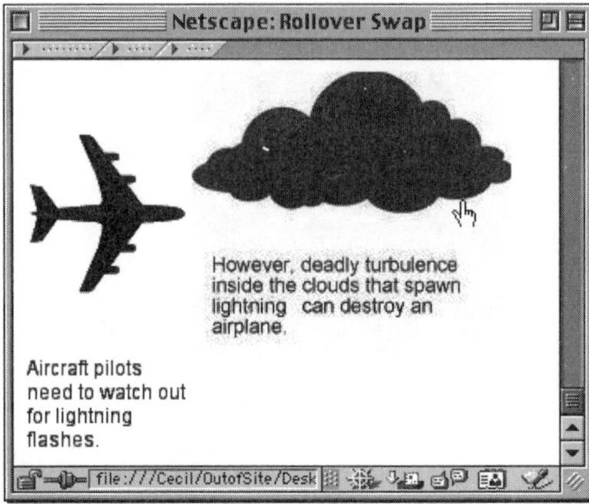

Only when the mouse pointer is actually over the right image does the thundercloud appear.

TABLE 15-1 Rollovers provide an animated connection between related concepts.

script in Appendix A at the end of this chapter uses two graphics, bolt.jpg and cloud.jpg, in the rollover and one graphic, airplane.gif, outside. A table is used for formatting. Table 15-1 shows the Web page before and after the mouse pointer is placed on the graphic. The text under the airplane image is in the bottom row of the table; however, all text associated with the changing graphics is actually graphic text embedded in the graphic image. In this way, it is possible to bring up the text message along with the changing images.

There are no instructions on the Web page to move the mouse pointer over the rollover. At some point in using Web pages for teaching and learning, students need to *assume* graphic elements may have more information—whether it is a pop-up alert message or even a link to a whole new page. In reading a book, students are not instructed to read the words one after another nor is there a special instruction to look at the graphs, charts, and illustrations. They are *expected* to do so. Unannounced surprises are much more interesting than those fully anticipated and provide a sense of exploration on a Web page. Suggestions to *explore* the page and similar helpful hints better connect the act of moving the mouse around a page and finding information than simply stating a hand and eye coordinated action.

Learning to See Things in a New Light with Rollovers

An important part of a university education is learning how to see things in a different light. Were a college education simply a repetition of common sense, there would be little reason to bother with higher education at all. However, that is not the case. Fields such as Women's Studies and Ethnic Studies are often faced with transforming stereotypes, and one use of rollovers is transforming the way students see things.

For example swapping graphics might be incorporated to let the student change the stereotype by his actions. The original graphics are swapped for the same graphic image with different textual content. The student first sees a set of images connected with both typical and stereotypical occupational choices, and the change in the *message* does not occur *until the student does something*. The text that appears on the rollover is part of the graphic with the image that appears. When the mouse is rolled off the image, the original image reappears. However, that image now has more than a single typical or stereotypical label seen *well below the image*. In this way the student can then see the image with a different set of assumptions without having a message to tell him that. What text remains well below the images is no longer connected to them. Like a magic trick that has been revealed, the audience now sees the *reality* of the situation "beneath the image."

Besides providing alternative interpretive schemes for stereotypes, rollovers can be used much in the same ways as layers and alert boxes to give additional information to connect one idea or concept with another. In multiple-choice questions, rollovers can be used to provide indications of correct answers and explanations of incorrect ones. The simple swap/rollover script used for the page shown in Table 15-1 can be adopted to any images. All that is required are two different images for each rollover.

Changing Image Size

One of the limitations of using image swapping is that the second image will be forced to the same size and proportions of the first image. If the first image is high and narrow, and the second one is low and wide, the second graphic will be distorted to the size of the first image. To correct this problem, make sure that both images are of identical size. This may mean that one image has a lot of white space around it to fill in the area it would not take up. Otherwise, there will be distortion problems. Table 15-2 shows what happens when two different size graphics are used and how they should work.

ImageStyler generated the second set of graphics in Table 15-2. It automatically made all the corrections so those different graphic images of different dimensions could be used in a rollover. Graphic programs like *Fireworks* and *PhotoShop* can also make the corrections. One simple way to do that is to enlarge the *canvas size* (not image size) so that both graphics fit on the same size canvas. Then crop the canvas to minimize white space but keep the graphics the same dimensions.

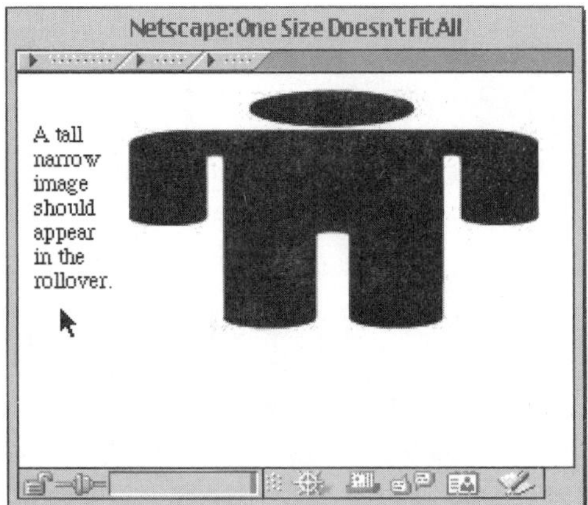

Initial images in a rollover define the size of the space used.

Images that have different dimensions will be forced to the size of the first image, and distortions are likely.

To prevent distortion, the first image has to be the same image size including white space around the viewable graphic.

When the second graphic comes up, it appears to be a different size from the first one, but both are identical even though much of the first one is taken up by white space.

TABLE 15-2 Image distortion occurs in rollovers if the graphics are a different size. This is corrected by adding white space around the images so that the *viewed* images are different while the graphic dimensions are identical.

Cascading Style Sheets

Cascading Style Sheets (CSS) are used to define certain style attributes of a page. Several style sheets can be used to define a Web page and thus they *cascade over one another*—hence the name. For anyone who has a background in Web page design, basic HTML is an extremely awkward way to design a Web page. By creating style sheets, faculty members are able to create Web pages or even courses using a style and design that best suit their needs. Once a style sheet is completed, it can be used over and over again, and so in addition to being a good design tool, it saves time.

At the time of this writing, Internet Explorer and Netscape Communicator diverge. With Version 4 of Internet Explorer, Microsoft introduced truly dynamic style sheets that could be changed by the user on a Web page. As was seen in Chapter 14, Internet Explorer and Netscape Communicator use different ways of dealing with layers, and the two major browsers have differences in the way that their Version 4 series of browsers dealt with CSS. Version 5 of Internet Explorer had even more enhancements for CSS and Microsoft's conception and interpretation of the CSS specifications. What specifications are used by either major browser or new browsers that may become available is unknown at this writing. However, a good place to find out about current specifications for CSS can be found at **http://www.w3.org**, the World Wide Web Consortium (W3C). When new specifications are announced for just about anything dealing with standards for Web-based languages, W3C will have it. In this section, the CSS discussed works on both browsers without any special script. Only a limited subset of CSS is examined, and for a fuller examination of CSS attributes see **http://www.w3.org/Style/**.

Using Style

Cascading Style Sheets work either *inline* or as *style sheets*. The inline use of CSS is discussed because it provides a quick introduction to using CSS. However, for the most part, the discussion centers on using style sheets because of their usefulness for larger Web page projects such as lessons or courses.

One of the primary tags used with style sheets is <SPAN>. Something like the <DIV> tag, the <SPAN> </SPAN> combination acts like a text receptacle separate from but part of a Web page. The text in the <SPAN> element can be defined with a style all its own. A <DIV> block is a bit different in that it will break up the middle of a paragraph, but a <SPAN> element can be inserted in the middle of it.

However, the main use of <SPAN> and <DIV> in this section is to see how they can be used in defining styles. The property within the <SPAN> tag that signals a definition is *style*. For example, the following line of script would provide a line with 12 point navy blue text:

```
<span style = "font-size: 12pt; color: navy">
```

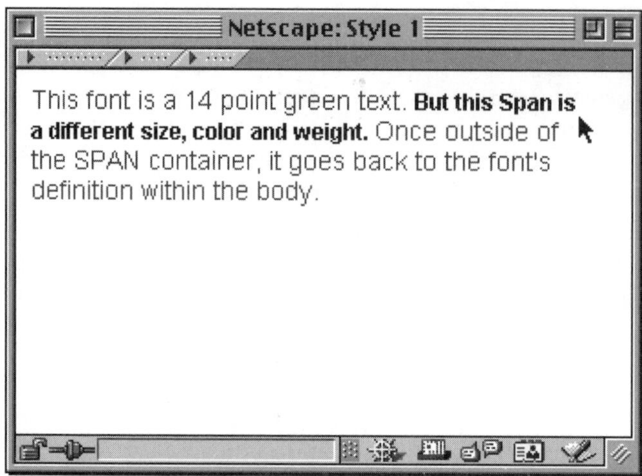

FIGURE 15-1 The darker text is within a SPAN container.

All of the text within that span container (everything between <SPAN> and </SPAN>) will have a 12 point navy blue text, regardless of other definitions around it. A sample script in Appendix B at the end of the chapter shows how the SPAN container works.

Figure 15-1 shows the Web page as it appears on the screen. Notice that although the font within the <SPAN> tags (the bolder darker text) did not conform to the color, weight, and size of the <FONT> tag definition, it did retain the font face. Because the default font is a serif font, it is important to note that text within a SPAN does retain the other definitions not changed in the style definition. In this case, the nondefault font face is retained. (See listing in Appendix B.)

Style Sheets

In some cases, the design requires a style throughout the whole page. With a single, global definition in the HEAD area of a page, you can define one or more styles using either existing tags or ones you create. To begin, define the <SPAN> tag with a built-in style so that whenever <SPAN> is used in a page, just the <SPAN> tag alone is enough to change the style. (See Appendix C at the end of the chapter for a listing.) See Figure 15-2.

Redefining Tags

In much the same way that the <SPAN> tag can be globally defined, so too can other tags. This can be done with points and other familiar page measurements. For example, setting up a series of heading levels and a whole new style for links may be useful for a style sheet. In the script in Appendix D at the end of this chapter, note that the link tag is <A> used in <A HREF=. . . >. Instead of getting underlined text, a bold text in a terra-cotta color called "firebrick" is used. When the tags

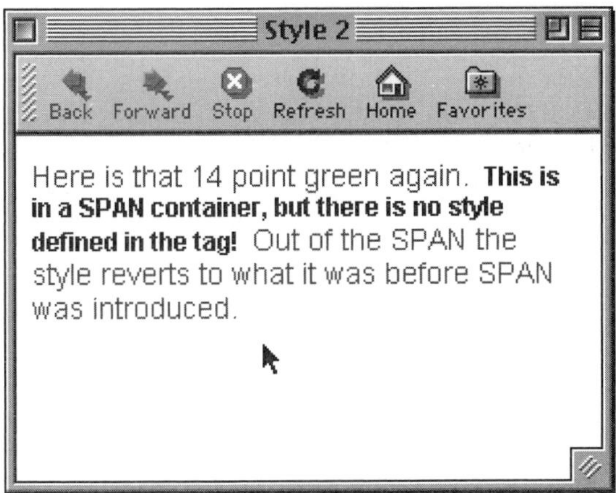

FIGURE 15-2 Style sheets can be used to define groups of text within a SPAN.

are used in HTML, the newly defined styles for the tags are invoked. Figure 15-3 shows these new styles.

Class

This next section deals with making unique styles without reference to any tag at all. Good page formatting is possible because one is not restricted by the limitations of standard HTML choices or redefining existing tags. However, it is important to understand that this does not mean that Web pages should be used for long stretches of text that replace books, articles, and other paper documents. Formatting text on Web pages should be for a small, clear explanation, and longer text documents need to be left on paper. It takes students about three times as long to read text on the screen as it does on paper, and most students have the good sense to print out long textual passages. If it is the instructor's intention that the student print out a long scroll of text, she should have a special link to that page and instructions to print the page. Otherwise, it is much more useful to provide students with printed pages that they can use in conjunction with a Web page. The resolution of printed pages is far greater than screen resolution, and lessons can be designed to give the student something to read before responding to an interactive Web page.

Creating unique style definitions in style sheets uses the following format:

```
.defName {feature: definitions}
```

When used to define a style, the leading period or dot [.] is dropped and just the definition name is used. Generally, use a defined label or name with the *class* attribute of a tag. For example, a paragraph uses the <P> tag, and so to introduce a style to a paragraph, one would write

```
<P class=defName> The text goes here. </P>
```

In many of the examples in this book, the <P> tag has been used to create a paragraph line break with an added space. However, using CSS, the <P> tag becomes a container to define the text within and it expects a </P> tag to close the defined block. The <BODY>, <SPAN>, and <DIV> tags can also contain a defined class to format text. Of course, the <P. . . > with the class definition still inserts a paragraph line break.

Figure 15-3 has a good deal of formatting in it and some new elements. First, using all caps has been discouraged as a general style because it is difficult to read and looks amateurish. However, given some added spacing between the letters, it can be used effectively as a header. CSS allows letter spacing to be specified, and so more creative use of text in page design is possible. Also, the style definition includes a text transformation so that whatever is written in the defined style is transformed to uppercase letters. Notice that the word "Theory" in the script is written in uppercase and lowercase (Appendix E), but in Figure 15-4 it is all in uppercase or all caps. Finally, a nonstandard font is used as the first font in the list, *Bauhaus 93*. Notice how it was placed in quotation marks. If the user does not have that font, the script looks for substitutions in Arial and Helvetica, two standard fonts on most computers.

Second, notice that the margins are different for the two heads and the body text. This provides more flexibility in setting up a page to make the heads distinct but not divorced from the rest of the page. For the body font, the first line is indented, and any subsequent paragraph with the same style would indent *only* the first line of the paragraph.

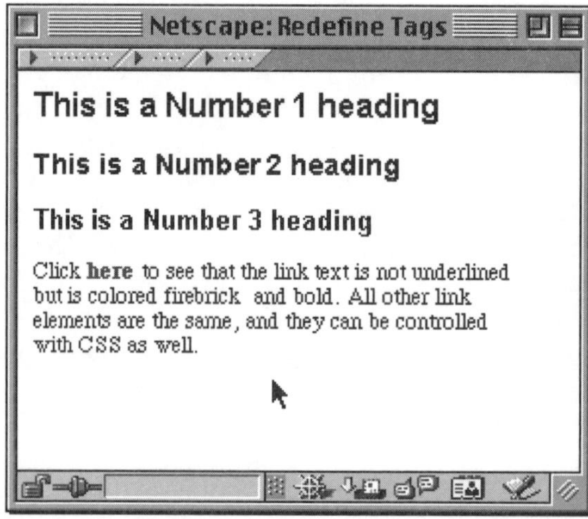

FIGURE 15-3 Redefining tags allows customized styles for specific requirements on a page.

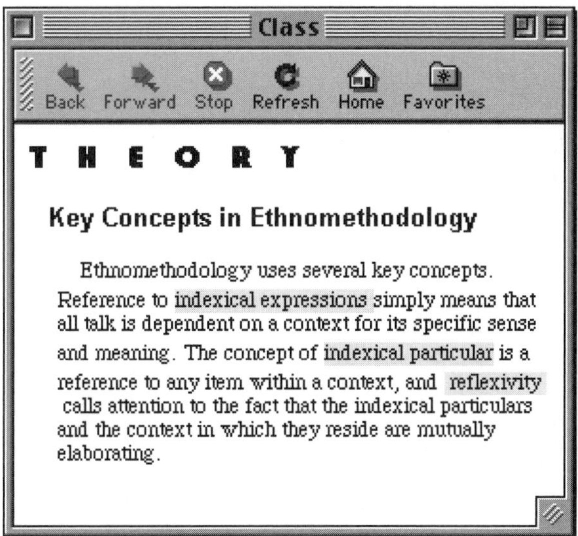

FIGURE 15-4 Using style sheets, far more style elements can be put into a page for increasing clarity and focus.

Finally, each concept in the page appears as though it is highlighted with a yellow marking pen. Simply making the background color for the style definition yellow did this. Each concept in the page is placed in a <SPAN> that changed only the background color. Because students regularly mark their reading with colored markers, this simulates what they do on paper and helps bring attention to the concepts. (See Appendix E at the end of the chapter for a listing.)

Borders and Backgrounds

Page decorations can be useful for making text and graphics stand out in useful and interesting ways. Various borders and backgrounds can enhance a message or make it look pretty bad. Figure 15-5 shows what some backgrounds and borders look like. The importance of borders and backgrounds is that they can be used for enhancing a page, but all too often they are used because they are available. This is especially true with background images, as can be seen in Figure 15-5—the message is virtually unreadable because the checkerboard background gets in the way.

In examining the listing, the main element that is different is the script for bringing up a background image. The format,

```
image: url (graphic.jpg)
```

indicates that the graphic is in the same folder as the HTML for the Web page, but a fuller address (for example, http://www.stateu.edu/Prof/images/graphic.jpg) could be used if needed. Otherwise, the script looks very much like the script used

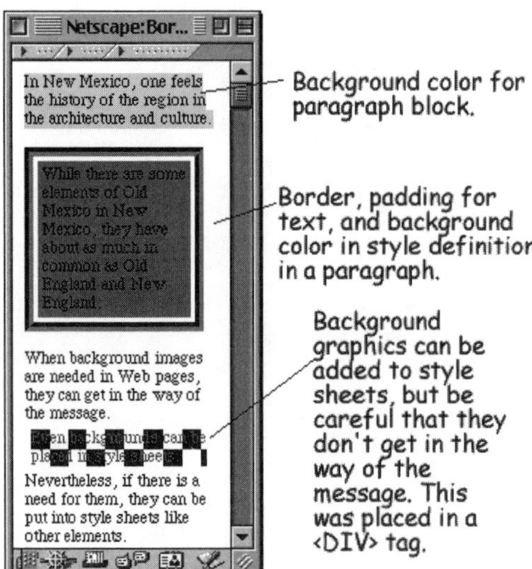

FIGURE 15-5 In using borders, background colors, and backgrounds, do not pull more attention to the border or background than the content.

in defining the other style characteristics. (See Appendix F at the end of the chapter for a listing.)

The *padding* attribute works something like *margin* except it defines the margins within the borders rather than the page. Without a three-pixel padding (3px), the text was difficult to read. In fact, in one of the worst cases of design misdirection, the label warnings on tobacco ads appearing on cigarette packages, on billboards, and in print advertisements use a thick border to clutter the words—with the help of all caps and underlined sans serif text (Tufte, 1997, 65). For example, Figure 15-6 shows how the misuse of style can distract from the message using the same anticlarity design of the tobacco companies on their warning labels.

Table 15-3 shows a sample of the various CSS attributes and their properties and a quick way to look up some commonly used ones. For a full listing of CSS attributes and properties, see **http://www.w3.org/TR/WD-CSS2/indexlist.html.** Also, if any of the attributes or their properties do not work on one browser, try another. At the time of this writing, a few attributes worked only on one browser or another. Also, be sure the browser in use is Version 4 or newer—preferably newer.

WARNING! THE DESIGNER GENERAL HAS DETERMINED THAT BAD DESIGN CAN DESTROY YOUR WEB SITE

FIGURE 15-6 We can learn from intentionally distracting and confusing design. Cigarette warnings are a good example.

Name	Meaning	Properties	Example
color	color of font	#00000–#FFFFFF or names	h3 {color: green}
background-color	color of block background	#00000–#FFFFFF or names	p {background-color: pink}
background-image	linked background image	uses selected image file as background	h2 { background-image: url(cloud.gif)}
font-family	name of font or fonts to be used in style.	"font name" or fontname, generic names include "serif, sans-serif, monospaced, fantasy, cursive"	span {font-family: "Book Antigua", Times, serif}
font-style	font name	normal, italic, oblique	body {font-style: normal}
font-variant	font's variation from normal	normal, small-caps	h3 {font-variant: small-caps}
font-weight	intensity level of font	normal, bold, bolder, lighter, 100, 200, 300, 400, 500, 600, 700, 800, 900	.chub {font-weight: 800}
font-size	size of font	point, pixel, percent, or em value, number, description [small, large] or relative size [larger, smaller]	p {font-size: 130%} h1 {font-size: xx-large} h3 {font-size: 16pt}
text-indent	indents first line of text paragraph	point, pixel, percent, em	h5 {text-indent: 0.5em}
text-align	sets text alignment	left, right, center, justify	p {text-align: right}
text-decoration	adds feature to text	none, underline, overline, line-through, blink	.changeout {text-.decoration: linethrough}
text-transform	changes case of fonts	capitalize [first letter of every word only], uppercase, lowercase, none	.shout {text-transform: uppercase}
margin-top	distance of text block from top of page	point, pixel, percent, or em value	p{margin-top: 30px}
margin-bottom	distance of text block from bottom of page	point, pixel, percent, or em value	h1{margin-bottom:2 em}
margin-left	distance of text block from left of page	point, pixel, percent, or em value	body{margin-left: 20pt}
margin-right	distance of text block from right of page	point, pixel, percent, or em value	p{margin-right: 10%}
margin	sets all margins to specified widths	point, pixel, percent, or em value	body{margin: 2em} body {margin: 75%}
border-width	width of box border line	thin, medium, thick	h1{border-width: solid medium blue}
border-color	defines color of border	#00000–#FFFFFF or names	p {border-color: tan}
border-style	defines kind of border to be displayed	none, dotted, dashed, solid, double, groove, inset, outset	p {border-style: outset}

TABLE 15-3 Use this table for a quick lookup of some common CSS attributes and their values.

Creating and Using External Style Sheets

Once a style sheet has been prepared, it could be quite complex, or there might be several different style sheets for different courses or lessons. Rather than having to rewrite a new style or even cut and paste an existing one, it is much easier to use external style sheets. An external style sheet is a text file that contains styles that have been defined, much in the same way that external JavaScript text files can be brought in and used without having to rewrite to script again. The format used is the following <LINK> tag:

```
<link rel="stylesheet" href="templateBio.css"
  type="text/css" >
```

The file is referenced by HREF, just as with other links, and the file name can be whatever classification system the instructor wants. In this example "template-Bio.css" is used to suggest a template for a biology class that has its own set of styles and designs. See Appendix G at the end of the chapter for an example of creating and using an external Cascading Style Sheet.

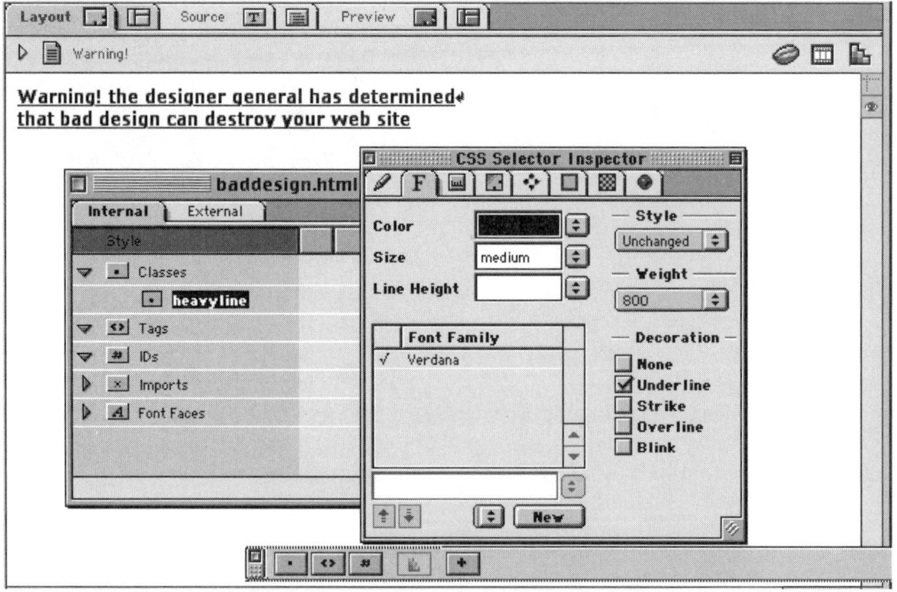

FIGURE 15-7 Adobe *GoLive* automatically generates CSS code.

Web Design Tools and CSS

Having gone through a good deal of CSS code, it may appear a trifle backward to now suggest using a Web development tool for CSS. I would certainly suggest using *Dreamweaver* or *GoLive* for CSS, but in this case, learning something about CSS code actually helps when using a Web design tool. Each of the elements redefined in Web design tools writes CSS code. However, understanding what the codes do greatly helps to create and use CSS in the Web design applications. Figure 15-7 shows two CSS windows in Adobe *GoLive* used in developing CSS. Note the dot [.] definition in the left window and how the font characteristics are selected in the right window.

Summary and Review

Rollovers and Cascading Style Sheets are fairly subtle but important tools to help create learning-rich Web pages. Most of the use of rollovers is to light up buttons on Web pages, and this can be a useful way of engaging students. However, a far better use for rollovers is to provide additional insights and juxtapose images and thoughts to show relationships, or alternative interpretations or to make some connection that *reacts to* a student's activity. Rollovers can be important tools in helping students make transitions, see connections, and broaden perspectives. They can still be used to light up a linking image, but they should not be assigned solely to minor or even trivial tasks. Rather rollovers should enhance ways of helping students see transformations.

Excellence in page design is invisible. To the viewer or reader, fonts, the page, text, images, colors, layout, and all the rest flow effortlessly *for the person looking at it*. The content of the page comes forth, and there is no attention to the surround and context of the page. It looks and feels right, and so there is nothing to do but read it. However, when a poorly designed page is before a student, there is difficulty and discomfort. Somehow, the design gets in the way of the page's content, and while a reader may not know what's wrong, she will sense it in a level of discomfort and even confusion. Just like the next-to-impossible-to-read design used in cigarette warning labels, poor design draws one's attention away from the content.

With Cascading Style Sheets, it is possible to design an excellent page. Although a good simple page is possible using standard HTML (and a few tricks), using CSS just about any design technique is possible. The font set is limited by what the student's computer has on board, but because several variations of a font (for example, Arial, Helvetica, sans serif) can be found on just about any computer hooked up to the Internet, there is very little reason to limit Web page design to non-CSS HTML and old browsers. Because establishing good connections and communication is an essential part of the learning process, using Cascading Style

Sheets aids in the communication and connections necessary for a solid learning-centered Web page.

Glossary of Terms

Cascading Style Sheet A sheet consists of one or more style definitions, and a single page may have several sheets. The sheets are cascading in that when multiple sheets are on the same page, different style sheets may attempt to affect the same text. *Cascade* refers to the order in which conflicts of style are resolved—the precedence and hierarchy of the sheets.

External Style Sheet When Cascading Style Sheets are placed in a separate text file and called into a page using the <LINK> tag, they are considered external.

Rollover Graphic swapping when the mouse pointer rolls over an image programmed to replace itself with another image.

Text background colors Both text colors and the background for each text letter on the screen can be defined in a style sheet. When the sheet is applied, only that text with the CSS definition will have the defined background color. The background color of CSS overrides that of the page, a cell, or a layer.

Text borders Using CSS, it is possible to provide a defined border as part of a style sheet. All text influenced by the sheet is bordered.

Reference

Tufte, Edward. *Visual Explanations* (Graphics Press: Cheshire, CT: 1997).

Appendix

A. Table 15-1

The following script uses the term "swap" as the function names. Essentially, all a rollover does is to *swap* graphics when the mouse pointer is on top of the graphic and when it rolls off. That means that there must be two event handlers each time the swap or rollover occurs. First, when the pointer is detected over the graphic, there must be an event handler to deal with that action. Second, when the mouse pointer is rolled off the graphic, a second event handler needs to launch a function.

```
<html>
<head><title>Rollover Swap</title>
<script language="JavaScript">
var storm1=new image()
storm1.src="bolt.jpg"
var storm2= new image()
storm2.src="cloud.jpg"
function swap1() {
```

```
document.storm.src=storm1.src
}
function swap2() {
document.storm.src=storm2.src
}
</script>
</head>
<body bgcolor="white">
<table border=0 cellspacing=0 cellpadding=0 cols=2
  width="60%" >
<tr>
<td><img src="airplane.gif" border=0 align=center></td>
<td><a href="#" onMouseOver="swap2()"
  onMouseOut="swap1()"><img src="bolt.jpg" name="storm"
  border=0 ></a></td>
</tr>
<tr><td><font face="Arial,Helvetica">Aircraft pilots need
  to watch out for lightning flashes.</font></td>
</tr>
</table></body></html>
```

The JavaScript is used to put the images in variables named *storm1* and *storm2*. These variables are then "loaded" with the images to be swapped by attaching the *src* attribute and equating them with image names (for example, storm1.src="bolt.jpg"). The two functions, *swap1()* and *swap2()*, define the page elements as being one of the two variables loaded with the graphic images. In the body of the script, event handlers for both *onMouseOver* and *onMouseOut* fire one of the two functions. That is all there is to it. However, it is very important to name the *image src* tag in the body of the script. The name, *storm*, is used for the document to identify in which image holder the swap will occur. (The term *image holder* is used here to mean the tag where the image to be swapped is first defined.) So while the name property is usually not needed when an image is inserted in a Web page, in using rollovers it is essential to include it.

B. Span Container

See Figure 15-1 to see how the page is configured in the browser.

```
<html>
<head><title>Style 1</title>
</head>
<body><font face="Arial,Helvetica" color="green" size=+1>
This font is a 14 point green text.
<span style="font-size: 12pt; color: navy; font-weight:
  bold">
```

```
But this Span is a different size, color and weight.
</span>
Once outside of the SPAN container, it goes back to the
   font's definition within the body.
</font></body>
</html>
```

C. Redefining SPAN

See Figure 15-2 for a screen shot of how the script affects the page.

```
<html>
<head><title>Style 2</title>
<style>
span {font-size: 12pt; color: navy; font-weight: bold}
</style>
</head>
<body><font face="Arial,Helvetica" color="green" size=+1>
Here is that 14 point green again.
<span>
This is in a SPAN container, but there is no style
   defined in the tag!
</span>
Out of the SPAN the style reverts to what it was before
   SPAN was introduced.
</body></html>
```

D. Redefining Style Tags.

Figure 15-3 shows a screen shot of the listing.

```
<html>
<head><title>Redefine Tags</title>
<style>
h1 {font-size: 16pt; font-weight: bold; font-family:
   Arial, Helvetica, sans-serif}
h2 {font-size: 14pt; font-weight: bold; font-family:
   Arial, Helvetica, sans-serif}
h3 {font-size: 13pt; font-weight: bold; font-family:
   Arial, Helvetica, sans-serif}
a { text-decoration: normal; color: firebrick; font-
   weight: bold}
</style>
</head>
</body>
```

```
<h1>This is a Number 1 heading</h1>
<h2>This is a Number 2 heading</h2>
<h3>This is a Number 3 heading</h3>
Click <a href="#" onclick="alert('That link is a bold
   fire brick!')">here </a> to see that the link text is
   not underlined but is colored firebrick and bold. All
   other link elements are the same, and they can be
   controlled with CSS as well.
</body></html>
```

E. CSS/Class

The script for Figure 15-4 breaks each style definition into separate lines. This helps clarify what is in the style for later editing and changes. Also, notice how the leading period or dot [.] is dropped when the definition is used as a class.

```
<html>
<head><title>Class</title>
<style>
.spacedHead {font-size : 16pt;
font-family: "Bauhaus 93", Arial, Helvetica;
font-weight: bold;
text-transform : uppercase;
letter-spacing: 16pt; }
.head1 {font-size: 13pt;
margin-left: 10px;
font-family: Arial, Helvetica, sans-serif;
font-weight: bold; }
.textBody {font-size: 12pt;
margin-left: 15px;
text-indent: 1em; }
.highlight {background-color: yellow}
</style>
</head>
</body>
<p class=spacedHead>Theory</p>
<p class=head1>Key Concepts in Ethnomethodology </p>
<p class=textBody> Ethnomethodology uses several key
   concepts. Reference to <span class=highlight>indexical
   expressions </span>simply means that all talk is
   dependent on a context for its specific sense and
   meaning. The concept of <span
   class=highlight>indexical particular</span> is a
   reference to any item within a context, and <span
   class=highlight> reflexivity </span> calls attention
```

```
  to the fact that the indexical particulars and the
  context in which they reside are mutually elaborating.
</body></html>
```

F. Figure 15-5, Borders and Backgrounds

```
<html>
<head><title>Borderlines and Backgrounds</title>
<style>
.checkboard {color:lightslategray; background-image:
  url(checkbd.gif)}
.southwest {background-color: navajowhite}
.southofborder {border: groove green medium; background-
  color: red; padding: 3px}
</style></head>
<body>
<P class=southwest >In New Mexico, one feels the history
  of the region in the architecture and culture.</p>
<P class=southofborder>While there are some elements of
  Old Mexico in New Mexico, they have about as much in
  common as Old England and New England.</p>
When background images are needed in Web pages, they can
  get in the way of the message.
<div class=checkboard>Even backgrounds can be placed in
  style sheets.</div> Nevertheless, if there is a need
  for them, they can be put into style sheets like other
  elements.
</body></html>
```

G. External Style Sheets

To set up the external file, use only the script for the style sheet. Omit the <STYLE> tags. For example, the following script is saved as a text file, "desert.css," using a text editor such as Notepad or Simple Text.

```
.desert { font-family : Arial, Helvetica, sans-serif;
color: moccasin;
background-color: saddlebrown;
text-indent:0.5em}
a { text-decoration: none; color:tomato; }
```

Next, to use the external style sheet, all that needs to be done is to include the <LINK> tag as shown in the following script:

```
<html>
<head><title>CSS Template</title>
<link rel="stylesheet" href="desert.css" type="text/css">
</head>
<body bgcolor="white" class=desert>

Once a style has been developed for a certain effect, a
link to the style sheet saved as a text file will give
you what you want. This one is placed in the BODY tag,
and it includes the <a href="#"> Link style </a> as well.

</body></html>
```

Note that the CLASS attribute is declared in the <BODY> tag so that the entire Web page is subject to the style sheet's design. The style sheet could have been called up in any other appropriate tag as well.

Chapter 16

Organizing Web Pages and the Future of Web Technology in Higher Education

In a thoughtful and provocative article Alistair Fraser (1999) noted that he was *horrified* at the idea of the Web being nothing more than another access to traditional pedagogy. Citing Marshall McLuhan, Fraser notes that new technologies are often used to do nothing more than shovel the same old stuff with a new delivery system. The resulting *shovelware* could be done with books, videos, articles, lectures, or some other traditional method. If that is the case, why bother?

Why indeed? If by *traditional pedagogy* Fraser means standing up in front of a class and talking while students take notes, his point is doubly valid. It is valid in that such disconnected teaching really involves the student very little, and a good videotape with lots of filmed examples could probably be substituted with a better chance of students comprehending any major point the professor wants to make. Fraser's point is also valid in that a *single method* of communicating to students, such as a lecture, is wholly devoid of imagination. This is not to say there are no good lectures. There are even great lectures, but lectures are *still* only one way of communicating to students. That and reading books make up the great bulk of a university education. Small group discussions, labs, and some actual research make up the rest of what passes for pedagogy in higher education.

For Fraser, universities now have interactive *computer visualization* over the Web to aid in communicating the *mental models* of one's discipline. Universities also have a new tool in computer visualization—an interactive visualization—for developing metamodels. The metamodels are the models used *to think about models.* In this book metamodels have been borrowed heavily from the works of

Edward Tufte in terms of design and Erving Goffman for interaction. Other developing metamodels lie within technology that empowers both students and faculty to engage the learning process. With interactive, real time, hypertime, or slow motion, what are the ways we can set up learning situations that will help students learn in ways we have not yet even envisioned? What could be done to enhance lectures, involve students, and make the learning experience a better one? None of the new technology is going to help if good pedagogy is not a key element of it. For the most part, good pedagogy is not part of the modern university—some single technique, usually the lecture, is. Therefore, one role of the Web may be to introduce good practices that could be done *without* the Web. The new technology and good pedagogy are reflexive with each defining and building on the other. For example, the University of South Florida's *A Teachers Guide to the Holocaust* (http://fcit.coedu.usf.edu/holocaust/default.htm) employs a rich array of text, pictures, sound, pop-up windows, and video for anyone interested in the Holocaust. The site has the feel of an online museum, rather than a book or lecture, where the viewer is invited to explore.

In an online article Jakob Nielsen (1998) argues that the concept of an e-book (electronic book) is not a good metaphor. An e-book concept tends to connect a computer with the capability of hypertext links, interaction, navigation, search, and connections to the Internet with that of a static printed book. Nielsen argues, that books are married to the linear flow of text and that this tradition must end. By having an array of choices there is a dynamic dimension between the reader and the medium. More options are available for approaching a problem and although the same information and understanding may be the end result no matter what route is taken, a sense of self-direction and choice resides in the process. Even better, the same topic can be understood from several perspectives and approaches to be analyzed and developed.

Throughout this book there has been an attempt to do two things regarding the issues discussed by Fraser and Nielsen. On the one hand, beginning with the concept of a *third generation Web site*, an invitation is made to rethink ways of organizing learning experiences—lessons. On the other hand, *good practices* in teaching and learning need to be incorporated in Web-based learning. Although both Fraser and Nielsen are correct in urging educators and others to think of new metamodels for using Web and Internet technology, one is hardly a Luddite for seeking to use research findings on nontechnology learning and employ them with Web technology. Likewise, the use of the Web is not an either/or proposition with good traditional methods. A good lecture by a professor holding a stick to emphasize a point is superior to sluggish presentations using the best new technology with video, graphics, and sound effects. Preparation, enthusiasm, and engagement are important ingredients. If Web-based components are *usefully* incorporated as part of a lecture or in some way complement a lecture, it would be foolish to abandon *either* the lecture or the Web material for a course because they represent two different mediums and techniques. The same is true with books. They have far superior resolution, take less time to read, and are more portable. In time, e-books may indeed replace paper ones as their resolution increases and their bulk decreases. In the meantime, though, a sensible mix based on the *best current technology and practices in pedagogy*, both old and new, needs to be considered.

Final sets of issues to consider in this chapter are administrative ones. There needs to be some kind of infrastructure and overall plan within a university so that faculty has the equipment and support to get what they need. Expectations can be modest or great, but one sure way to fail is when faculty needs come up short to what a university hopes to accomplish. Of the technologies available for teaching and learning in higher education, the Web and Internet represent only one set. If the Web is to be used as part of an overall strategy, the support for it in terms of personnel and equipment needs to be in place before it can be effective. However, the first order of business is to see how Web pages can be placed on servers.

Using FTP and Organizing a Local Web Site

Once a set of Web pages has been created on a computer, they have to be sent to a server. When the pages are on the server, they can be read from anywhere on the Internet. The good thing about a server is that, for the most part, it acts just like a desktop computer. *A server is a computer* with server software and is configured to store and send files. The term *server* denotes both software and hardware. An NT Server, for example, refers to a server with Microsoft NT Server software. Sun, Compaq, Hewlett-Packard, Dell, or Gateway could manufacture the hardware server. It does not matter as long as the hardware can operate the software. A Web server denotes the hardware server has Web server software. Servers generally have larger storage capacity and different I/O ports than typical desktop computers; however, the difference is not as great as some believe. A typical desktop computer is easily set up as a server. For example, an iMac comes with built-in server software. Connected to a cable modem, even an iMac could be set up as a server—the point being there's little difference between desktop computers and servers. Servers store files in any file hierarchy the creator designs. That means it is possible to test all of the files on a desktop computer before sending them to a server. Once on the server they can be expected to act the same way on the server as on the computer used to develop them. Figure 16-1 shows how the file order on the desktop computer is mirrored on the server computer.

Before sending pages to a server, be sure to send them in the same relative order as they have been arranged and tested on the desktop computer. That means if Page B goes into Folder A on the desktop computer, Page B should go into Folder A on the server. It is not a difficult task, but it is the source of more problems and broken links than just about anything else. Relative links need to be maintained and the only way to do that is to be sure the folder and file arrangement is the same.

Many Web site development programs, including *Front Page, Dreamweaver,* and *GoLive*, provide excellent tools for creating a *local site*. A local site is simply the site organized on your desktop computer to be transferred to the server as mod-

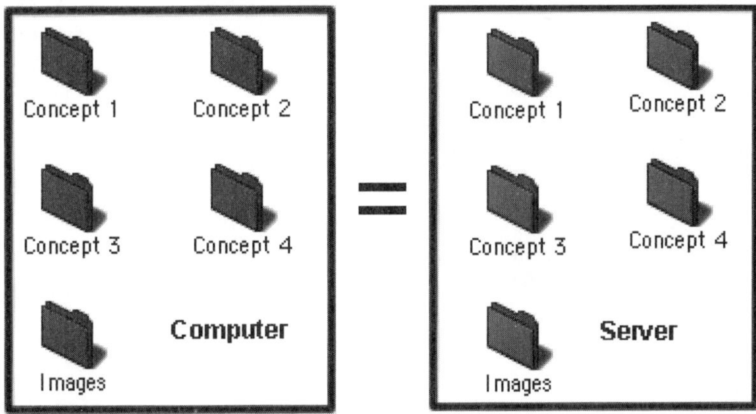

FIGURE 16-1 Files on the server and desktop computer should mirror one another.

eled in Figure 16-1. The information for transferring the Web pages to the *remote site* (the server) is put directly into the program so that the application program sends the pages it develops to the server. This can be sent without using a separate FTP program, saves time, and helps keep everything consistent. Figure 16-2 shows *GoLive's* setup for linking local and remote sites.

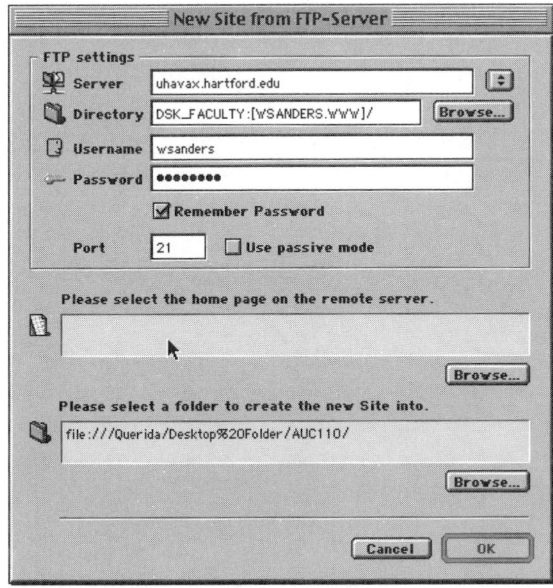

FIGURE 16-2 Adobe *GoLive* provides a built-in FTP for sending pages between local and remote sites.

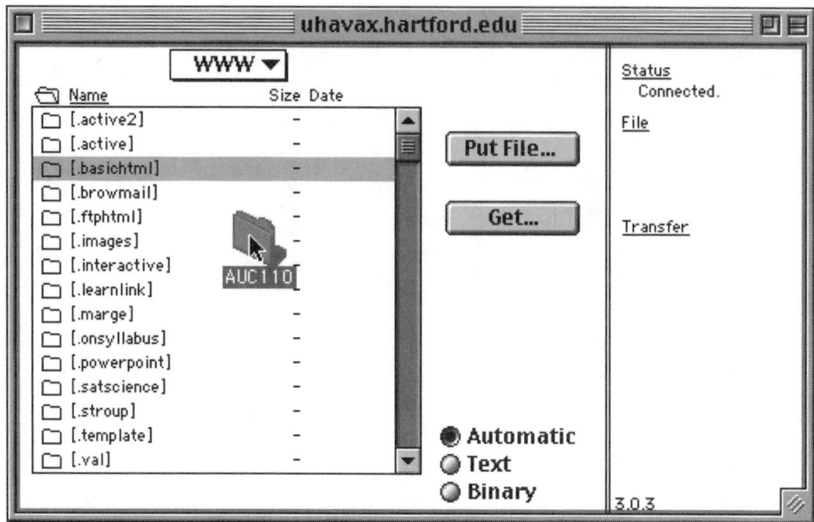

FIGURE 16-3 Placing folders and files on remote servers is as easy as it is to move them from one local drive to another. *Fetch,* a Macintosh FTP application, shows the contents of all levels of the user's folder. Students cannot access this area.

The most common way that files are transferred between a desktop computer and a server is File Transfer Protocol—FTP. It is very similar to transferring files between a hard disk on a computer and any other place such as a floppy disk, a *Zip* drive, or some other storage medium. The special software required for FTP transfer is freely available for both Windows and Macintosh computers. For Windows a popular FTP program is called *Windows Sockets File Transfer Protocol Client* available at **http://www.csra.net/junodj/ws_ftp.htm**. For the Macintosh, a program called *Fetch* is the most commonly used FTP program available free from **http://www.dartmouth.edu/pages/softdev/fetch.html**. With both *Windows Sockets FTP* and *Fetch* it is possible to use "drag and drop" to put files and folders on a remote server. In Figure 16-3, a folder called "AUC110" is shown being dragged from the local desktop to the server. All of the Web pages and graphics in the folder on the server will use the same relative links as on the desktop. So even without a good Web page development program it is possible to easily organize and put Web pages on a server.

The setup and use of these FTP utilities are very simple. *Windows Sockets FTP* shown in Table 16-1 shows how this popular program displays local and remote files.

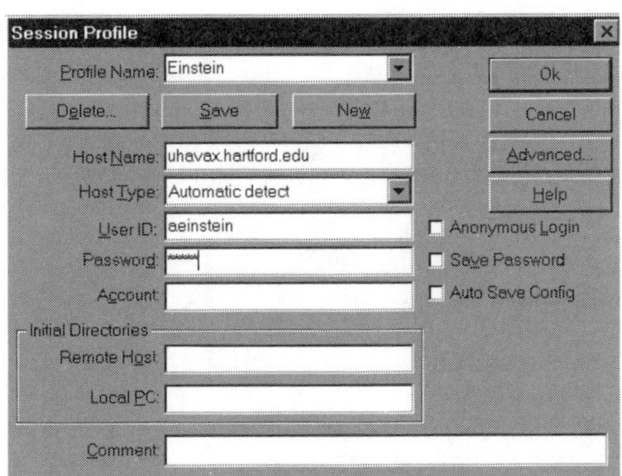

Using Windows Sockets FTP it is simple to set up a connection between the desktop computer and server.

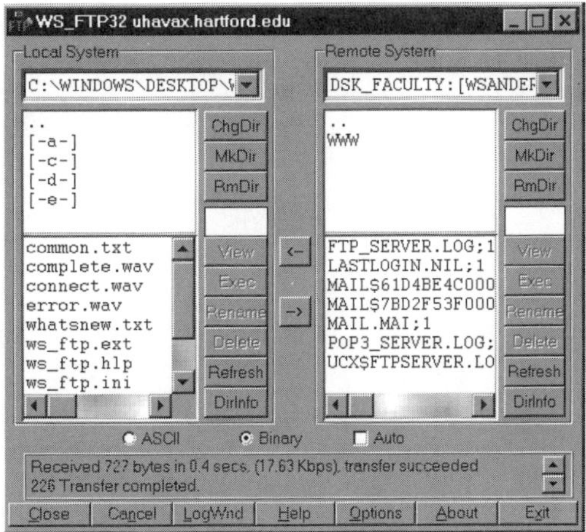

Two windows display the local and remote systems. Files can be transferred back and forth by clicking on the arrows between the windows.

TABLE 16-1 With *Windows Sockets* it is easy to establish links between the desktop computer and the server.

Editing and Updating Pages on the Server

Once all of the pages for a lesson or course are on the server, they will need to be periodically updated. This was found to be particularly true with the syllabus. An online syllabus is a great tool for adding material during the course of a semester as new information becomes available or the professor finds that some changes need to be made for better student understanding. For example, a course dealing with contemporary political issues may want to add links to pages on the World Wide Web that bring in new information during the course of a semester. The links need to be added to the syllabus, and that is generally a simple matter, especially if the page to be changed is on the local computer. All that needs to be done is to make the changes on the local computer and FTP it to the remote (server) computer. However, sometimes a page will not be on the computer one is using, such as one from a campus lab or a home office. Using Netscape Communicator, all that is required is to go to the URL of the page and select **Edit Page** from the **File** menu. That will bring the remote page, graphics and all, into Netscape *Composer*. From *Composer*, the page may be edited and then "published" directly from *Composer*. It works just like FTP except that it automatically sends all the graphic files, including new ones that may have been added, to the server. So rather than having to go

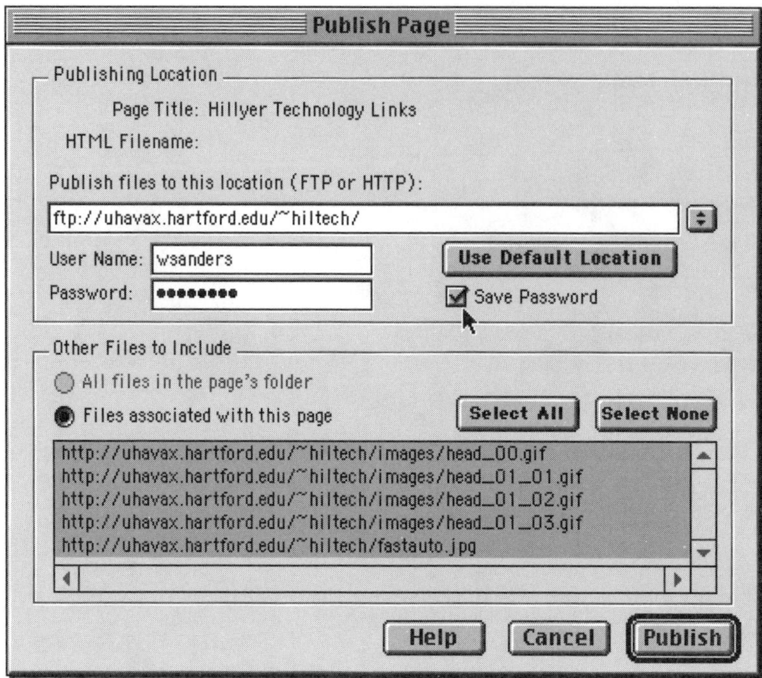

FIGURE 16-4 When a Web page is sent to a server using *Netscape Composer*, all of the associated files are sent as well.

through a complex process with several steps and several different applications, all of it can be handled with a single application. Figure 16-4 shows the Publish page from *Composer* after it has been edited and is ready to be placed back on the server. Notice in the window labeled **"Publish Files to this location (FTP or HTTP)"** that FTP is used. All that does is to indicate that File Transfer Protocol is used to place the files in the desired address. Most servers are set up to transfer using FTP, and although the default is HTTP for a page that has been edited and set to be published, it is important to remember to change it to FTP. *Front Page, GoLive*, and *Dreamweaver* have a similar capability, but one's primary Web page development program may not be available on every computer, but a browser like Netscape Communicator usually is.

Shockwave and Other Plug-Ins

One of the important tools that students will need in their browsers is an array of "plug-ins" for their browsers. Fortunately, most of these plug-ins are free because they enable the client to view Web pages created with certain commercially sold software such as Macromedia *Flash* and *Director*. One of the most important plug-ins at this writing is *Shockwave* freely available from www.macromedia.com. A simple step-by-step set of instructions shows how to set up and use the plug-ins, and so there need be no concern about overcomplicating the procedure.

Plug-ins are available for a variety of different enhancements for Web pages. The *Shockwave* plug-in is a key one for multimedia materials put on Web pages for interactive learning. Developing materials for dynamically combining video, animation, sound, and an interactive response system requires programs such as *Flash* and *Director*, both of which can be configured to operate on the Web when both the student's computer and the server have interpretive software for *Shockwave*. Many faculty who master *Flash* or *Director* for CD-ROM-based presentation or have technical development staff do it for them are often perplexed when their software does not work when ported over to the Web, even when using the Web-based version of the courseware. Usually, the problem resides with the university server not having the right software for playing *Shockwave*. Sometimes the university technology services department is not aware of the problem and assumes that it is due to the lack of a proper client plug-in. When using these more robust forms of multimedia, it is essential that there is good communication between the professor and her students, who need to know about getting the right client plug-in. In addition, the professor needs good communication between herself and the right computer services personnel.

Placing a *Shockwave* file into a Web page is easy with a good Web page editor. For example, after creating a *Flash* file that morphed from the word "Leaf" into the image of a leaf as a demonstration to visually and dynamically show the relationship between symbols and objects, it was saved as a ".swf" file. The .swf extension indicates that the file is a *Shockwave* file for *Flash* and will work on the Web. Next, using the <EMBED> tag in HTML, the movie is placed on the page. When the Web page opens, the *Flash* animation is automatically played. Buttons or other objects that can be manipulated by students as well can control these files. As can be seen from the following script, getting the material in a Web page is quite simple.

```
<html>
<head><title>Word and Image</title></head>
<body bgcolor="white">
<embed src="leaf.swf" width="200" height="250"
  loop="false">
</embed>
</body></html>
```

Basically, the <EMBED> tag acts very much like a tag to place an image on the page. Instead of putting in an image, though, it puts in a movie. The file name "leaf.swf" is analogous to a name like "leaf.gif" for a standard image file. Usually, though, all of the code can be generated from *Flash* using the Publish option. Both the Web version of the *Flash* movie (.swf) and the HTML are generated automatically. All parameters can be changed in *Flash* or the HTML tags.

QuickTime and RealVideo Players

Two players available free online for both Windows and Macintosh computers are QuickTime and RealVideo. Each can play sound and display video, and each has a stand-alone player that can bring in movies from the Internet and players embedded in Web pages. The QuickTime player has a pull-down menu of streaming video sites, and the RealPlayer has a similar array of video links. It is possible using streaming video to create a virtual television station.

As access to broadband connections increases, the speed at which data can be transferred across the Internet will be fast enough to have higher-quality online video. Very soon, the Web will be able to be used as a world wide broadcasting system, and using low-cost production software and hardware, faculty can produce video and audio to be seamlessly integrated into Web pages.

Using Cookies, CGI, and ASP for Data Storage and Retrieval

One of the major drawbacks in the way Web pages work is that although they can be accessed from anywhere in the world, getting information and storing it are a bit more involved and complex. For example, suppose students are given an assignment to collect survey data for a research methods course. Once the data are all collected they are sent to a central site where the students can collect all of the data of the other students, analyze it, and demonstrate their knowledge of data collection and analysis. The problem lies in the fact that each time the Web browser or computer is turned off, the data in the computer are lost. Other than emailing the data to each class member, there is no very good way to store the data using standard HTML.

Cookies

One interesting and even odd way of storing data across the Web is with "cookies." Using JavaScript text files can be written to a user's hard drive with cookies, but cookies are dependent on the same person using the same computer and same browser. Because several different students in different classes will use computers in a university computer lab, storing information in cookies is a bit awkward and risky. If two different students from the same class use the same computer and Web pages storing cookies to the hard disk, one student's work will be confused with another's. Usually, cookies are placed on a computer by a remote computer that wants to know the identity of the local computer. This can be handy for checking to see whether students using the same computer have taken an exam, completed a lesson, or done some other task. However, cookies are severely limiting and limited in what they can do. Unless there is a clear understanding that the same students in the same course use the same computer all the time, cookies are not much help.

CGI

Storing and passing information on the Web have depended on Common Gateway Interface or CGI. Using CGI it is possible to store everything from a student's test results to her essay on Keats. Once a CGI storage and retrieval system has been established, they can serve as valuable course administrative and student learning databases. Reading and writing to a storage computer (server) using CGI programs, usually written in a language called Perl, involves HTML forms and is controlled by JavaScript on the client's computer. Having the right technology support staff to set up the CGI and Web pages to store and retrieve the data is crucial to an effective course with database capability. Some educational packages include a CGI module, such as Blackboard.com **(http://www.blackboard.com/).** For the professor and instructional technology staff, these all-in-one educational packages have great administrative tools, but they sometimes have limited design options.

ASP

A newer alternative to CGI is a system called Active Server Pages. These have many of the advantages of CGI, but they are written in a language closer to HTML and JavaScript. Identified by .asp extensions, ASP offers many of the solutions of CGI without having to have additional server programming in addition to the Web server.

Administration of Instructional Technology

Enough administrative issues exist in instructional technology to raise the *Titanic*, but this section touches on only a few. The most essential issues in Web-based education in universities involve:

- Student access to the Web
- Faculty acceptance of Web-based learning and learning-centered pedagogy
- Support for development and maintenance

These issues are baseline ones that vary with the universities and colleges, but unless they are addressed and dealt with effectively, having success with instructional technology is nearly hopeless. Good strategic plans for technology are dependent on a clear understanding of these essential issues, for if any one of them is found wanting, there will be serious problems in making Web-based learning a reality.

Student Access to the Web

The World Wide Web is always changing, and in order to access it students need to be able to have access to it in its changing format. For the most part phone lines and modems are a very poor way to use the Web, especially one rich in multimedia and graphics. Having access through the Web with only a 56.6k modem means that most of the interactive, engrossing courseware developed is largely wasted, and other than good email access, paper-based materials are less frustrating.

Universities and colleges, for the most part, have at least a T1 level of speed, and some have far more than that. Home cable modems provide comparable speeds to a T1 line and even can exceed T1 speeds under certain circumstances. (T1 lines run at about 1.5Mbps and cable modems up to 5Mbps. In reality, rarely do either have those speeds, but compared to phone modems, they are up to 100 times faster.) Newer technologies are being introduced, including wireless ones. In 1999, Apple Computer introduced "AirPort," a wireless local area connection to up to 10 computers at a speed of 11Mbps, which is fast enough for most of the "heavier" applications. However, as with most fast wireless connections, computers have to be relatively close to the wireless port. The port itself is hardwired to the Internet through a T1 or similar connection. For classroom use of the Web, wireless connections have the potential for making every classroom a computer lab.

Residential colleges and universities are providing connections through T1 or T3 access directly to the dormitories. For completely or even mostly residential institutions, students have excellent access in this manner. Where all students are required to have computers, the situation is ideal. However, more and more students are going to urban commuter campuses where their best chance for high-speed access to the Internet is through university connections. Some institutions are experimenting with "plug-in" rooms where students bring their computers with them and plug into a high-speed university connection. Most others, though, are using university computer labs. Both open and classroom computer labs with high-speed Internet access are extremely valuable for low-income students who have no computer or for students without portable computers. It is in these settings where the students can access rich and robust Web-based learning.

The great hope of some universities is that with computers on the Internet students can access "anytime, anywhere" education. Institutions such as the University of Phoenix and Western Governors University have elaborate superstructures and some infrastructures for the "virtual university." Ironically, these universities probably have the worst student access to the Web because most of them use phone modems. This is not to belittle what these early efforts in Web-based education have done, but rather it is to point out that good access to rich multimedia Web pages is more often found at the traditional universities and colleges. With Internet 2 becoming available for very high-speed communication for certain universities and research-oriented activities, the availability of and demand for more broadband connections increase.

Administratively, several issues regarding student access to the Web require consideration and action. The first and most important is the wiring of the university. Wiring classrooms and dormitories to the Internet through high-speed connections is essential. It is a costly investment, but with a fiber optic backbone to the buildings and CAT 5 copper and/or fiber optics to the ports, most of the high bandwidth graphics, sounds, videos, and dynamic multimedia on the Web can be accessed effectively. The high cost of fiber optic connections from the port to the computer has limited full use of fiber optics, but in the future, fiber optic connections directly to computers may be both affordable and necessary. (CAT 5 copper connections can handle about 100Mbps, and with T1 lines generating 1.5 Mbps at the time of this writing, CAT 5 copper can handle connection speeds for the foreseeable future.)

One hesitation factor in extending wiring has been the promise of wireless connections. As broadband wireless solutions become more available, such hesitation may prove to be grounded. However, most high-speed wireless connections at the time of this writing were short-range, such as Apple Computer's AirPort. Therefore, even with more wireless connections in the future, there is still a need to have a fully wired environment for the base wireless port in the buildings.

Faculty Acceptance of Web-Based Learning and Learning-Centered Pedagogy

A more difficult administrative issue with faculty is why they should bother with Web-based learning or the concept of a learning-centered pedagogy. Under just about every circumstance, even the ideal, getting good materials on the Web requires extensive and intensive faculty efforts. It will take time, learning, and usually a good deal of trial and error before there is a successful Web-based lesson, let alone a course or program. Experience shows that faculty needs the following in order to accept Web-based course material:

- Evidence that the benefit to the student is greater than what is currently being done
- Support in the form of course design and technology
- Equipment, software, and Internet connections
- Models and exemplars of courseware, especially in their discipline
- A reward system that recognizes faculty efforts using Web-based content delivery and enhancement
- Time for learning (including learning support) how to prepare and develop materials for the Web

These items greatly oversimplify the many concerns that will come into play. In the pages of the *Chronicle of Higher Education*, debate over the use of instructional technology is heated and vocal. Of all of these arguments and issues, the foremost surrounds the benefits derived by students. If the benefits are minimal, vague, and unsupported, *there is absolutely no reason* to go to the time and expense to develop Web courseware. This is why it is important to connect good learning-based pedagogy to instructional technology. If a lecture is the best way that students will learn, it makes no sense to simply take a lecture and put it on the Web. Likewise, if a Web page is nothing but a long string of text, hyperlinked or not, books do a better job—they have higher resolution and are easier to carry around.

What is essential to Web-based learning is a learning strategy underlying it, not a technology strategy.

A surprise and benefit of the introduction of instructional technology has been the opening of debate over pedagogy. Long dormant in universities and colleges, especially the major research universities, the discussion of the role of teaching and learning has heated up and been focused. One residual outcome is a dual introduction to both technology and pedagogy in environments where they have not been discussed in a long time.

Another surprise has been the acceptance and exploration by older faculty. Many faculty members who had been written off as "deadwood" in universities have been energized by the introduction of the Web. Far from being created by younger faculty, who first came to know the Internet and Web as students, many of the most interesting and successful multimedia productions have been created by full professors who have taken a recent interest in computers and the Internet. To some extent this should not come as a surprise. Younger faculty do not want to rock any academic boats, and they tend to have their hands full trying to get their research done, grants written, publications out, and courses developed. Accomplished professors, on the other hand, have reached full rank, and they are looking for new challenges. All they need is a little help and support in developing course materials for the new technology.

Support for Development and Maintenance

Faculty should not have to become computer experts. For years a convoluted code had to be delivered to the computer each time a command was issued. Known as CLI or Command Line Interface, this code was an extension of the old mainframes. In 1984, Apple Computer introduced the Macintosh with a graphic interface, and shortly thereafter, Microsoft introduced Windows. The evolution of the "user-friendly" computer was not necessarily mirrored in "user-friendly" computer staff at universities, however.

Computer support at universities meant support of administrative computing—handling finance, records, and the like. Working with complex databases and protocols for maintaining and distributing data, the old systems until very recently used the old-fashioned CLI. Still many finance and database systems on university networks are so convoluted that only those who have been trained or have become accustomed to a Byzantine set of instructions and nonintuitive keystrokes knew how to use them. As a result of this history the computer staffs often viewed with contempt faculty who used their "user-friendly" Macintosh and Windows computers, and believed that serious computing could be accomplished only by those who understood the mysteries of the mainframe.

After the personal computer revolution in the early 1980s and the introduction of the Macintosh and later Windows, there seemed to be a split between the "toy" computers of the faculty and the "real" ones controlled by university computer staffs. However, as the desktop computers became more powerful and the mainframes went from filling rooms to fitting under desks, the major difference between the two types of computers lay in the fact that the mainframes and connected terminals *were connected*.

Everything about computing changed when the Internet and the World Wide Web were made generally available in the early 1990s with the introduction of the Web browser. Not only were the faculty members' computers connected, they were connected to the whole world, not just to computers on campus. In order to be connected, faculty came to rely again on the campus technology staff. The staff maintained the routers, servers, IP/TCP codes, and other highly technical connective skills, resources, and information. However, the faculty had changed since the old days of the mainframes and the hermetically sealed computer rooms. They understood a lot more about computers, and a number of faculty from diverse fields became quite knowledgeable about not only their computers but also how to use them for their classes.

At this point a changed (and sometimes charged) university faculty came *back* into communication with computer services staff. The computer staff, who considered themselves the foremost experts on all things *computeresque,* were confronted by a number of faculty who knew some part of computing far better than IT staff. For example, in one case I watched in horror as computer services staff explained to faculty how to use a word processor. Not only did many of the faculty know more about using the word processor than did the computer staff, but the staff used perfectly horrid examples of grammar, page design, and how to make presentations.

For their part, once the faculty decided they knew as much about computers in their area of expertise, they proceeded to browbeat, bully, and generally place the computer services staff in the role of unresponsive dinosaurs of the "old ways." In fact, like everyone else, computer staff was working hard to keep up with all of the changes being wrought by the Internet revolution. Rather than a centralized computer with communication through terminals or terminal emulators, *distributed computing* meant that there was no center. Every node on the Internet was both self-contained and interfaced simultaneously. Client computers could become servers and vice versa. Some departments (usually in the sciences) set up their own systems bypassing the computer center altogether. Intranets were popping up within the university all the way down to the department level while the university was scrambling to set up its own Intranet.

Suffice it to say that *the nature of support for computers in universities has fundamentally changed*. Computer staff know virtually *nothing* about course design, pedagogy, and whether something found on the Internet has any validity for a course or not. Faculty have no clue what TCP and IP are and what they do even though they are at the core of Internet computing. A new type of interface staff is developing. Collectively, these people are *instructional technology designers*. They know about pedagogy and course design using multimedia on computers. Most importantly, they can communicate with both computer staff and faculty. They can explain clearly to the computer center faculty course requirements in terms of server space, CGI programming, and plug-in support. However, they also understand the limitations of computer resources and what is possible and what is not.

They can relate to faculty in terms of what they want to effectively present to students and help them prepare courseware. At the same time they understand ways to use the least amount of bandwidth to effect the outcome desired by faculty. The development of this area of support is critical to the growth and effective implementation of Web-based courseware. It is an area and field clearly in the process of self-definition and invention. It is as much a phenomenon of the larger changes in society as it is of university needs to help students learn.

Summary and Review

This chapter began with the concerns of a *horrified* faculty member, and it ends with administrative concerns of putting together the framework for Web-based learning. In between the discussion covered what it takes to get faculty work from their desktop computer to a server and new emerging Internet and Web technologies. The university model of teaching and learning has not changed fundamentally since the concept of a university education was democratized into a meritocracy. Under that ideal—sort of Darwinian survival of the fittest—professors organized and presented a corpus of knowledge and students *worked hard* to succeed to master the corpus. To ensure only the fittest survived, an artificial bell-shaped curve was superimposed onto education, weeding out those who were at the lower end of the curve. Under this system, in a class full of half-wits high grades would be given to the top tier of half-wits, whether they really learned anything or not. Likewise, in a class of brilliant and creative students, failing grades would be given to the less-than-brightest, even though they learned everything any professor could wish for.

Many faculty members saw through this facade of artificial standards and made adjustments so that learning was more important than curves. This is especially important because the democratic ideal of equal education for all was becoming a reality. Nontraditional students, often a code word for ethnic minorities and older women, were coming to college in large numbers for the first time. Inner-city colleges and universities were desperate to succeed with students from low-income families who had little or no tradition of higher education in their histories. The institution's enrollment and funding were dependent on the success of these students. However, no one was quite sure how or why students learned, even though most professors believed that studying and doing assignments were the key. Students had to pay attention and listen for the nuances of meaning, and the more care and engrossment they gave to a course, the more they got out of it. Some students seemed to learn differently from others, some in groups and some individually. Eventually, a set of practices was identified that seemed to work when it came to student learning. The *professors were right.* The students had to study, to become involved and engrossed in what they were learning. However, while in the middle of technological, social, and political revolutions during the latter part of the twentieth century, most professors taught as professors taught in the nineteenth century. At the beginning of the twenty-first century, they still do.

Recognizing this state of affairs and doing something about it have been the topic of this book. It should be clear to the reader that if education fails to get students to *learn*, it has failed, period. Doing the same thing in colleges and universities for centuries and passing it off as pedagogy amount to self-delusion at best and fraud at worst. Trying out another system of thinking about teaching and learning is an attempt to break a cycle that has persisted for far too long. There is no guarantee that using the good practices recommended by the American Association of Higher Education (AAHE) are much better than traditional lectures, and there certainly is no guarantee that the new and emerging technology of the World Wide Web is a panacea to students' failure to learn. However, if students are not learning very much or very well under current conditions it probably is a good idea to try something new.

Glossary of Terms

FTP File Transfer Protocol is generally through a utilities program (for example, *Windows Sockets FTP, Fetch*) that allows the transfer of files on one's own computer to a Web server.

Metamodel A model used to develop other models. In the context of education and technology metamodels refer to a guiding framework in which models of learning are cast.

Relative links HTML links expect a folder (directory) in a certain position on the computer relative to the position of the linking page. The link may be at a higher or lower level than the page, but the directory must be in the same relative position on the server as on the developing computer for them to work. *Absolute links* are those links that include the full URL of the target (for example, http://memory.loc.gov).

Shovelware This term is a pejorative one to describe putting material on the Web as content with none of the interactive capabilities or other features of the Web. The content is "shoveled" onto the Web page for students to examine.

Zip drive Zip drives and disks are actually brand names of the Iomega Corporation. However, they have come to be synonymous with most-high capacity (100mb or greater) removable disk media.

References

Fraser, Alistair B. "Colleges Should Tap the Pedagogical Potential of the World-Wide Web" Chronicle of Higher Education. August 6, 1999, p. B2.

Nielsen, Jakob. "Electronic Books—A Bad Idea." *Jakob Nielsen's Alertbox,* July 26, 1998. http://www.zdnet.com/devhead/alertbox/980726.html.

Appendix A

Web Color Names

aliceblue
antiquewhite
aqua
aquamarine
azure
beige
bisque
black
blanchedalmond
blueviolet
brown
burlywood
cadetblue
chartreuse
chocolate
coral
cornflowerblue
cornsilk
crimson
cyan
darkblue
darkcyan
darkgoldenrod
darkgray
darkgreen
darkkhaki
darkmagenta
darkolivegreen
darkorange
darkorchid
darkred
darksalmon
darkseagreen
darkslateblue
darkslategray
darkturquoise
darkviolet
deeppink
deepskyblue
dimgray
dodgerblue
firebrick
floralwhite
forestgreen
fuchsia
gainsboro
ghostwhite
gold
goldenrod
gray
green
greenyellow
honeydew
hotpink
indianred
indigo
ivory
khaki
lavender
lavenderblush
lawngreen
lemonchiffon
lightblue
lightcoral
lightcyan
lightgoldenrodyellow
lightgray
lightgreen
lightpink
lightsalmon
lightseagreen
lightskyblue
lightslategray
lightsteelblue
lightyellow
lime
limegreen
magenta
mediumaquamarine
mediumblue
mediumorchid
mediumpurple
mediumseagreen
mediumslateblue
mediumspringgreen
mediumturquoise
mediumvioletred

midnightblue
mintcream
mistyrose
moccasin
navajowhite
navy
oldlace
olive
olivedrab
orange
orangered
orchid
palegoldenrod
palegreen
paleturquoise
palevioletred
papayawhip
peachpuff
peru
pink
plum
powderblue
purple
red
rosybrown
royalblue
saddlebrown
salmon
sandybrown
seagreen
seashell
sienna
silver
skyblue
slateblue
slategray
snow
springgreen
steelblue
tan
teal
thistle
tomato
turquoise
violet
wheat
white
whitesmoke
yellow
yellowgreen

Index